VALUES AN

MIND ASSOCIATION OCCASIONAL SERIES

This series consists of occasional volumes of original papers on predefined themes. The Mind Association nominates an editor or editors for each collection, and may cooperate with other bodies in promoting conferences or other scholarly activities in connection with the preparation of particular volumes.

Publications Officer
M. A. Stewart

Secretary
R. D. Hopkins

RECENTLY PUBLISHED IN THE SERIES:

Desert and Justice
Edited by Serena Olsaretti

Leviathan *after 350 years*
Edited by Tom Sorell and Luc Foisneau

Strawson and Kant
Edited by Hans-Johann Glock

Identity and Modality
Edited by Fraser MacBride

Impressions of Hume
Edited by Marina Frasca-Spada and P. J. E. Kail

Ramsey's Legacy
Edited by Hallvard Lillehammer and D. H. Mellor

Transcendental Arguments
Problems and Prospects
Edited by Robert Stern

Reason and Nature
Essays in the Theory of Rationality
Edited by José Luis Bermúdez and Alan Millar

Values and Virtues

Aristotelianism in Contemporary Ethics

Edited by
TIMOTHY CHAPPELL

CLARENDON PRESS · OXFORD

OXFORD

UNIVERSITY PRESS

Great Clarendon Street, Oxford OX2 6DP

Oxford University Press is a department of the University of Oxford.
It furthers the University's objective of excellence in research, scholarship,
and education by publishing worldwide in

Oxford New York

Auckland Cape Town Dar es Salaam Hong Kong Karachi
Kuala Lumpur Madrid Melbourne Mexico City Nairobi
New Delhi Shanghai Taipei Toronto

With offices in

Argentina Austria Brazil Chile Czech Republic France Greece
Guatemala Hungary Italy Japan Poland Portugal Singapore
South Korea Switzerland Thailand Turkey Ukraine Vietnam

Oxford is a registered trade mark of Oxford University Press
in the UK and in certain other countries

Published in the United States
by Oxford University Press Inc., New York

British Library Cataloguing in Publication Data

Data available

Library of Congress Cataloging in Publication Data

Data available

Typeset by Laserwords Private Limited, Chennai, India
Printed in Great Britain
on acid-free paper by
Biddles Ltd, King's Lynn, Norfolk

ISBN 0-19-929145-4 978-0-19-929145-8

Contents

Notes on Contributors

Christopher Miles Coope is Senior Fellow in the School of Philosophy at the University of Leeds. He has published on ethics and applied ethics; one recent paper is 'Peter Singer in Retrospect', *Philosophical Quarterly*, 2003. His book *Worth and Welfare in the Controversy over Abortion*, and a paper in *Philosophy* ('Death Sentences'), will appear in 2006.

Linda Zagzebski is Kingfisher College Chair of the Philosophy of Religion and Ethics at the University of Oklahoma. In addition to several edited books, she is the author of *Divine Motivation Theory* (Cambridge University Press, 2004), *Virtues of the Mind* (Cambridge University Press, 1996), and *The Dilemma of Freedom and Foreknowledge* (Oxford University Press, 1991), as well as numerous articles and book chapters in epistemology, ethics, and philosophy of religion. She is President of the Society of Christian Philosophers and past President of the American Catholic Philosophical Association.

Fred D. Miller, Jun. is Professor of Philosophy and Executive Director of the Social Philosophy and Policy Center at Bowling Green State University. He has been a visiting professor at the Johns Hopkins University, the University of Washington, and the University of Waterloo, and a visiting scholar at Harvard University, the Institute for the Research in the Humanities at the University of Wisconsin, Jesus College, Oxford, and the Centre for Ethics, Philosophy, and Public Affairs at St Andrews University. He was President of the Society of Ancient Greek Philosophy from 1998 until 2004. He is the author of *Nature, Justice, and Rights in Aristotle's Politics* (Oxford University Press, 1995), and co-editor of *A Companion to Aristotle's Politics* (Blackwell, 1991) and *A History of the Philosophy of Law from the Ancient Greeks to the Scholastics* (Springer Kluwer, 2006).

R. A. Duff is a professor in the Department of Philosophy at the University of Stirling, where he has taught since 1970. His paper in this collection is part of a larger project on the character and conditions of criminal liability. He has published *Trials and Punishments* (Cambridge University Press, 1986), *Intention, Agency and Criminal Liability* (Blackwell, 1990); *Criminal Attempts* (Oxford University Press, 1996), and *Punishment, Communication and Community* (Oxford University Press, 2000).

Hallvard J. Fossheim is a lecturer in Philosophy at the University of Oslo. His research focuses primarily on Plato and Aristotle.

Adam Morton holds the Canada Research Chair in epistemology and decision theory at the University of Alberta. His current work concerns the intelligent reaction to limitations in one's reasoning powers: how to think about the fact that your head is only human sized. He has also taught at Princeton, Ottawa, Bristol, and Oklahoma. His most recent books are *The Importance of Being Understood: Folk Psychology as Ethics*, and *On Evil* (both Routledge).

Timothy Chappell is Professor of Philosophy at The Open University. He has also taught at the Universities of East Anglia, Manchester, Dundee, and Oxford, and has held visiting positions at the Universities of British Columbia, Edinburgh, and St Andrews. His other books are *Aristotle and Augustine on Freedom* (Macmillan, 1995), *The Plato Reader* (Edinburgh University Press, 1996), *The Philosophy of the Environment* (ed., Edinburgh University Press, 1997), *Understanding Human Goods* (Edinburgh University Press, 1998), *Human Values: Essays in Consequentialist and Non-consequentialist Ethical Theory* (co-edited with D. Oderberg, Macmillan, 2004), *Reading Plato's Theaetetus* (Hackett and Academia Verlag, 2005), and *The Inescapable Self* (Orion, 2005).

Paul Russell is Professor in Philosophy at the University of British Columbia, where he has been teaching since 1987. He was born in Glasgow, Scotland, in 1955. He is a graduate of Queen's University at Kingston (B.A.), Edinburgh University (M.A.), and holds a Ph.D. from Cambridge University. He has been a research fellow at Sidney Sussex College, Cambridge (1984–6); a visiting assistant professor at the University of Virginia (1988); a Mellon fellow and a visiting assistant professor at Stanford University (1989–90); a fellow of the Institute for Advanced Studies in the Humanities at Edinburgh University (1991 and 1996); visiting associate professor at the University of Pittsburgh (1996–7), and visiting professor (Kenan Distinguished Visitor) at the University of North Carolina at Chapel Hill (2005). His principal research interests include problems of free will and moral responsibility, and the history of early modern philosophy (particularly David Hume). He is the author of *Freedom and Moral Sentiment: Hume's Way of Naturalizing Responsibility* (Oxford University Press, 1995; Oxford Online Scholarship, 2003).

Christine Swanton is Senior Lecturer in Philosophy at the University of Auckland, and author of *Freedom: A Coherence Theory* (Hackett, 1992; winner of the Johnsonian Prize, 1990), and of *Virtue Ethics: A Pluralistic View* (Oxford University Press, 2003). She has published extensively in moral theory, including work on virtue ethics, role ethics, Hume, and Nietzsche.

Karen Stohr is Assistant Professor of Philosophy at Georgetown University. Her main research area is ethics, with a focus on Aristotelian virtue ethics and Kantian ethics. She is also interested in social and political philosophy, feminism, and bioethics, particularly in the Catholic tradition. Her present research concerns the virtue of practical wisdom, moral risk and responsibility in childbirth, moral obligations to improve the moral perfection of others, and latitude and mandatory aid in Kantian ethics. Recent publications include: 'Practical Wisdom and Moral Imagination in Sense and Sensibility', forthcoming in *Philosophy and Literature*; 'Moral Cacophony: When Continence is a Virtue', *The Journal of Ethics* (2003); 'Virtue Ethics and Kant's Cold-Hearted Benefactor', *Journal of Value Inquiry* (2002); and 'Recent Work in Virtue Ethics', with Christopher H. Wellman, *American Philosophical Quarterly* (2002). She is also a member of the Ethics Committee at Providence Hospital in Washington, D.C.

Sandrine Berges holds a Ph.D. from Leeds University. She teaches in the Philosophy Department at Bilkent University in Ankara. She is currently working on legal and political philosophy in Platonic dialogues.

Johan Brännmark currently holds a position as researcher at the Department of Philosophy, Lund University. He has taught at Umeå University and been a Fellow at the Swedish Collegium for Advanced Study in the Social Sciences, Uppsala. His dissertation,

'Morality and the Pursuit of Happiness' (Lund, 2002), was a study in Kantian ethics. He is now working on value theory.

Theodore Scaltsas is Professor of Ancient Philosophy, University of Edinburgh. His books include *Substances and Universals in Aristotle's Metaphysics* (Ithaca, 1994) and *Unity, Identity and Explanation in Aristotle's Metaphysics* (co-edited with D. Charles and M. L. Gill, Oxford, 1994). His most recent publications are on the topics of plural subjects, relations, and ontological composition. He is the director of Project Archélogos.

Talbot Brewer is an associate professor in the Corcoran Department of Philosophy at the University of Virginia, and a faculty fellow at the University of Virginia's Institute for Advanced Studies in Culture. His recent publications include, 'Virtues We Can Share: Friendship and Aristotelian Ethical Theory', *Ethics* (2005), 'Maxims and Virtues', *The Philosophical Review* (2002), 'The Real Problem with Internalism about Reasons', *Canadian Journal of Philosophy* (2002), 'The Character of Temptation: Towards a More Plausible Kantian Moral Psychology', *Pacific Philosophical Quarterly* (2002), 'Savoring Time: Desire, Pleasure and Wholehearted Activity', *Ethical Theory and Moral Practice* (2003), and 'Two Kinds of Commitments (and Two Kinds of Social Groups)', *Philosophy and Phenomenological Research* (2003).

Introduction

Timothy Chappell

After twenty-four centuries, Aristotle's influence on our society's moral thinking remains profound even when subterranean. Much of the finest work in recent ethics has been overtly Aristotelian in inspiration, especially, of course, in the area of virtue ethics—but not only there. Many writers who would officially distance themselves from Aristotle and his contemporary followers are none the less indebted to him, sometimes in ways that they do not even realize.

This volume brings together some of the best recent work in Aristotelian ethics and virtue ethics. The authors write on a wide variety of topics; yet what is striking, when their essays are presented together, is how strong the thematic connections are between them. It becomes obvious that the very diverse research programmes that they are pursuing are none the less parts of a single conversation.

Christopher Coope bases his argument on a survey of the development of 'Modern Virtue Ethics' since Elizabeth Anscombe's classic paper, 'Modern Moral Philosophy' (*Philosophy*, 1958). Coope follows Anscombe's lead in more than his title. His survey is not merely informative about how the argument has developed, but also highly perceptive—and provocative—about where, as he sees it, the argument has gone wrong.

We could say, with only a hint of paradox, that Coope is dubious about modern virtue ethics for Aristotelian reasons. Unlike some of the other contributors, Coope shares Anscombe's doubts about contemporary moral theory. His worry is that to develop virtue ethics as another genus of moral philosophy, *alongside* consequentialism, deontology, and other rivals, and competing with them to give the best account of a supposedly uncontroversial notion of 'moral rightness', is to miss the most important point of doing virtue ethics in the first place—which is to demystify our discussions of moral matters by giving an analysis of the key notions, including that of moral rightness.

As Anscombe saw—like Nietzsche before her, and Bernard Williams after—our specially moral concepts have a very mixed and peculiar historical freight. Yet even at this late stage, Coope suggests, it is still possible for us to return to a simpler and more straightforward way of thinking about ethics. This is where Aristotle can help us. On the Aristotelian approach, as Coope develops it, our key concepts will be, not 'moral virtue' but simple *good sense*; not 'special moral obligation', but *acting reasonably*; not a high-defined, moralistic notion of '*true* or *real* happiness' but *being fortunate*; even, perhaps, not 'ethics' but *ta prakta*—matters for practical decision. As Coope puts it, 'the connection between simple practical rationality and goodness is obscured by conventional moral fervour'. Anscombe's and Foot's sort of approach clarifies the connection by dropping the fervour.

In Coope's view, this return to the Aristotelian notion of *good sense* is what Anscombe and Foot were proposing. By comparison, he sees most modern virtue ethicists as relapsing into just the conventional ways of doing moral philosophy that virtue ethics might, with better luck, have displaced. As a result, he claims, there is little beyond labels and emphases to distinguish too much modern virtue ethics from other approaches. Moreover, virtue ethics as now mostly practised has, Coope believes, been influential in spreading some important errors: above all, as he puts it, 'the cardinal virtue of justice, "more glorious than the morning or the evening star", has become damagingly marginalized'.

While Coope criticizes modern virtue ethics for treating justice as a minor virtue, he also freely admits to seeing a problem about whether justice is (or at least can be argued to be) a virtue at all. But there is, he insists, no paradox: 'there is a world of difference. For justice, *if* it is a virtue, can only be a cardinal, pivotal, or key virtue.' Though justice, if it is a virtue at all, will have to be a cardinal one, that fact does not foreclose the question what reason *I* can have to realize *to allotrion agathon*, 'someone else's benefit' (*Republic* 343c5), which is what justice often seems to involve doing.

As Coope observes, the force of Glaucon's challenge was always obvious to Foot and Anscombe: they understood very well that it was a central problem for ethics to justify justice. (See Anscombe 1958: 40; and Foot 1978: 125.) One way in which Coope thinks things have gone downhill in modern virtue ethics is the increasing lack of grip on this problem about justice.

To judge by their contributions to the collection, Linda Zagzebski and Fred Miller are two contemporary writers on virtue ethics who escape this criticism. As we might expect from her title—'The Admirable Life and the Desirable Life'—**Linda Zagzebski** begins her chapter by raising the question of how virtue and flourishing are connected. If we can show that there is a tight connection between virtue and flourishing, that may help us to answer two important questions in ethics. One of these is the metaphysical question 'What grounds the moral?'—the question of what rightness and goodness consist in, and why. (Obviously this is a broader question than Coope's question 'Why be just?'—but, equally obviously, it is a related question.) The other is the motivational question 'Why be moral?'—the question why anyone should *want* to have the virtues.

Zagzebski is as sceptical as Coope about the prospects for attempts, however ingenious, to solve these two problems by devising accounts of flourishing and virtue that dovetail with each other so perfectly that there can *never* be a serious clash between them. She also thinks that such ingenuity would be misplaced anyway. This is because she rejects the most widely accepted view—the one found, for example, in Foot and Hursthouse—about how the concept of flourishing grounds the concept of virtue. On that view, flourishing is the basic concept and virtue the problematic one; and success with our two questions means arriving at an understanding of virtue that makes sense of it relative to the concept of flourishing. For Zagzebski, by contrast, our account of virtue is not built upon the foundation of flourishing in the first place. Virtue and flourishing are both concepts that presuppose something else as their theoretical foundation. This something else is the *exemplars* of virtue which for Zagzebski provide 'the hook that connects our theory [of ethics] to that part of the world with which the theory is concerned'—'the ethical domain' (Zagzebski, this volume, p.55).

Zagzebski is working here with an analogy between the reference of ethical and of natural-kind terms. Kripke, Putnam, Donnellan, and others have famously argued that the reference of natural-kind terms—'gold' and 'water' are the usual examples—is not fixed by learning the meaning of a relevant description (e.g. 'heavy yellow fusible metal', or 'clear liquid found, in impure forms, in rivers, lakes and seas'). Rather, the reference of such terms is learned *directly*, by ostension. We learn to use 'water' by seeing a sample of water, and understanding that 'water' refers to 'anything of the same essential kind as *that*' [said while ostending the water]; or else, at second hand, we learn to use natural-kind terms ('uranium', 'the bonobo') by learning to use them in the same way as those who have (explicitly or implicitly) performed such a process of ostension. Just likewise, Zagzebski proposes, with our ethical exemplars: direct reference to these exemplars has exactly the central and basic place in our ethical discourse that direct reference to 'gold', 'water', 'uranium', and so forth has in our scientific discourse.

Zagzebski's exemplarist proposal gives us an Aristotelian ethical theory in which reference comes first, and descriptions come second. We shall often be able to refer to exemplars of central ethical concepts, even though we cannot explain *why* they are examplars of those concepts by giving full descriptive accounts of the concepts. So, for instance, with practical wisdom: 'Aristotle has quite a bit to say about what the virtue of *phronesis* consists in, but he clearly is not confident that he can give a full account of it'; but 'fundamentally, this does not matter, because we can pick out persons who are *phronimoi* in advance of investigating the nature of *phronesis*. The *phronimos* can be defined, roughly, as a person *like that.*'

As Zagzebski says, one thing that her exemplarism makes good sense of is the Aristotelian emphasis on imitation in moral education: more on that in Fossheim's essay, below. Zagzebski's proposal also seems to have important anti-sceptical implications: if the *foundation* of our theory of ethics is provided by our direct contact with instances of (genuine) goodness, then it is hard to see room for the idea that our whole theory might be systematically mistaken about what is good and bad. (Contrast Anscombe 1958: 57 as quoted by Coope p.46, this volume.) Again, Zagzebski's exemplarism enables her to copy Aristotle's derivation of pleasure and desire from the notion of the *agathos*. For her, as for Aristotle, what is truly desirable or pleasant is what admirable people desire or find pleasant. Here the admirable people are, of course, the exemplars, and those who approximate more or less closely to them.

Finally, Zagzebski's exemplarism brings us something like an answer to the question 'Why be moral?' Zagzebski develops two lines of thought about this question. The first is that, if virtue and other (truly) desirable things are—as she takes them to be—distinct and separable components of the human good, then it is no more surprising that some unpropitious circumstances should create tension between *these* two components than between any other two: 'the difference between flourishing and living virtuously is due to luck', but 'this is just another case of the general truth that the compatibility of most of the important components of a good human life is a matter of luck' (this volume, p.61). In this sense, the question 'Why be moral (if you also want to flourish)?' is not much more pressing than the question 'Why play rugby (if you also want healthy knee-joints when you are eighty)?'

This, of course, does not yet show that virtue is something that we reasonably want as well as flourishing, in the way that we might reasonably want rugby as well as healthy knee-joints. Part of Zagzebski's response to this more basic challenge is already clear: it is to argue that what is *truly* desirable is what the admirable desire—and they desire virtue. Spelling this out further, she adds an argument that anyone whose life we find admirable is bound to be someone that we find 'attractingly imitable'. As a matter of the structure of our concepts, exemplars of the admirable are *introduced* into our understanding as examples that we are motivated to imitate. This does not mean that our motivation to imitate those whom we find admirable, and so be moral, will always be our *overriding* motivation. But it does mean that, for anyone who is capable of admiring the right exemplars, there is always *some* motivating reason to be moral.

In 'Virtue and Rights in Aristotle's Best Regime', **Fred Miller** comes at the problem of justice from quite a different angle. Putting that problem into what is arguably its only proper context, the political one, he recasts the problem about the place of justice in virtue ethics, as a problem about the place of rights in the best regime.

'A serious issue for modern virtue ethics', Miller begins, 'is whether it can justify the respect for individual rights.' In a virtue ethics, this justification will surely have to come from the virtue of *justice*, if it comes from anywhere. Conversely, there will be little content to the virtue of justice if it does not ground respect for individual rights. Moreover, if modern virtue ethics is supposed to be a theory of, *inter alia*, moral obligation—a point on which Miller displays none of Coope's diffidence—then it can hardly allow that an agent can be completely virtuous, yet simply disregard the rights of others.

So if Aristotle had a plausible theory of virtue in the community—i.e. a theory of justice—then it must have committed him to a substantive theory of individual rights. The trouble is that most commentators have seen little or no sign of anything like a rights theory in Aristotle's *Politics*. In his close study of Aristotle's *Politics* and related texts, Miller's aim is to assemble the evidence that they have been missing.

Miller's argument is structured around the two main objections to the thesis that Aristotle has a theory of rights. The first objection is that Aristotle, like other ancient philosophers, had no concept of rights. Sometimes, as in MacIntyre 1981: 67, this conclusion is inferred from the premiss that Aristotle, like other ancient philosophers, had no word for 'rights'. Second is the objection that even if Aristotle does have (something like) a concept of rights, still rights on Aristotle's conception will necessarily be very feeble in comparison with rights as they are understood by modern rights theorists. For Aristotle (so the objection runs) shares Plato's holistic inclinations, and with them his readiness to sacrifice the interests of individuals to the public interest.

On the first objection, Miller begins by pointing out that the 'lexical' argument is simply a *non sequitur*. Speakers of a language which lacks a (single) word for *x* need not, just for that reason, lack the concept of an *x*. For example, English has the one word 'uncle' where Urdu has separate terms for 'father's brother', 'mother's sister's husband', etc., and no one word to cover all these relations. This does not show that English- and Urdu-speakers have different uncle-concepts.

Anyway, as Miller goes on to show, it can easily be argued that pretty well all of our rights-talk *is* translatable into ancient Greek. Miller makes this point by considering Hohfeld's well-known taxonomy of four sorts of rights (claim-rights, liberty-rights, authority-rights, and immunity-rights), and showing how a direct translation of each of Hohfeld's four terms into Aristotle's Greek might plausibly be provided (respectively, as *to dikaion*, *exousia/exesti*, *kyrios*, and *adeia/ateleia*). After some clarification of his position against criticisms of Vivienne Brown's, Miller goes on to argue in close textual detail that the core of Aristotle's notion of rights is something very like the Hohfeldian notion of a claim-right.

Finally, Miller addresses the second objection to his thesis—the claim that even if Aristotle does recognize something like rights, they will have no real argumentative weight because Aristotle is also theoretically committed to something like Plato's political holism. Miller argues that this objection misreads Aristotle. Though Aristotle is certainly no modern liberal, he is not a Platonic holist either. His best regime is based on a moderate individualism, central to which is a commitment to ensure the possibility of the best life—the life of complete virtue—for *each* citizen in the state. This will be impossible unless each citizen's rights are respected. The idea that Aristotle may be committed to *some* sort of individual rights, but that these rights are too easily overridden to be worth very much, is therefore mistaken.

If Miller is right, then clearly an Aristotelian virtue ethics can solve the problem about justice with which we began. It can do this by showing how, once we are set up in civil society, the aim of making the best life possible for all will necessarily lead us to deal justly with each citizen—and in particular, to assign each citizen his rights.

The key to the solution is the move from the individual to the political context. Given that this move works so well, it is natural to wonder whether virtue ethics might not be equally fruitfully applied in another context, closely interrelated with the political: the context of law. Many legal theorists have had this thought. The approach to the philosophy of law called 'virtue jurisprudence', which argues that ideas of virtue and vice ought to play a central role in our understanding of the proper aims and principles of systems of law, though not the majority approach, is certainly an influential one. But is such an approach really plausible, as a general way of understanding how the law works (and/or should work)?

This is the question taken up by **Antony Duff** in 'The Virtues and Vices of Virtue Jurisprudence'. His answer to the question is carefully qualified. He sketches some of the ways in which the virtue-jurisprudential approach has been applied to the criminal law. One application has been seen in claims that the proper ground or object of criminal liability is the vice displayed in an offender's action. Duff finds these claims over-ambitious and over-general. None the less, he does think that virtue theory can play a useful and important role in legal philosophy, provided we move to a level of greater detail. Duff is cautiously optimistic about the prospects for a virtue-jurisprudential analysis of two well-known criminal defences, namely duress and provocation (the latter being, however, only a partial defence). Duff shows how we can best understand these defences in roughly Aristotelian terms, as involving action motivated by an appropriate emotion that is strongly, and reasonably, aroused—would be aroused, as jurists say, in the 'reasonable person'—but that is also apt to destabilize or mislead even a person of moderate virtue.

If this *can* be done, it is tempting to extend the treatment. Perhaps criminal law should admit a wider emotion-based defence, not limited to the emotions of fear and anger but covering crimes understandably motivated by any appropriately, and strongly, felt emotion? Duff shows how such an excuse could be articulated, but is careful not to commit himself definitively on the issue of whether such a defence should be admitted in general. He clearly thinks that this style of defence is bound to face serious problems. After all, he has already noted of provocation that the virtue-jurisprudential analysis of this defence tends to raise the question of what counts as a *virtuous* response to provocation. But violence is hardly ever going to be the response to provocation that the virtues *enjoin*; indeed, it won't often be a response that the virtues even *permit*. This doubt about the emotion-based version of the provocation defence seems likely to generalize, casting doubt on any emotion-based defence whatever. All the same, Duff leaves the issue open; as is shown by the list of questions with which he ends his discussion of emotion-based defences, he doubts that a single clear verdict on the viability of all such defences is available. Here as elsewhere, there will be cases and cases.

The possibility of a defence of 'emotional duress' brings Duff back, finally, to the claim which he began by rejecting. For might that possibility not seem to pave the way back to the virtue-jurisprudents' more ambitious claim that *all* criminal liability is grounded in vice? Duff rejects this idea: we can, he suggests, make use of virtue-based notions to think specifically about the defence of emotional duress, without thereby committing ourselves in general to a virtue-based view of criminal liability.

No doubt one of the original stimuli to the development of virtue jurisprudence was a remarkable piece of exemplarism, to use Zagzebski's term, which is deeply embedded in the English common-law tradition. This is the common law's frequent appeal to the judgements of the 'reasonable person' (historically, the 'reasonable man'). Duff discusses this sort of appeal in passing in his chapter, sounding a sceptical note about it. Perhaps, he suggests, we would be less confused about the real nature and the consequences of this appeal if we stopped invoking the imaginary figure of the 'reasonable person' to ask 'would the reasonable person have done this?', and instead asked ourselves simply 'was it *reasonable* to do this?'

Zagzebski would presumably reject this suggestion of Duff's. She would say that our appeal to the reasonable *person* is not just verbally different from Duff's appeal to the *concept* of reasonableness. The difference between the two appeals is that the appeal the reasonable *person* is an appeal to an exemplar, a reference-fixing sample of reasonableness (or practical wisdom). Now the nature of reasonableness is, in the end, fixed by direct ostension of such samples. Hence, to appeal to the concept of reasonableness when we could appeal to the reasonable man is to settle for the explanatorily second-best; for the concept of reasonableness is derivative from paradigm samples of reasonableness, and cannot be well understood in isolation from them.

If Zagzebski is right about this, the 'reasonable person' might have a more prominent place than Duff allows in virtue jurisprudence—a place parallel to the place of the *phronimos* in Aristotelian political and ethical theory. It will also be easy to see how acquiring the virtues, and especially the rather elusive but utterly central virtue of practical wisdom, is likely to be more a matter of imitating the virtues' exemplars than of learning whatever rules—if any—the virtues generate.

Zagzebski's interest in the notion of imitation in ethics is shared by **Hallvard Fossheim** in 'Habituation as *Mimesis*'. Fossheim is concerned with a question about Aristotle's account of moral habituation. What is it, according to Aristotle, that gives us our first motivation to pursue 'the good and the noble'? How can 'the learner', as Fossheim calls the person who is beginning to acquire moral concepts, come to love the noble? One influential answer to this question has been that it happens when we follow the advice of others who are more morally advanced than ourselves. Another has been that the practice of virtue leads to the enjoyment of virtue. But the first of these answers seems to beg the question. Unless we are already inclined to virtue, it is hard to see why we should *want* to follow others' advice, however morally wise they may be. And the second answer merely prompts a further question: *why* should the practice of virtue lead to the enjoyment of virtue?

We might answer that the practice of virtue brings enjoyment because it is characteristically associated with pleasure. If this were right, then the association between virtue and pleasure would be extrinsic in the learner. But we know from Aristotle that the association is supposed to be intrinsic in the person of full virtue; so the association account would still need to explain how extrinsic pleasure becomes intrinsic. (Maybe, on the association account, this transition could only happen by way of some sort of self-deception—a suspicion one might also entertain about Mill's account of the same transition in *Utiliiarianism*, chapter 4: 'What was once desired as an instrument for the attainment of happiness [*sc.* virtue], has come to be desired for its own sake.')

In any case, Fossheim prefers a different and less indirect answer from that offered by the association account. Fossheim's striking idea—one that has been surprisingly under-exploited in the literature—is that the human instinct to imitate is one of the main sources of our original motivation to be moral. Fossheim develops this idea by reference to Aristotle's main discussion of *mimesis*, in the *Poetics*. He concedes, of course, that this instinct can only be a beginning: in particular, it does not account for the intellectual understanding that comes with practical wisdom, which for Aristotle is a crucial component of full virtue. He also admits the obvious point that the human instinct to imitate can set us in the direction of vice, if we are surrounded by bad exemplars. But that just underlines the truth of Aristotle's famous remark (*NE* 1103b24) that in ethics 'education is the main thing—indeed, it is the only thing'. If Fossheim is right, moral education has to involve imitation—'practical *mimesis*', as he calls it—because the point of the process is as it were for the actor to grow into his mask: 'we end up *being*— bringing fully to reality—what we began by merely *imitating*'.

Fossheim's interest in the learning processes that are involved in acquiring the virtues is shared by **Adam Morton**. In his chapter 'Moral Incompetence', Morton's thesis is the very Aristotelian claim that there is much more to being a good person than meaning well. We also need what Morton calls 'moral competence', and he uses a series of engaging examples to diagnose and describe moral *in*competence—a 'broad category of action and thinking . . . which is responsible for much of the harm that well-intentioned people do'. Moral incompetence is, broadly, the lack of a 'capacity to handle specifically moral aspects of problem-solving'. Its opposite, moral competence, is the presence of this capacity, and—to a degree—can be learned.

(A lack of) moral competence seems close to what we colloquially call (a lack of) nous or gumption. Since, as a problem-solving capacity, moral competence has an obvious intellectual element, it may also be close to what Aristotelians call practical wisdom. Hence, an obvious question about moral competence and incompetence—compare my own contribution in the subsequent chapter—is the question whether they have any genuine unity. 'Perhaps the conclusion to draw' from Morton's examples 'is simply that moral decisions can be hard, so that a variety of cognitive failings can cause us to bungle them'. Complexity defeats human understanding in most matters—so it is no surprise if it defeats it in moral matters too. If bafflement in the face of complexity is all that moral incompetence comes to, we need not posit a specially *moral* sort of incompetence to explain the facts that moral complexities sometimes get the better of us, and that some of us are better at dealing with moral complexity than others.

In response Morton argues, first, that there is a specifically moral form of (in)competence in dealing with complexity: 'a person can be capable of performing reasonably well at thoughtful tasks in general, but be a persistent bungler of moral problems.' This is so because—although there is no such thing as 'a specific moral faculty, failure of which can be dissociated from general intellectual failure'—still, 'among the large and varied bundle of competences that allow us to handle life's problems', some specific combinations 'are particularly relevant to finding acceptable ways through moral problems'. It is the lack of these combinations of competences that amounts to moral incompetence.

Second, Morton observes that, if we try and tell the story of how moral competence can be acquired, two accounts look most plausible—the Aristotelian and the Kantian—both of which necessarily leave room for the possibility of a specifically moral inability to cope with complexity. Moral incompetence is inevitably possible on the Aristotelian account of how moral competence is acquired, because this involves the imitation of exemplars, the stockpiling of relevant experience, the development of a sense of what experience *is* relevant—and so on; all of which are obviously fallible processes. Likewise, the Kantian account of the acquisition of moral competence is basically an account of how we learn to subsume particulars under generalities, which we then learn to test. This account, too, since it invokes processes and abilities that are necessarily fallible, is sure to leave room for the possibility of specifically moral incompetence.

So is moral competence a virtue? In particular, is it the virtue of practical wisdom? Morton notes three disanalogies that someone might see between moral competence and more typical virtues. None of them, he thinks, disposes decisively of the thesis that moral competence *is* a virtue, provided we understand that it is a virtue of a rather non-standard kind. (An intellectual rather than a moral virtue, perhaps?—as, of course, Aristotle suggests.) But, Morton concludes, what really matters is not how we classify moral competence, but that we see its vital importance to human flourishing.

A different way of asking whether moral competence, or practical wisdom, is a virtue, is to ask whether it is *one* virtue. This is the question that I raise in my chapter 'The Variety of Life and the Unity of Practical Wisdom'.

A problem about the Aristotelian virtue of 'practical wisdom', as this is normally understood in the contemporary literature, is that it can seem an entirely shapeless virtue—so shapeless as barely to be a virtue at all. Typical virtues, like courage and temperance, are particular dispositions with particular fields of operation. By contrast practical wisdom, *phronesis*, is defined by Aristotle (*NE* 1140b5–7) as 'a truthful disposition', one which is accompanied by reason and practical, and which is 'concerned with what is good or bad for humans'. It sounds, then, like practical wisdom is simply a disposition *to get things right in action*. But it is hard to see why we should want to say that there is any *one* disposition to do that. And there are at least three reasons not to say it. First, the *unity problem*: the 'things' that need to be 'got right in action' seem too various for it to be possible that a single disposition could apply to all of them. Second, the *overlap problem*: either a disposition *to get things right in action* will crowd out the other virtues—it will do all their work, leaving them with nothing to do; or else this disposition itself will get 'crowded out'. And third, the *triviality problem*: a disposition to 'get things right in action' sounds trivial and vacuous. Positing such a disposition explains nothing, and does not make practical wisdom something that we can discuss or teach in any rational way. Appeals to such a disposition in ethical theory will be mere hand- (or wand-) waving.

In my chapter I examine two responses to this set of problems about practical wisdom. The first is (what I take to be) Aristotle's own response, the doctrine of the mean; the second is one form of the modern doctrine of particularism. I reject both responses: they do not help us to understand the nature of practical wisdom, and anyway are implausible in themselves. I then offer my own response. This involves me in rethinking the relation of belief and desire in motivation (cp. Brewer's discussion in Chapter 14). In most recent philosophy, this relation has been understood in Humean terms—desire as the engine; belief as the steering-wheel of motivation. I reject this picture, and offer an alternative picture on which our only intrinsic motivations to action are not desires, as Hume thought, but the perceptions of mutual relevance, between (sets of) desires and beliefs, of the strong sort that we call *reasons to act*. Now although perceiving our reasons to act is often very easy, it is not always—perhaps, even, not usually. Hence there can be such a thing as *skill* in perceiving our reasons to act, by skilfully conjoining our beliefs and desires. This skill, I propose, is what practical wisdom is. No doubt my account makes practical wisdom a very general thing, and to that extent leaves unfinished business at the end of the chapter. None the less, the account does explain how practical wisdom can be a genuinely unitary disposition, with a particular and definite shape, that can be related to the other virtues without raising the overlap problem. Further, my account of practical wisdom does not make it trivial to invoke that disposition for explanatory purposes, especially when the account is conjoined with a specific normative ethics—as it needs to be, though I do not attempt to spell this out here.

Though Hume's ethics is reasonably well established as a source for virtue ethics in general, it is no surprise—given Hume's well-known anti-cognitivist tendencies—that Hume is rarely thought of as someone who has much to tell us about practical wisdom. **Paul Russell**, in his chapter 'Moral Sense and Virtue in Hume's Ethics', is candid about the thinness (or at least scatteredness) of the evidence, but tenacious in his pursuit of the thesis that there is more of a place than is generally realized for something very like practical wisdom in Hume's ethics. Russell meticulously assembles the disjoined textual evidence for a number of important claims about Hume's views on the virtues. Thereby he shows that Hume had subtle and interesting views about a number of central topics in virtue ethics: not only about practical wisdom but also about moral education, the relation between the good and the noble or admirable, and the places and relative functions of pleasure, desire, belief, and reason in ethics.

Russell focuses on Hume's foundational notions: 'virtue' and 'moral sense'. He shows that Hume regards virtue as continuous with our other admirable qualities, including our natural abilities such as intelligence, and even including physical beauty. Unlike Aristotle, Hume does not see virtue as picked out by any special relation to the will. Virtue is, simply, whatever *mental quality* excites the admiration of our moral sense—a simplification in Hume's moral theory that has attracted much criticism, for example, in Foot 1978: 74–80. Russell does not deny that Hume defines virtue in this simple way; but he does insist that so defining virtue need not prevent Hume from making any distinctions at all. Naturally, Hume sees some differences between qualities like loyalty and qualities like beauty, especially in respect of the usefulness of punishment for reforming them.

The relation of moral sense to the moral virtues is also different from its relation to other admirable qualities. It may be true for Hume that—to use a metaphor that he favoured—a person's moral virtues attract the approbation due to a sort of 'moral beauty'; this idea is strikingly reminiscent of Aristotle's emphasis on the noble person (*ho kaloskagathos*) as the moral ideal. None the less, the response of our moral sense to moral virtues is typically more complex, and more intellectually based, than its response to such simple admirable qualities as good looks or agility.

Of course, there are some parallels. Both with justice and with good looks, there is a simple feedback mechanism: we approve of others' approval of us, and so we approve of ourselves being just or handsome, because these are qualities that excite others' approval of us. But there are also differences. In the case of the moral virtues, the approval of others is not just desired because it is pleasant, but because it is felt to be justified (both intellectually and morally). If we engage in moral reflection, we shall see that being just, or benevolent, meets the sort of standard of merit that we would like to have general currency in our society. This kind of exercise of moral reflection takes us to a much higher level of intellectual activity than the simple enjoyment of others' admiration for my good looks or agility. But such moral reflection is itself an exercise of what Hume calls 'moral sense'. This goes to show the inadequacy of the widespread 'thin' understanding of 'moral sense', as no more than Humean passion's intellectually blank response to any pleasing object.

Russell argues that Humean moral sense, so far from being characterized by simple acts of 'emoting', is the raw material of Humean moral reflection. As we learn to respond not only to the moral phenomena around us but also to ourselves, so we develop a capacity—at its best, discursive in form and intellectually sophisticated in character—for 'reviewing our own character and conduct from a general point of view'. This is moral reflection, and it serves for Hume 'as a master virtue, whereby a person is able to cultivate and sustain other, more particular virtues'; just as practical wisdom serves as a master virtue for Aristotle. Russell adds that Humean moral reflection is like Aristotelian practical wisdom in another respect, too: for it represents not the triumph of reason over passion (or vice versa) but the fusion of reason and sentiment in the interests of virtue. (With Russell's Humean fusion of reason and sentiment, compare the anti-Humean fusion of belief and desire in reasons that is sketched in my chapter.)

Hume has often interested virtue ethicists, including Philippa Foot, and not always as an object of criticism. Another philosopher whom many recent virtue ethicists have taken seriously—again, partly no doubt because of Foot's interest in him (Foot 1973: 81–95)—is Friedrich Nietzsche. In her chapter 'Can Nietzsche be Both an Existentialist and a Virtue Ethicist?', **Christine Swanton**'s answer to her own question is an emphatic 'yes': she sees Nietzsche's thought as a rich, powerful, and underrated resource for virtue ethics.

As Swanton begins by acknowledging, there might seem to be insurmountable obstacles to seeing Nietzsche as a virtue ethicist. Some of these obstacles stand in the way of seeing Nietzsche as *any* sort of ethicist, given his willingness to undermine the very idea of 'morality' by providing it with a genealogy, or indeed to attack it head-on by his characteristic method of argument-as-vituperation. At times, quite clearly, Nietzsche sees morality as the *enemy*.

None the less, we might reject—as Swanton does—the reading of Nietzsche as an advocate of immoralism. We can still read Nietzsche as a critic of morality, and thereby make sense of the Nietzschean idea that 'morality is the enemy' in a way not so very far from Christopher Coope's thesis in Chapter 1. Nietzsche's willingness to raise fundamental questions about the whole phenomenon of morality by looking at its history is one of the most obvious things that Nietzsche shares with mainstream virtue ethicists. (With Anscombe 1958: 26's 'the teeth don't come together in a proper bite', compare this: ' "How much the conscience formerly had to bite on! What good teeth it had!—And today? What's the trouble?'—A dentist's question" ' (Nietzsche 1968: 24). Though Anscombe never alludes to it, it is hard to believe that she had not read this aphorism.) Until the revival of modern virtue ethics, no philosopher for literally centuries—not since Hobbes's time at the latest—had seen the problem about how to vindicate morality, and particularly justice, as clearly as Nietzsche. So even if Nietzsche has no place (and would want no place) in any study of morality that presupposes 'the special sense of "moral"', Swanton is surely right to insist that he has a place of honour in the history of the broader Aristotelian inquiry into what counts as human flourishing.

Here, however, we come to a second obstacle to Swanton's reading of Nietzsche. This is that virtue ethicists typically base their account of human *happiness* on an account of human *nature*; whereas Nietzsche seems to have little use for either notion. He is uninterested (it might be said) in the notion of human nature, because, like other existentialists, his principal interest is not in generalizations about the mass of men but in the free and undetermined individual (compare Sartre's famous slogan 'Existence precedes essence'). And he is uninterested in the notion of human happiness, because he thinks that it is better for humans (some of them, at least) to be *great* than to be happy.

Swanton rebuts these criticisms of her reading. To take the second point first, Nietzsche's contempt for happiness- or pleasure-based moralities such as utilitarianism hardly shows that Nietzsche is uninterested in the more basic Aristotelian notion of *flourishing*. It merely shows that he thinks—plausibly enough—that there is more to flourishing than happiness or pleasure. As for human nature, it is, of course, obvious that Nietzsche does not offer the sort of triple-decker psychology (desires–*thumos*–intellect) that we find in Plato and Aristotle, or use such a psychology as the basis for a theory of the virtues. But what Nietzsche does give us, as Swanton demonstrates in detail, is a subtle and complex picture of the virtues and vices of an existential individual. The root of all these virtues is self-love or self-acceptance (here one is reminded of the role of 'moral reflection' in Paul Russell's account of Hume); and the root of all the vices is the urge to escape or run away from oneself. For this picture to be worth having, it needs to have some general application—to apply to more people than just Nietzsche himself. But it obviously won't have this general application unless people are sufficiently alike for there to be at least *some* sense in speaking of a 'human nature'. Nietzsche too, then, for all his acknowledged differences, can still be classed as a philosopher who offers us an account of the character-traits that we need to avoid or develop if we wish to flourish, and one who bases this account on a subtle, interesting, and very original psychology ('out of my writings there speaks a *psychologist* who has not his equal'—Nietzsche 1979: 45). To say this much is to say that Nietzsche is a virtue ethicist.

What, then, might be *practical wisdom* for Nietzsche? Swanton herself notes a striking parallel between the place of practical wisdom in Aristotle's ethics, and the place of integrity in the existentialists': 'Integrity . . . is the expression of practical choice as opposed to a drifting into modes of behaviour and comportment which deny, or are an escape from, self. Like Aristotle's practical wisdom, integrity is the precondition or core of virtue.'

Right though Swanton surely is about this parallel, it *is* a parallel, and not an identity-relation, between practical wisdom and integrity. So the question

remains open what an existentialist such as Nietzsche should say about practical
wisdom itself. It might seem unsurprising if Nietzsche said *nothing* about
practical wisdom: compared with the exciting traits that he usually emphasizes—charisma, spontaneity, authenticity, creativity, imagination, 'overflowing',
and so forth—practical wisdom seems a rather grey virtue. (One thinks of Blake:
'Prudence is a rich ugly old maid courted by incapacity.') But in fact this line
of thought is mistaken. It is quite clear, above all perhaps in *Zarathustra*, that
the possessors of Nietzschean excellence are supposed to be practically wise. No
doubt they will have much need of practical wisdom if they are to acquire the
integrity, the happy relationship to themselves, that is central to Nietzsche's
ethical thought. This will be so even if this practical wisdom is, in them, largely
an unconscious and inarticulate thing, more to be admired than explained; or if
explained, then better understood through a narrative than through a theory.

   This important existentialist idea that narrative can be a mode of ethical
understanding, and an accompanying stress on the use of the imagination as an
essential part of the exercise of practical wisdom, has become very influential
in virtue ethics. The influence is obvious in **Karen Stohr**'s chapter, 'Manners,
Morals, and Practical Wisdom', in which she develops a rich account of some
important but often-neglected aspects of practical wisdom by looking closely
at the narratives of Jane Austen's novels. Specifically, Stohr focuses on good
manners—an obvious form of what Adam Morton would call moral competence.
She argues that 'it is not simply a happy accident' that good manners and good
morals are ordinarily found together in the world of Jane Austen's fiction: rather,
'a person's manners are the outward expression of her moral character'. The
capacity to behave appropriately in social settings is properly understood as a
virtue, according to Stohr (and Austen): genuinely good manners 'contribute to
and are expressive of morally important ends, the ends to which someone with
full Aristotelian virtue is committed. They thus form an essential component of
virtuous conduct.' Hence, Stohr argues, 'there is an important sense of 'good
manners' in which having them is possible only in conjunction with the right
moral commitments'; further, 'the capacity to behave in a well-mannered way is
a proper part of virtue and that insofar as a person lacks this capacity, she falls
short of full virtue'. And both claims are at home in the context of Aristotle's
account of *phronesis*.

   In this collection's second philosophical essay on literature, **Sandrine Berges**'s
chapter 'The Hardboiled Detective as Moralist', Berges begins by reaffirming the
widely accepted claim that good novels can be morally valuable. She first presents
this claim in the way that it is usually presented by such authors as Nussbaum,
with reference to a familiar canon of classic novels by authors such as Henry
James. She then substantiates the claim by referring to a refreshingly unfamiliar
canon: novels by authors such as Ian Rankin, Marcia Muller, and Jean-Claude
Izzo, who write in the genre of the hardboiled detective novel. If Berges is right,

there is much to be learned morally from crime novels too. Maybe most of us will even get more from crime novels than from Henry James.

What is more, Berges argues, the ethical guidance we may extract from hardboiled detective novels is typically just the kind of Aristotelian ethics praised by Nussbaum. The hardboiled detective, as Berges depicts him, typically shows a predilection for particular cases, and a rejection of generalizing rules; he tends to care most about what is going on around him, and to be influenced in his action by this caring. Also, his character typically evolves and matures from one novel to the next because of what he has gone through. The hardboiled detective is not only a moralist, Berges concludes, he is an Aristotelian moralist: an exponent of practical wisdom.

This claim faces two objections. The first is that crime fiction breeds paranoia: an avid reader is led into seeing crime and corruption everywhere, which surely undermines crime literature's credentials as a suitable part of a course in moral improvement. But, Berges replies, 'Seeing evil everywhere is only paranoia if there is a fantastic element to one's vision'; 'It is not paranoid to deplore the omnipresence of racism in the streets and in the police force, nor is it paranoid to suspect that some politicians are in cahoots with the mafia.' Rather, becoming aware of the evil in our society is a vital precondition of learning to resist it.

The second objection is that crime novels, and their heroes, are too *dark*: the world of the crime novel, typically an urban wilderness, is a hopelessly pessimistic place, and the hardboiled detective herself is a damaged, cynical, estranged, and battle-scarred loner. Even if the hardboiled detective is (in a way) an exemplar of virtue, or at least of the virtue of practical wisdom, she is a very double-edged exemplar: it is far from obviously true that we want to be like her, even if we admire her. But that, Berges insists, is not the end of the argument. We should look beyond the hardboiled detective's thick-skinned virtues, to the state of society that made such heavy-duty psychological body-armour necessary. Maybe what the exemplar of the hardboiled detective should lead us to do is not so much imitate her, as transform the society that produced her.

Berges and Stohr provide studies of the ways in which different sorts of literature can become studies of that key theme in Aristotelian ethics: practical wisdom. Aristotle famously says (*NE* 1144a9) that practical wisdom is not concerned with the nature of the good or the aim of life, but with 'what is towards the aim' (*ta pros ton skopon*)—with identifying means to the good, and/or instances of the good.

Despite practical wisdom's focus on means and instances of the good rather than on the good itself, it is obvious that the nature of practical wisdom is bound to be determined by the nature of the good. We can hardly know what counts as instantiating the good, or as a means to the good, unless we know what the good *is*. In earlier essays in the collection, the nature of the good has perhaps been a somewhat peripheral theme. In their different ways the last three chapters, by

Johan Brännmark, Theodore Scaltsas, and Talbot Brewer, all speak to this theme rather more directly.

Johan Brännmark, in his chapter 'Like the Bloom on Youths', considers the prospects for hedonism, the view that pleasure is the good. Brännmark rejects hedonism, but he sees its natural pre-reflective appeal: 'Even if [hedonism] is not where all of us end up, it is where most of us start.' Brännmark's project, we might say, is to explain the appeal of hedonism without accepting it. As he himself puts it, he wishes to 'explore the possibility of an Aristotelian pluralist account of the human good in which pleasure is *good*, yet is not just another item on the list of goods'.

A hedonist might argue, as Hume seems to, that pleasure and the absence of pain is the only good, since it is the only thing that is never sought for the sake of anything else. But the key question for the theory of well-being, Brännmark argues, is not the question (one which Aristotle asks as well as Hume) what goods are final and non-instrumental. Even if pleasure and the absence of pain is the only thing that is never sought as a means to anything else, this does not prove that it is the only good. Rather, the key question about any putative good is another question that Aristotle also asks: namely, whether a good human life would be complete without it.

This question leads Brännmark to a two-level conception of human well-being. It is obvious that a life would be incomplete without some sort of pleasure; but it is also obvious that a life would be incomplete without the kind of goods that are typically listed in 'objective list' theories. The best response, Brännmark suggests, is to give a place in our theory to items of both sorts. But then how shall we connect the two sorts of items to each other? Brännmark's answer deploys a particular sort of hedonism, Fred Feldman's, in which the central cases of pleasure are the *enjoyment*-pleasures. Enjoyment, unlike sensational pleasure, is always enjoyment *of something*: it is an attitude to an object, not a simple, non-relational feel. Thus, Brännmark suggests, we can analyse the pleasures that really matter as being defined at least in part by their objects. In lives that display full well-being, there will not only be plenty of instances of goods from the 'objective list', there will also be an *enjoyment* of those goods. The full realization, within a life, of the value of goods from the list will be dependent upon the person's enjoying those goods. Conversely—and here Brännmark parts company with the hedonists—the full realization of the value of the enjoyments that come in a person's life will depend upon the condition that those enjoyments should have prudentially worthwhile objects. This makes pleasure, as Brännmark concludes, 'a kind of prudential master-value—even if it is not, *pace* hedonism, the only good there is'.

Theodore Scaltsas, in his chapter 'Mixed Determinates', also examines Aristotle's concept of pleasure, though his exploration takes him in another direction. Scaltsas is concerned with a theme that he argues can be traced through different domains of Aristotle's thought: the anti-Platonic theme that the best state is not necessarily a pure one. Aristotle never makes this theme into an explicit principle, which helps to explain why it has evaded interpreters, who tend to share Plato's instinct—from the attractions of which Aristotle is working to free himself—that the best state must be some unadulterated state of a transcendent being. What Aristotle tells us, by contrast, is that even 'the pleasant by nature'—the truly pleasant—cannot be found, even in the best human life, without some admixture of pain and impurity. Aristotle tells us something parallel about the good and the true: that the naturally good, the really good, is not found without some admixture of the bad; and that the true—what we really ought to believe—is not free of admixture with the false.

This is surprising, since Aristotle says (for instance) that the 'pleasant that is *not* by nature' involves conflict; the contrast that we naturally expect is that the 'pleasant that *is* by nature' will *not* involve conflict. Yet, Scaltsas argues, there is conflict even in the 'pleasant by nature'; but it is a different sort of conflict from the kind found in the 'incidentally pleasant' and the 'apparently pleasant'.

On Scaltsas's interpretation, Aristotle makes room for this possibility by using the concept of *being determinate* (*to hôrismenon*) to characterize the real, the best, or what is by nature. His resolution is achieved by offering a very sophisticated analysis of the way that the determinate can, despite its determinateness, nevertheless admit of degrees. This allows for the determinate to be mixed with its opposite (the bad, painful, or false), while differentiating this sort of admixture and conflict from the conflicts inherent in what is not 'by nature', which is indeterminate. Thus the difference between conflict due to different degrees of determinacy and conflict due to indeterminacy is used by Aristotle to characterize the differences between the best states that can be achieved in the moral and the cognitive domains from the worst states. The upshot is a moderation of the kind of ideal of life that it will be realistic for us to accept. If Aristotle as Scaltsas reads him is correct that, even in the best life possible for us, there is no chance of achieving complete freedom from the bad, the painful, or the false, that puts limits on what kind of good life we ought to seek; though, of course, as Scaltsas is careful to stress, this does not come near meaning that there is no clear ideal of life to aim at at all.

In a way, **Talbot Brewer**'s chapter 'Three Dogmas of Desire' concludes the collection as Christopher Coope's began it: by taking some contemporary orthodoxies and showing how they need to be questioned—and can most fruitfully be questioned by drawing on the deeper resources of the virtue-ethical tradition. 'Virtue ethicists'—Brewer writes—'have done moral philosophy a useful service by deepening and enriching the reigning conception of moral psychology. I believe that they can repeat this service in the case of the concept of desire.'

Just as Coope's title and opening echoed Anscombe, so Brewer's title and opening echo Quine. Quine famously questioned two dogmas that are, or were, central to modern empiricism. As his title indicates, Brewer's aim is to question three dog-mas about the nature of desire: three insufficiently questioned views about desire, which are central to contemporary Anglo-American ethics and action theory. The first dogma is a belief that *desires are propositional attitudes*; the second is that *desires are distinguished from other propositional attitudes by direction of mind–world fit*; the third is that *any action can be explained as the product of a belief/desire pair*. (With Brewer's attack on this third dogma, compare my own in Chapter 7.)

The central problem with the first dogma, Brewer thinks, is that so many desires are clear counter-examples. In the end, Brewer argues, *no* desires really fit the propositional model; but he begins with the simpler point that when, for instance, I desire some person, there is no finite and determinate set of propositions that I want to be true. What I desire is *that person*, and this desire simply cannot be translated into any set of desires that this, that, or the other should happen between myself and that person. It is essential to desiring a person that you do not *stop* desiring him or her, once any such proposition has come true. There is an influential contemporary view of desire that makes it simply a functional feedback mechanism, designed to alter the world until the world fits the proposition that the desire is a propositional attitude towards—*and then stop*. Since desire for a person—if it is genuine—*never* stops in this sort of way, the propositional account of desire cannot be right.

These remarks already show part of what Brewer thinks is wrong with the second dogma: its implicit functionalism. He also questions the uncritical way in which, for the proponents of the three dogmas, it seems to be simply *given* that one's present desires are reason-providing. Mightn't there be something radically wrong with those desires?

To develop further his case against all three dogmas, Brewer draws on Plato, Gregory of Nyssa, and Aquinas to sketch a radically different conception of desire. This he calls the *ecstatic* conception of desire, because on this model, one is constantly led to 'stand outside' one's previous understanding of what it is that one is desiring. One of Brewer's own examples is Augustine. The 'longing that serves as the unifying thread of Augustine's *Confessions*, and that he eventually comes to regard as the desire for God', takes very different forms during Augustine's life: 'Yet Augustine thinks that we would lose sight of the possibility of conversion (and the coherence of this and many other life-stories) if we fail to see that the longing for God is present from the beginning of our lives, and that many human pursuits are unsatisfying displacements of a longing whose real nature is opaque to, or at least unacknowledged by, its possessor.' Our conception of desire needs to object-based, not proposition-based, because a central part of what is going on, in the most important cases of desire, is that we are attempting to gain a better understanding of *what* the thing is that we desire: 'our grasp of [our desires]' objects always exceeds our explicit articulation of their objects, and hence presents us with an occasion for further articulation of our own concerns'. But this attempt is not even visible to the propositionalist, who will be able to see no deeper unity between Augustine's various desires than is given by writing them out to specify their propositional objects. This, Brewer suggests, is a radical failure on the part of the three-dogmas' picture of desire.

The example of Augustine might suggest that the problem is purely theological, therefore dispensable for anyone who doesn't go in for theology. Though Brewer is happy to deploy theological examples, he is also at pains to show that the problem is *not* purely theological: it is a completely general problem about making adequate sense of the objects of desire. The picture 'obtains, for instance, in the pursuit of ideals of artistic or philosophical excellence': 'The objects of such desires are fugitive: as the light of self-understanding pierces more deeply into the desire, the desire itself extends so as to outdistance our achieved articulation of its object.' It also 'permits a more illuminating account of loving desires for other persons than propositionalism'. The evaluative-attention approach, as Brewer also calls his own outlook, 'provides a way of crediting the thought that personal love essentially involves desire, without committing us to the claim that it essentially involves a project of remaking the world in the image of one's thoughts'. By contrast, the propositional translations of what we mean by talking about the desire for another person 'all seem to omit something critical'.

Thus, Brewer concludes, we can begin to see the possibility of a quite different, and a more illuminating, account of the desires that relate us to our own ideals and our loved ones than is available through the lens of the three dogmas. And this is worth having because, even if we can't follow Anscombe's advice and simply drop ethics, at least pro tern, still it is important for us to see that the three-dogmas' approach to desire is not ethically neutral, but embodies, expresses, or supports a certain particular view of what the good life is for us. That view can be challenged; to show how fruitful it can be to develop a virtue-ethical challenge to that view is one of Brewer's chapter's most important achievements. Virtue ethics, if he is right, will not only transform our conceptions of morality, of practical wisdom, and of pleasure, but of desire and deliberation as well.

1

Modern Virtue Ethics

Christopher Miles Coope

I will begin by stating three theses which I present in this paper. The first is this: that virtue ethics, insofar as it remains a valuable new approach in moral philosophy, is misleadingly so described. The description fails to single out what is of interest. The second is that the difference between this new approach and other so-called moral theories is not at all to be called a mere difference in emphasis or focus. Again I must add: insofar as the approach remains of value. For it was intended to be something radical, and only as such was it worth anything at all. The third is that the cardinal virtue of justice, once thought 'more glorious than the morning or the evening star', has become damagingly marginalized. It no longer has a starring role. I shall point out some consequences.

I

A virtue ethicist, if we must use this description, could be characterized as a moral philosopher who thinks that we have more to learn from Plato and Aristotle than from Kant and Bentham, Moore and Ross. We might talk about the Greek turn, or perhaps the Greek *return*—without of course supposing that Greek thinkers in these matters were all of one mind. I suppose that many of us count as virtue ethicists by this hospitable criterion. However, when the phrase 'virtue ethics' first came on the scene a number of people, I suspect, must have had a certain sinking feeling—without perhaps quite realizing why. The thing, we supposed, was almost bound to go to the bad. This gloomy assessment has I think proved quite realistic. This paper tells the story.

What is now called 'virtue ethics' is everywhere said to owe its origin, or at least its revival, to Elizabeth Anscombe's article 'Modern Moral Philosophy' (Anscombe 1958).[1] A series of deservedly famous articles by Philippa Foot, starting from that year, continued the work. In fact, this new approach in ethics was more or less the achievement of The Somerville Two, as we might call them.[2] A return to the consideration of the virtues was only part of the story—think, for example, of the work done on the concepts of intention and wanting, on the concept of good/bad/indifferent, and on the connection between goodness and choice. There were no particular anxieties about orthodoxy: no suggestion that it would be improper for the subject to advance in a somewhat Unscombean direction. The new approach, such as it was, even lacked a name. For many years, no one so far as I am aware talked about 'virtue ethics'. And this title, when it eventually emerged, was singularly ill-chosen. If a name had been needed, *good-sense ethics* would have been far more suitable. In this first section I want to develop this claim, for it will well characterise the advance that had been made. If we are to detect a decline we must first establish what was once achieved.

Good-sense ethics would have been a better name for two reasons. First, the very word virtue has a pious, if not faintly ridiculous, aura in our modern world. 'Virtues ethics' would have been better, or 'the ethics of the virtues' (or 'excellences'). The phrase *good sense* entirely lacks this aura. 'Good sense' is here intended as a colloquial phrase for 'practical wisdom' or *phronesis*, and *phronesis* is not one of Aristotle's 'moral' virtues (to use the traditional translation). It is somewhat unfortunate that Rosalind Hursthouse, perhaps the most noteworthy of recent writers on these topics, has taken to translating *phronesis* as *moral wisdom*, thus bringing back the unwanted associations (Hursthouse 2003: 2, 3). Admittedly it is not really clear what Aristotle has in mind by *phronesis*. Sarah Broadie says that his discussions on the subject 'can often seem maddeningly obscure' (Broadie and Rowe 2002: 5).

But second, and much more important, good sense was clearly the fundamental thing for the Greeks. They considered practical wisdom the master-virtue: man was a rational animal, and his excellence lay in rationality. It is the return to this thought which made the revolution so revolutionary. For years people had been saying: 'But that can't have anything to do with ethics—it is just a matter of prudence!' We were now to say (more or less): 'That is not a matter of

---

[1] The present paper is intended as a tribute to Elizabeth Anscombe, who taught me while I was at Oxford. As it happens, her tutorials (they lasted all afternoon) were not about moral philosophy at all but, at my request, were entirely about Wittgenstein. In her book on the *Tractatus*, which we discussed for many hours, she described Wittgenstein's family background thus: 'The children were brought up in an atmosphere of extreme contempt for most kinds of low standard. The whole generation had an unusual fire about them.' These phrases, the *contempt for low standards*, and the *unusual fire*, have remained with me ever since as apt descriptions of her own character.

[2] For Philippa Foot's attractive obituary of Elizabeth Anscombe see Foot 2001a.

prudence—so it can have nothing to do with ethics!' This is the big break. We were not just to be virtue ethicists but phronesists.[3]

Elizabeth Anscombe's paper sought to undermine a certain way of invoking 'ought' and 'must', where these notions were thought to have a unique moral role. What she said is often mischaracterised. It is a complete mistake to describe this as a flight from deontic terminology in favour of the aretaic (as one sometimes hears). There is no suggestion in her work that she wished somehow to lighten our lives by replacing the stick-concept of duty by the carrot-concept of goodness—a perfectly comical idea. Anscombe had absolutely nothing against 'ought' and 'must'—how could she have had? She said (naturally enough) that these everyday terms were 'quite indispensable' (1958: 5, 1981 reprint: 29). They come in in all sorts of ways. Nor need we imagine that she would have wished to ban a term like 'wrong', a rather general term which has many rationally innocent applications. She simply suggested that it is often helpful to be more specific. Nor again need we suppose that she would have had us abandon the thought that justice 'required' this or that—the payment of one 's bills, let us say—or that the paying of bills was a duty of justice. She was merely inveighing against those who invested notions of 'Ought' and 'Must' and 'Duty' (capital initials supplied) with a purely mesmeric force. The habit of so doing, she claimed, was an unappreciated consequence of having abandoned the presuppositions of a law conception of ethics, a conception such as we find in Stoicism or Judaism, where of course the *ought* need never have been mesmeric. This 'historical' part of her paper I am going to regard as something of a side issue. But we should note at least this. The point at issue is not well expressed by reciting (the association is all too familiar): 'If God does not exist then everything is permitted.' It would be less misleading to say to say that if God does not exist then *nothing* is permitted. For the very concept of *permitted*, where that word has inherited a certain tone, simply falls out of consideration—or at least *should* do so.

People have regularly criticised virtue ethics, saying that it is not very good at what is called 'action guidance', at telling us what we *ought to* do, and great efforts have then been made to provide an answer. But this criticism is quite indeterminate until we are told what kind of 'ought' is in play, the mesmeric kind or some other. In fact, it was the notion of force itself which was critical to the new outlook. For the question of the force of the *oughts* of ethics seemed to have found an answer, in outline if not in detail, via the notion of good sense and its defect, foolishness. How else indeed could it have been answered?

I say 'in outline if not in detail' because it is obvious that the picture we were given in 'Modern Moral Philosophy' was only intended as a sketch, with many

---

[3] It now appears that Elizabeth Anscombe herself used 'good sense' in the above way. See the posthumous collection, Anscombe 2005: 197. I also note that Herbert McCabe chose 'good sense' as a translation of Aquinas's *prudentia*, thinking in particular how Jane Austen would have understood this phrase (McCabe 2002: 152–3, 196).

gaps to be filled in later (perhaps much later) when more work had been done and we had acquired more insight. However, the question of force is gradually fading from the minds of modern virtue ethicists, and this is an enormous but unnoticed impoverishment. We retain the virtues-talk but not what made that talk of interest.

It was possible to do moral philosophy without this dodgy notion of *ought*, Elizabeth Anscombe said: as witness the example of Aristotle, to whom our very notion of 'morality' would be quite alien. The word *moral*, she said,

'just doesn't seem to fit, in its modern sense, into an account of Aristotelian ethics . . . . If someone professes to be expounding Aristotle and talks in a modern fashion about 'moral' such and such, he must be very imperceptive if he does not constantly feel like someone whose jaws have somehow got out of alignment: the teeth don't come together in a proper bite' (Anscombe 1958: 2, 1981: 26).

This point seems to have been taken in. Kathleen Wilkes was later to write in a similar vein: 'Plato and Aristotle are not discussing our notion of morality at all. . . "Morality", in the contemporary sense of the term, is not something that Aristotle wished to discuss as such' (Wilkes 1980: 355). And in the same year Bernard Williams said (appreciatively) that 'the system of ideas' in Plato and Aristotle 'basically lacks the concept of "morality" altogether, in the sense of a class of reasons or demands which are vitally different from other kinds of reason or demand' (Williams 1980: 251). More recently, D. S. Hutchinson in *The Cambridge Companion to Aristotle* referred to the *Ethics* as a treatise on 'how to be successful' (1995: 199). 'How to be successful' must surely sound very jarring to the modern moral ear. It belongs more with happily 'non-moral' concern or reminder expressed in the New Testament: 'What does it profit a man. . .' (Mark 8:36). Now if these characterizations of Aristotle are anywhere close to the truth, we can see straight away that what his *Ethics* is a theory *of* is not at all what either *Principia Ethica* or *The Right and the Good* purports to be a theory of. It is interesting to see how Albert Schweitzer, long ago and from a somewhat different tradition, had also got the message. A running head in his *Civilization and Ethics* rather startlingly proclaims: 'Aristotle Substitutes his Doctrine of Virtues for Ethics' (Schweitzer 1923: 47, 49).[4]

---

[4] Williams's chapter 'Morality, the Peculiar Institution' in *Ethics and the Limits of Philosophy* echoes 'Modern Moral Philosophy' in more than one way. See especially 1985: 174, where his target is a special and dubious notion of moral obligation shared by 'a range of ethical outlooks' which he calls morality. Williams' criticism (precisely Anscombean in form) is that the difference between these outlooks is so much discussed that we fail to notice what is of importance, the difference between all of them 'and everything else'. In Anscombe this latter remark has to do not so much with the mesmeric idea of obligation but with the defect for which she coined the word *consequentialism* (of which more later). Remarkably, almost on cue, Williams provides his own denunciation of this defect (1985: 185). He finds it characteristic of what he calls *morality* that it tends to overlook the idea that certain courses of action have to be ruled out from the beginning (1985: 185): an odd claim, since this is of course so plainly untrue of the man said to have given 'the purest, deepest, and most thorough representation' of what Williams calls 'morality', namely Kant (1985: 174).

The *Nicomachean Ethics* does not itself start out with a discussion of the virtues. It starts, and indeed ends, by taking up the tremendous question, what it is to be truly fortunate. I talk about *being fortunate* rather than the more usual *flourishing*, since the former seems to be a broader notion, and it is the broader notion we want here. It is a broader notion, since a person who flourishes can become yet more fortunate if something he wishes to happen, quite independently of his flourishing, comes about—and even if, as might be, he can never know that it comes about. (I am assuming we exclude things only wanted through ignorance). It would be unnatural and confusing to insist that this fulfilment could not be independent of his flourishing and must instead be counted a part of it. That said, an account of the difficult concept of flourishing must be an important step in answering the broader question as to fortune. The notion of good sense in acting must be related to the answers we give. It has always been one of the key advantages of this turn to the virtues to have revived this issue. And it has been important that our account of flourishing and good fortune be uncontaminated with contemporary thoughts of 'morality'.[5]

It is also possible to approach the topic of good sense and good fortune in microcosm, as it were. This approach is particularly useful because it will not seem to an unreconstructed modern reader as if the virtues are involved at all, and this is all to the good. *Prima facie*, a man acts *well* all the time—almost as regularly as his heart acts well. A man constantly acts well without anyone supposing him a saint: when he opens a tin, looks at his watch, visits the bank or the grocer, takes an umbrella when it looks like rain. In real life there will hardly ever be a realistic doubt to be raised against this presumption. We may often be unduly complacent, but not here. What after all is action 'for'? What is the

---

As to 'What does it profit a man . . . ' we find John McDowell making a pious mystery out of it (1998: 90). He writes: 'Obviously we are not meant to answer "The profits are outweighed by counterbalancing losses." The intended answer is "Nothing". At that price, whatever one might achieve does not count as profit.' We should resist such edification. The consequences of the loss of one's soul as depicted in the New Testament make grim reading, as a critic such as Antony Flew would regularly want to remind us, and crass and manifest 'outweighing' is exactly what comes to mind.

5 Would a man be fortunate if what he wanted came about, *even when* the satisfaction of his aims involved the wronging of others? I am inclined to think so (subject of course to the ignorance proviso). Here I take issue with Philippa Foot's recent thoughts on this topic. In her *Natural Goodness* (2001: 94), she considers the case of the murderers Frederick and Rosemary West 'who did not even spare their own children'. She asks whether someone who had made it possible for the Wests to get their way, undetected for the rest of their lives, would have *benefited* them. Philippa Foot suggests that such assistance could not count as a benefit, even if the Wests were not in the least wracked by guilt, ran no risk of consequent misfortune, and considered their horrible activities pleasurable if not something of an achievement. This, she argues, is something we can learn, not by moralising, but just by thinking about the concept of benefit. Can this be right? There are plenty of people in our community who 'do not even spare their own children'. Doctors who help to dispose of such children—which perhaps have Down syndrome—are said, surely not unreasonably, to be providing a benefit to these people, in intention and often in effect, even if at their children's expense.

ergon of action—the point of acting? Voluntary actions, beyond mere doodlings, are purposive. An action can thus be successful or not successful. Goodness in action is connected with getting results. One wanted to pay the bill, and such-and-such an action constituted the appropriate bill-paying. One wanted to displease Sally, and Sally was duly displeased. So far forth, these are good action, though of course the wider context might tell a different story, might show them to have been unwise. And all this of course has nothing to do with the philosopher's thought that 'satisfaction is good', whatever that would mean, but is closer to the truism that it is a merit in a medicine to be effective. This view of goodness in action is itself truistic. Yet we shall find—in a way which is both interesting and to be expected—that people are not easily convinced of it. Philippa Foot remarks: 'I remember protest at a convivial philosophical gathering when I remarked as someone started to drink a glass of wine that he was acting well' (Foot 2001: 76). In fact, insufficient appreciation of harmless pleasures is a fault under temperance, a point already appreciated by Aquinas (ST II-IIae, q142, A1; A6, ad2). Temperance is not at all a gloomy virtue.[6]

To spend money on something one enjoys is to spend it *on a good cause* (not in every case of course, but in the vast majority of cases in the ordinary run of life). This is a satisfactorily unimpressive thought. Yet the connection between simple rationality of this kind and goodness tends to be obscured by conventional altruistic expectations. Rosalind Hursthouse's chosen example of 'acting well' involves giving someone a present (1999: 68–9). *That* is what gets 'the tick of approval' as she puts it. It is however completely misleading in any virtue ethics worthy of the name to cling to such 'virtuous' examples. We should be giving the tick of approval to the opening of a can of beans. And if we must continue to talk of 'moral reasons', then *in order to make one's supper* must be allowed to count.[7]

The fact that ordinary human actions so often count as good actions simply *qua* successful is quite striking when we think that an action, even a successful action, can be bad in many different ways. It can of course be penny wise and pound foolish. But more than that, it can be an action of a bad kind, or some circumstance can make it bad, or it can be done for a bad motive, or it can

---

[6] That temperance requires us not irrationally to miss out is appreciated by Michael Slote, discussing the doctrine of the mean (Slote 1997:184). Aristotle seems not to realize the extent to which people can be unreasonably buttoned-up, perhaps because he thinks that not enjoying bodily pleasures sufficiently must be a consequence of insensitivity, a rare condition, rather than of profitless ascetic teaching which *might* be quite common: NE 1119a. Chastity is a virtue allied to temperance. And once again, it need not be thought of as exclusively nay-saying. 'An act of intercourse occurring as part of married life is an exercise of the virtue of chastity unless something prevents it from being so,' writes Elizabeth Anscombe (1981: 89).

[7] The notion of supererogation can be misleading here. For it suggests that an action good-to-do-but-not-bad-to-omit cannot be something merely sensible, but must instead be a 'virtuous' action in the degenerate everyday sense, like giving a present. But perhaps this notion is more at home in what Anscombe called 'a law conception of ethics', with its distinction between counsels and commands.

be thought bad by the agent. If anything like this is correct, one might begin to wonder how one could possibly act well save in the rarest circumstance. But then, so many people—and indeed organisms generally—are pretty healthy day to day, and yet one only counts as healthy if one simultaneously satisfies several criteria.[8]

It might be thought that merely picking up an umbrella when it looks like rain would not have any 'moral worth'—save perhaps in quite peculiar circumstances, where one has to overcome one's umbrellophobia. Michael Slote for example remarks that although it may be 'smarter or wiser or more prudent to provide oneself with a better lunch or take pills to relieve one's headache, . . . "morally better" is not a phrase that naturally comes to mind in connection with such actions' (1997: 185). But perhaps all this shows that we should jettison the idea of a peculiarly *moral* sort of worth—or indeed of something called 'a moral point of view'.[9]

Let us return to the question of the force of *ought* and *must*, the force let us say of agreeing, after deliberating what to do, that one ought to or must do such and such. It has always been an indispensable and salutary part of good-sense ethics to find justice a problematic virtue in this regard, and here, of course, it is the *Republic* rather than the *Nicomachean Ethics* which has been a central text. Justice often stands in the way of the projects we would naturally wish to pursue, and would therefore seem to be a self-defeating quality of character, like timidity or a burdensome obsession, rather than something we need. This problem is one of the glories of good-sense ethics. It might seem odd to pick out a problem and call it a glory, but some problems just are fruitful. It is the irritating grain of sand that creates the pearl. Of course, with the mesmeric *ought* at our disposal this intellectual difficulty about justice would not have arisen: or rather, what is important about it would have been covered over.

One might of course believe that it is important never to act unjustly, without being able to say *why* it is important. Presumably Glaucon and Adeimantus were in this position. In fact, it would seem to have been Elizabeth Anscombe's view that 'the situation at present is that we can't do the explaining [*sc.* why a good man is a just man]; we lack the philosophic equipment' (Anscombe 1958: 16–17, 1981: 40). And here we do not have to do with some supposed 'moral' sense of importance. It is, incidentally, very misleading to describe this difficulty as a

---

[8] To go by the World Health Organization criterion of health (and surely *they* should know) no one would ever count as healthy.

[9] Useful economy: whether we are expounding Aristotelian ethics or not, the adjective 'moral' should not be introduced into our philosophical terminology if it is possible to avoid it. Let us try to do without 'the moral life' (widespread), 'moral wisdom' (Hursthouse 2003:1), 'moral responsiveness' (Swanton 2003: 2), 'moral experience', 'moral significance', 'the moral universe as a whole' 'the moral domain' (all Swanton 2003: 8–9), and so on. Likewise with 'ethical', as in 'the ethical outlook' (Hursthouse 1999: 229) or 'the ethical consciousness' (Williams 1985: 33). Bernard Williams's very proper unease with the adjective 'moral' (Williams 1981: p. x) managed to coexist with his fondness for using it ('morally distasteful', 'moral cost', 'moral reason', etc.).

matter of 'Why be moral?' - or again by talking of 'ethical scepticism' (Bernard Williams's chosen phrase, 1985: 24). It is a problem specific to justice. Since it is hardly going to arise for the other three cardinal virtues it is not a problem for ethics generally. Ethics is about acting well, and the question 'Why act well?' is not readily comprehensible.

Given this problem about justice as a virtue, given that is to say that this is regarded *as* a problem, it is clear that good-sense ethics is as far removed from let us say 'an ethic of caring' as one could possibly imagine. The objection that a virtue's standing is problematic if it is merely 'another's good' could hardly impress us if 'caring' were accepted without a qualm as the only or the principal virtue. It is not of course that good-sense ethics is particularly *un*caring. In the peculiar silliness of our time, good sense will perhaps be thought to underwrite a distinctively 'male' ethic, despite the crucial role played in its modern origin by *Miss* Anscombe and *Mrs* Foot, as it was once academically the custom to refer to them. As has frequently been observed and is quite obvious in any case, good-sense ethics is not to be thought of as egoistic or macho. It is simply not as un-egoistic as certain popular doctrines which feel free to pile on impressive altruistic demands: the doctrine, for example, that there is a reason ('there just *is* a reason', 'this is just what we *call* a reason') for a man to do good to other people irrespective of what he cares about or needs to care about, a stipulation based no doubt on what people who want to cut a good figure—one thinks in particular of the secular clergymen of the academy—can be got to say.

Someone who teaches a child to look both ways before crossing a road is not inculcating supposedly 'realistic' no-nonsense me-firstism. John McDowell (1980: 365) illustrates the attitude of those who have doubts about justice and charity as one of brutal tough-mindedness: 'That's a wishy-washy ideal suitable only for contemptible weaklings. A real man looks out for himself, etc.' In fact, elementary good sense itself would suggest that what is called a selfish life is hardly going to be a flourishing one. Individuals need suitable friends and they therefore need to be un-calculatingly friendly. They also need certain emotional susceptibilities, to sympathy for example (and also to disgust and indignation), all of course to be governed by good-sense. People defective in this regard are unlikely to flourish. Perhaps they would do well to be moderately soppy about spaniels; good-sense would not rule out such a thought. Moreover, as we have pointed out, a man can be unfortunate simply because he does not get something he wants, and what is wanted in this connection can so easily be another's good. Pretty well everyone loves, cares for the good of, *some* others—and interestingly these need not be relatives or even friends, for attachment is somewhat anarchic. And the ability to love is deeply important to each of us, as part of our nature. We should note incidentally that we especially need to meditate on that Aristotelian question 'What is it to be truly fortunate?' if we are to love those we love *well*, for it is their good fortune which we care about. Good-sense ethics is not then *un*caring. Indeed, ordinary un-calculating neighbourliness is plainly a good-sense virtue. It is a conceptual, rather than some kind of ideological, truth that an individual's good sense is specially related to his *own* good, and to his *own* projects, and to the good of those *he* cares about, and need not take in the good or the projects of the individual whose name is listed next to his in the telephone directory.[10]

The virtues of good sense both enable and ennoble. They represent a kind of strength, and strength both helps us to do well and is an aspect of doing well—as it is with health. So we should not suppose that good-sense ethics is 'merely utilitarian' in the popular sense—that it is merely concerned with results rather than with fineness of character. For good sense is not only 'productive'; we are to see it as admirable, at least when it is present in some more than the usual degree. We see this distinction between the merely useful and the fine even among artefacts. A paper plate is merely useful, but we talk of *fine* wines, as something crafted and rare, and connoisseurs will admire their qualities. A fine character is crafted too—and rare. Foolishness is not only apt to be damaging, it will be regarded as contemptible. A businessman who makes a rash investment will not only regret his loss, he will be ashamed to think that he could have been so careless. The latter indeed might cause him the greater grief. 'It is not so much the money—it is the thought that I could be such a damn fool.' The fine life is the wise life: it is the judicious pursuit of what is worth pursuing. (Thus a *fine* life, a *flourishing* life, and a *fortunate* life will be distinct but related notions.)

I talked just now about *elementary* good sense. It is important to see that there can be such a thing. All the same, I do not wish to suggest that what Hume in his essay *On Suicide* calls 'plain good sense and the practice of the world, which alone serve most purposes of life. . . ' is all the good sense there is. Reasoning-what-to-do has a provisionality built in: what is sensible to do in the light of a restricted set of aims can become manifestly foolish when further aims are introduced. Our knowledge of what is of benefit to us, though real, is limited in scope. It is possible, too, that there is an element of indeterminacy in the notion of good sense, because of its relation both to wanting and to welfare - but not I think too much to rob it of its pivotal role. We need to distinguish between flourishing in inessentials and flourishing in essentials (Anscombe 1958: 18, 1981: 41). So *good* sense should not be assumed to be a matter of *common* sense, except in regard to what might be called 'local' matters or again matters of outline expressed in homely proverbs. It is because the path of good sense can be so unobvious that education cannot limit itself to the bare exhortation to be rational. Aristotle himself writes as if the knowledge of what's what in this matter can be profound and difficult to obtain, and seems not to have come to the same

---

[10] Glaucon's talk at *Republic* 359c of 'the self-advantage which every creature by its nature pursues as a good' is an unfortunate distraction. Someone can easily be tempted to be unjust out of an outgoing concern for others, or even by way of preventing injustice by, let us say, conspiring to punish the innocent. These are often the more interesting cases for our enquiry. Why is it important, even in *these* cases, to be constrained by what justice requires?

conclusion in the *Nicomachean* and the *Eudemian Ethics*. His account of 'the good for man' is no doubt unsatisfactory; a modern Aristotelian can hardly help being 'neo' in this regard. Elizabeth Anscombe herself saw immense problems in the concept of human 'flourishing' (1958: 18, 1981: 41, her scare quotes). That it should be a problematic concept is hardly surprising, since like so many concepts in this area it is tied up with modality. Doing well is defined in relation to potentialities, of what might be in store for us (or more generally, for creatures of the kind under discussion).

II

Let us now think about the concept of a virtue generally. Once we have recognised the existence, intelligibility, and importance of the ethics of good sense we can relax somewhat as to what counts as a virtue. This will save a certain amount of unnecessary distraction. We need not insist that all virtues are *good-sense virtues*, such as courage or temperance, virtues which a fairy-godmother would bestow on the child in the cradle.[11] We might indeed think—we could hardly *not* think—that the notion of a good-sense virtue had a certain unique place in our lives and our philosophical ruminations. But as to the concept of a virtue more generally we could afford to be fairly inclusive, for nothing much would hang on how we delimited it. Analogously, we can show the same inclusiveness in regard to what is to count as a reason for acting. We can relax when a philosopher insists that there just *is* a reason to do this or that—to help the little old lady cross the road, etc. For we can talk if necessary about good-sense reasons.

Perhaps there are virtues which are not good-sense virtues, which we might call the *compliance* virtues, reflecting standard interests in how one has reason to wish others to be. We could here talk of 'amiable characteristics': we would like to live among people who exhibit them. It is useful to think in this connection of the way we bring up our children. Not all the qualities we would like to install in our children are put there simply for their benefit, for we have to live with them for many years. A good deal of moral education, though of course not all of it, will involve an attempt to install the compliance virtues - so as to produce a satisfactory product. Some virtues would perhaps belong in both lists: coming under compliance *and* good sense. We should expect some overlap, for a certain readiness to fit in and be outgoing is likely to be needed if one is to have a good chance of flourishing. 'Docile' is an interesting adjective here. Is docility a virtue? Someone who is not teachable is unlikely to flourish, *and* is unlikely to

---

[11] A sensible fairy-godmother will not for a moment suppose that the gift of these virtues is sufficient to ensure that the child flourishes. Or indeed, though this is less obvious, that they are necessary for flourishing either. We all know how chance plays its part.

be compliantly malleable. He would therefore be bad from both the internal and external perspective.

Just as there are qualities of character we need as individuals so too there are such individual qualities which we-as-a-community need to support and instil. So we have as it were a notion of communal good sense. Evidently the requirements of communal good sense do not straightforwardly translate into a good-sense requirement on each individual. Persuasion and enforcement tends to fill the gap.

We should not think of a compliance virtue as necessarily maiming. Sometimes we might reasonably expect its net effect on the agent's own good to be neutral, offering a balance of advantage and disadvantage. But it could also turn out that some virtues, in this broad sense, can be expected to harm the one who has them.[12] I am of course assuming, as I indicated, a fairly easy-going conceptual latitude in characterising a virtue. If we can talk literally of the virtues of a pruning knife, as Socrates does in the *Republic*, then the most *general* notion of a virtue will not be tied to the idea of flourishing, for a pruning knife cannot flourish. There is nothing however to stop us adopting a narrower account in the case of the human virtues. If we wish to think of ethics in an interesting, non-manipulative way, we *will* be concerned with the good-sense virtues. And similarly, if we expect ethics simply to answer the question, which each individual addresses to himself: 'How ought I to live?'—where the *ought* is neither mesmeric nor egoistic.

Good-sense ethics regards the individual as an end in himself. This assertion should not be thought to represent some sort of moral stand, as perhaps it would in Kant. It is not part of a manifesto. It is not even supposed to be a particularly impressive remark. Any organism has a good of its own, but is also good for the purposes of other organisms. Most organisms for example are part of the food chain. And so many are suitable hosts for parasites. Some organisms make good pets. We can perhaps think of 'a good human being' quite externally if we are so minded—as a farmer might understand 'a good cow' or 'a good sheepdog'. A good cow, a cow that would be regarded as admirable at an agricultural show, would not necessarily be a flourishing cow, though we would certainly expect the concepts to overlap. Cows and sheepdogs are bred for a purpose. This is not of course to say that the average farmer is likely to be unconcerned about the good of his animals. He will probably not have the dog put down the day it ceases to function. The important thing to see is that there *is* this external point of view, and that like the internal perspective, it too generates criteria of being admirable.

---

[12] Or as Swanton 2003: 294 puts it, they can 'characteristically be inimical to agent flourishing'. Nietzsche thought so too. The philosopher who has most whole-heartedly embraced what I would call a compliance conception of the virtues is Pincoffs 1985. From this perspective, the problem of evil in theology arises because God appears not to be the God we would have designed if the opportunity had arisen.

People, like farm animals, can be regarded as admirable specimens in this way. A virtue is a good quality of a thing. But good for whom or in respect of what? Philippa Foot writes:

'Good qualities are exactly those which are of some interest or use, and it is not surprising that *someone* has a reason to choose good F's and G's where F's and G's are the kind of thing one can choose. In general very many people will have reason to choose to have good ones, since the good will be judged from some standard point of view. But not everyone will have these reasons, since he may not have standard desires and interests, *and may not be the one whose desires and interests are taken into account*'

(Foot 1978: 151, italics in last sentence added).

Marx once suggested, perhaps not too earnestly, that *weakness* was a virtue in a woman (Raddatz 1979: 64). Well, even a joke, even a bad joke, has to be intelligible. And what Marx said would be quite intelligible if weakness indicated something compliant or controllable. By contrast, it would be entirely unintelligible, at least without further explanation, if weakness meant an inability to walk about, to grasp things or to lift them.

What is important is not just the *list* of traits classified as virtues, but the *point* of classifying something as a virtue; and this point might not always be the same from virtue to virtue. We can make a similar remark about reasons for action. Ethics-talk and reasons-talk is in part domestication. We should not be especially shocked by this, but just aware of it. Moral philosophy, indeed philosophy generally, is a cards-on-the-table sort of thing. The question is whether, once we have all the cards on the table, we still want to set up an ethic which makes use of the broad conception of the virtues thus conceived, rather than of a narrower good-sense-based conception. 'A disquisition on the virtues' rather suggests a tedious literary essay, something written for gentlemen with time on their hands by other gentlemen in the same predicament. Would a virtue ethics of this broad kind, lacking the tighter discipline that good-sense ethics reintroduces, have much interest? I very much doubt it. However, I rather fear it is what we have got.

III

At first—way back in the late 1950s—a virtue ethicist would have been someone who found more of interest in 'Modern Moral Philosophy' than in modern moral philosophy. That article was disconcerting, and hence one expected to learn something from it. Turning to modern virtue ethics, what a contrast we find. It can only be called concerting. Modern virtue ethics has become something soothing, edifying and familiar. It has grown up in the polluted atmosphere of contemporary expectations (assumptions, presuppositions, confusions, distractions) and naturally enough has quickly become tarnished by them. Michael

Slote (1997: 175) purports to be 'adapting ancient ideas of virtue to the requirements of current-day ethical theory', and it shows: 'We do best to consult and
draw upon our current-day thinking about what is ethically admirable and what
counts as a virtue' (1997: 184–5). The latest virtue-ethics outlook is standardly
introduced to us as representing a mere difference in emphasis or focus.[13] In
Rosalind Hursthouse's justly praised *On Virtue Ethics*, the newly arrived theory or
outlook is presented in this way—in her case at the very outset (1999: 1). Virtue
ethics is to *emphasize* character. That sounds like a matter of minor adjustment,
and nothing in the least radical.

Emphasizing character has in practice meant a lot of talk about 'the virtuous
person'. Such a description could only be applied to the most impossible prig.
'Virtuous' would be a safe word for us only if we were equally happy to talk of a
virtuous pruning knife—or indeed a vicious one. 'Virtuous' has acquired quite
the wrong associations, as has 'vicious.' Laziness may be a vice, and it would
certainly be accepted as such by modern virtue ethicists, but we could hardly call
a man vicious merely on account of being lazy. 'Vicious' has become a word for
dogs which bite. It is true and important that we sometimes need to reclaim old
terminology that has been spoiled by modern usage, like so many of the virtue
terms indeed, such as prudence, justice and temperance. But are we to toil on
behalf of 'virtuous'? It seems hardly worth the effort.

One of the most agreeable characteristics of the Anscombe turn was to rid
ethics of this horrible 'virtuous' aspect, the competitive academic sermonising
about doing good to all sentient beings and ecosystems, and all that muttering
about Mother Teresa (on the part so often, it must be said, of those who do
not care a bit about what she stood for). There are two distinct ways in which
a piece of work in moral philosophy can be agreeable, the intellectual way and
(as it were) the 'moral' way, and of course I have in mind the first. I think here
in particular of Bradley's remark that 'moralism is bad for thinking', quoted
by Elizabeth Anscombe in her *Intention*.[14] Here it might instantly be objected
that Elizabeth Anscombe was a frightfully moralistic writer herself. Did she not
pen a famous protest against the proposal to give Mr Truman, a man 'with a
couple of massacres to his credit', an honorary degree at Oxford, and publish it

---

[13] Thus several times in Baron, Pettit, and Slote (1997). See the Introduction (1) with its talk of
emphasis, focus and standpoints. Also Marcia Baron's remarks in this volume about the 'hallmarks
of virtue ethics' in terms of what is emphasised or favoured (35). And see Slote's contribution (175),
where once again the difference is said to be one of emphasis, or (177–8), where it is a matter of
focus. In Zagzebski 1996: 78 too the difference is a matter of focus.

[14] Anscombe 1957: 11: I should give the context. 'It is very usual to hear that such-and-such are
what we *call* 'reasons for acting' and that it is 'rational' or 'what we *call* rational' to act for reasons;
but these remarks are usually more than half moralistic in meaning (and moralism, as Bradley
remarked, is bad for thinking); and for the rest they leave our conceptual problems untouched,
while pretending to give a quick account. In any case, this pretence is not even plausible, since
such remarks contain no hint of what it is to act for reasons.' Something of the kind surely is
what we should say in reply to the supposedly definitive suggestion that such-and-such are what we
call virtues.

at her own expense? Was she not accused of 'high mindedness' on account of it (see Anscombe 1981: 64)? This is a useful objection, for it helps us to clarify what is at stake. The demands of justice are minimal, almost humdrum, demands. One is not to cheat anyone, one is to pay one's bills, one is not to lie or steal, one is to keep contracts. One is not to seduce the queen, kill the king and usurp the throne. No one could make such banal claims in order to impress.

This un-moralising advance however could hardly have been expected to last, and was lost within a generation. The key notion of good fortune or *eudaimonia* was given a moral slant: '*Eudaimonia* in virtue ethics is indeed a moralised concept' writes Hursthouse (2003: 7). Goody virtues were soon being invoked (or invented or emphasized) by the dozen. In particular, much was eventually made of an alleged virtue, variously known as charity or benevolence. This particular slant was not there from the beginning of the new turn in ethics. The supposed virtue of charity for example did not put in an appearance at all in Philippa Foot's earliest papers. Here the talk was of 'the cardinal virtues, prudence, temperance, courage and justice'.[15] The new generation of virtue ethicists however all went for charity or benevolence. The list of 'character traits that are called virtues' in Rosalind Hursthouse's *Ethics, Humans, and Other Animals* sets out without demur: 'benevolent, altruistic, generous, compassionate, kind . . .' (Hursthouse: 2000: 147). Yet charity had inexplicably been left out by Aristotle. It would not be enough to point out that everyday friendliness could be regarded as an Aristotelian virtue; nor Aristotle's 'liberality'. Charity would have to be something bigger. I am tempted to call it the *grand* charity Michael Slote complains of 'the absence, in Aristotle, of any commitment to generalised humanitarianism' (Slote 2000: 335). Why this curious omission? How could Aristotle (to say nothing of Plato and the rest) have failed to notice what now seems to so many to be the most vivid and obvious of all the virtues? What have we learned since his day, and how did we learn it? There seems to be an enormous change—not to be characterised as a difference of emphasis! About all this there has arisen a not-to-worry complacency.

Rosalind Hursthouse for example admits that charity is not an Aristotelian virtue 'but all virtue ethicists assume it is on the list now' (1999: 8). A suspiciously heart-warming consensus! It is as if Aristotle, unlike us, lacked decent standards. However Elizabeth Anscombe was alive when this claim about 'what all virtue ethicists assume' was written, and charity is not even indexed in the relevant

---

[15] In the papers reprinted in Philippa Foot's *Virtues and Vices* that are concerned with the virtues, there is no mention of charity at all before 'The Problem of Abortion and the Doctrine of Double Effect', published in 1967, where it comes into her presentation of a distinction between harming and not helping (Foot 1978: 27). It is easy to see how this lapse came about, but the supposed virtue of charity need not have been brought in to make her point, because we can evidently owe help under justice. Indeed what is said to be a matter of charity is so often a matter of justice instead, a point emphasized by Philippa Foot herself in her Gilbert Murray Memorial Lecture (Foot 1993: 12)

volume (Volume III) of her *Collected Philosophical Papers*: it is hard to see in its pages any evidence of such a virtue.[16]

To be sure, in any discussion of charity we need to ask what a speaker has in mind by it. The shifting sands in this regard tend to make any discussion unsatisfactory. Thus charity for Aquinas is not quite what people expect it to be. In Aquinas it is an aspect of charity to love oneself. Suicide can represent be a defect against this virtue under this head. Charity in this particular aspect would seem to be what I have called a good-sense virtue. One would need a good deal of charity on a desert island. We have to observe this caution as to what the speaker has in mind even in reading a contemporary author. It is possible the Rosalind Hursthouse for example has changed her view about what counts as charity, for in her first book, *Beginning Lives*, she had listed it as an Aristotelian or good-sense virtue. 'His [Aristotle's] answer is: "If you want to flourish/be happy/be successful you need to acquire and practice the virtues—courage, justice, benevolence or charity, . . . " ' (Hursthouse 1987: 225). This suggests that she then had in mind something like Aristotle's 'liberality', and what I called 'everyday friendliness', rather than the grand conception. And even in her later book, *On Virtue Ethics*, Hursthouse is reluctant to accept what a utilitarian would doubtless want to call charity—that is to say, impersonal benevolence—as a virtue (2001: 224–6). She is right to have her doubts. One might even wonder whether was an amiable characteristic. Would one not rather want to avoid someone thus endowed?

Having made this allowance, there remains a problem. It must seem to many that Aristotle had this blind spot about something so many people want to call charity. Why this oversight? It would be a great distraction to say 'Well, what would you expect? He said all those disgraceful things about women!'. We are not discussing his attitudes or his character. Nor more interestingly do we have to suppose that he must have recognised all the virtues there are. Perhaps he missed out on humility. But we can show, perhaps, why he *should* have included it, and why the neo-Aristotelian *will* include it. For a well-judged appreciation of our incapacities and limitations (which I suppose humility to be all about) is pretty important if we are to have a chance of doing well. This can hardly be thought foreign to the Greek mind when we remember 'Know thyself!' And what characteristically—though of course not always—needs correcting is the propensity to overestimate. Furthermore, this virtue evidently involves an Aristotelian mean—somewhere between *hubris* and Heepishness. That humility

---

[16] There is a passing reference to charity in her essay, written while an undergraduate, 'The Justice of the Present War Examined' (reprinted in Anscombe 1981). This was however an article written primarily for a Catholic readership. In the posthumous collection (Anscombe, 2005) justice is of course indexed, but charity not at all. Amusingly, this has, since I wrote these words, become a matter of reproach. Simon Blackburn ends his review of this collection headed 'Simply Wrong', with what he calls 'a parting kick.': 'The index lists eleven pages for justice, and none at all for altruism, benevolence, charity, compassion, mercy, sympathy, or love' (Blackburn 2005: 12). On whom does the kick land?

has been thought a virtue in particular by Christians is not in the least surprising, since they tell us, with a certain plausibility, that we are especially prone to act badly. Socratic thoughts as to how anyone could err willingly may have done something to conceal this flaw in our nature from those under his influence. Whatever we are to say the omission of humility from the lest of virtues, there is a clear contrast with the case of charity. There is simply no need to shout Aristotle down, or move him over, or think of him as primitive or behind the times, saying that all we virtue ethicists assume that *humility* is on the list now.[17]

Ethics, unfettered by the discipline imposed by the appeal to good sense, tends to extravagance. It has frequently been noticed for example how claims about human rights yield to inflationary pressures. We have been vividly aware of this since Bentham's animadversions on 'the rights of man'. The only thing inhibiting the really big claim when we are unfettered is that we might feel badly about not living up to it. And this drawback is evidently not serious, for if the claim is sufficiently big—or as we might nowadays prefer to say, inclusive—we will not be *expected* to live up to it, and that neatly solves the problem. That trouble removed, we might as well adopt the ethics of Peter Singer straight away.[18] In fact we could do somewhat better, and proclaim to the world the mother of all axioms: 'If you can do good to anything at all, that is what you must do!' It is only a matter of time till some philosopher puts his name to this axiom—as the farthest reach of the expanding circle. So why not get in first? After all, how could one possibly refuse to do good to something? To make it better of its kind? Or to repair it? The world is surely *a better world* if a lawn mower can now be expected to start. It contains one more good-state-of-affairs. We could imagine the existence of a corresponding virtue, *ameliorance* it might be called. However, there is a price. The stringency of a demand must be repaid in the coinage of explanation. Where there is a 'have to' we want to hear about its force. An account must exist, must be possible, even if we are at present not wholly able to provide it.[19]

It is possible to talk seriously about a virtue of charity without indulging in the merely extravagant claim. Peter Geach can do so, for example, because for him charity is a *theological* virtue, that is to say something comprehensible as a

---

[17] Aquinas actually contrived to find humility in Aristotle's list of virtues. Anthony Kenny (2004: 105) points out how 'by an astonishing piece of intellectual legerdemain', Aquinas was able to claim that humility was 'not only compatible with but a counterpart of the alleged Aristotelian virtue of magnanimity'—referring us to II IIae, 161, 1, ad 3.

[18] For an appreciation of which see my Critical Study 'Peter Singer in Retrospect' (Coope 2003).

[19] I rashly thought that ameliorance was an invention all of my own. But then I came across the following description of 'the environmental virtues': 'The environmental virtues can be understood as being virtues not just because they are dispositions to promote human-centred ends, but also the ends of the flourishing and integrity of ecosystems, species, and natural objects (sentient and non-sentient) for their own sakes' (Swanton 2003: 94). This almost amounts to ameliorance. All that is lacking is the inclusion of artefacts. How could it be right to discriminate against them?

virtue given a certain background, as indeed it is defined in the (instructively short) entry in the *Oxford Dictionary of the Christian Church*. Geach writes:

'If charity is love of God above all things in the world and of our neighbours for God's sake, charity is to be prized only if there is a God: otherwise it is a pathetic delusion like Don Quixote's love for Dulcinea. The word "charity" bears other senses, but it is dubious whether in these senses charity is a virtue at all' (Geach 1977: 17).[20]

Nietzsche also saw things clearly here. He writes contemptuously in *The Twilight of the Idols*:

'They [the English—he had in mind George Eliot in particular] have got rid of the Christian God, and now feel obliged to cling all the more firmly to Christian morality. . . [But] when one gives up Christian belief one thereby deprives oneself of the right to Christian morality' (Nietzsche 1968: 80).

Nietzsche if he had been around today would surely have noticed the way in which secular environmentalists feel free to adopt ideas of 'stewardship' while denying the background assumptions which give this notion sense. Clearly, a reasonable virtue ethic needs either to be Geachean or Nietzschean. In the early days of its revival it was more or less so. But what a falling away there has been. Nietzsche would have talked of decadence: meaning here the replacement of good sense by goodyness.

IV

It has become the practice to describe virtue ethics as if it were a rival 'theory' of (something we call) morality to set against the two familiar 'theories', utilitarianism and deontology. It would seem that the very phrase 'virtue ethics' was introduced with this comparison in mind. This wish to get established in the theory business has proved most unfortunate, as has been a certain homely togetherness. We reported above the claim that virtue ethics simply offered us a mere difference of emphasis. Differing emphasis is supposed to distinguish the three moral theories (or perhaps families of moral theories). Indeed the difference in emphasis can appear more minor by the minute. Rosalind Hursthouse says,

---

[20] Geach, we should note, is quite ready to recognise the virtue of kindness to animals. See e.g. Geach 2001: 94: 'Man is an animal, and sympathetic reaction to the feelings of other animals is part of our natural make-up.' He adds 'like other emotional reactions this needs regulation by right reason'. If Geach is right, it might be better to say 'a good man *is* kind to animals' rather than 'a good man *ought to be* kind to animals'. The elimination of the *ought* will help to circumvent difficulties people have had with Kant's views on this subject. A propensity to be kind to animals would not so much *be* a virtue as an intimate by-product of a virtue, of a certain combination of sympathy and control that as social beings it would be maiming to lack. Charity as a love of God would have to be something completely different, as the idea of sympathy for God, the incarnation apart, seems not intelligible.

for example, that what is called emphasising character is now, after a few years of dialogue, no longer such a distinctively virtue-ethical activity: rival theories, wanting to be in on the action, have gone in for a little character emphasis on their own account (1999: 4). Indeed, she expresses the hope that all three theories might some day merge. There is surely an unhealthy ecumenism about all this.

As we know, it was for years assumed that everyone must ultimately line up with one or other of the two philosophical parties, perhaps indeed from the cradle.

> For every boy and every girl
> Who walks on earth beneath the sun,
> Is either a deon-tol-ogist
> Or else a u-tilly-tarian.

There was now to be a 'third way', 'a new kid on the block' as Hursthouse has put it.[21] Step forward *virtue ethics*. 'Virtue-based ethics,' she wrote (1991: 223), not without a hint of pride, 'is now quite widely recognised as at least a possible rival to deontological and utilitarian theories'. This innocent-sounding remark comes from Hursthouse's significant article 'Virtue Theory and Abortion'. I say 'significant' because it is offered as a model: it seeks to answer familiar criticisms of the new approach, and to display how attractively—I think this is the expected word—this approach can handle an important controversy. Not surprisingly this virtues-and-abortion article has since been frequently anthologised: it can be seen to fulfil not only a theoretical but a practical need. Fellow virtue ethicist Michael Slote calls it 'ground breaking' (Slote 1997: 237). We shall have more to say about it.

One might wonder why this talk of a third way should be unwelcome: don't we need fresh thoughts? The trouble arises when we ask 'the third way *to where?*' or better 'the third way *to do what?*' The answer is not hard to find. It is to determine *what actions are right*, or at least to give a general outline of how such questions are to be answered—precision not to be expected, and all that. The idea that the three 'theories' provide rival answers to this single question comes out very clearly in Rosalind Hursthouse's abortion article, and later in the book *On Virtue Ethics*. Each theory is expected to 'specify right action' as Hursthouse puts it (1999: 164), to indicate which action gets that 'tick of approval' (1999: 69). Chapter One of *On Virtue Ethics* is actually *called* 'Right Action.' A criterion is to be provided (though heaven help us, *not* an algorithm). Each rival candidate theory is meant to come up with an answer of the form: 'An action is right iff. . . .'

The trouble with all this has nothing to do with an objection to theory *per se*. It is sometimes said that modern virtue ethics itself is 'anti-theory', but insofar

---

[21] Hursthouse 2000: 146; Slote 1997: 233. I would myself suggest 'prematurely ageing kid on the block, with obesity problems'.

as one can understand this thought, it is quite possibly a sinister sign as we shall see. Rather, the problem is that it has always been quite indeterminate what the established, supposedly rival, theories have been trying to do. And once this question has been addressed, it is then unclear whether we should, post Anscombe, be trying to do it at all.

Consider this heavy use of the word 'right.' As the word appears in moral philosophy, it is hopelessly ambiguous—as has been frequently pointed out. Sometimes it seems to mean obligatory, sometimes permissible, sometimes admirable.[22] One could hardly think of such logical differences as unduly refined or academic. Moore's utilitarianism and Ross's deontology, once thought of as exemplars of the two established theories, both purport to indicate what it would be for an action to be 'the right action' (with allowance of course for joint winners). For Ross reverently follows Moore, merely adding in some further duties, leaving Moore's maximizing duty in reserve to take up the slack. Kant perhaps on the other hand seems to have no concept of a winner at all: he is attempting to provide a filter. What comes through his filter are actions which are *all* right—that is to say permissible. This is true, perhaps surprisingly, of Mill as well—to go by the account of moral obligation he gives in the last chapter of *Utilitarianism*. As we can see, then, there is an enormous difference in regard to the simple preliminary question 'What are these two established theories supposed to be theories *of*?' One would have thought that by now people would have given up talking in terms of right action in this traditional but confusing way; in particular, that they would have given up the use the phrase 'the right thing to do', a phrase which surely only has application in narrow contexts And our reason here should not simply reflect a worry about exotic cases of 'moral dilemma', so relished by the more serious philosophers of the day, cases where every course open to an agent is allegedly wrong, so that there is *no* 'right thing'. It should reflect instead the fact that neither good sense nor justice is perpetually directive.[23]

This is not all. A modern virtue-theorist will want to add that what is determined as right *must morally be such*, otherwise we would not have a *moral* theory; and then some account of this qualification falls due. Utilitarianism

---

[22] Hursthouse 1999: 26 (obligatory), Zagzebski 1996: 233 (permissible), Swanton 2003: 240–1 (admirable).

[23] At one place Hursthouse does seem to recognize that virtue ethics is not really commensurate with the other two theories. She says (1999: 69): the phrase 'right action' as it appears in present day philosophical writing is not one the virtue ethicist 'is happy with'; instead the virtue ethicist 'favours' talk of acting well. However, she suggests, virtue ethicists should go along with what they are unhappy with, just to maintain a fruitful dialogue 'with the overwhelming majority of modern moral philosophers'. But the point is surely: to get our fundamental concepts straight. We are not concerned with linguistic discomfort. The virtue ethicist certainly needs—dialogue or no dialogue—the concept of *wrong or wrongful action*, where this indicates an action which is unjust. (Our problems here are very usual. Julia Annas for example (2004) takes it for granted that virtue ethics is concerned with something called the right thing to do, quite generally, and simply argues that we cannot expect 'a theory' to tell us which these golden actions are.)

and deontology both left the force of the moral must entirely unexplained. Thus they hardly deserved to be called theories at all. Modern virtue ethics however, in setting itself up as a rival, seems to have fallen in line with this low intellectual expectation—to have settled for explaining in ways which do not really explain. The contrast with what I have called good-sense ethics is striking. Elizabeth Anscombe, as we have seen, wanted to reject 'the moral' in its present-day use, as marking a special category of obligation or permission. This would make her view, thought of as a virtue ethics, quite incommensurable both with the utilitarian Moore *and* with the deontological Ross. She would not be offering a better answer to the question they posed. She would be rejecting it.

Of course, we *might* take the question 'When is an action right?' to be the question 'Just when is an action permissible under justice?' We would set up a system of rules, though some of them would contain the un-rule-specifiable qualification 'reasonable'—as in 'the bill is to be paid in a reasonable time'. (This unspecifiability is well dealt with in Anscombe 1958: 15–16, 1981: 38–9.) Naturally, we would also hope to provide some account, at least in outline, why *these* rules rather than others. And we would have to say something about the attitudes of mind which justice requires. However this would not give us a theory of virtue ethics, since although justice is *a* virtue, there are others.

The question now would be: does the notion *permissible* used in this way transfer out of the realm of justice to the virtues generally? 'Permissible under justice' seem to have a clear sense, for there is something law-like about this virtue, as its name suggests (a law-*likeness* which is intelligible without presupposing an actual lawgiver). By contrast 'permissible under patience' (let us say) sounds quite unnatural.

If push came to shove, we might try setting up a criterion in the approved style suitable for good-sense ethics: 'An action is not foolish iff. . . ' (and so on). But we would then have travelled so far from 'the other two theories' that we should not be setting up as a rival at all, still less as a rival differing only in what is 'emphasised'. As Amélie Rorty (1980: 3) remarks about 'the Kantian and utilitarian systems': 'The problems of those systems do not arise, and can barely even be formulated, within Aristotle's ethics.' This remark is still apt, I have suggested, even in the case of the loosely Aristotelian approach to moral philosophy, the approach which was to develop into, or rather decline into, modern virtue ethics.

V

Mention of justice leads naturally to the last of the three main criticisms of modern virtue ethics presented in this paper. Recent developments have led to a sidelining of this cardinal virtue. In part, this must be a result of our willingness to 'adapt ancient ideas of virtue to the requirements of current-day ethical thinking', in Michael Slote's ominous words, already quoted. The idea that injustice, as a criticism of actions or dispositions as opposed to social arrangements, had rather been lost sight of in current-day ethical thinking was one of the main complaints levied by Elizabeth Anscombe in her talk 'Does Oxford Moral Philosophy Corrupt Youth?' (Anscombe 1957).[24]

It might seem paradoxical to complain that justice as a virtue has been sidelined when we have ourselves admitted that there is a problem about its standing: whether indeed justice should be counted as a good-sense virtue *at all*. But there is a world of difference. Justice, *if* it is a virtue, can only be a cardinal, pivotal, or key virtue. It is hard to think of this pride of place as a mere prejudice. We think of the way it is proclaimed to the world in the opening sentence of the Institutes of Justinian. Yet virtue ethicists, if they so much as notice the matter at all, are now seeking to confine uppity justice to her place. But it is time, I shall argue, that justice once again be given her due.[25]

Perhaps the notion of justice is an embarrassment for modern virtue ethics, in that it does not seem in any interesting way to require a resort to the preferred formula: 'an action exemplifies virtue X if it is what someone with X would do'—or something along those lines. This sort of formula might seem to be needed in the case of temperance or patience, and perhaps very many other virtues: at least we cannot very well list the actions required. Justice seems to be an exception: we *can* do something to define justice via the actions (or omissions) required of the individual, though the connection might be a little complex to describe. Elizabeth Anscombe says—hardly surprisingly: 'A just man is a man who habitually refuses to commit or participate in any unjust actions for fear of any consequences, or to obtain any advantage for himself or anyone else' (1958: 16, 1981: 40). Or as Hobbes put it, 'A just man . . . is he that taketh all the care he can, that his actions all be just' (*Leviathan*, 15). Of course one might also want to say something about the spirit in which the just man acts, what he cares about, and what he finds contemptible, as Hobbes indeed recognized in the passage from which that quotation comes. But this is something in addition. Philippa Foot, in a recent essay, has said that if a virtue ethicist is someone who teaches that acts are in the first instance to be appraised via 'dispositions, motives, and other 'internal' elements' then she has never been a virtue ethicist: 'for me it is *what is done* that stands in this position' (Foot 2004: 2). Thoughts

[24] This talk, we can now see, was a kind of 'trailer' to 'Modern Moral Philosophy'. As a distinctly puzzled youth, I can remember hearing it when it was broadcast on the Third Programme.

[25] It would be wrong to blame the denaturing of the virtue of justice entirely on modern virtue ethics. Things were already beginning to go awry at the time of Hume and Leibniz, and had gone pretty well off the rails by the time of Rawls. It would take too long to go into this here.

about the centrality and special character of justice must surely underlie her remark.[26]

Given any recent book-length treatment of virtue ethics we can crudely put our sidelining conjecture to the test by looking up the references to justice in the index. Most of what we find will be quite piffling. Often the word justice simply features in a tedious list: 'kindness, charity, sympathy, sensitivity, empathy, charm, uxoriousness, fondness, justice, concern, compassion . . . ' etc. In two well-known virtue-ethics books I was led to the idiomatic phrase *does justice to*—as in 'does justice to his dinner'. All this triviality and nonsense would not matter in the least if there had been, here or there, a few pages of serious discussion. But where were they? In the forty pages of Copp and Sobel's 2004 survey article on virtue ethics the words *justice* and *injustice* are nowhere to be found.[27]

Rosalind Hursthouse excuses the virtual non-appearance of justice as a topic in her book by saying—with a curious echo of Plato's Socrates at the end of Book I of the *Republic*—that it is a difficult concept (1999: 5–6). It is indeed a virtue with many parts or aspects to it, unlike (I imagine) courage or patience. But practical wisdom and happiness are difficult concepts too, as indeed is the concept of a virtue. Elizabeth Anscombe thought the topic difficult ('Justice I have no idea how to define': Anscombe 1958: 4, 1981: 29) but this did not tempt her to give up on it. Peter Geach devotes a good chapter to justice in *The Virtues*, even though he too finds the concept difficult, indeed 'immensely problematic' (1977: 110).

The thought that virtue ethics has to compete with two rival 'theories' has certainly contributed to the devaluation of justice. Justice seems to be the province of the rival firm, the deontologists, who are always rabbiting on about rules, boundaries and what is forbidden. *Don't*ologists they should surely be called. It is here we come to the bad supposition, mentioned above, that our 'virtue' account of ethics should be anti-theory: that is to say, should be unsystematic head-to-toe and have no place at all for fairly determinate don'ts. What is called 'the morality of simple rules' will be dismissed with cool disdain, with an impressive appeal to Aristotle where this is thought necessary (Slote 1997: 176, 180). To be sure, Aristotle suggests that we must be content to speak 'about things which are only for the most part true' (*Nicomachean Ethics* 1094b). But this very pronouncement must surely be regarded as a case in point: *it* is only for the most part true, since Aristotle himself denied that the judgment 'adultery is bad' is only true for the most part. He claims both in the *Nicomachean Ethics*

---

[26] Philippa Foot has also indicated to Michael Slote in a personal communication that she prefers not to be described as a virtue ethicist. (Review of *Natural Goodness*, in *Mind* (2003) 131.)

[27] At first sight, Slote's *Morals from Motives* (Slote 2001) might appear an exception to my 'index test'. Here we find a whole chapter nominally about justice, and a section of a later chapter. But there is no discussion of justice as a virtue. Instead we are treated to a (distinctly optimistic) conjecture that truly 'caring' people will not (or not often?) wrong others.

(1107a15) and the *Eudemian Ethics* (1221b20) that actions of certain kinds are always bad. It is therefore a mistake to contrast Aristotle the Flexible with Kant the Inflexible. (For an example of this mistaken contrast confidently deployed, see Galston 2003: 52.)

Aristotle's homely analogies with health and sailing should be carefully handled here. We need to attend to the broad difference between guidance about what to *do* and what *not* to do. There may be no sensible rules instructing us just where to sail, but there are surely many sensible rules telling us where *not* to sail: straight onto the rocks for example.

This animus against rules, lines and boundaries is very curious, but an observer of modern virtue ethics can hardly miss it.

> 'What's the good of Mercator's North Poles and Equators,
> Tropics, Zones, and Meridian Lines?'
> So the Bellman would cry: and the crew would reply
> 'They are merely conventional signs!'

Perhaps it is thought that a resort to 'a simple rule'—such as Just Say No in relation to rape—would represent unimaginativeness or intellectual idleness in the face of life's complexity.[28]

But there is not only the deontological rival to be considered. Looking over our shoulders at the other rival firm, it becomes necessary for us not to be outdone in virtue by the demands of the utilitarianism of boundless sympathy. So we invent this virtue charity about which we have been talking, along with a host of tributary caring virtues. By contrast, mere justice will now seem an ungenerous, Shylockian, sort of thing. (The bad thought of a justice which *demands* punishment, rather than sometimes permitting it, no doubt contributes to this discomfort.)

Suppose as virtue ethicists we *wanted* to sideline justice. It is easy to see how it would be done. First of all we would greatly augment the list of virtues. Let us try our hand at it: considerateness, graciousness, cleanliness, orderliness, punctiliousness, politeness, earnestness, inwardness, outwardness, openness, awareness, audacity, productivity, domesticity, proclivity, proportionality, propinquity, perspicuity, sensitivity, serendipity—these at the very least. We would hope that justice will hardly be noticed among the throng.[29] It is quite characteristic of

---

[28] There is perhaps an expectation that virtue ethics is bound to be rule-repudiating. Alasdair MacIntyre commented that more than one critic of his *After Virtue* had 'misrepresented that book as a defence of "a morality of the virtues" as an alternative to "a morality of rules"' (MacIntyre 1988: ix).

[29] We need not suppose that no new or hitherto unremarked 'moral' virtues can ever be described. *Tidiness*, as a propensity of character, seems very evidently an Aristotelian moral virtue, a quality we evidently need, with attendant vices on either side: the (usual) sloppiness and the (rarer) obsessional straightening-up. It is a virtue the author lacks. Much of the message of this paper could be expressed in epitome: *tidiness is a virtue, benevolence ain't.* Someone might ask, scandalized: 'Does this mean that tidiness is more important that benevolence? What an extraordinary thought!' But the question makes no sense. There is no such thing as importance in the abstract.

modern virtue ethics to produce huge lists. Being something of a beginner, I only managed twenty. However Rosalind Hursthouse achieves a score of twenty-three or so, and I bet she was not really trying (2000: 147). She warns us, knowingly, that it is 'not a complete list'. In another work Hursthouse (2003: 6) gives us a list of thirty-two vices, 'unjust' not being included. Alliteration can prove hard to forgo. Edmund Pincoffs talks of a person who is 'careful, cautious, cheerful, clever, civil, cooperative, and courteous' (Pincoffs 1985: 117). No sign of 'chaste' needless to say: there are limits to this abundance. He ends his article by compiling an impressive catalogue of no less than 167 personality traits, put together with the industrious help of Robert Audi. This must surely be a world record.

Alongside the ever lengthening list, the sidelining ethicist will talk a great deal about 'richness', and rather generally urge the use of a large vocabulary.[30] Rosalind Hursthouse credits the thought that 'we need an enriched ethical vocabulary' to Bernard Williams (1991: 228). Even without the adornment of such an authority, the idea is hard to resist. Fancy advocating limitation and impoverishment! Or worse, reductiveness! Amid all this copiousness of menu, that charming virtue charity, curiously unknown to Plato and Aristotle as we have said, will be chalked up on a blackboard like a chef's special.

Next, we should be sure, as diligent sideliners, to give very petty examples of injustice, assuming that it is to be mentioned, such as Christine Swanton's example of cake-cutting (2003: 244). In fact, one ought to insist that injustice is always something like a cake-cutting mishap; or is something that only a tiresome child would call unfair. Attention to analogies with punishment say, and idioms like 'doing justice to,' can help. Given sufficient trivialization it is hardly surprising that people can frankly admit that they are about to do something unjust, indeed very unjust.[31]

---

[30] Hursthouse 2000: 148 talks of 'the large vocabulary of the virtues and vices'. Hursthouse 1987: 219–20 complains that 'Many moral theorists do moral philosophy in terms of a very limited vocabulary'. Judith Thomson is here praised: 'rather than allowing only the blanket description "wrong", she uses "unjust", "callous", "selfish", etc.'. 'We have, in fact, an enormous vocabulary with which to describe people and their actions in ways relevant to morality. . . There is a particular way of doing moral philosophy which exploits this rich vocabulary. . .'

[31] Lord Halifax, Foreign Secretary during the Second World War, found that there had been a leak from the Foreign Office typing pool. He went straight there and said 'I am going to do something very unjust, but necessary in the interests of national security. There has been a leak from this pool, and I do not know which of you it is. And therefore I am going to sack you all.' This story, told by Isaiah Berlin, is presented by J. R. Lucas as an example of a 'treating alike' which is unjust (Lucas 1980: 171). But the interest lies elsewhere, for it is already obvious that one can treat alike unjustly. The interest is twofold. We need to note the assumption, regularly in evidence, that someone can propose to 'do something very unjust' without the least dishonour. That is what is important for our purposes here. But also that, in truth, the action in question was plainly *not* unjust, as Lord Halifax I suspect at least half realised. It was surely all right for him to sack a secretary in such a sensitive job, seeing that he had reason to suspect that she was a security risk. Each secretary was presumably in this position. The action only appears unjust by inept analogy with punishing the innocent.

If the petty-examples manoeuvre shows signs of faltering, we could try another: restricting scope. We could say that justice has solely to do with the sort of rights which arise out of a contract. Or that it has solely to do with ownership. ('What individual justice most naturally refers to are moral issues having to do with goods or property', Michael Slote 2002.) Admittedly, this is not a recent development. Both restrictions are already in evidence in Hume. It is possible to be even narrower. It will be said that justice is only about that rather special thing: the fair division of common possessions or things belonging to the community, what Aristotle called 'distributive justice' (1131b28). It is possible to slice and say 'only' in this way because, as I said, it is natural to think of justice as having parts, and in particular because there is, as Aristotle himself pointed out, a narrow sense of justice of which distributive justice itself is a part. (This narrow notion is perhaps not as narrow as one might think. Elizabeth Anscombe says of it that it covers 'distribution, property, debts, desert and punishment and is equivalent to fairness in dealing with other people,' Anscombe 2005: 196).

Related to this restriction of scope, with its focus on property and promising, is the thought that injustice must be an infringement of a waivable right—offering us a quick proof that voluntary euthanasia is not unjust, save where some special circumstance makes it so. But surely the interesting thing about what is called, perhaps misleadingly, the right to life, is that it might not be (properly regarded as) waivable. A trump card sometimes has to be played. The scope of the requirements of justice might then be wider than one might at first have thought, and wider in regard to issues of central importance. Consider here the way that in our legal tradition the consent of the one killed has not been regarded as a defence to a murder charge.[32]

Lastly, and in a complementary way, we might try cutting off various bits of justice in order to pretend that they are something else, 'honesty' say, or 'veracity'. Both this technique and the last are skilfully deployed by Rosalind Hursthouse (1999: 6) in a passage devoted to cutting down the claims of justice. Lying is not unjust, it is *dishonest*, says Hursthouse firmly, the italics bristling on the page. And though murder might indeed be unjust, we should not be too impressed by that: 'What is wrong with killing, when it is wrong, may be not so much that it is unjust, violating the right to life, but, frequently, that it is callous and contrary to the virtue of charity.' Rather surprisingly: she thinks that the supposedly bad thought that lying is unjust (rather than dishonest), together with the stress on injustice as the key defect in regard to murder, is an indication that the topic of justice as a virtue is/has become 'corrupted'. Hursthouse also complains that the concept of justice involved is 'vague', though I think this must be a rather desperate measure seeing that the concept of *any* virtue—temperance, fortitude

---

[32] I discuss this matter further in my *Worth and Welfare in the Controversy over Abortion*, Part Five (Coope 2006).

etc.—must surely be vague. All in all, it is hard not to conclude that she has lost the idea of justice as a cardinal virtue altogether or wishes to repudiate it.[33]

Given the impoverishment of the concept of justice, the so-called virtue of charity, already given prominence as we have seen, will be brought in to cover up the gaps. Thus helping the wounded stranger by the roadside is said (Hursthouse 1999: 6) to be a matter of 'charity' rather than justice. But why should we go along with that? When Elizabeth Anscombe wrote her well known two-page paper 'Who is Wronged?' (Anscombe 1967) she assumed that someone could be *wronged* by the mere failure to be given aid. That was part of the background to the paper. The question remained to be answered whether someone would be wronged simply because a resource (a drug, a boat) was used with less than maximal life-saving efficiency. How can it simply be asserted that the duty to helping the stranger by the roadside comes under charity rather than justice?[34]

As we have seen then, the cardinal virtue of justice has been in one way or another demoted or marginalised. In the rest of this paper we shall count the cost.

VI

It is a small step from the somewhat informal demotion of justice, as merely one virtue hardly noticeable among so many, to an actual invitation to injustice. No doubt this invitation would be muted and accompanied by agonising. The work of Rosalind Hursthouse, as deservedly the best known proponent of modern virtue ethics, is worthy of note in this regard too, so I shall continue to dwell on it. A virtue ethicist, on her account, is at least to regard it as an open

---

[33] Rosalind Hursthouse, in a personal communication, has pointed out to me that the remark about killing and charity was directly inspired by a passage in Philippa Foot's article 'Euthanasia', a passage which as it happens I had quite overlooked (see Foot 1977: 53). Foot takes it for granted in this article that the right to life is waivable—so that a killing would not be unjust where this right is waived, though it might be contrary to some other virtue (charity being her example). Even if we accept that the right to life is waivable—which we should be slow to do as I have indicated—it still seems to me important to preserve the thought that murder is a great injustice, and we should not allow ourselves to be distracted by the thought that murder in certain cases might be other bad things too, or by the thought that certain killings might not be unjust at all, at least in the primary way, but nevertheless bad for other reasons (which is surely correct).

[34] One way of demoting justice is to promote it: enormously to inflate (and distort) its scope. Another way—perhaps the ultimate triumph—is to rob justice of its distinctiveness, and *turn it into* what is called charity. Simone Weil, without the excuse of unacquaintance with Plato, stands accused on both counts. (1) *Inflation*: 'Justice means seeing to it that no harm comes to men' (Weil 1962: 30). (2) *Name stealing*: 'From my earliest childhood I had also the Christian idea of love for one's neighbour, to which I gave the name justice; a name it bears in many passages of the Gospel and which is so beautiful' (Weil 1951: 18). Weil was writing of course before our modern virtue ethicists were born. The resources she here provides for them are yet to be exploited, though Slote 1997: 275 is already talking of justice as 'universalized benevolence'. There is an eighteenth-century precedent in Godwin: 'It is just [i.e. required by justice] that I should do all the good in my power.'

question whether to act unjustly, seeing that the alternative might be (what the virtue ethicist is to call) unkind (Hursthouse 1991: 227). This would represent a 'problem'.

Rosalind Hursthouse initially became involved with virtue ethics when she wrote her substantial study of the abortion issue, *Beginning Lives*, published in 1987. On the whole, *Beginning Lives* is surely one of the better books among the very large crop on this contentious subject. But when finally, after 334 pages (out of 355), she has to be done with preliminaries, to climb off the fence and provide some sort of a conclusion, what do we find? Something of the form: 'Alas (dreadful sorry, and all that) it is sometimes all right to do a wrong'.[35] (Practical books of abortion-help sometimes take this line, advising troubled women to write apologetic letters to their unborn offspring explaining what they are about to do to them. See for example Vanessa Davies 1991: 94.)

This astonishing (and yet not so astonishing) conclusion in this early work seems to have had a profound influence on Hursthouse's subsequent thinking about the new ethics. The idea that one is seriously to consider doing what is unjust from time to time is made more acceptable to the sensitive ethicist by the thesis that after deciding to go for it, the agent does not 'emerge unscathed'. One presumably factors that in. The idea that it can be all right to wrong others is still being propounded years later in Hursthouse 2000: 149. Here she begins by saying that 'the virtues cannot be simply defined as dispositions to follow particular rules such as. . . respect the rights of others. . .' This is reasonable enough. But she immediately goes on to talk of the way the virtuous 'tailor' these rules. An invitation to *tailor* the rule which enjoins us to respect the rights of others is an invitation to wrong these others. To be sure there are, apparently, certain limits: we are not even to contemplate 'killing . . . a human being *simply on the grounds that this would be the most effective way of maximising the interests of others*' (italics added). To which the only response can be: 'Gee, thanks'. How far we are from Elizabeth Anscombe's 'Modern Moral Philosophy'—or indeed Aristotle's remarks about murder, adultery, and other unconditionally wrong forms of action.

How little there is about justice in *Beginning Lives*. All the index references to justice bar one are to Judith Jarvis Thomson's well-known article on abortion (Thomson: 1971). The sole remaining reference, perilously close to the chapter where Hursthouse has finally to state her view, to 'stick her neck out' as she puts it (1987: 331), gives as an example of injustice an action which is quite possibly not an injustice at all. (Someone is wasting his life, and although

---

[35] In fairness I should quote her actual words: 'Circumstances may make it necessary to do what is, in itself, wrong.' However, 'it would be appropriate to regret that circumstances made it necessary to do this thing' (Hursthouse 1987: 335). I have altered the order of these remarks, but not in a way which misrepresents her position. We should note that she does not talk about doing *a* wrong, or about *wronging*. That is surely an indication that the notion of justice is only insecurely in the frame.

it would be kind to interfere I am said to owe it to him not to do so. Wouldn't it depend what 'interference' amounted to?) The only other two examples involve dishonesty and promise breaking. Now *Beginning Lives* is about (what is arguably) homicide. And the natural response is to say: the discussion of justice is insufficiently rich. Ironically, the richness test fails here—where it really counts. There is *no* mention of the virtue of justice in this final chapter, despite the fact that pretty well everyone who objects to abortion thinks that it involves an enormous injustice. But we *are* told about 'such character traits as strength, independence, resoluteness, decisiveness, self-confidence, responsibility, being serious (as opposed to being light-minded), being in control of one's own life'! In an article published later in a *festschrift* for Philippa Foot (Hursthouse 1995: 70–1), 'the virtue ethicist' is displaying 'the resources of her character trait vocabulary', listing ways in which a woman's choice to have an abortion at seven months 'in order to go on holiday' might be objected to. *Unjust* is conspicuously absent. The main worry seems to be that she might be tempted to kill for a lark. A virtue ethicist is depicted as entertaining an ever-so-serious thought: that 'killing babies. . . is a serious matter, never anything to be undertaken lightly' (Hursthouse 1995: 72). One begins to feel that it would call for a ceremony or solemn ritual.[36]

The thought that justice as a virtue was being sidelined in modern virtue ethics first struck me when reading Hursthouse's article 'Virtue Theory and Abortion', since this is offered to its readers, as I said, as a sample of the way modern virtue ethics can be of practical use. The general message here is that the abortion issue has become so intractable because people on all sides will insist on talking about rights and what is owed. But what has gone missing in this article is the thought that if an action is unjust then it must be bad, *whatever* else, good or bad, can be said about it. We do not need to lay on a further sensitive discussion of 101 other vices, hard-heartedness or whatever, in case the action might also exhibit them. Suppose we are considering whether it is all right to kill *this* aunt for *that* amount of her money. Once we have worked out that the killing is compatible with justice (if that is what we conclude after prayerful reflection) there will be time enough to ask whether it is nevertheless callous, light-minded, ungrateful, flighty, thoughtless, shallow, self-indulgent, or a waste of a valuable resource.[37]

Rosalind Hursthouse exhibits a disabling mistake in regard to the question what it is to be 'an unjust agent,' a mistake which seems to me quite natural

---

[36] The missing phrase from this quotation is 'or indeed taking human life at any stage'. I left this out because this raises further questions: clearly 'taking human life' might sometimes be all right—for the police in certain situations for example—and here it would not at all be corrupting to insist that this is nevertheless a serious matter, that enquiries need to be undertaken after the event, and so on.

[37] Hursthouse 1991: 234 can actually say 'virtue theory quite transforms the discussion of abortion by dismissing the two familiar dominating considerations as, in a way, fundamentally irrelevant'. One of these 'dominating considerations' is of course whether abortion is murder under the description: the killing of a child. If that can be dismissed as irrelevant, if only 'in a way', this sort of virtue theory is surely bankrupt.

to modern virtue ethics. She says that someone faced with what she calls a tragic dilemma might choose to act unjustly, but would still not be acting '*as* (in the manner). . . the unjust agent does.' Instead he would act 'with immense regret and pain instead of indifferently or gladly, as . . . the unjust one does' (Hursthouse 1999: 73–4, italics in text. This must be a considered opinion, since essentially the same passage had occurred in 1995: 65.) But clearly an agent who has thought things out, and is prepared to wrong others—even in a regretful spirit—is *already* an unjust agent; that is of the essence of the concept.

Rosalind Hursthouse in a letter has pointed out to me that I failed in an earlier draft to notice the distinction she makes: between 'acting unjustly' and merely 'doing what is unjust', and I have altered what I had written above accordingly. But what of this distinction itself? Aristotle indeed contrasted doing what is unjust and acting unjustly (NE1134a17) but he seems to have in mind the case of someone who does what is unjust when carried away by passion, a very different matter. Not so here. We are concerned here with choice. The suggestion that we are to leave open the possibility of killing the innocent, saying that although we would indeed be wronging them—doing what is undoubtedly unjust—we might not for all that be *acting unjustly*, appears to my mind a bookish prop for the ways of the world.

It was possible for Hursthouse to fall into this difficulty, I suspect, because the passage I quoted is made more complex by an interwoven thesis, which I carefully filtered out, about 'the callous agent', 'callous' being very much one of her words. We are told in one breath as it were about the callous and the unjust agent. Now there is indeed *a way in which the callous agent acts*. Callousness is incompatible with sensitivity. Injustice however is perfectly compatible with it: more than that, injustice—the 'higher injustice' we could call it—might actually be induced by sensitivity. When we hear the description *acting in the manner in which the unjust agent acts* we should surely protest that there is no such thing. We might indeed be inclined to write out a long list of alternative 'manners': callously, forgetfully, regretfully, agonisingly, frivolously, piously, altruistically, etc. Without a vivid awareness of this difference between callousness and injustice one will be seriously hampered in writing about 'tragic dilemmas' and the alleged need to wrong.[38]

Among the many ways in which an unjust agent may be motivated are some which might sound admirable, responsible etc, as we have seen. Neglect of this

---

[38] One cannot help suspecting an academic or literary form of self-indulgence in all this agonizing about dilemmas. People who live humdrum lives in a university love to imagine cases in which even they, as more or less virtuous persons, would 'have to' do some unspeakable crime against humanity, and how they would then wring their dirty little hands—having first held them aloft for us all to see—and confess that their lives had been forever 'spoiled', adding perhaps, in case we are not convinced of their sincerity, that they were contemplating suicide, perhaps in some public place to the strains of Mahler. This may all sound profound and sensitive, but in reality it is only a ride on a ghost train. Philippa Foot, in conversation, once offered the perfect phrase to describe this sort of thing: bourgeois Satanism.

evident possibility tends to trivialize or domesticate the virtue, for it is then quite easy to overlook the possibility of 'virtuous' injustice. Pincoffs for example discusses failings in truthfulness—which would appear, in the main, to mean lying. These failings are characterised several times on one page as *acting for one's own advantage* (1985: 123). But it is an elementary fact of life that quite monstrous lies (to say nothing of betrayals, murders, swindlings, torturings, etc.) can be undertaken for 'moral' reasons. Bernard Williams discussion of 'Justice as a Virtue' (Williams 1981) is also of interest here, for he is engaged in telling us—quite reasonably of course—that people can have various motives for acting unjustly (he has in mind *making an unfair distribution*). Aristotle had been wrong, he says, to put this all down to 'graspingness'. Williams points to other possible motives, 'lust, malice, anger' (85), 'fear, jealously, desire for revenge' (86). One can even act unjustly out of laziness or frivolity (91). But it is noteworthy that no warm, cuddly or liberal motive gets a mention—a striking oversight, made easier by focussing on a narrow cake-cutting example of injustice. It cannot be that these two philosophers were unaware of the possibilities. We have here to do with a mind-set.

This mind-set helps make possible the assumption, so often made, that the wicked are almost of another species, quite different from the likes of us. John McDowell (1995: 150) can say without irony: 'Of course, decent people (like us) think. . .' Or consider the way Hursthouse discusses how 'we' might attempt to 'recommend the life of virtue' to the wicked—or 'convert' them (1999: 174, 176). 'We' don't want the life of the ruthless and powerful, thank goodness!—even though they are apparently happy (1999: 177). 'Few of us (by which I mean myself and you, my readers) are likely to be steeped in vice. . .' (1999: 174), even if our aspirations to live well are so often unrealised (1999: 223). The person steeped in vice, one feels, is an alien being found under damp stones or at the bottom of a well.

Again, Hursthouse seems anxious to tell us—and one first wonders how she knows and then wonders what she means—that the wisdom that underlies (neo-) Aristotelian ethics cannot all be made manifest to individuals outside our charmed circle, however rational and clear-sighted they might be: 'There is no possibility of 'justifying morality from the outside' by appealing to something 'non-moral', or by finding a neutral point of view that the fairly virtuous and the wicked can share' (1999: 179). Leaving aside this obscure claim about insights supposedly unrecognizable from a neutral point of view, how can we safely suppose that 'the wicked' are as it were foreigners? Our togetherness breeds a false sense of security. How can we have the slightest assurance that a room-full of virtue ethicists will not include a fair proportion of 'the wicked'? Isn't that rather to be expected? It is this kind of them-and-us thinking that leads us to suppose that any practice 'we' are comfortable with cannot be a grave injustice.

Contrast Anscombe (1958: 14, 1981: 37): 'Rather generally it must be good for anyone to think: "Perhaps in some way I can't see, I may be on a bad path, perhaps I am hopelessly wrong in some essential way." That is surely a thought we need to carry around with us, and not forget when we enter the study.'

VII

We cannot leave this review of the legacy of 'Modern Moral Philosophy' without a word about 'consequentialism'. The word was actually coined in that paper (Anscombe 1958: 12, 1981: 36), but is now often, and confusingly, used in a different way.[39] Can't we say that pretty well all modern virtue ethicists, of one stripe or another, are consequentialists in Anscombe's original sense? Don't they all teach, as it were, that anything goes if the price is right? Would Anscombe have said, rather as in her article (1958: 1, 1981: 26), that the differences between them 'are of little importance'? I fear she would. Consequentialism, as she named it, is the natural outcome of a devotion to the supposed virtue of charity in its grand contemporary sense with its attendant, mesmeric, can-do-no-other, ought. One concludes—first of all in amazing and ingenious imaginary cases, but later perhaps for real—that one simply 'has to' wrong others in quite fundamental and elementary ways.

Consider first Christine Swanton. She writes that 'we cannot claim that certain features *always* contribute positively (or negatively) to the virtuousness of the act' ((2003: 242, her italics). We can only talk, she suggests, of what is true characteristically. The important phrase here is the 'or negatively'. What we are told, insofar as it is clear, seems to be Anscombe-consequentialist. The fact for instance that one is procuring the judicial condemnation of the innocent will not always, on this view, 'contribute negatively' to the virtuousness of the action. In the case of other modern virtue ethicists, while one might suspect consequentialism, matters are less evident.

The trouble is that one has to proceed by examples of what is in all circumstances prohibited. Elizabeth Anscombe included sodomy (1958: 10, 1981: 34), but it is clear by now that the virtuous person will regard this as an innocent pastime—though not to everyone's taste. But what about killing the innocent (as it is called)? Is someone a consequentialist who says boldly that we may kill whenever the pay-off is large enough? That is to say when 'charity' or 'social responsibility' requires it? Michael Slote (2001: 96–8) for example thinks that it sometimes all right (perhaps one's duty?) deliberately to kill the innocent.[40] He explains that although one must not of course kill someone

---

[39] Curiously, Anscombe herself later used the word in the way now conventional: Anscombe 2005: 271.

[40] These pages in Slote, and those surrounding them, are not very lucid or definite. They are perhaps written with a certain tact. But after several read-throughs it seems to me that this is what we are supposed to learn. See also Slote 1996: 95 and Slote 1997: 225.

merely to save three others, that is only because the number to be saved is too small. Roughly how many savings would justify the killing of the innocent he does not tell us, and it might not be quite decent for the caring ethicist to ask: this number, I presume, would be something that only the virtuous person (knife in hand) would know. What Slote (2001: 66) calls 'humanitarian caring' would be at the back of it.

All this however would not be enough to render Slote an Anscombe-consequentialist. As I said, we cannot establish out that an ethicist meets this standard merely by pointing to examples: that he thinks it all right on occasions to kill the innocent, or punish the innocent, or lie to patients about their illnesses when they demand an honest answer, or torture prisoners in police custody, etc. For we might find him saying the very next day that a truly virtuous person would never on any account hit a woman, quite unthinkable, that this would always count as dastardly, etc. (*Dastardly* is surely a modern-virtue-ethics sort of word, an item from that ever so rich vocabulary.) One needs therefore to consider an ethicist's general approach. There is for example a suggestion in Slote (2001: 38) that an action is 'morally acceptable' if it does not exhibit 'malice or indifference to humanity'. This, given the likely understanding of *malice* in this context, seems to indicate consequentialism straight away.

Rosalind Hursthouse thinks that one would be 'seriously lacking in virtue' if one has come to consider the world to be such that one is forced quite often—'not infrequently'—to lie or to kill (1999: 86). Again she maintains that 'a too great readiness to think that 'I can't do anything but this terrible thing, nothing else is open to me' is a mark of vice, of a flawed character' (1999: 87, footnote, italics omitted). All this suggests a consequentialist attitude; for after one has checked, and double checked, to be quite sure one has not been 'too ready', one is presumably to go ahead. One is not to lie or to kill the innocent *too often*.

That said, she seems willing to see invariable badness in regard to at least one kind of action: an action involving the sexual abuse of children, so much in people's thoughts these days. This—even with the young person's consent—is certainly *not* regarded by the virtuous as an innocent pastime.[41] Does this show us, after all, that she is not a consequentialist? No. The evidence is insufficient. She sets up her example in a way which seems to indicate that she has not yet appreciated what the debate is about. For she takes as her example the sexual abuse of children *for pleasure*—as something which no 'genuinely virtuous person' would do (Hursthouse 1999: 87). This is presented as something of a bold conjecture in her book, for she says that she is rather going out on a limb in making it. For all that, the example is plainly irrelevant; it is not what Elizabeth Anscombe and other anti-consequentialists have had in mind by a description of an action. Supposing I say earnestly that one must never, ever,

---

[41] At least not yet. I write in September 2005.

frame a defendant for trivial reasons—one should not even *think* of it. This is not even the beginning of an anti-consequentialist stand. The rider 'for trivial reasons' destroys this suggestion entirely. The vehement assertion that it is an outrage to abuse a child for pleasure simply invites the response 'And what about *for money?*' 'What about *when needed for one's "psychological health"?*' 'What about *in the interest of life-saving research?*' A genuine anti-consequentialist, an 'absolutist' if you like, will say of actions falling under certain kinds—and what is called child abuse might well be such a kind—that they are not to be done for any reason whatsoever. And certainly, one will not be counted as repudiating consequentialism if one merely says what everyone admits: that actions are always bad when done for a bad motive or in a bad spirit. 'Doing such-and-such *out of spite*' would always be bad, but this description is not a sample of the always-bad relevant to the discussion about kinds of action in 'Modern Moral Philosophy'.

2

The Admirable Life and the Desirable Life

Linda Zagzebski

1 INTRODUCTION

Recently virtue ethicists have given a lot of attention to the connection between two senses of a good life: the moral sense and the sense of a happy or flourishing life. Socrates insisted that a virtuous life is both necessary and sufficient for happiness, a claim that is as hard for us to accept as it was for the jury in Socrates' trial. Still, many moral philosophers continue to exercise their ingenuity in arguing that the moral life is at least necessary for the happy life, even if not sufficient, but even this weaker claim is unconvincing to many. It seems to me that whenever someone makes a claim that stretches credibility and it continues to influence countless reflective persons for millennia, it is worth examining the motives behind it. My conjecture is that the reason for the insistence that the moral life is the happy life is that it has the potential to solve two important problems in meta-ethics. One is the problem of what grounds the moral. The other is the why-be-moral problem. I suspect that it is hopeless to argue that there is a necessary connection between virtue and flourishing as a way to solve either one of these problems, although I won't say it is impossible. In this chapter I shall propose a different approach to the construction of an ethical theory. One of its consequences is that virtue is necessary for flourishing, but that is because both virtue and flourishing are connected to something else that is the key to solving both the grounding problem and the problem of why be moral.

How would an argument for a necessary or nomological connection between virtue and flourishing solve the grounding problem? It is typically assumed that 'the moral' *needs* grounding, whereas flourishing does not. That assumption may be supported by the naturalistic view that everything evaluative either reduces to, or supervenes upon, the natural. If a notion of flourishing can be devised that contains nothing evaluative in it, and if it can also be shown that there is some law-like connection between flourishing in this sense and moral virtue, that would be treated as an advance in our understanding of what virtue is. I find this line of thought dubious on all counts, but one can understand the motive.

The second problem motivating the desire to find a necessary connection between virtue and flourishing is the why-be-moral problem. The idea here is that we take for granted that there is something vaguely called flourishing or happiness, that everyone is motivated to have. By contrast, not everyone is motivated to be virtuous. If we can show that there is a necessary, or at least a very tight, connection between virtue and flourishing, and if the non-virtuous person is at least moderately rational, we shall have given her a motive to be moral.

The grounding problem and the why-be-moral problem are quite different, but I think that they lie behind much of the discussion of the relation between virtue and flourishing. Some theorists are more interested in one problem than the other, and theorists with different interests tend to talk past each other. However, there are also some theorists who aim at a position on the connection between virtue and flourishing that can handle both problems. Rosalind Hursthouse and Philippa Foot, for example, propose a naturalistic account of flourishing that makes human beings continuous with plants and non-human animals (Hursthouse 1999; Foot 2001). Hursthouse goes on to argue that being virtuous is the 'best bet' for flourishing. Calling something a 'best bet' or a 'reliable bet', as she also does, is clearly an appeal to motive. On Hursthouse's account, flourishing is both a ground for the virtues and a state that normal human beings presumably desire to have: virtue is tied to flourishing both in the course of nature and in human motivation. Similarly, when Philippa Foot argues that there is a deep conceptual connection between happiness in one sense and virtue, her favourite example (Foot 2001: 94–5) is of some very brave men who were killed for opposing the Nazis, and wrote letters home shortly before their executions (Gollwitzer *et al.* 1956). Their letters express regret that they will never see their families again, but there is no regret for their actions. Foot argues that there is a sense in which they sacrificed their own happiness, but also a sense in which they did not. Her case for the claim that there was a sense in which they did not depends upon interpreting their lives from their own point of view as expressed in their letters. Foot concludes that the *concept* of happiness in one of its senses is linked with the concept of virtue. Notice also that the sense of happiness she is interested in has to do with the kind of life a person would be motivated to live. At a minimum, a happy life is such that someone who has lived it does not die regretting it.

Foot's example is interesting, but I find it hard to conclude from it either that there is a concept of happiness that includes virtue or that the happiness the Nazi opponents had when they were about to be executed is the sort of happiness most people are motivated to have. So it is hard for me to see that the example succeeds at helping us with either the grounding problem or the why-be-moral problem. I suspect that attempting to solve both problems with one account of the relationship between virtue and flourishing is problematic because the issue needs to be formulated one way if the background concern is the question 'why be moral?', and another way if the background question is 'what grounds the moral?'

If the issue is 'what grounds the moral?', then flourishing has to be defined in a way that makes it a metaphysically more basic state than the moral. For the naturalist, flourishing must be as close to a biological notion as possible, and Hursthouse and Foot explicitly use a botanical model of flourishing. A flourishing human is analogous to a thriving tomato plant.

But it is questionable whether *this* notion of flourishing is the one that can help with the why-be-moral problem. Even if it can be demonstrated that there is a tight, perhaps necessary, connection between virtue and flourishing in the biological sense, that is not the sense of flourishing that connects to the motivational structure of the non-virtuous person. If there is any sense of flourishing that we can count on everyone to be motivated to have, it is the psychological sense: *enjoyment*. Hursthouse does include having characteristic human enjoyments in her account of flourishing, but her argument that virtue is a reliable bet for flourishing works as well as it does only because she puts much more in her notion of flourishing than psychological states that the non-virtuous will find desirable.

It is no accident, then, that the issue of the relation between virtue and flourishing is often formulated instead as the issue of the relation between virtue and happiness, as we see in Foot. The latter formulation is more heavily motivated by the why-be-moral problem. But that formulation has the opposite problem since it is very hard, probably impossible, to defend the claim that happiness in the sense everyone wants can serve the function of grounding virtue.

The eudaimonist can hit the jackpot and solve both problems at once if she can defend the Aristotelian view that flourishing in the biological sense and happiness in the psychological sense are components of the very same state or property of the person's life. I shall not say this is impossible, and I think Hursthouse, Foot, and others have gone some distance towards accomplishing it, but it is notoriously very difficult to pull off. What is even more difficult is to show that living virtuously is closely connected with this state. The empirical evidence seems to be against it.

But, before looking at such evidence, why not ask ourselves the question 'what would we lose if it turned out that virtue is *not* necessarily connected to flourishing in any of the senses just mentioned, and perhaps isn't even a reliable bet for flourishing?' I have suggested that what we would lose is a particular argument for the grounding of virtue in the natural, and a particular way of answering the why-be-moral question. But if there is another answer to these problems somewhere in the neighbourhood, then we need not try so hard to exercise our ingenuity in insisting that virtue makes a person flourish.

We are still left with the problem of how to formulate the question. I suggest that the question should be asked in terms of the two most basic evaluative attitudes we have towards human lives: we admire them; and we desire them. We find some lives admirable and some lives desirable. I don't think there is anything more basic than admiring and desiring in our attitudes towards the good of lives and other objects of value (although this is not to say that the root of value is *in* our attitudes). But the fact that there are two basic evaluative attitudes is puzzling. Why would there be two fundamentally different ways in which a life can be good? There must be *some* reason why 'good' is appropriately applied both to the admirable and to the desirable, and so the impulse to look for a connection between them is appropriate. Of course, it is possible that we shall find that *good* is not a univocal concept when applied to human lives, but, if so, we shall not find that out simply by noticing that the desirable differs from the admirable. We shall have to look more deeply. The question I want to ask, then, is this: what is the connection between the admirable life and the desirable life? This question is motivated neither by the grounding problem nor by the why-be-moral problem. It arises solely from curiosity about the evaluative realm and its apparent bifurcation into two kinds of value. But I think that my proposed answer will show a way to solve both problems. In order to do that, let me start with the method I want to use, what I call exemplarism.

2 EXEMPLARISM[1]

Let me begin with two observations about the constraints we face in constructing an ethical theory. One is that any ethical theory must be compatible with a list of particular judgements of which we are more certain than we are about any ethical theory—for example, 'it is wrong to punish a person for a crime she did not commit', or 'Arthur Schindler did an admirable thing when he protected Jews from the Nazis', and many others. Some of these judgements are quite general and some are more particular, but they all have a central place in our moral thinking because we make them with so much confidence: we would reject any ethical theory that had the consequence that one of them is false. I believe that among the judgements we would put in this category are judgements about the identity of paradigmatically good persons. Almost everyone knows about some of the paradigms—Jesus Christ, Socrates, the Buddha—but there are also paradigms known only to a small circle of acquaintances, and there are probably many such people.

The second observation I would make about the construction of an ethical theory is that we cannot define everything in a fixed domain using conceptual analysis. Unless we are willing to accept conceptual circularity, either some moral concept or concepts will be basic, or the foundation of the theory will refer to something outside the domain. That means that either something is good in the most basic way and we cannot expect an argument for its goodness, or the structure of moral theory rests on something (allegedly) outside of ethics—for example, God's will, human nature, or rationality. If reference to exemplars of good persons can be incorporated into the foundation of a theory without going

---

[1] This section, on exemplarism, is a shorter version of the argument of Zagzebski 2004: 40–50.

through concepts, that would permit us to avoid the problems with a purely conceptual foundation. Furthermore, we would not want a theory to consist solely of a system of concepts and their relations, and of judgements using these concepts, anyway. There is a domain of human life and experience outside the theory that the theory is intended to explain. A moral theory needs a 'hook' to connect it to what the theory is about. We have a model for constructing a theory of this kind in the theory of direct reference, which became well known in the 1970s as way of defining natural kind terms such as 'gold' and 'water'. I propose that we adapt this approach to the task of defining the basic concepts of ethics.

Leaving aside differences of detail between the various versions of the theory of direct reference, Saul Kripke (1980), Hilary Putnam (1975), Keith Donnellan (1966), and others proposed that a natural kind such as *water* or *gold* or *human* should be defined as whatever is the same kind of thing or stuff as some indexically identified instance. For example, gold is, roughly, 'whatever is the same element as *that*', water is 'whatever is the same liquid as *that*', a human is 'whatever is a member of the same species as *that*', and so on. In each case the demonstrative term 'that' refers to an entity to which the person doing the defining refers directly—in the simplest case, by pointing.

One of the main reasons for proposing definitions like this was that often we do not know the nature of the thing we are defining, and yet we *do* know how to construct a definition that links up with the thing's nature. We may not know the nature of gold, and for millennia nobody did, but that did not prevent people from defining 'gold' in a way that fixed the reference of the term and continued to do so after the nature of gold was discovered. In fact, we would not call the discovery that gold is the element with atomic number 79 a *discovery* unless we thought that modern speakers are knowledgeable about the nature of the same stuff of which pre-modern speakers were ignorant. If 'gold' did not refer to the same thing both before and after such a discovery, it is hard to see how we could claim that there is something about which the discovery was made. The theory of direct reference explains how the referent of the word 'gold' remained invariant after it was discovered what makes gold what it is.

This proposal began a revolution in semantics, because it has the consequence that competent speakers of a language can use terms of various sorts[2] to refer successfully to the right things without referring *via* a descriptive meaning: 'gold' and 'water' do not refer to whatever satisfies a given description. There is no need, on this view, for speakers to associate descriptions with natural kind terms; it is even possible that they succeed in referring to water and gold when they associate the wrong descriptions with terms like 'water' and 'gold'.[3] On the best-known

---

[2] Initially the discussion focused on natural-kind terms and proper names; later the theory was applied to a broader range of terms. The extent of the class of terms which can refer directly is not important for my purposes.

[3] On one version of the theory, natural-kind terms have *no* meaning; they are purely denotative (cp. Mill's theory of proper names). On another version of the theory, natural-kind terms do have

versions of the theory, what users of such terms need to count as competent is not mastery of any such repertoire of descriptive concepts, but to stand in a particular causal relation: to be related, by a chain of appropriately reliable communications, to actual instances of water and gold. It is not even necessary that every speaker be able to identify water and gold reliably themselves, as long as some speakers in the community can do so, and the other speakers can rely on the judgement of the experts.

A second consequence of this theory is that there are necessary truths that can only be known *a posteriori*. If a natural kind is defined as 'whatever shares the same nature as some indexically identified object', then under the assumption that the chemical constitution of water is essential to it, the discovery that water is H_2O is a discovery of the nature or essence of water. It is necessary that water is H_2O, but that truth is *a posteriori* because it takes empirical observation to discover it.

If we look carefully at the way Aristotle defined *phronesis*, or practical wisdom, I think we find a remarkably similar procedure, but without the well-developed semantics of the theory of direct reference. Aristotle has quite a bit to say about what the virtue of *phronesis* consists in, but he clearly is not confident that he can give a full account of it. And what is more important for my purposes here, he thinks that, fundamentally, this does not matter, because we can pick out persons who are *phronimoi* in advance of investigating the nature of *phronesis*. The *phronimos* can be defined, roughly, as a person *like that*, where we make a demonstrative reference to a paradigmatically practically wise person. So Aristotle assumes that we can pick out paradigmatic instances of practically wise persons in advance of our theorizing. Presumably Aristotle thought that there was a lot of agreement about the identity of the *phronimoi*, but I doubt that he thought it necessary that every competent speaker of Greek be able to identify the *phronimoi* reliably, just so long as the *phronimoi* were recognizable by the community—which is to say, by educated Athenian men.

If we overlook the obvious chauvinism, I think that Aristotle was basically right about this. Just as competent speakers can successfully refer to water or gold, and make appropriate assertions about these natural kinds whether or not they know any chemistry, so competent speakers can successfully talk about practically wise persons. They can do this even when they can neither describe the properties in virtue of which somebody is a *phronimos*, nor even reliably identify the *phronimoi* in their community. Like 'water', '*phronesis*' and '*phronimos*' (and the English 'practical wisdom' and 'practically wise person') are terms that each speaker associates with paradigm instances. The *phronimos* is a person *like that*, just as water is a substance *like that*.

If I am right about this, the traditional charge against Aristotle that his definition of *phronesis* is circular is misplaced. Aristotle may have been attempting

---

meanings, but these meanings are not 'in the head': the speaker need not grasp them as a means to finding the referent. See Putnam 1975.

a way of defining *phronesis* directly, parallel to the way of defining 'water' in the theory of direct reference. Perhaps Aristotle did not actually have this in mind, but he might have. At least, it seems to me to be consistent with his exposition of *phronesis,* and, in any case, I think this interpretation aids his theory.

Let me now return to the issue of how an exemplarist moral theory can be constructed. A moral theory consists in part of a system of concepts. Some concepts in the theory are defined in terms of others. But, as I have said, unless we are willing to accept conceptual circularity, some concept or concepts will either be undefined or will refer to something outside the domain. Most moral philosophers have done the latter. The basic evaluative concept in their theory is defined in terms of something allegedly non-evaluative, such as human flourishing in the biological sense. The alternative I am suggesting is to anchor each moral concept in an exemplar. Good persons are persons *like that,* just as gold is stuff like that. The function of an exemplar is to fix the reference of the term 'good person' or 'practically wise person' without the use of any concepts, whether descriptive or non-descriptive. Reference to an exemplar then allows the series of conceptual definitions to get started. So the system of conceptual definitions of the most important concepts in our moral theory—*virtue, right act, duty, good outcome*, etc.—is linked to the world the system is about by indexical reference to a paradigmatically good person. As with other theories based on direct reference, indexical reference is the hook that connects our theory to that part of the world with which the theory is concerned—in this case, the ethical domain.

If all the concepts in a formal ethical theory are rooted in a person, this will explain why narratives about, and descriptions of, that person are morally significant. It will remain an open question what it is about the person that makes him or her good. When we say that water is whatever is the same liquid as the stuff in this glass, we are implicitly leaving open the question what properties of the stuff in this glass are essential (or even related) to its being water. For the same reason, when we say that a good person is a person like that, and we directly refer to Socrates or to St Francis of Assisi, we are implicitly leaving open the question of what properties of Socrates or Francis are essential to their goodness. Perhaps there are non-evaluative properties of these persons that are sufficient to determine their moral goodness; perhaps not. Perhaps their goodness is not determined by any descriptive properties we know how to apply and that is why we need narratives. Perhaps (as I have argued in Zagzebski 2003) the distinction between evaluative and non-evaluative properties is itself problematic. The exemplarist approach has the advantage that none of these matters needs to be settled at the outset. We need to observe the exemplar carefully to find out what the relevant properties are. If we take narratives to be detailed and temporally extended observations of persons, then we can say that exemplarism gives narrative an important place within the theory analogous to the place of observation in scientific theory. Perhaps it is even possible to discover necessary truths in ethics analogous to the discovery that water is H_2O and that gold is the element with atomic number 79.

How do we identify exemplars? I propose that it is through our experience of admiration. As I understand emotion, an emotion is a state of feeling a certain way about an object perceived in a distinctive way. (See Zagzebski 2003; Zagzebski 2004: ch. 2.) For example, pity is a state of feeling what we call pity for something that is perceived as pitiable. Love is a state of feeling the characteristic way we call love towards an object perceived as lovable. An emotion has both an affective aspect and a cognitive aspect. As our beliefs change our emotions change, since the way we perceive the object is affected by other things we come to believe. Admiration is the emotion of admiring what we see as admirable. I don't think it is possible to describe what admiration feels like any more than we can describe what love, pity, or any other emotion feels like, but we can say some things about it. We find the admirable attractive in a way that, given certain conditions, we would imitate or emulate. So the admirable is what we might call the imitably attractive. We do not always have the desire to imitate because imitation is often incompatible with our own situation or abilities, or is incompatible with something else we want, but there is an attraction that makes imitation the natural thing to do given the right conditions. The power to move us is present in the emotion of admiration.

We can make a mistake when we pick out exemplars because we pick them out by an emotion that may or may not fit its objects. Just as we can pity someone who is not pitiful, fear something that is not fearsome, or hate something that is not hateful, we can admire someone who is not admirable. We know that because we change what and whom we admire over time and we assume that if we no longer admire someone we once admired, our former emotion of admiration was inappropriate. It did not fit the object. This is disanalogous with the way natural kinds are initially identified. Presumably, whoever designated 'gold' as 'whatever is the same element as that' could not make a mistake, since pointing, unlike an emotion, is not something we can make a mistake about.

But one of the interesting consequences of the theory of direct reference is that reference can succeed even though there are massive mistakes among most of the individuals in the community, who may associate the wrong descriptions with a natural kind term like 'gold', 'diamond', or 'uranium,' and who may not even do a very good job of identifying examples of the kind. What the theory requires for successful reference is that a person is connected by a chain of communication with actual instances of the kind. Nowadays, we defer to the experts in the community for the identification of kinds like diamond and uranium, and for telling us the nature of the kind. In contrast, we often do not agree on who are to what as experts at identifying good people, so our situation is closer to that of linguistic communities in a pre-scientific age. But even communities that did not have experts who could reliably identify instances of chemical elements and animal species probably succeeded in referring to those elements and species. But they probably did not make massive errors, even in a pre-scientific age with no reliable experts to correct them. In contrast, doesn't it seem possible for the members of a society to be radically mistaken in their emotion of admiration, systematically admiring people who are not admirable and failing to admire those who are, thus failing successfully to refer to admirable people when they use moral discourse?

I think this question should be divided into two. The first question is whether this could happen in some other society; and the second question is whether we can think of it as happening to ourselves. I shall not rule out the possibility that it could happen some time and somewhere, although I doubt it. Human beings are too much alike to support such radical error across the board. What undeniably does occur is that a society's view of the admirable person is skewed by exalting a certain image or prototype—the warrior, the successful moneymaker, the star of film or sports, the healer, the adventurer, and so on. What also undoubtedly occurs is that a whole class of persons is ruled out of the class of exemplars because of their sex or race or ethnicity. An interesting account of the psychology behind this is given in Koonz 2003. As I interpret Koonz's evidence, there is very wide correspondence between the people we admire and the people the Nazis admired, and they recognized most of the same virtues in exemplars that we recognize. But human beings have the capacity to rule out of the moral community whole groups of people, and the Nazis, as well as many others throughout history, exercised that capacity.

If we ask the second question whether *we* can be radically mistaken in our admiration, I think we have to give a different answer. Taking seriously the possibility that we are radically in error in our emotion of admiration leads to a global moral scepticism that we have no choice but to resist. It is illuminating that even when people point out that we have serious disagreements with Nazis, members of warrior cultures, and contemporary adolescents in the way we identify some of the exemplars, I have never heard anyone conclude that maybe the Nazis and adolescents are right and we are wrong. It is taken for granted that we are right, and I think that we have no choice but to respond that way. This is the reaction we would expect if I am right that we should take those people we identify as clear examples of exemplars (as well as clear examples of anti-exemplars) as fixed points of reference in the construction of an ethical theory. In any anti-sceptical system of thought, we have to place basic trust in ourselves, and that includes trust in our emotion of admiration. We need to assume that those we strongly admire, upon reflection, are admirable, and those we find strongly reprehensible are, in fact, reprehensible.[4]

Let us now go back to the two meta-ethical problems that are behind the desire to maintain that the admirable life is closely connected to the desirable life: (1) what grounds the moral? and (2) why be moral? Exemplarism answers the first question by grounding the moral, not in a concept but in direct reference to exemplars of goodness perceived in the emotion of admiration. The other

---

[4] Cp. Fossheim's chapter in this volume.

concepts of interest to ethics can be defined by reference to exemplars. To see exemplars as admirable is to feel some attraction to imitating them. Morality does not require that we imitate them in ways that are incompatible with our own personality, vocation, and historical circumstances, but collectively they set a standard for the admirable life. I have said that to admire them includes some motive to imitate them. The reason we do not is usually that we think the moral life is lacking something desirable. We suspect that the admirable life and the desirable life split apart. For a fuller answer to the why-be-moral problem, then, let us return to the connection between the admirable life and the desirable life.

3 THE LIFE OF THE EXEMPLAR

If 'good person' is defined by direct reference, it is plausible that 'good life' is defined by direct reference as well. It is a life *like that*— which is to say we know it when we see it. A good life will be a life that is attractive *either* in the sense of being admirable or in the sense of being desirable. However, I doubt that we define 'good life' independently of the way we define 'good person'. We imitate persons whom we regard as exemplars, and we imitate lives which we regard as exemplary, and these are not independent activities. We identify certain persons as exemplars partly because we find their lives exemplary, and we identify certain lives as exemplary partly because they are the lives of the persons we admire. A person is not independent of her life, although there is a partial independence in that the way a person's life goes is not wholly under her control.

I suggest that the virtuous person is the standard for both the admirable and the desirable. Admirable traits are the traits of admirable persons. The life lived by a virtuous person is admirable. There are many such lives since, unlike 'water', the term 'good' permits of many variations. A desirable life is a life desired by an admirable person and, again, there are probably many such lives. If an admirable life is not the same as a desirable life, it is because the life an admirable person actually lives is not the same as the one she desires to live. That is possible if there are circumstances beyond her control that prevent her from living the life she desires.

If the difference between an admirable life and a desirable life is the difference between the life an admirable person lives and the life she desires to live, the difference must be due to luck, or circumstances beyond her control, but that is surely too simple an explanation of the difference. Often when a virtuous person lacks some feature of a flourishing life, such as health and enjoyment, it really *is* within her power to have health and enjoyment. So we need to examine cases.

Swanton 2003: 82–3 offers three examples of persons who lead virtuous but not flourishing lives. One is an aid worker in the jungle who suffers repeatedly from malaria and dysentery, is often exhausted and discouraged, does not have the comfort of religious belief, and dies prematurely. The second is a bipolar artist who is extremely productive during her manic phases, but eventually commits suicide while in deep depression, having achieved no recognition for her work. The third is an environmentalist who is not taken seriously during his lifetime and dies in despair. His work finally bears fruit after his death.

In Swanton's judgement all of these lives are admirable, but none is flourishing. I agree with her about that. I would add that since none of these lives is flourishing, none is desirable. The hard part is determining what follows from that judgement.

Swanton takes these cases to be counter-examples to what she calls the 'eudaimonist thesis'—the thesis that, necessarily, a virtue *characteristically* leads to flourishing. As we have seen, one proponent of the eudaimonist thesis is Rosalind Hursthouse, who argues (1999: 172) that virtue is a 'reliable bet' for flourishing. Swanton maintains, to the contrary, that these three lives display traits that are certainly virtues, and yet possessing these traits is not a 'reliable bet for flourishing', for these three clearly are not flourishing (2003: 81).

But how can we be sure, about any of these lives, that possessing the traits they display was not a reliable bet for flourishing? I imagine that what Swanton has in mind is something like this: 'none of these lives *ever was* a reliable bet for flourishing; it could have been predicted that these agents would not flourish, and furthermore, that they would not flourish in part *because* of the virtues they displayed.' But this claim is very hard to evaluate. The aid worker, the artist, and the environmentalist fail to flourish because of the way their personal traits combine with circumstances beyond their control. I think we should take a closer look before we can say confidently that these three lives falsify the eudaimonist thesis.

If a desirable life is what is desired by admirable (that is, virtuous) persons, then the various elements of a desirable life are integrated in the motivational structure of such a person. The virtuous person desires the admirable life, and so it is desirable to be admirable. I assume that the virtuous person also desires the standard uncontroversial elements of a desirable life such as health and long life, friends, creative work, enjoyment, and so on. Living an admirable life may sometimes be incompatible with some of these other features of a desirable life. But that is just an instance of the general truth that given some set of contingent circumstances, any one element of a desirable life can be incompatible with another. This is not a special problem for the relationship between virtue and flourishing; it is also a problem that arises between and among the uncontroversial elements of flourishing such as health, friends, and enjoyment. The pleasures of a good life can harm our health; spending time with our friends can detract from creative activity; living an intellectually rich and creative life can be stressful. Living a healthy life can take time away from any of the other components of flourishing, including friends and creative activity, at least for those persons whose health requires considerable attention. And so on.

So, in particular circumstances, it may not be possible to have all of the elements of a desirable life—something must be sacrificed. If the virtuous person makes a sacrifice of her health or comfort for the sake of some other component of a desirable life, she surely is aware that the sacrifice *is* a sacrifice; that's what it is, and the virtuous person is not deluded. None the less, the way she lives her life is what she is motivated to do, all things considered. The virtuous person does do what she wants to do, given that she finds herself in circumstances in which she cannot have everything she would desire if she could write the script of her life herself.

As I have said, I am not sure how to evaluate the claim that virtue never was a good bet for flourishing in these cases. Obviously the aid worker, artist, and environmentalist have sacrificed some important elements of flourishing—a normal span of life and freedom from certain sorts of misery. Furthermore, they might have predicted that themselves. And yet they were willing to make the sacrifice. Are they living a life they find desirable? Clearly not, because nobody wants to lead a life of misery and die an early death. Yet I assume, from Swanton's brief descriptions of them, that they would find a life in which they did *not* pursue their art or humanitarian work even less desirable. That is, from their point of view, it would not be desirable to gain a longer life and greater comfort at the price of sacrificing their respective commitments to humanitarian aid, an artistic vocation, and environmental work.

So all three are in a bind: given their circumstances, no matter what they choose to do, they will miss out on some element of a desirable life. But notice that if they choose to forgo their admirable endeavours, then *by their own choice*, they miss out on key elements of what they regard as the desirable life; whereas if they pursue their admirable endeavours, they miss out on these key elements because of circumstances that they do *not* choose. I can see how, from the point of view of the virtuous agent, the lives these people lead are as desirable as *they* are able to make them given their circumstances.

My position is eudaimonist in one respect but not another. I think the eudaimonist is roughly right that the difference between the flourishing or desirable life and the virtuous or admirable life is filled by circumstances beyond the agent's control. However, the agent always has choices, and some of these would permit her to have more of the uncontroversial elements of a flourishing life, such as health and long life, than the choices she actually makes. The choices she makes permit her to have a more admirable life, but since living admirably is also an element of a desirable life, it follows that either way she will have more of some element of a desirable life and less of another. But the point I want to stress is that the two kinds of life she could choose have a different relation to luck: if she chooses a life she knows makes it probable she will have health, pleasure, and long life, but forgoes the life of virtue, she loses an element of a desirable life through choice. If she chooses a life of virtue, but knows that the life she has chosen makes it improbable she will have health and long life, she loses an element of a desirable life through bad luck. There is an indirect connection between her choices and her lack of flourishing, but she does not choose to be miserable and die young. By contrast, choosing to lose her life of virtue is the only way she can lose it.

So the eudaimonist is right that the difference between flourishing and living virtuously is due to luck. But this is just another case of the general truth that the compatibility of most of the important components of a good human life in a given set of circumstances is a matter of luck. And, in any case, the basic idea of eudaimonism is wrong. 'Flourishing', 'living a desirable life', is not a foundational concept in ethics, in relation to which we are to understand what virtue is. Instead, on my proposal, the foundation of ethics is not a concept at all. Rather, the foundation is provided by exemplars of goodness, direct reference to which enables us to define 'virtue', 'a desirable life', and 'an admirable life'. In Zagzebski 2004 I have argued that we can use the exemplar to define the other basic concepts of interest to ethics, such as a good outcome, a right act, a virtuous act, and a duty, but I shall not comment on that part of my theory here.

4 'WHY BE MORAL?'

Let us now return to the question 'why be moral?' I have already said that if the non-virtuous person admires the virtuous, there is some attraction to the latter that can give the non-virtuous person a motive to imitate the moral life, at least up to the point that it does not seem seriously to threaten such goods of life as friendship, health, long life, and freedom from suffering. So I think that exemplarism give us an answer to the why-be-moral problem if all we are looking for is a motive not to be vicious. But what about the motive to be exceptionally virtuous, like Mother Teresa or the three people described by Swanton? I think that moral philosophers often make the mistake of thinking that the question is answered if we can show that the moral life is desirable from the point of view of the exemplar, the superlatively virtuous agent. But that does not give us a motive to be like the exemplar since the real question for us is whether to adopt the point of view of the exemplar. Foot faces this problem in her discussion of the men who were executed for opposing the Nazis. She argues that there is a sense in which they were happy because they did not regret their actions, but the claim that they were happy depends upon seeing their lives from their own point of view. I fail to see how that gives any of us a motive to imitate these men. If their lives are happy only from a point of view we do not already have, then the natural response will be to say, 'Well, I admire these men's ability to sacrifice their own lives and not regret it, but I'm afraid that if *I* did what they did, I *would* regret it.'

It is much more difficult to link up the motive to be exceptionally virtuous with the motives of ordinary people than to give people the motive to be good in the ordinary way. The only way I know of to motivate ordinary people like ourselves to excel in virtue is to use narratives that reveal the interconnections among the different elements of a life, often revealing that what even ordinary people admire commits them to choices that in certain circumstances end tragically. So would a non-virtuous or ordinarily virtuous person want to imitate a person who lives heroically, or is committed to a cause, or pursues a talent as far as possible even when it may end in suffering, perhaps tragedy? Yes, I think so. Of course, no one wants to imitate the bad luck, but we might want to imitate a life that leaves it to luck whether it ends tragically.

A more likely scenario is that the ordinary person lacks the passion of Swanton's three exemplars and would not choose such dramatically distinctive lives as they choose, but would still want to imitate their virtuous traits. I am not suggesting that everyone would respond this way; but I think that there are enough commonalities in the motivational structure of all normal humans that no one can even understand what morality is about unless they have some motivation to follow it, a motive that does not arise from reason or the apprehension of general moral principles, but from the normal human ability to feel the emotion of admiration.

In summary, I propose that exemplars of virtue determine what we mean by both the admirable and the desirable. The ground of ethics is not a concept, such as virtue, flourishing, or some other; rather, it is a set of individual exemplars direct reference to which determines the scope of the discourse of ethics. Exemplars of virtue are admirable persons, and to see them as admirable is to feel some attraction to imitating them. An admirable life is a life led by an admirable person. A desirable life is a life desired by an admirable person. Admirable persons desire an admirable life, so the admirable is desirable. Admirable persons also desire the uncontroversial elements of flourishing such as health, friends, and enjoyment. It is a sad fact of life that often we cannot have it all. A fully desirable life is not within the reach of everyone. We cannot imitate luck, good or bad, and so we cannot imitate the lives of persons who do have a fully desirable life, but we can imitate that part of a desirable life that is imitable. What is imitable includes the admirable.

3

Virtue and Rights in Aristotle's Best Regime

Fred D. Miller, Jun.

1 INTRODUCTION

Virtue ethics, as a theory of moral obligation, holds that an action is morally correct in so far as it is an expression of moral virtue, for example, in so far as it is courageous, generous, or just. Virtue has an irreducible role in moral theory in that the correctness of a virtuous action cannot be explained on a more basic level, that is, in terms of duties derived independently of virtue (for example, from the categorical imperative or the principle of utility). A serious issue for modern virtue ethics is whether it can justify the respect for individual rights. If it cannot, this would seem to be a crucial lacuna for a theory of moral obligation. Moreover, it would present the disturbing prospect that an agent could act in a completely virtuous way yet disregard the rights of others. This essay attempts to make a start on addressing this issue by examining the relation between virtue and rights in Aristotle. It argues that Aristotle's virtue ethics serves as the basis for a system of political rights, the most perfect embodiment of which is the best regime.

The reasoning is as follows: the best regime is the 'most correct' of those which are called 'correct', 'just without qualification', and 'according to nature' (*Pol.* III.7.1279a17–21, 17.1287b37–41; IV.8.1293b25). In correct (or just) regimes—as contrasted with deviant (or unjust) ones—the rulers aim at the common advantage rather than their own private advantage (III.7.1279a28–31). However, Aristotle repeatedly equates justice with the common advantage (*Pol.* III.12.1282b16–18; *NE* V.1.1129b14–19, VIII.9.1160a13–14).[1] The best regime therefore upholds the just claims of citizens. But a right is a claim of justice which an individual has against other members of the community. The

---

[1] In this context 'just' refers to *universal* justice (or lawfulness), which aims at the common advantage in the best regime, and which is identified with complete virtue in relation to others (*NE* V.1.1129b14–27). Distributive justice and corrective justice are specific virtues or parts of complete virtue (2.1130a14, 22–4, b30–1131a1).

highest good for the individual citizens as well as for city-states is 'the life of virtue, which is equipped to such an extent that its possessor can partake of virtuous actions' (*Pol.* VII.1.1323b40–1324a2). Therefore, in the best regime, political authority is exercised so as to secure the rights of all the citizens to share in virtuous actions.

This interpretation of Aristotle is, however, controversial. It faces two objections in particular. First, it is commonly maintained that Aristotle, like other ancient philosophers, had no concept of rights, so that it is anachronistic to understand their political theories in these terms. Consider the following even more sweeping declaration by Alasdair MacIntyre:

There is no expression in any ancient or medieval language correctly translated by our expression 'a right' until near the close of the Middle Ages: the concept lacks any means of expression in Hebrew, Greek, Latin or Arabic, classical or medieval, before about 1400, let alone in Old English, or in Japanese even as late as the mid-nineteenth century. (MacIntyre 1981: 67)

This view is shared by other scholars such as Leo Strauss and Michel Villey, who agree that the ancient Greek *dikaion* and the corresponding Latin *ius* may be translated 'right', but maintain that it is a mistake to translate these terms by the substantive expression '*a* right'. For, they argue, the ancient terms refer only to an objective condition of justice, namely, the correct assignment or relation of things to persons, and thus could not be used for *subjective* rights, that is, to rights which are *possessed* by individuals.

The second objection says that, even if it could be shown that Aristotle had a concept of rights, such a right would necessarily be very feeble in comparison with rights as they are understood by modern rights theorists. For if, as argued above, Aristotle equates justice with the common advantage, then he is primarily concerned with the public interest rather than the well-being of individuals, and he would agree with Plato that the legislator should see 'that the city-state as a whole has the greatest happiness' rather than being concerned with the happiness of the individual citizens (*Republic* IV.421b). Thus, Aristotle, like Plato, would be inclined to sacrifice the interests of individuals in order to promote the public interest.

Sections 2 and 3 will take up the first objection; section 4 will deal with the second.

2 ARISTOTLE'S LOCUTIONS FOR 'RIGHTS'

Regarding ancient Greek, MacIntyre is correct that there is no *single* expression that can be correctly translated as 'a right'.[2] This does not, however, show that

---

[2] Modern Greek does have an all-purpose word for a right: *dikaiôma*.

the ancient Greeks did not have a concept of rights. There is no word in English that means the same as the German *Schadenfreude*, but English-speakers readily understand what it means: enjoyment of another's misfortunes. (Curiously, ancient Greek does have an equivalent term: *epichairekakia*.) Bruno Snell used a 'lexical' claim like MacIntyre's to argue that Homer lacked psychological concepts such as mind, agent, or consciousness because he did not have precise counterparts for these modern terms.[3] Against this, Bernard Williams (1993: 34; cp. Knox 1993: 43–4) contends that 'beneath the terms that mark differences between Homer and ourselves lies a complex net of concepts in terms of which particular actions are explained, and this net was the same for Homer as it is for us'. In the case of rights, it needs to be considered whether there is similarly a complex net of concepts which was substantially the same for the ancient Greeks as it is for moderns.

The modern analysis of rights by the legal theorist W. N. Hohfeld is a useful paradigm because it is theoretically neutral. That is, it sets forth the logical implications of rights-claims without making strong assumptions concerning their philosophical underpinnings. His analysis has been accepted not only by legal theorists but also by moral and political philosophers as an account of moral rights.[4] Hohfeld (1923) distinguished four senses in which one person *x* might have a 'right' in relation to another person *y*: a claim, a privilege (or liberty), power (or authority), and immunity. Each of these relations involves a correlative relation of *y* to *x*: first, *x* has a right in the sense of a *claim* against *y* to *y*'s øing, in which case *y* has a correlative duty to *x* to ø (for example, the right to repayment of a debt); second, *x* has a right in the sense of a *liberty* (or *privilege*) to ø against *y*, in which case *y* has no claim against to *x*'s not øing (for example, the liberty to consume one's own property); third, *x* has a right in the sense of a *power* (or *authority*) to ø against *y*, in which case *y* has a liability to *x*'s øing (for example, the authority to arrest someone); and fourth, *x* has a right in the sense of an *immunity* against *y*'s øing, in which case *y* has a disability to ø in relation to *x* (for example, immunity against being required to testify against oneself).

It is noteworthy that Aristotle, like other Greeks in the fourth century BC, used the following locutions corresponding to Hohfeld's different senses of 'rights':

---

[3] Snell 1953: 8 argues that Homer lacked the later concepts of a unified body, because he lacked a term that referred to the body as a whole: 'This objective truth, it must be admitted, does not exist for man until it is seen and known and designated by a word; until, thereby, it has become an object of thought.' Along similar lines, Snell argues, 'Homer has no one word to characterize the mind or the soul.' In a recent discussion, Richard Gaskin (2002: 151) marshals criticisms of 'the so-called lexical method, upon which Snell relies, namely the principle that if a culture lacks a word for a thing, then it does not recognize that thing's existence'.

[4] A caveat: Hohfeld's theory is not *entirely* neutral (which would be impossible), but it is applicable within a wide range of modern rights theories (Lockean, deontological, rule utilitarian, etc.).

Hohfeld	Aristotle
claim	*to dikaion*
liberty, privilege	*exousia, exesti*
authority, power	*kyrios*
disability, immunity, exemption	*adeia, ateleia*

The notion of a *claim* plays an important role in Aristotle's discussion of the just distribution of political offices in *Politics* III. He remarks that individuals similar by nature necessarily have 'the same just claim' (*to auto dikaion*) according to nature (III.16.1287a12–14).[5] The notion of liberty or privilege has an especially important role in Aristotle's authoritative definition of a citizen as 'one who has the liberty or privilege (*exousia*) to share in deliberative or judicial office' (III.1.1275b18–19).[6] The notion of *authority* or *power* is needed to explain the nature of political office. For example, 'Solon seems at any rate to grant the most necessary power to the people, namely to elect and audit the offices, for if it did not have the authority (*kyrios*) over this, the people would be a slave and an enemy [of the constitution] . . .' (II.12.1274a15–18).[7] The notion of *immunity*, on the other hand, limits the authority of office-holders: market officials cannot prohibit commerce because the law grants merchants the immunity (*adeian*) to buy and sell in the marketplace (cf. *NE* V.4.1132b15–16). An exemption (*ateleia*) may also be granted to citizens in certain cases, for example from military service or taxation (see *Pol.* II.9.1270b1–6).[8] Thus Aristotle uses locutions corresponding to all four of Hohfeld's rights-relations. This shows the weakness of the 'lexical' argument from the premiss that Aristotle lacks a single word corresponding to the generic English substantival noun 'right' to the conclusion that he does not have a concept of rights.

The 'just claim' locution (*to dikaion*) is the most important, because it captures what is essential to a right: a claim of justice against others. The next section will argue that this relation is at the core of political rights as Aristotle understands them. But first it is necessary to get clear about this relation. One obvious difficulty is that not all duties entail rights. For example, the commandment in the Mosaic code not to covet one's neighbour's ox does not imply that the neighbour has a right not have his ox coveted. Likewise, for Aristotle, not all duties will involve correlative rights. For example, if some friends contribute

---

[5] For other occurrences of *to dikaion* see *NE* V.4.1132a19–24; *Pol.* III.1.1275a8–10, III.9.1280b11, 12.1282b18–30, IV.4.1291a39–40.

[6] For other occurrences of *exousia* and *exeinai*, see *Pol.* IV.4.1291b40–1, 5.1292a41, IV.6.1292b35–7, V.12.1316b3–5.

[7] For other occurrences of *kyrios*, see *Pol.* II.12.1274a15–18, III.14.1285b10, 15.1286b31–3, VII.3.1325a35.

[8] The term *akuros* is also used for a disability, see *NE* VII.9.1151b15, *Rhet.* I.15.1376b11–29, *Ath. Pol.* 45.3–4.

equally to buy a pizza, each of them has a just claim against the others to an equal share of pizza, which entails that each of the others has a duty not to take more than their fair share. But duties of charity do not entail rights. Even if someone has a duty of charity to give some pizza to a homeless person, the recipient would not thereby have a right to it. Similarly, even if someone has a duty based on moderation to abstain from eating all his entire portion, the others would not thereby have a right to the remainder.

In an earlier work I tried to solve this problem by treating the duty as a necessary condition for the just claim: *x* has a just claim against *y* to ø *only if Y* has a duty to *x* to ø. The rationale for that was that the just claim is 'in some sense more basic than, and helps to ground, the correlative duty' (Miller 1995: 95–6).[9] Vivienne Brown has persuasively objected, however, that this proposal departs in a significant way from Hohfeld's scheme where claims and duties are true correlatives. Moreover, as Brown points out, this gives rise to a theoretical problem: 'there would need to be either an alternative sufficient condition for a claim-right or a theoretical account of the two different kinds of duties so that those that are correlative to a claim-right can be differentiated from those that are not' (Brown 2001: 274). It seems clear that the latter is the appropriate strategy: a just claim has as its correlative a duty of justice (as contrasted, for example, with a duty of charity). But, if so, then there is no reason to weaken the requirement by treating the duty as a mere necessary condition for the just claim. Rather, we should make it necessary *and sufficient*, and say that *x* has a just claim against *y* if, and only if, *y* has a duty of justice to *x*. Other kinds of duties that *y* might have (based on other virtues such as bravery, temperance, or generosity) do not involve correlative just claims.

Another issue concerns the content of the right in question. As noted earlier, *x*'s just claim to *y*'s øing involves *y*'s correlative duty to *x* to ø, for example to repay a debt. This suggests that the claim-holder is essentially passive and the duty-holder essentially active. On this basis, Brown has also objected that there is a problem with talking about one having 'a claim to have or do something—to disputed goods, to citizenship, to act as a defendant or prosecutor in a court of law, to political office.' She argues that this entails transposing the action denoted by the just claim from the right-holder to the duty-holder, so that *x*'s just claim is not that *y* øs but that *x* can ø. What was, on the Hohfeldian analysis, a merely 'passive' right has thus been transformed into an 'active' right. Hence, Brown contends (2001: 274), 'the duty-holder's action is thus sidelined to merely accepting or not preventing the right-holder's action'.

This objection fails, however, to take into account two features of the Hohfeldian analysis. First, the Hohfeldian analysis is purely formal, so that the substitution instance for ø may be passive as well as active. For example,

---

[9] I there propose a similar treatment for the other three relations. The present chapter seeks to clarify and correct my earlier discussion in a number of ways.

y's correlative duty to ø may be the duty to be ruled by *x*. Hence, the just claim of *x* to rule over *y* is equivalent to the just duty of *y* to be ruled by *x*. Since just claims may be of either sort, active or passive, there is no systematic sidelining of duty-holders. Second, it should be kept in mind that an ordinary 'right' is analysable into many distinct Hohfeldian relations. For example, *x*'s property right to a house involves a host of such relations, including the claim against any other individual *y* not to enter it without *x*'s permission, the liberty (privilege) to use the house without *y*'s permission, the authority to offer it for sale to *y*, the immunity against *y*'s selling the house without *y*'s permission, and so forth. Similarly, an ordinary 'political right' such as the right to office will include a panoply of Hohfeldian elements. For example, it includes the liberty (or privilege) right to hold an office combined with a just claim against others not to prevent one from occupying it. Holding an office also entails the authority of the office-holder to issue commands, which persons subject to the authority have a duty to obey. Thus, political rights typically imply duties, including duties of non-interference and duties of obedience.

Finally, it is noteworthy that *to dikaion* is also mentioned in connection with the settlement of legal disputes. Aristotle says that judges are called mediators, on the grounds that 'if one gets the intermediate, one will get the just. The just (*to dikaion*), then, is something intermediate, if in fact the judge is' (*NE* V.4.1132a22–4). In applying corrective justice the judge aims at a kind of equality by taking away the unfair gain of one party and transferring it to the other. 'Whenever a whole is divided into two, people say that they have their own (*ta hautôn*) when they receive the equal' (1132a27–9). It should not be supposed (as Brown 2001: 291 does) that 'having one's own' means here that the parties have merely got 'what is equal' in accordance with principle of 'what is just'. For Aristotle states at 1132b12–13 that 'to have more than one's own (*ta hautou*) is called gaining and to have less than one had at the beginning is called losing'. In contrast when neither party ends up with more or less than before, 'they say they have their own (*ta hautôn*) and are neither gainers nor losers' (1132b16–18). Hence, by 'having one's own' after judgement Aristotle clearly means being restored to one's original position, i.e. to one's position prior to the allegedly unjust transfer. Corrective justice implies that the victim has a just claim to receive compensation and the perpetrator has a just duty to provide compensation. The legal dispute is thus resolved justly when each party receives *to dikaion*— in this case, what belongs to it.[10]

---

[10] Brown (2001) objects that 'there is no mention here of rival claims or of disputing parties'. However, in fact, a few lines earlier Aristotle says, 'That is why, when people dispute (*amphisbêtousin*), they turn for refuge to the judge' (1132a19–20). Again, 8.1135b31–5 mentions disputes over whether one party has suffered injustice from another.

3 VIRTUE AND POLITICAL RIGHTS (POLITICS III)

In *Politics* III Aristotle considers the controversy over the regime or constitution (*politeia*),[11] which he defines as 'the ordering of the city-state with respect to its offices, especially the one that has authority over all' (*Pol.* III.6.1278b8–10). Elsewhere he expands this definition: the constitution determines how offices are distributed, what element has authority (*kyrion*), and what is the end of the community (IV.1.1289a15–18). He treats the constitutional controversy as a dispute over political offices among rival groups in the city-state, including the multitude (i.e. the poor), the wealthy, and the virtuous. This resembles a legal dispute over an inheritance with each party claiming to be the legitimate heir. It is important to keep two main points of view in following Aristotle's argument: the dispute is among citizens or members of the city-state (*polis*); and the dispute is fundamentally over political offices. In this dispute each party claims that it has a just claim to political offices based on a principle of justice.[12] The political case is unusual because the parties only partially agree about what justice is, as Aristotle observes in the *Nicomachean Ethics*: 'for everybody agrees that justice in distributions must be according to merit in some sense, but not everybody means the same sort of merit; democrats mean free birth, oligarchs wealth (or some of them noble birth), and aristocrats virtue' (*NE* V.3.1131a25–9; cf. *Pol.* III.9.1280b21). That is, they all agree that

(1) It is just for offices to be distributed in proportion to one's merit (*axia*).

But the parties disagree over the standard by which merit is to be gauged. The general principle on which all parties to the dispute agree is that the citizens have just claims against each other proportional to their merit. But they disagree about what standard of merit is appropriate for distributing political power.

The political import of (1) becomes clear from a passage in which Aristotle develops the argument of the oligarchs:

---

[11] The word *politeia* is difficult to translate. Sometimes the meaning is closer to 'regime', e.g. when Aristotle identifies the *politeia* with a community (*koinônia*, *EE* VII.9.1241b13–15) or with the government (*politeuma*, *Pol.* III.6.1278b11, 7.1279a25–7). But sometimes its meaning is closer to 'constitution', e.g. when he calls the *politeia* the ordering (*taxis*) of the city-state (III.6.1278b8–10, IV.1.1289a15) or the form of the compound (*eidos tês syntheseôs*, III.3.1276b7–8).

[12] Brown 2001: 292 objects that the disputation in *Politics* III has nothing to do with individuals' political rights: 'the disputants are not individual rivals for office but the parties, classes, or partisans who are disputing self-interestedly about the constitution, and it is against these factional disputants that Aristotle's own argument is being directed.' This objection assumes that either the dispute is between political factions or between citizens belonging to different groups but not both. But it is clear that the partisans in question are arguing on behalf of individual citizens. E.g. if the multitude has authority, as the democratic partisans argue, then individuals will have the right to be members of the assembly, council, and juries (see III.11.1282a37–8).

If they came together and formed a community for the sake of possessions, then they would share in the city-state to the extent that they did so in property, and the oligarch's argument would seem to be strong. For it is not just for one who has contributed one mina to share equally in a hundred minas with the one giving all the rest... (*Pol.* III.9.1280b25–30)

Aristotle objects that the oligarchs are mistaken in thinking that the proper end of the city-state is the accumulation of wealth. His own view is that the proper end of the political community is the life of virtuous activity. He supports this conclusion by criticizing opposed theories of the city-state, for example the *Lycophron's* view that law is 'a contract (*synthêkê*) and guarantor of just claims among one another (*engguêtês allêlois tôn dikaiôn*) but not the sort of thing to make the citizens good and just' (1280b10–11). This sort of association is a mere alliance which can exist when its members are far apart from each other, and the mere fact that the members live close to one another does not make it any more of a city. The same goes for associations formed for the sake of intermarriage or the exchange of goods, even when there are laws against injustice in transactions. In all these cases individuals in different families could pursue the aims of the association regardless of whether they live together or separately. The argument recalls that of *Politics* I.2. The family arises by nature in order to fulfil the daily needs of its members, and villages are formed to satisfy longer term needs. But in order to meet the highest human ends families must combine into a city-state: 'The community composed of villages that is complete is the city-state. It reaches a level of self-sufficiency, so to speak; hence while it comes into being for the sake of living, it exists for the sake of living well' (1252b28–30). Similarly, in *Politics* III.9, Aristotle maintains that the city-state is 'the community-in-living-well of households and families, for the sake of living well: for the sake of a complete and self-sufficient life' (1280b33–5, cf. 1280b39). Aristotle equates living well with a life spent in virtuous or noble activities (see 1280b5–6, 39, 1281a1–4). Hence, we arrive at Aristotle's own teleological principle:

> (2) The end of the city-state is virtue.

But even though the oligarchs are fundamentally mistaken about the ultimate aim of the city-state, their argument rests on an important premiss which Aristotle takes on board:

> (3) Those who contribute more to the end of the city-state have greater merit.

This premiss, conjoined with Aristotle's own view, yields Aristotle's interim conclusion:

> (4) 'Hence those who contribute most to such a community [justly] have a larger share in the city-state than those who are equal or superior in freedom and birth but unequal in political virtue, or those who are superior in wealth but inferior in virtue.'   (1281a4–8)

True enough, Aristotle does not use the language of 'just claim' (*to dikaion*) here,[13] but this locution will appear on the scene before long.

Indeed, in *Politics* III.12 Aristotle repeats the point that justice involves a distribution of equal things to equal persons, and paraphrases another misguided argument about political justice:

> Perhaps someone would say that offices should be distributed unequally in accordance with any good whatever, provided that in all other respects the men do not differ but are similar, on the ground that those who differ have a different just claim and merit claim. But, if this is true, those who are superior in complexion and height any good whatever will have an excess of political just claims (*pleonexia tis tôn politikôn dikaiôn*). But is not this obviously false? (1282b23–30)

The expression 'an excess of political just claims' looks like an oxymoron, because *pleonexia* is equated with injustice in the particular sense, for example, distributive injustice (see *NE* V.1.1129b1–2). The expression may be contrived to suggest the incoherence of the position being criticized. Aristotle regards this view as mistaken because it assigns political rights on the basis of a mistaken standard of justice of justice. But this view is also a mistaken application of a principle which he accepts:

> (5) A principle of political justice assigns political just claims to rule (i.e., political rights) to citizens in proportion to their merit.

This is supported by means of an analogy involving the distribution of flutes. If someone is superior to others in playing the flute, it does not matter if he is inferior in other respects, such as birth or beauty: 'Still he should be given the outstanding flutes. For superiority in birth and beauty must contribute to the work; but they contribute nothing' (1282b41–1283a3). This recalls premiss (3): those who contribute more to the relevant end have greater merit. As in the case of the flutes, justice requires that offices be distributed in accordance with merit.

It might be doubted (as it is by Brown 2001: 286) that *tôn politikôn dikaiôn* should be translated as 'political just claims' at 1282b29 on the grounds that no Greek locution is used here for the 'duty' which is the required correlative for a just claim (in the Hohfeldian sense). But it becomes clear in the sequel that the just claim to rule entails a correlative duty to obey. Aristotle takes up the issue of whether it is just for one person to rule or for many citizens to share in governance according to law. He sets forth the argument for the latter:

> Some people think that it is not at all according to nature for one individual to be the authority over all the citizens where the city-state consists of similar individuals. For it is necessary that individuals similar by nature have the same just claim and the same claim of merit according to nature.... Therefore, it is just not to rule any more than being ruled, and hence, it is just to rule and be ruled in turns. (III.16.1287a10–14, 16–18)

---

[13] As is pointed out in Brown 2001: 283–4. But see *Pol.* 1282b26–30 discussed below.

The phrase 'it is just to rule and be ruled in turns' implies that justice requires a situation in which the parties take turns holding office. Taking turns is the just solution when all the citizens are equal but not all can rule simultaneously. When individuals do hold office they have a just claim to rule and the others have a duty to obey. That is

> (6) A citizen has just claim to rule another citizen if, and only if, the latter has a duty of justice to obey the former.

Subsequently Aristotle affirms the thesis about the justice of ruling in turn, with an important qualification:

But from what we have said it is clear that among similar and equal persons it is neither advantageous nor just for one person to have authority over all, regardless of whether there are laws or not and he is a law unto himself, whether he and they are good or not, and even whether he is better than they are in virtue, unless it is in a certain way. (III.17.1287b41–1288a5)

The exceptional case is one in which one individual possesses extraordinary virtue, to such an extent that the other citizens are not even proportionately equal to him. Indeed, the others cannot attain his level even by pooling their virtue together. In such a case, justice requires that this exceptional individual should become an absolute king:

When a whole family or even some individual person happens to be so eminent in virtue that this exceeds the virtue of all the others, then it is just in that case for it to be a kingly family and have authority over all, or for this individual to be king. . . . It is surely not appropriate to execute or exile or ostracize this sort of person, or [to claim] that he deserves to be ruled in turn. . . . So it only remains for this sort of person to be obeyed, and to have authority without qualification and not by turns.   (1288a15–19, 24–6, 28–9)

When there is no such incomparably superior individual, however, the former result obtains, which is described again in *Politics* VII:

Among similar persons the noble and the just are [exemplified by ruling and being ruled] in turn, for this is equal and similar: [assigning] what is not equal to equal persons and what is not similar to similar persons is contrary to nature, and nothing contrary to nature is noble. That is why when someone else is superior in terms of virtue and the power to enact the best things, it is noble to follow this person and just to obey him. (VII.3.1325b7–12)

It is clear from these passages that political justice, for Aristotle, has the following implication for public policy:

> (7) Hence, if all the citizens are equal and similar with respect to virtue, they should take turns in having the just claim to rule and the just duty to obey; but if one citizen is incomparably superior in virtue to all the

others, then the former should always have the just claim to rule and the latter always has the duty of justice to obey the former.[14]

To sum up, Aristotle's argument in *Politics* III relies on the following crucial claims: justice assigns ruling and being ruled to individuals on the basis of their merit (*axia*); and the correct standard of merit for the city-state is virtue. Moreover, x has a just claim to rule y if, and only if, y has a just duty to obey x. On the basis of these claims, Aristotle concludes that if x is incomparably superior to y in terms of virtue, then x has a just claim to rule y and y has a duty to obey x. But if x and y are equal in terms of virtue (and cannot rule simultaneously), then justice requires that they take turns ruling, in which case, alternately, one has a just claim to rule and the other a just duty to obey. The result of applying justice in a political context then is a network of just claims and correlative just duties which are essential to a system of political rights.

4 VIRTUE, JUSTICE, AND RIGHTS (*NICOMACHEAN ETHICS* II–V)

Granted that Aristotle's theory of political justice can accommodate rights in the sense of the just claims of the citizens, what sort of rights will these be? Will they have anything like the force of a right as understood by modern political theorists? To answer these questions, we must examine the underpinnings of Aristotle's virtue ethics. Following a brief overview of Aristotle's theory of virtue, we shall discuss the place of justice in Aristotle's virtue ethics. Because justice is associated with the 'common good' or 'common advantage', it will be necessary to consider carefully how Aristotle understands these expressions. For, if the individual's well-being is somehow swallowed up in, or overshadowed by, the common interest, individual rights will play, at best, a negligible or marginal role in Aristotle's moral theory.

Aristotle's account of virtue presupposes a moral psychology which divides the human soul into two parts: rational; and non-rational (*NE* I.13.1102a26–1103a10).[15] The non-rational is subdivided into a vegetative subpart, involved in nutrition and growth, that operates automatically and is oblivious to reason; and a desiring subpart, that is capable of obeying or disobeying reason. The soul exemplifies virtue or excellence when it is ruled by reason: that is, when the

---

[14] Aristotle adds the qualification (*Pol.* III.13.1284a3–8) that the virtue or political ability of this individual is not comparable (*symblêtê*) to that of the others, because if x was only proportionately superior to y, they could arguably arrive at a just power-sharing arrangement.

[15] This summary is somewhat simplified but adequate for present purposes. Cf. *EE* II.1.1119b26–1220a13. Aristotle says this psychology is set forth in his external (*exôterikoi*) or non-technical discussions. This 'exoteric' psychology resembles Plato's in dividing the soul into departs, although its relation to Aristotle's own psychological theory in *De Anima* is controversial. For further discussion see Miller 2002.

rational part is functioning properly and the non-rational follows its guidance. For example, I want to take a walk because I know by means of reasoning that walking is good for my health. There are two main kinds of virtue or excellence (*aretê*): intellectual virtue (for example, theoretical wisdom or practical wisdom), which belongs exclusively to the reasoning part of the soul; and moral virtue (for example, generosity or temperance), which involves the control of the rational part over the desiring part. This connection between virtue and the rule of reason seems to be anticipated by Aristotle's preliminary sketch of happiness as rational activity of the soul in accordance with virtue (*NE* I.7.1097b24–1098a20).

Moral virtue (together with vice, its opposite) is, according to Aristotle, a state or condition of the soul which is acquired by repeated action: 'we learn by doing, for example, people become builders by building and lyre-players by playing the lyre; so too we become just by doing just acts, temperate by doing temperate acts, brave by doing brave acts' (II.1.1103a32–b2). There is more to acting virtuously than merely behaving in a particular way in particular circumstances. 'The agent also must be in a certain condition when he does them: in the first place he must have knowledge, second he must choose the acts, and choose them for themselves, and thirdly his action must proceed from a firm and unchangeable character' (4.1105a30–3; cf. *EE* VIII.3.1248b34–6).

Aristotle goes on to offer a formal definition of virtue[16] as 'a state involving deliberate choice, which lies in an intermediate relative to us and which is determined by reason' (6.1106b36–1107a2). There are three parts of the definition of note. First, the genus of virtue is a state involving deliberate choice. Virtue is a state (or disposition) rather than a passion (for example, feeling fear or being confident) or capacity (for example, being able to fear or be confident). For people are not praised or blamed because of their feelings or natural capacities, but they are praised or blamed for the choices they are inclined to make (for example, how they respond to a perilous situation).

Second, the differentia of virtue involves an intermediate relative to us. The main idea is that to feel or to act is to choose among alternatives involving a continuum of greater or less. In a perilous situation we can feel more or less afraid and more or less confident, and we can follow safer or more dangerous courses of action. We can choose an amount that is more, or less, or intermediate, when compared to other options.

For example, it is possible to feel fear and confidence and appetite and anger and pity and in general pleasure and pain both too much and too little, and in both cases not well; but to feel them at the right times, with reference to the right objects, toward the right people, with the right aim, and in the right way, is what is both intermediate and best,

---

[16] Following Aristotle's own practice moral virtue will be called simply 'virtue', as distinguished from 'intellectual virtue'.

and this is characteristic of virtue. Similarly with regard to actions also there is excess, defect, and the intermediate.   (1106b18–24)[17]

Courage represents an intermediate condition between cowardice (the disposition to feel too much fear and too little confidence) and foolhardiness (the disposition to feel too little fear and too much confidence).

Third, the intermediate selected by virtue is determined by reason. Aristotle adds that this is the reason which a practically wise person (*phronimos*) would use to determine the intermediate. There is thus a close connection between moral virtue and practical wisdom. He claims elsewhere that 'It is not possible to be good in the strict sense without practical wisdom, nor practically wise without moral virtue' (VI.13.1144b31–2). This claim assumes a distinction between virtue in the strict sense (*kyriôs*) and merely natural virtue. Someone may be naturally brave in the sense of being inclined to face risks without flinching or falling back, but still may overreact or underreact, lacking the inability to judge correctly what level of response is appropriate to the situation. This correct judgment requires practical wisdom (*phronêsis*), which enables the agent to make a true judgement about what level of response is intermediate relative to him.

It should be emphasized that virtuous acts, according to Aristotle, are per-formed 'for themselves' (*di' auta*), i.e. for their own sakes (*NE* II.4.1105a32). This distinguishes his virtue ethics from other moral theories that might take the virtues on board. For example, a version of hedonistic egoism which holds that individuals ought to seek the greatest pleasure and least pain for themselves over their whole lives might also recommend that individuals act virtuously—temperately and courageously and even justly—on the grounds that such virtues will make individuals more effective in promoting their own utility. But if an agent does an act simply because it is instrumentally valuable, it is not on Aristotle's view a truly virtuous act, even if it resembles one. He characterizes an act done for its own sake as noble (*EE* VIII.3.1248b19–20, *Rhet.* I.9.1366a33–4). A recurring theme in Aristotle is that a virtuous act is noble because it has a noble end: 'Courage is noble. Therefore, the end also is this sort of thing; for each thing is defined by its end. Therefore, it is for the sake of the noble that the courageous person endures and does acts according to courage' (*NE* III.7.1115b21–4).[18]

Unfortunately Aristotle does not say very explicitly what he means by 'noble' (*kalon*).[19] He does indicate, however, that to have a noble aim is to be ruled by

---

[17] Cf. III.1.1119a16–18, IV.1.1120a9–13, 1121a1–21.

[18] Reading *ho andreia kalon* at 1115b21. The received text begins 'For the courageous person too courage is noble . . .'. On the idea that an act is noble because it has a noble end, see also *NE* IV.1.1120a23–4, 2.1122b6–7, 6.1126b29; VI.12.1144a26; *EE* III.1.1229a4, 1230a29–31; VIII.3.1249a5–6.

[19] A good discussion is Rogers 1993.

the rational part of the soul: 'The appetitive element in a temperate man should harmonize with reason; for the noble is the mark at which both aim, and the temperate man craves for the things he ought, as he ought, and when he ought; and this is what reason directs' (IV.12.1119b15–17). Moreover, Aristotle's discussion of temperance suggests that the noble involves a recognition of, and respect for, our nature as human beings. The vice of self-indulgence involves overindulgence in slavish or brutish pleasures, especially those of touch and taste: 'Self-indulgence would seem to be justly a matter of reproach, because it belongs to us not as human beings but as animals' (10.1118b2–3). The opposed, less common, vice of insensibility involves an aversion to pleasure: 'such insensibility is not human. Even the other animals distinguish different kinds of food and enjoy some and not others; and if there is any one who finds nothing more attractive than anything else, he must be something quite different from a human being' (11.1119a6–10).

As indicated above, virtue itself is noble because it has a noble end. Hence, the recognition of and appropriate response to a noble action or trait of another person is itself noble. For example, when Aristotle discusses generosity, which involves the giving and taking of wealth, he points out that people may fail to be generous even though they give a lot to others. 'Their giving is not generous; for it is not noble, nor is done for the sake of the noble, nor is it done in the right way; sometimes they make rich those who should be poor, and will give nothing to people of moderate character, and much to flatterers or those who provide them with some other pleasure' (IV.1.1121b3–7). Those who make gifts in order to reward flatterers are aiming at pleasure rather than at the noble. A person who makes a gift to a deserving person is doing something noble because the act involves a recognition of, and appropriate response to, the recipient's moral character.

Similar considerations underlie Aristotle's controversial discussion of the virtue of pride (*megalopsychia*), which involves thinking that one is deserving of great things (for example, honours and offices) when one is, in fact, deserving of them (IV.3.1123b1–2). Although Aristotle's exposition of pride is sometimes derided as a celebration of moral narcissism, his main point is that virtuous agents must recognize and respond appropriately to nobility in themselves as well as in others. While vain people are manifestly fools and ignorant of themselves, the unduly humble hold back 'even from noble actions and undertakings, regarding themselves as unworthy, and likewise from external goods' (1125a25–7). In this sense pride is 'the ornament of the virtues' (1124a1–2). In so far as agents recognize and respond appropriately to their virtues (for example, courage and temperance) they become more efficacious moral agents. Pride is thus a higher order virtue which magnifies the agent's virtue. Aristotle contrasts the virtuous person who is merely well born. The *eugenês* may enjoy great honour but only the *megalopsychos* is entitled to it. 'Those who without virtue have such goods neither justly (*dikaiôs*) regard themselves as deserving (*axiousin*) great things, nor are they correctly called proud; for these things imply complete virtue' (1124a26–8). It is noteworthy that pride, the crown of the virtues, is here tied to justice, which now needs to be considered.

The virtue of justice has a central place in Aristotle's political philosophy: 'justice has been acknowledged by us to be a communitarian virtue, which necessarily entails all the others' (*Pol.* III.13.1283a38–40). Aristotle views just acts as on a par with temperate and other acts that are done for the sake of the noble or for their own sake (see *EE* VIII.3.1248b16–22, 1249a5–9). Yet justice looks like a vexing counter-example to Aristotle's thesis that every virtue is a mean between two opposed vices, because it has only one opposite: injustice. Another complication is that the word 'just' is evidently used ambiguously, given the fact that the term has different opposites when used in different contexts. Sometimes it is opposed to 'lawless' (*paranomos*) and other times to 'taking too much' (*pleonektês*). For Aristotle justice in the first sense, i.e. 'lawful' (*nomimos*), is *universal* justice, and in the second sense, i.e. 'equal' or 'fair' (*isos*), is *particular* justice. Particular justice takes the specific forms of distributive and corrective justice, and the previous section argued that these forms of justice imply just claims or rights. The focus in this section is on universal justice.

In a pregnant passage Aristotle characterizes universal justice as lawfulness:

The laws in all their enactments on all subjects aim at the advantage either of everyone in common or of the best persons or of those who have authority based on virtue (*kat' aretên*), or something of the sort; so that in one sense we call those acts just that tend to produce and preserve happiness and its components for the political community. (V.1.1129b14–19)

Although this passage presents textual problems,[20] the general point seems reasonably clear. Acts are just in the universal sense when they conform to the laws, and the laws aim at the advantage of the political community. By 'advantage' is understood what produces and preserves the happiness or good life of the citizens. The laws can do this in various ways. In the ideal case they promote the common advantage of everyone. Failing this, they promote the advantage of a subset of citizens, for example the best citizens who possess moral virtue or of a virtuous ruling class. Alternatively, the laws aim at the advantage of those who have authority on some other basis, for example in oligarchy (where the basis for authority is wealth) or democracy (where it is free birth). The laws command and forbid specific types of acts. A given prescription, for example not

---

[20] One problem is that *kat' aretên* is omitted in manuscript K^b perhaps because it was regarded as redundant. However, the best persons and those who have authority based on virtue are not necessarily the same groups, since not all of the virtuous may possess authority. Another problem is whether 'common' in modifying 'advantage' applies to the first disjunct, i.e. 'to everyone', alone or to the other disjuncts as well. Only the former interpretation is consistent with the use of 'the common advantage' in *Pol.* III.7 to apply to the advantage of the subjects as well as the rulers. Therefore, the translation here retains *kat' aretên* and restricts 'common' to the first disjunct.

to commit adultery, falls under both the specific virtue of temperance and the universal virtue of justice as lawfulness. Aristotle adds that the laws may not, in fact, promote the advantage of the political community; this depends on whether they are rightly or wrongly framed.

Universal justice turns out to be the same as complete virtue. 'It is complete because he who possesses it can exercise his virtue towards others also and not merely by himself; for many persons can exercise virtue in their own affairs, but cannot in their relations to others' (1129b31–1130a1). Universal justice comprehends all of the virtues in so far as they exercised towards other persons. Aristotle notes that 'justice, alone of the virtues, is thought to be another's good, because it is related to another; for it does what is advantageous to another, either a ruler or a partner' (1130a3–5). This statement seems to overlook specific other-regarding virtues such as generosity, which involves giving to and taking from others. However, Aristotle is here stating an opinion about justice, what some think to be the case, which points to a truth that he states more precisely, namely that justice is concerned with the well-being of the political community.[21] This is also indicated by Aristotle's subsequent remark that 'the things that tend to produce virtue taken as a whole are those of the acts prescribed by the law which have been prescribed with a view to education for the common [sc. advantage]' (2.1130b25).

The close connection between universal justice and the common advantage[22] raises several problems for Aristotle's account of justice. *Problem 1:* is universal justice an exception to Aristotle's general thesis[23] that the virtues are intermediate states between extremes in all cases? It would seem that a law or action either aims at the common advantage or it doesn't. It makes no sense to say that a law or action promotes the common advantage excessively. Accordingly, when Aristotle classifies constitutions in *Politics* III.7 he divides them into two main groups—the just and the unjust—not into three. *Problem 2:* does the virtue of justice apply to one's self? The claim that justice aims at the common advantage suggests that it does, but the statement that justice (both universal and particular) is exercised in relation to others (*NE* V.2.1130b1–2) implies that it does not. The latter implication is supported by the intuition that an agent cannot act unjustly towards himself. If so, justice differs from friendship, a virtue which agents properly exercise towards themselves as well as others (*NE* IX.4 and 8). What accounts for this special feature of justice? This may be called 'the asymmetry problem'. *Problem 3:* can universal justice conflict with the just claims of individuals? The particular forms of justice result in just claims belonging

---

[21] The claim that justice is another's good is found in Plato's *Republic* IV.343c.

[22] Political justice is identified with the common advantage at *Pol.* III.12.1282b17–18. See also *NE* IX.8.1169a8–11: 'if all were to strive towards what is noble and strain every nerve to do the noblest deeds, everything would be as it should be for the common [advantage], and every one would obtain for himself the goods that are greatest, since that is what virtue is.'

[23] The thesis is explicit at *NE* IV.7.1127a16–17. On this problem, see Hardie 1980: 201–3.

to individuals. Distributive justice implies that individuals have just claims to honours, offices, property, and so forth according to their worth, and corrective justice restores to individuals property to which they have a just claim but which they have lost as a result of unjust exchange. But if universal justice is concerned with the common good, might it be possible to bring about this end by assigning goods in a way that did not satisfy the just claims of individuals? This would seem to be especially possible if the common good were understood in utilitarian terms, as the greatest good for the greatest number. These three problems, as we shall see, all have a bearing on the issue of whether Aristotle's theory of justice includes a concept of rights.

Problem 1: how is justice an intermediate state? Aristotle takes a couple of stabs at solving this problem. His first suggestion is that 'just action is intermediate between doing injustice and being done injustice; for the one is to have too much and the other to have too little' (5.1133b30–2). This will not do, because acting justly is supposed to be an intermediate between two extreme *actions*, and being treated unjustly is not an action but a *pathos*. Aristotle concedes that justice differs from the other virtues: 'Justice is a sort of mean but not in the same way as the other virtues, but because it relates to an intermediate amount' (1133b32–3). A related argument is that in the case of injustice 'one term becomes too great, the other too small, as indeed happens in practice; for the man who does injustice has too much, and the man who is done injustice too little, of what is good. In the case of evil the reverse is true; for the lesser evil is reckoned a good in comparison with the greater evil' (3.1131b17–20). This would be persuasive only if acting unjustly consisted in having too much and being treated unjustly consisted in having too little. But there is clearly more to acting unjustly than having too much. For example, if a parent treats two children unfairly, the favoured child may be no more responsible than the disfavoured child for the unfair treatment. To be deemed unjust, the beneficiary must have voluntarily helped to bring it about that he has too much, or at least been an accessory (for example, by refusing to return his excessive share).

Aristotle's second, more satisfactory, solution emphasizes the role of the just distributor who is 'a doer, by choice' of what is intermediate (5.1134a1–3) and of the unjust distributor who does what is excessive or deficient (6–8). The virtues of justice and injustice pertain to the distributor rather than the recipient of just or unjust shares:[24] 'It is plain too that the distributor does injustice, but not always the person who has too much; for it is not he to whom what is unjust belongs that does injustice, but he to whom it belongs to do it voluntarily, i.e. the person in whom lies the origin of the action, and this is present in the distributor not the receiver' (5.1136b25–9). Justice turns out to be a sort of intermediate

---

[24] The reference to a distributor (*dianemôn*) here does not mean that the solution is confined to distributive justice as narrowly defined in *NE* V.3. 'Distributor' refers here more widely to anyone who assigns shares and thus applies to any case of justice or injustice.

because the distributor may assign a share greater than, or less than, what the recipient has a just claim or right to. Justice is the state by which the distributor assigns to each recipient what he has a just claim or right to. Normally there are at least two recipients, so that an unjust distribution is vicious in both respects: it is simultaneously excessive and deficient in that one party receives more than, and the other less than, he has a just claim or right to. In some cases the distributor also happens to be one of the recipients, for example when one party takes advantage of another. The recipient then acts unjustly but *qua* distributor not *qua* recipient.[25] It is by using the just claims or rights of the recipients as a benchmark that Aristotle is able to show that justice is an intermediate between extremes.

Problem 2: the asymmetry problem. Given that justice promotes the *common* advantage, it might be supposed that 'if a man distributes more to another than to himself, knowingly and voluntarily, he does himself injustice' (1136b19–10). But this conflicts with the intuition that it is morally permissible to relinquish the share that one deserves. Not only that, but 'the decent person may turn out to get more of some other good, for example of honour or unconditional nobility' (1136b21–2). If the distributor assigns more to himself than he deserves, he acts unjustly; but if he assigns to himself less, he does not. To explain this asymmetry, Aristotle argues that we must refine the definition of doing injustice: to say that one person does injustice to another is not merely to say that the one harms the other with knowledge of the person acted on, of the instrument, of the manner, and so forth. We must add that he does so *contrary to the wish of the person acted on* (1136b4–5). If *x* knowingly harms another person *y*, then *x* does an injustice to *y* provided that it is contrary to the wishes of *y*.[26] This qualification is significant because it enables individuals to waive their own just claims even though they cannot waive the claims of others. Someone who waives a just claim, for example to payment of a debt, is not voluntarily doing injustice to himself (see 11.1138a23–8).

Moreover, Aristotle associates the virtue of equity (*epieikeia*) with the willingness to waive one's just claims: the sort of person who is 'not a stickler for justice in a bad sense, but tends to take less [than his share] although he has the law to support him, is equitable, and this state is equity, which is a sort of justice, and not a different state' (1137b34–1138a3).

[25] Aristotle adds, truly but misleadingly, 'In the unjust act to have too little is to be done an injustice; to have too much is to do injustice' (5.1134a12–3). Although someone is done an injustice by someone if and only if someone does an injustice to someone, being done an injustice is not a deficient action, as noted above.

[26] This is related to another puzzle, namely whether someone can be done injustice voluntarily. Aristotle contends that one cannot, although one can voluntarily permit an unjust assignment of shares, but this is not the same thing as being done injustice voluntarily. Aristotle gives an example from Homer, *Iliad* 6.298–301, where Glaucus gave Diomedes golden armour in exchange for bronze, although the golden armour was worth more than ten times as much. Aristotle argues that Glaucus gave his own property and it was in his power to give it to Diomedes, so that he was not involuntarily done injustice by Diomedes (1136b9–11). In this case Glaucus may have acted foolishly but he was not done injustice involuntarily because he did not act contrary to his own wishes.

Aristotle's treatment of the asymmetry problem indicates an important parallel between treating people unjustly and violating their rights. Just as individuals cannot violate their own rights, they cannot do themselves injustice according to Aristotle. For individuals can waive their own just claims but not those of others.[27] That is why a distributor who voluntarily assigns less to himself than he deserves does not treat himself unjustly, although he would act unjustly if he did this to someone else. Thus on Aristotle's view just claims involve an element of consent similar to modern rights.

Aristotle applies this solution to apparent counter-examples, for example the prohibition against suicide or self-mutilation. Regarding suicide Aristotle notes that 'the law commands a man not to kill himself, and what it commands one not to do it forbids' (1138a6–7).[28] Similarly, he who though anger voluntarily stabs himself does this contrary to right reason, and this the law does not allow; therefore he is does injustice. But towards whom? Surely towards the city-state, not towards himself. For he suffers voluntarily, but no one is voluntarily done injustice. This is also the reason why the city-state punishes; a certain dishonour attaches to this man who destroys himself, on the grounds that he is doing injustice to the city-state (1138a7–14).

Citizens have duties to the city-state, for example to perform military services in its behalf, and it has correlative just claims or rights against the citizens. Any citizen who violates the just claims of the city-state can be punished with dishonour (*atimia*), a legal sanction involving the loss of civil rights including the right to a proper burial. The implication of this discussion is that although individuals can perform self-regarding unjust actions such as suicide, they cannot treat themselves unjustly, i.e. violate their own rights.

Problem 3: can universal justice override the just claims of individuals? This depends on what it means to say that universal justice aims at the common advantage (*tôi koinôi sympheron*).[29] This expression may be interpreted in two quite different ways. The first is *holistic*: the common advantage is the good of the whole city-state, which resembles an organism in that it has an end which is

---

[27] Cf. Hardie 1980: 210: 'a man may show an equitable character by waiving his strict legal rights when he has the law on his side'.

[28] Literally the text reads, 'The law does not command a man to kill himself, and what it does not command it forbids' (Revised Oxford Translation). Rendered this way the claim has puzzled many commentators, because Aristotle elsewhere says that the law permits actions although they are not commanded, e.g. in buying and selling (4.1132b16) and because it conflicts with Aristotle's own solution to the asymmetry problem. In the *ou keluei* construction, the *ou* can be adherescent, negating the dependent infinitive, meaning '*x* commands *y* to not ø' (See Smyth 1920: § 2693.) Jackson 1879: 122 correctly understands the point of the passage as 'What the law *bids* is *dikaion*, what the law *forbids* is *adikon*'. In an illuminating discussion of this passage Young (forthcoming, *ad* 1138a7) points out that 'neg-raising' (whereby negation of the main verb is transferred to the dependent verb) is found in other languages, including English. For example, when people say, 'I don't want to go,' they typically mean that they want to not go, not that they lack a desire to go.

[29] The discussion of problem 3 draws briefly on Miller 1995: ch. 6, which may be consulted for further discussion.

distinct from, and superior to, the ends of its individual members. Just as the end of Socrates' eyelashes (protecting his eyes from foreign material) is subordinate to the end of Socrates (rational activity), Socrates' own end is subordinate to the end of the city-state as a whole. The other interpretation is *individualistic*: to promote the common advantage is simply to promote the ends of the individual citizens. The city-state is happy or flourishing if and only if the citizens are happy. Because the best regime is fully just, it must take seriously the fact that its members are distinct individuals and must respect the interests of each and every citizen. The individualistic interpretation was succinctly defended by Zeller 1897: ii. 224–6: 'In politics as in metaphysics the central point with Plato is the Universal, with Aristotle the Individual. The former demands that the whole should realize its ends without regard to the interests of individuals: the latter that it should be reared upon the satisfaction of all individual interests that have a true title to be regarded.'[30]

Aristotle himself understands Plato's ideal regime in the *Republic* as holistic. Against the 'hypothesis that it is best for the entire city-state to be one as far as possible', Aristotle argues that

...as it becomes more one it will no longer be a city-state; for the city-state is with respect to its nature a sort of multitude, and if it becomes more one it will be a household instead of a city-state, and a human being instead of a household; for we would say that a household is more one than a city-state, and one [human being is more one] than a household; so that even if one could do this, it ought not to be done; for it would destroy the city-state.   (*Pol.* II.2.1261a16–22; cf. *Rep.* IV.422d1–4236, V.462a9-b2)

Aristotle objects that the city-state could not, and should not, possess the unity of a living, organic substance. Instead, the city-state must be composed of persons who are diverse in kind and perform diverse functions (1261a22–b10), and its aim should be self-sufficiency rather than unity (1261b10–15). Aristotle also criticizes the collectivistic aim of Plato's ideal regime:

Further, destroying even the happiness of the guardians, he says that the lawgiver ought to make the city-state as a whole happy. But it is impossible for a whole to be happy unless most or all or some of its parts possess happiness. For being happy is not the same as [being] even; for the latter can belong to the whole, even if neither of its parts does, but being happy cannot. But if the guardians are not happy, which others are? For at any rate the artisans and the multitude of vulgar persons are surely [not happy].   (*Pol.* II.5.1264b15–24; cf. *Rep.* IV.419a1–421c6, V.465e4–466a6)

In rejecting Plato's ideal, Aristotle promulgates a comparatively weak necessary condition: the city-state is happy only if most or all or some members of the

---

[30] Zeller cites *Pol.* II.5.1263b36, 1264b17, and VII.9.1329a23. More precisely, the position ascribed by Zeller to Aristotle is *moderate individualism* holds that the activities which regard other-regarding virtuous activity as essential to the individual's ultimate good. In contrast, *extreme individualism* would understand advantage in terms of self-confined goods such as wealth, honours, and pleasure which each individual possesses to the exclusion of others.

city-state are happy. This disjunctive requirement is satisfied by deviant regimes which promote only the advantage of the rulers (see III.7.1279b30–1). But the first two disjuncts—'most or all'—suggest two competing standards for the best regime, which correspond to alternative interpretations of the common advantage:

> *The overall advantage*   The city-state is happy only if most of the members are happy.
>
> *The mutual advantage*   The city-state is happy only if each of the members is happy.

The *overall* advantage is aggregative and thus permits trade-offs, sacrifices of the basic interests of some individuals in order to promote the advantage of others. The overall advantage could not be deeply committed to the rights of individuals. The *mutual* advantage, on the other hand, reflects the requirement of individualism that the happiness of *each* of the participants must be protected by political institutions. In rejecting Platonic happiness, Aristotle does not say which of these standards should be applied in the best regime. But whether or not Aristotelian universal justice implies a commitment to the just claims or rights of individuals depends on whether he understands the common advantage as the *mutual* advantage.

There is strong evidence that he does, in fact, understand the common advantage in this way in his description of the ideal regime in *Politics* VII–VIII. First, Aristotle says that 'the best regime is that order under which anyone whatsoever might act in the best way and live blessedly' (VII.2.1324a23–5). The expression 'anyone whatsoever' (*hostisoun*) implies that a regime will not be 'the best' if any individuals are excluded from a happy life.

Second, the citizens of the best regime are genuine members of the city-state rather than mere adjuncts such as slaves and vulgar workers (VII.8.1328a21–5).[31] If the citizens merely performed necessary functions, they would be indistinguishable from the adjuncts (cf. IV.4.1291a24–8). Genuine members must also partake of the end of the city-state (VII.8.1328a25–33, b4–5). Aristotle regrettably believes that many persons devoted to productive professions are incapable of leading the good life (1328b33–1329a2). On the other hand, when he describes the city-state as 'a community of similar persons for the sake of the best possible life' (1328a35–6), he implies that *all* its genuine members, i.e. citizens, partake in this end. This requirement is also asserted in support of universal property rights: 'a city-state should be called happy not by viewing a part of it but by viewing *all* of the citizens (*eis pantas tous politas*)' (1329a23–4). This is strong evidence for the mutual-advantage interpretation.

Third, Aristotle lays down a principle to guide the founder of the best regime:

---

[31] Aristotle denies that a city-state can be composed of slaves or beasts because these cannot partake of happiness (VII.8.1328a33–5 and cf. III.9.1280a31–4).

[A] city-state is excellent due to the fact that the citizens who partake in the constitution are excellent; but in our case all (*pantes*) the citizens partake in the constitution. We must therefore inquire as to how a man becomes excellent; for even if all (*pantas*) the citizens could be excellent without each (*kath' hekaston*) of the citizens [being excellent], the latter would be more choiceworthy; for 'all' (*to pantas*) follows from 'each' (*to kath' hekaston*). (13.1332a32–8)

Aristotle thus distinguishes between two principles which could guide the lawgiver:

> *All* the citizens (in a collective sense) should be excellent.
> *Each* citizen (as an individual) should be excellent.

'Each' is logically stronger than 'all', because 'each' entails, but is not entailed by, 'all'. For 'all' is compatible with the overall advantage, that is, a state of affairs in which the interests of some citizens are sacrificed in order to advance the happiness of most of the citizens. 'Each' requires the *mutual* advantage, that is, the promotion of the excellence of each and every citizen. It is noteworthy then that Aristotle describes the 'each' principle as the more choiceworthy. This requirement rules out the holistic view that the city-state is excellent even if some of the citizens only 'merge' their lives in the life of the city-state as a whole.[32] Such a condition, in which some citizens bask in the reflected excellence of others, may be consistent with the weaker principle that *all* the citizens be virtuous (in a collective sense of 'all'), but it does not meet Aristotle's more stringent requirement that *each* of the citizens attain excellence. Only a mutual-advantage interpretation of justice will satisfy this requirement. This stronger requirement clearly assumes that the happiness of the citizens is *compossible*—that is, that there are no deep, irremediable conflicts of interests among them—but this is precisely what distinguishes the best regime from the inferior regimes.

In conclusion, this section has argued that Aristotle's universal justice, which Aristotle characterizes as perfect or complete virtue, is committed to claims of justice comparable to individual rights. This interpretation helps to solve several puzzles in Aristotle's account: how justice conforms to Aristotle's general thesis that every virtue is an intermediate state between two extremes; why individuals can do injustice to other persons, but not to themselves, unjustly; and why there is no conflict between universal justice and particular justice even though the former aims at the common advantage.

---

[32] This includes the moderate holistic interpretation of Cooper 1990. If under such a constitution 'everyone in common' leads the best life, then even someone who is not himself a virtuous person and so not constantly exercising virtues in his daily life is none the less in a secondary way leading a virtuous life, by having his life merged in the life of the whole city which itself *is* a virtuous one, by reason (primarily) of the virtues possessed, and exercised in its political and otherwise communal life, by its ruling class. (See Cooper 1990: 240 n. 22.)

5 CONCLUSION

If the foregoing argument succeeds, then there is a place for both individual rights as well as virtue in Aristotle's best regime. It does not follow from this that Aristotle is a 'liberal' in the modern sense. For he assigns to the legislator the task of making the citizens good and capable of noble acts (*NE* I.9.1099b29–32, II.2.1103b27–9, X.9.1179a34-b31). Consequently, he advocates a public system of compulsory moral education (*NE* X.9.1180a29–30, *Pol.* VIII.1.1337a27–32). He approves of legislation regulating speech including shameful language, offensive jokes, and indecent speeches on stage, and pictures representing unseemly acts (*NE* IV.8.1128a30–1, *Pol.* VII.17.1336b8–17). He defends slavery (albeit 'natural' slavery) and the legal subordination of women (*Pol.* I.4–13). The productive class including farmers, artisans, and manual workers are also disenfranchised in his ideal regime.

Modern rights theorists would disagree sharply with Aristotle on many of these issues. None the less, as argued here, Aristotle's best regime aims at the perfection and the good life for *each and every citizen*. This assumes that the just constitution must satisfy a strong compossibility requirement: it must enable all the citizens to exercise complete virtue simultaneously. The best regime is thus committed to securing the rights of the individual citizens. In this way Aristotle offers an instructive precedent for reconciling virtue ethics and rights-theory.

4

The Virtues and Vices of Virtue Jurisprudence

R. A. Duff [1]

The revival of interest in virtue theory (in particular Aristotelian virtue theory) among moral philosophers towards the end of the last century had an impact on legal theory, in a revival of 'virtue jurisprudence'. Virtue jurisprudents argue that ideas of virtue and vice ought to play a central role in our understanding of the proper aims and principles of systems of law. At their most ambitious, they might claim that 'the aim of the law is to make citizens virtuous' (Solum 2003: 181), or 'to promote the greater good of humanity . . . by promoting virtue' (Huigens 1995: 1425). Such claims cause tremors in contemporary liberal hearts, redolent as they are of nineteenth-century 'legal moralism'[2] and of the more ambitious (and more frightening) species of communitarianism; they also reflect what I see as one of the vices of some virtue jurisprudence—a familiar philosophical *pleonexia* that leads one to portray as *the* key to understanding a particular matter a concept or idea which, in fact, has only a more modest, but still useful, role to play.

This chapter is not primarily concerned with this vice of virtue jurisprudence, since I have argued elsewhere against such over-ambitious claims for the significance of virtue and vice in relation to the law, and in relation to the criminal law in particular (Duff 2002; 2003). To reject such ambitious claims should not, however, be to reject virtue jurisprudence outright; we might find a more modest and limited, but still useful, role for some of the virtue jurisprudents' ideas in relation to particular aspects of the law. My aim in this chapter is to identify one such virtue of virtue jurisprudence: to show how notions of civic virtue and vice can illuminate an important aspect of criminal law doctrine, and play a useful analytical and normative role in our critical understanding of criminal law.

[1] Grateful thanks are due to the Leverhulme Trust for the Major Research Fellowship during which I wrote this chapter, and to participants in the conference on Values and Virtues in Dundee, and in a conference on Human Nature in Law and Political Morality in Cambridge, at which earlier versions of this chapter were read. I am also grateful to Suzanne Uniacke for discussions on some of the central themes of the chapter, and for allowing me to read her 'Emotional Excuses' (forthcoming, *Law and Philosophy*).
[2] See e.g. Stephen 1967: 152 ('criminal law is in the nature of a persecution of the grosser forms of vice'). On legal moralism, see Moore 1997: 69–78 and Feinberg 1988.

As a prelude to that discussion (which will occupy sections 2–4 of the chapter), however, we need some brief explanation of what virtue jurisprudence might amount to.

1 'VIRTUE JURISPRUDENCE'

The general question we have to ask is whether substantive notions of virtue and vice can play a useful role in our understanding of law—in particular, for my present purposes, in our understanding of criminal law. One could, of course, easily make it a truism that the criminal law is concerned to promote 'virtue' and to punish 'vice' by defining those concepts in purely behavioural terms: we could say that a virtuous citizen is one whose conduct is always, *inter alia*, in conformity with the law's (justified) requirements, whilst the commission of what the law (justifiably) defines as a crime manifests a civic vice. From this it would follow that the law aims to encourage those behavioural dispositions that constitute virtue, and to discourage those that constitute vice. But this would reduce virtue jurisprudence to a rhetorical flourish, by reducing virtue and vice to mere behavioural dispositions. If virtue jurisprudence is to say anything interesting, it must operate with more substantive ideas of virtue and vice that could provide a distinctive focus for the criminal law and its doctrines of liability.

The precise contours of those substantive ideas will depend on one's particular brand of virtue theory. I will draw on an Aristotelian conception of virtue, as virtue jurisprudents (including Solum 2003 and Huigens 1995, for instance) tend to do. Without going into detail, we can say that beyond dispositions of conduct, Aristotelian virtue also and crucially involves dispositions of perception, of emotion, and of deliberation: the person of excellent character will be disposed to notice the salient aspects of his situation, in the appropriate, value-laden terms; to respond to that situation with appropriate emotions—emotions that embody a proper conception of the good; and to deliberate appropriately about what to do, in the light of that conception. Given the central role of emotion in excellence of character, an Aristotelian account also distinguishes excellence from self-control (*enkrateia*), and vice from weakness of will. The person of excellence acts wholeheartedly in a way that the self-controlled person cannot: while the latter acts appropriately and for the right reasons, she has to resist contrary passions in order to do so, whereas in a person of excellence passion 'always chimes with reason'.[3] So, too, a vicious person is wholehearted in her pursuit of what is evil, whereas the weak-willed person is led away by his ill-trained passions from the good that he (in some sense) recognizes and desires. In what follows, the role of emotions in the Aristotelian picture will be of particular importance;

---

[3] Aristotle, *Nicomachean Ethics*, I.13, 1102b29. Here and elsewhere I use Rowe's translation in Broadie and Rowe 2002.

I shall also raise later the question of whether the distinctions between excellence and *enkrateia*, and between vice and weakness of will, should matter to the criminal law.

We can certainly give virtue, understood in such substantive terms, a significant auxiliary role in relation to the criminal law. We can ask, for instance, what virtues citizens will need if they are to act rightly in relation to the law—leaving open the questions of whether it should be the state's responsibility to foster or to promote such civic virtues, and, if so, how. (I take it that 'acting rightly' will, on any plausible conception of the duties of citizenship, include the possibility of disobedience.) We can similarly ask what virtues are needed by legal officials (legislators, judges, police, and penal officers) if they are to fulfil their responsibilities properly, and whether there are distinctive virtues that belong to such roles. (See Solum 2003 for an interesting preliminary sketch of the judicial virtues.) But this species of virtue jurisprudence does not give virtue an essential role *within* our understanding of law, as virtue jurisprudents aspire to do. Given an understanding of what law is and what it requires, we can go on to ask what virtues citizens or officials require, but that initial understanding of the law is not set in terms of virtue or vice. We can ask what virtues judges need if they are reliably to reach just decisions by just procedures, but only given a prior understanding of what constitutes a just procedure or a just decision—an understanding in which notions of virtue or vice need not, for all that has been said so far, play any essential or constitutive role.

What, then, would it be to give substantive notions of virtue and vice a constitutive, rather than a merely auxiliary, role in our understanding of criminal law? We can identify a range of possibilities.

First, we could suggest that criminal punishment should aim to induce or foster virtue, by 'correcting' those whose criminal conduct displays vice (see e.g. Huigens 1995 and Huigens 2002).[4]

Second, we could suggest that even if punishment should not aim to induce virtue, vice should be an essential ground of criminal liability: either it should be the object of liability, in that what offenders are criminally liable for is, or should be, the vice that their offending conduct displays; or it should be an essential condition of liability in that even if what offenders are directly liable for is, for instance, some criminal action, they are thus liable only on condition that that action displays or flows from a vice.[5]

Or third, we could suggest that virtue is partly constitutive of, and not merely auxiliary to, right legal judgement: that, for instance, the right legal decision

---

[4] One could also offer a virtue-theoretic reading of theories that portray punishment as a matter of moral education: Morris 1981; Hampton 1984.

[5] For the significance of the distinction between objects and conditions of liability, see Duff 2002: 155–60. For an ambitious claim that criminal liability is grounded in vice, see Huigens 1995. For less ambitious claims that vice plays a role in the grounds of criminal liability, see e.g. Finkelstein1995; Kahan and Nussbaum 1996; Gardner 1998; Tadros 2001.

can only be defined as that which a virtuous judge would reach (for a qualified version of this claim, see Solum 2003); or that courts can determine (as they often must in both criminal and civil cases) whether a certain course of conduct was 'reasonable' only by asking whether it was what a virtuous person might do—that the 'reasonable' can only be defined in terms of the virtuous person's conduct.[6]

Such suggestions, if offered baldly as general claims about the aims of punishment or the grounds of liability or the criteria of legal judgement, will strike many as quite implausible—both as descriptive or analytical claims about our existing law, and as normative claims about how our law ought to function. But that is not the best way to understand them; to offer them in those terms is to fall into the *pleonexia* noted above. A more plausible approach for virtue theorists is to argue that substantive notions of virtue and vice play an essential role in some more particular legal context, or in relation to some particular legal doctrine;[7] and then to see whether and how far the claims of virtue jurisprudence can be extended to other, more general, aspects of the law.

This is the approach that I shall take here. I shall argue in sections 2–3 that we find an essential, constitutive role for notions of virtue and vice in relation to two specific criminal law defences—duress and provocation. I shall then argue, in section 4, that this account of these two defences generates a broader type of defence, which would cover other kinds of case. In section 5 I shall ask what support this line of argument can provide for an ambitious virtue jurisprudence of criminal liability.

2 DURESS AS AN ARISTOTELIAN DEFENCE

Suppose that someone is plausibly threatened that he and/or his loved ones will be seriously harmed if he refuses to commit a specified crime; he commits the crime, and successfully pleads duress as a defence at his trial. Our concern here is not with cases in which duress justifies what the defendant did—cases in which, given the threat, committing the crime was the right, or at least a straightforwardly permissible, thing to do. Nor is it with cases in which the defendant is excused because the threat was so destructively terrifying that he ceased to function as a deliberating, rational agent at all—as when, for instance, someone betrays secrets under severe, continuing torture. Rather, our concern is with less dramatic cases in which whilst the agent should (ideally) have withstood

---

[6] Feldman 2000 gives prudence and carefulness (as an aspect of benevolence) a defining role of this kind.

[7] See e.g. Solum 2003: 204–6, who argues that in cases in which 'equity' is necessary—cases in which a strict application of the legal rules would produce injustice—we must define the legally correct decision as the one that a virtuous judge would make.

the threat, and was not rationally incapacitated by it, we think that she should none the less be excused for giving in. Consider, for instance, someone who commits perjury because she has been plausibly threatened with quite serious injury by the defendant's friends.[8]

According to English law, one who acts under such a threat has a defence only if 'a sober person of reasonable firmness sharing the characteristics of the defendant' would have acted as she did in response to such a threat.[9] This is one of several contexts in which the figure of the 'reasonable' person plays a role in determinations of criminal liability—a role that causes both confusion and controversy when people ask which of the defendant's characteristics we should ascribe to this 'reasonable person', and why judgements of the actual defendant's guilt or innocence should depend on the hypothesized conduct of this imaginary being. The role of the 'reasonable person' is, in fact, to generate an answer to the question of whether the conduct or the response of this actual defendant was 'reasonable'—a question that we might do better to ask directly, rather than mediating it through the construction of the 'reasonable person' to whom the actual defendant is then compared. In the context of duress, we can plausibly offer an Aristotelian account of what makes a response to a threat 'reasonable' and thus excusable. As we shall see, the norm of reasonableness imports a justificatory dimension to the defence; but the defence is in the end still an excuse for doing what one should not have done.

The first, and most obviously justificatory, dimension of the defence is that the defendant was motivated by a 'reasonable' emotion—in this case, fear. To call her emotion 'reasonable' is to say both that it is a type of emotion that plays a proper part in human life, and that it was reasonably felt on this occasion. What she feared—the threatened harm—was indeed fearful, i.e. worthy of being feared; and the strength of her fear was not grossly excessive.[10]

Second, that reasonable emotion would reasonably, properly, motivate something like what the defendant actually did—an action whose relevant description would at least overlap with the description of her actual action. It would properly motivate her, it would give her a good reason, to act so as to avert the

---

[8] *Hudson and Taylor* [1971] 2 QB 202. Some argue that duress can exculpate only by justifying: Westen and Mangiafico 2003. I cannot discuss that argument here, though I think it misguided. Others hold that duress as a legal defence is always an excuse: Fletcher 1978: 829–35; Dressler 1989; Gardner 1998. Although I prefer the broader usage, on which duress sometimes justifies and sometimes excuses, one can see a rationale for limiting the term to excuses. When an agent is justified in giving in to a threat, his actions ' in themselves are . . . counter-voluntary; for no one would choose anything of this sort for itself'; but 'on this occasion and in exchange for these particular results [they are] voluntary' (Aristotle, *Nicomachean Ethics* III.1, 1110a18–20, 1110b6–7)—that is, he acts in accordance with his own rational will. By contrast, when his action is excused, his will is 'overborne' (see *Hudson and Taylor*, at 206): he is coerced against his rational will.

[9] *Graham* [1982] 74 Cr. App. R. 235, at 241.

[10] In the simplest kind of case, her fear is simply appropriate. In more complex cases, which I cannot discuss here, we might think her fear slightly excessive, but not unreasonably so given the immediacy of the threat: we can't blame her for not keeping an entirely cool head.

threat—which is what she indeed did.[11] Since we are not dealing with duress as a justification, however, it must also be admitted that her action as fully described was not appropriate. Although she had good reason to act so as to avert the threat, that did not give her good reason (or good enough reason) to commit that crime, even to avert the threat.

But, third, she did not display vice, though she did display a lack of 'superhuman excellence' (*Nicomachean Ethics* 1145a20–30), in being tempted to commit such a crime to avert such a threat. For an appropriate attachment to the good that was threatened could tempt even a moderately (humanly) virtuous person to commit such a crime.

Furthermore, and fourth, the emotion that she properly felt is one that, when strong, is apt to destabilize—to disturb our rational deliberation: its motivational power is liable to exceed its rational authority.

In the light of all these factors, we may conclude that in giving in to such a threat, and committing this crime, this defendant did not display a lack of those modest levels of courage and self-control, and of commitment to the goods and rights that the criminal law protects, that citizens can properly demand of each other on pain of public condemnation and punishment.

We do not say that it was right, or even permissible, to give in. The defendant should still have resisted, and should now regret giving in.[12] She displayed a lack of true excellence or of true strength of will. But we do not condemn her failure to resist, since resistance would have required a degree of courage whose absence we cannot justly condemn.[13]

3 PROVOCATION AND THE LEGITIMATION OF ANGRY VIOLENCE

We can give an analogous analysis of provocation, which constitutes a partial defence to a murder charge—partial in that its success serves only to reduce the crime to manslaughter (Simester and Sullivan 2003: 342–60). A defendant is entitled to this defence only if (i) he was provoked into losing self-control, as a result of which he committed the fatal attack; and (ii) a 'reasonable' person

[11] Compare John Skorupski's 'Feeling/Disposition Principle' (Skorupski 1999: 38): if she has reason to feel fear, she has reason to do what fear characteristically disposes one to do, i.e. to take avoiding action.

[12] Cp. *Nicomachean Ethics* 1110b18–22 on the significance of regretting acts done through ignorance.

[13] See further Duff 2002a: 63–8. For similar accounts, see Dressler 1989; Gardner 1998. We might note that such an account can help to make sense of the claim that 'perhaps in some cases there is no such thing as "being constrained", but one should rather accept the most agonising death' (*Nicomachean Ethics* III.1, 1110a26–28). Perhaps there are some wrongs that it would display vice even to be tempted to commit, whatever the threat, and some that only a vicious person could actually bring himself to commit.

would or might have lost self-control, and acted as the defendant did, in response to such provoking conduct. Here, too, the figure of the 'reasonable' person causes confusion and controversy, in particular about which characteristics of the actual defendant should be ascribed to it.[14] But here, again, we can side-step at least some of the confusion by asking whether the defendant's own response was 'reasonable', and by giving an Aristotelian account of reasonableness—an account that will also show why the defence is rightly controversial (see Horder 1992).

The first stage in mounting this defence is to show that the defendant was motivated by a 'reasonable' emotion—in this case, anger: anger has a proper part to play in human life (so it must be claimed), and the defendant reasonably felt strong anger on this occasion, since what provoked the anger was indeed highly provocative. On one conception of the role of anger in a good human life, it might be said that one *should* feel strong anger in the face of some kinds of provocation—that not to be thus angered would display a lack of self-respect, or a lack of proper concern for what was attacked by the provoking action. On other conceptions, anger is a reasonable, but not a necessary, response—it is, we might say, permissible, but not positively virtuous. But it is crucial to making provocation even a partial defence to claim that strong anger was a reasonable response to the conduct that provoked it.

Second, that reasonable emotion would reasonably, properly, motivate an action similar in relevant respects to what the defendant actually did—an action whose relevant description would at least overlap with the description of his actual action. It is here that the problematic character of the provocation defence begins to appear, when we ask what kind of action such reasonable anger could reasonably motivate. We can agree that if he had reason to feel anger, he had reason to do what anger characteristically disposes one to do, i.e. to express his anger in some appropriate way.[15] But there are many ways of expressing anger, many of which do not involve physical violence. Merely to talk of expressing anger in some appropriate way does not, therefore, bring us close enough to what this defendant did to portray his violent response as at all reasonable. What underpins the provocation defence, we must suspect, is not just the thought that it is reasonable and appropriate to express the anger that one reasonably and appropriately feels, but that such expression properly takes the form of physical violence, as retaliation for the provoking action (a point explored by Horder 1992). That thought does ground the claim that the defendant's reasonable anger would have properly motivated an action like his actual action in relevant respects—a retaliatory action involving physical violence against the provoker.

---

[14] See recently *Smith* [2002] 4 All ER 289; Gardner and Macklem 2001.

[15] See n. 11 above, on Skorupski's 'Feeling/Disposition Principle'. It should be clear that as I am using the idea here, what anger 'characteristically disposes one to do' is a normative matter.

Third, the thought that violence might sometimes be a proper expression of anger also grounds the claim that whilst the defendant's actual action—the fatal attack that he actually committed—was not appropriate, since he did not have good (or good enough) reason to retaliate so violently, none the less he did not display real vice in being tempted to retaliate so violently, in response to such provocation. Someone who was properly attached to the good that the provoking action attacked might well (unless he had attained a superhuman excellence of character) be thus tempted.

Furthermore, and fourth, the anger that the defendant properly felt is, when strong, apt to destabilize—to disturb rational deliberation: its motivational power is liable to exceed its rational authority.

In the light of all these factors, we may conclude that, although this defendant still did wrong in responding so violently to such provocation, he did not display a serious lack of those modest levels of self-control, or of respect for the interests and rights that the criminal law protects, that citizens can properly demand of each other on pain of public condemnation and punishment.

According to this account of provocation, a defendant is entitled to this partial defence if his violence can be portrayed as an understandably excessive form of what would have been a fully legitimate response to the genuine (i.e. appropriately anger-inducing) provocation that he suffered. He certainly went too far, and should now regret that. But he went too far down a road that he could reasonably have gone some way down—whereas a truly vicious agent goes down the wrong road altogether.

This account suggests a very close analogy between the structures of the provocation and duress defences—so close, in fact, that we might wonder why provocation is only a partial defence (either formally in the context of murder, or informally when it serves as a mitigating factor in sentencing for other crimes). Why should not the provoked assailant have a complete defence, as does the person who acts under duress? One possible answer would be that the provoked killer's action is categorically wrong in a way that an action done under exculpatory duress is not. When we excuse the agent under duress, that is partly because we think that a sufficiently serious threat could have fully justified her action, whereas nothing could fully justify the retaliatory violence used by the provoked agent. (This may also explain why duress is not a defence to murder in English law—although, in line with the argument I have sketched here, it should perhaps reduce murder to manslaughter.)

One merit of this account of provocation is that it shows why the defence should be deeply controversial in contemporary law: not just because, as is often argued in the context of women who kill their violently abusive partners, it favours a distinctively male response to provocation, but because it legitimizes (or presupposes the legitimacy of) physical violence as an appropriate way to express anger. We can agree that anger, including powerful anger, can be appropriate—even that someone who was not strongly angered by serious wrongs done to him or others would be ethically lacking (see *Nicomachean Ethics* IV.5). We can also agree that anger can be appropriately expressed—that there will be anger-expressing actions that the angry person will be properly and 'characteristically' disposed to do. But this does not commit us to agreeing that physical violence against the provoker is an appropriate way to express anger, and we might plausibly argue that it is inappropriate—that anger should be expressed in other ways that show more respect for the requirements of civil society and for the moral standing of those involved (see Horder 1992: ch. 9; but contrast Byrd 2005). If we take this view, we shall no longer see the provoked killer's action as going too far down a road, the road of retaliatory physical violence, down which he could reasonably have gone some way. That is, we shall no longer think what the provocation defence requires that we think: that, whilst the killer's actual attack was inappropriate, some milder form of personal violence would have been appropriate. We shall think instead that he went down an entirely wrong road; and that he therefore merits no formal defence.

4 EXTENDING THE MODEL

The defences of duress and provocation privilege the emotions of fear and anger: if a criminal action is motivated by one of those two emotions (and the emotion is appropriately aroused), the defendant might have at least a partial defence. But our criminal law appears to make no such provision for actions motivated by other emotions. However, it is not clear why the kind of defence analysed in the last two sections should not be available more widely, for criminal actions motivated by other emotions that deserve respect and sympathy.

Consider just two examples. First, impoverished parents, trying to get by on ungenerous social security provisions, steal goods for their children. Had they stolen food to feed children who would otherwise suffer malnutrition, we might think the theft justified; but suppose they steal books and computing equipment for their children, to assist in their education. We might not now think the theft justified; but if it was motivated by love for their children, and distress at what they (quite reasonably) saw as the children's serious deprivation, we might think that they should have at least a partial excuse. (Compare Hudson 1995: 70–2 on whether the law should recognize a defence of 'economic duress'.)

Second, someone caring for a terminally ill friend who is suffering pain and distress that no treatment can properly alleviate, and who earnestly asks to be helped to die, finally gives in to the friend's pleas (despite her own belief that even such voluntary euthanasia is wrong), and administers a fatal dose of drugs—motivated by her love for her friend and compassion for his suffering. Some would, of course, argue that she is justified in acting as she does, but even those who agree with her that euthanasia—even of this type—is wrong might think that she should have at least a partial excuse; she is not a murderer, or not simply a murderer.

Of course, we would need to know much more about the details and context of these two cases before we could reach a firm view about the agent's culpability; but it seems plausible that in some versions of each case we could discern an exculpatory argument parallel to those that I sketched above for duress and provocation.

First, each agent is motivated by an emotion (love, compassion) that has a proper role in human life, and is appropriately and strongly aroused on this occasion. Such love for children or friends is itself admirable. What distresses the agents (their children's deprivation; their friend's suffering) is truly distressing, as a real evil. What they want (educational benefits; relief from suffering) is truly worth wanting as a significant good.

Second, such emotions could properly motivate something like what these agents actually did—actions whose relevant descriptions would overlap significantly with the descriptions of their actual actions. Those emotions give them good reason to obtain the necessary educational materials, or to try to relieve the friend's suffering. But what they actually did, we are assuming, was not justified; they did not have good (enough) reasons, respectively, to steal the materials and to kill the friend.

However, third, they displayed no real vice in being tempted to commit such crimes for the sake of such goods, or to avert such evils. An appropriate attachment to the goods that they sought to foster or to protect could tempt even a moderately (humanly) virtuous person to commit such crimes.

Fourth, the emotions that they properly felt are, when strongly felt, apt to destabilize—to disturb rational deliberation: their motivational power is liable to exceed their rational authority.

In the light of all these factors, we may conclude, in the same way as before, that, in committing these crimes, these agents did not display a lack of those modest levels of virtue and self-control, of respect for the interests and rights that the criminal law protects, that citizens can properly demand of each other on pain of public condemnation and punishment.

A further necessary condition for exculpation might be that each agent (reasonably) saw no other way of averting the threatened evil or of achieving or protecting the relevant good—that as she (reasonably) saw it, she had 'no choice' but to commit the crime.[16] But that condition, I assume, could be met in these examples, as it can be in cases of duress and provocation: the agent could quite reasonably see no other way out of her acute difficulties.

Thus, even if we think that it was neither right nor permissible to act as these agents acted, we can see reason to allow them at least a partial excuse. They should regret committing their crimes; indeed, they should repent them as wrongs. But

---

[16] Suzanne Uniacke made me recognize the importance of this point.

the crimes were motivated by worthy emotions and virtuous commitments, and to resist the temptation to commit those crimes, in those contexts, would have required a moral strength whose lack we cannot justly condemn.

If we understand the defences of duress and provocation in the Aristotelian terms suggested in sections 2–3, we can therefore see them as particular applications of a more general form of exculpatory claim: as exemplifying a kind of excuse that we should, I have argued, reject in the case of provocation, but that can be discerned, and should be accepted, in other cases of crime motivated by some appropriately, and strongly, felt emotion. So perhaps the criminal law, instead of privileging the particular emotions of fear and anger, should recognize a more general defence of this kind.

A simple formulation of such a defence, expressed in terms that connect with existing legal doctrines, might be that the defendant is not guilty (or is guilty of a lesser offence) if he acted under a kind of pressure, or under the influence of an emotion, that would (or might?) have led a reasonable person to act as he did. This would require the court to answer the questions that my account of the defence made salient. Was the defendant reasonably affected by his situation: was it reasonable to feel that pressured, or to feel that strong an emotion? Was it reasonable, given that feeling, to be tempted to commit that crime? Was the pressure such as to disturb rational deliberation and action? In acting as he did, under the influence of that emotion, did the defendant display a lack of those modest levels of virtue and self-control that the law can properly demand of us?[17]

It might seem that the American Model Penal Code provides just such a defence, at least in the context of murder:

A homicide which would otherwise be murder [constitutes manslaughter when it] is committed under the influence of extreme mental or emotional disturbance for which there is reasonable explanation or excuse. (American Law Institute, Model Penal Code (American Law Institute 1985) s.210.3(1)(b); see Commentary to Part II, ss. 210.0–213.6, 53–75.)

For could we not say that someone who is to be eligible for the defence I have sketched must be suffering 'extreme . . . emotional disturbance for which there is reasonable explanation', in that he must be reasonably (or not unreasonably) affected by a strong emotion that is liable to disturb rational deliberation?

Despite the general wording of this section, however, which suggests that any reasonably aroused strong emotion could ground the defence, it is, in fact, used only for cases that would previously have been pleaded either as provocation,

---

[17] I have formulated this defence, in line with existing legal doctrines, in terms of the 'reasonable person'. But see p. 90 above for the point that the role of the 'reasonable person' test is simply to determine whether this defendant's response was reasonable, and hence that, to avoid confusion, we might in the end do better to formulate the defence more directly in terms of the reasonableness of the defendant's response, without reference to the 'reasonable person'. (Contrast Zagzebski's 'exemplarism' in Ch. 2.)

or as diminished responsibility. But we should not see the general defence that I have sketched as one of 'diminished responsibility'. For someone who pleads diminished responsibility is claiming that, in virtue of some impairment of his capacities for rational thought and agency, his responsibility for the wrong that he did is, whilst not removed (as in cases of responsibility-negating insanity), at least reduced; he is not to be judged and condemned as a rational, responsible, agent.[18] By contrast, one who pleads the kind of defence I am suggesting here makes no such claim. Although part of her claim is that her deliberation and action were disturbed by the strong emotion that motivated her, she claims no impairment of rational capacities. She asks to be judged as a rational, responsible, agent, in the light of the reasons for which she acted and the reasonable emotions by which she was motivated.

There are plenty of further questions to be asked about this proposed general defence (we could call it a defence of 'emotional duress', to make clear that it is only available to agents who act against their better judgement, against their own rational will, under the influence of strong emotion). For which crimes should it be available, and should it provide a complete or only a partial defence? What other emotions might ground it, and should the law set any limits on the range of emotions that could ground it? Are there practical objections to allowing such a general defence, for instance that it might encourage people to commit crimes for which they really have no excuse, in the hope of faking such a defence? Are there further objections of principle, for instance that by allowing such a defence we would remove the law's persuasive or deterrent power just when it is most needed, by having the law say to those who are tempted to crime by some strong emotion that they can give in without thereby becoming liable to conviction and punishment?

To this last question, it might be replied that since it is an excuse rather than a justification, such a defence is addressed to the courts, telling them whom to convict or acquit, rather than to the citizens, telling them what they may or may not do (Alldridge 1990: 495–9; Gardner 1998: 597). However, apart from the fact that it is not clear whether we can sustain such a sharp distinction between 'rules for courts' and 'rules for citizens' (Duff 2002a: 61–8), it would be difficult to prevent citizens from realizing that such a defence was available, absent a practically and morally implausible kind of 'acoustic separation' (Dan-Cohen 1984; for useful criticism, see Singer 1986).

However, we cannot pursue these important questions any further here. It is time to return to virtue jurisprudence, to ask what support its general claims might gain from my account of duress and provocation in sections 2–3.

---

[18] That is why suggestions that women who kill their violent partners should plead diminished responsibility rather than provocation will be unacceptable to women who want to insist that they acted, and should be judged, as rational and responsible agents. See Gardner 2003: 157–61 and further references therein.

5 VIRTUE JURISPRUDENCE AGAIN

I have argued that we can give a plausible Aristotelian account of duress and provocation as defences. I have not argued here that this account is better (more illuminating, or making more plausible moral sense) than those generated by other theories of criminal liability—for instance, than the sort of account that would be offered by those who ground criminal liability in choice, and who would argue that we must explain such defences in terms either of some impairment of the agent's rational capacities, or of her lack of a fair opportunity to exercise her capacities (Hart 1968; Moore 1997: ch. 13; Morse 1998). But suppose that such an argument could be provided, and that we should accept the Aristotelian account of the duress and provocation defences. Does this offer any support to the larger claims of virtue jurisprudence?

What excuses the defendant who acts under duress is that her action flows from motives, from emotions, that are virtuous or at least non-vicious, and that it does not display a serious lack of the modest kinds of civic virtue (of courage, of respect for the interests and rights that the law protects) or self-control that citizens can properly demand of each other. In short, her action does not display the kind of vice or weakness that her fellow-citizens can properly condemn. This analysis does seem to give substantive notions of virtue and vice a substantial role in relation to at least this significant aspect of the criminal law. There would, no doubt, be relatively few cases, even if we extended the defence in the way suggested in section 4, in which such a defence would be offered. But once notions of virtue and vice have been given this foothold within the criminal law, it might be hard to resist the argument that they are essentially involved, albeit more often implicitly than explicitly, in the grounds of criminal liability in general.[19]

For, the virtue jurisprudent can now claim, if we ask why virtue and vice should play this role in the analysis of duress and provocation, why we should excuse the agent whose action does not display a serious lack of minimal civic virtue or the active presence of civic vice, the only plausible answer is that such vice or lack of virtue is a general basis of criminal liability. What makes an agent criminally liable, when he is criminally liable, is not just the fact that he committed a criminal action, but that in doing so he displayed a kind of civic vice, or serious lack of even minimal civic virtue, that makes him deserving of public condemnation. He can avoid such condemnation by showing, as someone who acts under exculpatory duress can show, that although his action was criminal

---

[19] Compare Huigens's arguments (Huigens 1995 and 2002)—though his account of virtue and vice differs from that assumed here, in that he focuses on the quality of the agent's practical reasoning and his conception of the good, and does not give the importance that I give to the role of emotions.

(since it was not justified), it did not display the relevant kind of vice. In most cases no direct reference need be made to this dimension of the agent's criminal liability, since proof of the standard elements of a crime usually constitutes proof of the relevant kind of vice. But what justifies holding the agent criminally liable is still the vice displayed in his action—as is shown by the fact that he must be acquitted when his criminal action does not display such vice.

There is something to the virtue jurisprudent's argument here. A person is justly convicted of a criminal offence only if her commission of the crime displayed a serious lack of civic virtue (of that kind and degree of virtue that citizens can properly demand of each other on pain of public condemnation and punishment), or a culpable civic vice (vice of a kind that merits her public condemnation by her fellow citizens). However, it is still not clear how substantial a role this gives to substantive notions of virtue and vice in our understanding of the grounds of criminal liability.

First, it is not yet plausible to claim that vice is *the object* of criminal liability: that what offenders are convicted, condemned and punished *for* is the vice that their actions display. The most we can plausibly say is that vice is *a condition* of liability: that offenders are convicted, condemned, and punished for their wrongful actions, *on condition* that those actions displayed a relevant kind of vice.[20] The person who pleads duress, or one of the other types of emotion-based excuse suggested earlier, seeks to be excused for the particular crime (theft, assault, or whatever) that he committed. If his plea fails, it is for that crime, not for the vice displayed in it, that he is convicted.

Second, virtue and vice are relatively lasting character traits. We cannot have a virtue or a vice just for a day or a week. In determining a defendant's criminal liability, however, courts are not interested in whether her criminal action displayed a lasting vice. Of course, to see her as a rational and responsible agent at all, we must assume that the emotions, beliefs, and intentions from which her action flows have some diachronic identity and structure. But the court is not interested in whether those structures are structures of vice.

Third, the virtue ethicist should be interested not just in whether we are virtuous or vicious, but in what specific virtues or vices we display. She will want to distinguish, for instance, the coward from the avaricious person; the bully from the bad-tempered person who is too quick to anger; and so on. She will also want to distinguish the vicious person from the weak-willed person, and the truly virtuous person from the self-controlled person.[21] Such distinctions do not, however, figure in legal determinations of criminal liability. The law does not classify crimes by reference to the vices that they display. What count in law as

---

[20] On the distinction between objects and conditions of liability, see n. 5 above. The suggestion that the objects of liability are actions is itself neither clear nor uncontroversial: see Duff 2004.

[21] Or she will do so if she draws her inspiration from Aristotle. I take it, however, that virtue theorists who do not distinguish weakness of will from vice will still want to distinguish such weakness from other kinds of vice.

instances of the same crime might display what would count from the perspective of virtue theory as quite different vices or defects. An assault, for instance, might display cruelty, or excessive anger, or hatred, or cowardice (if, for instance, it was committed under duress that was not serious enough to excuse it, or from fear of losing face with one's peers), or greed (if it was committed as part of a robbery, for instance, or for pay). Again, it might display a kind of weakness of will rather than an entrenched vice. But none of these discriminations, crucial as they are for virtue theorists, will be relevant to the offender's fate at his trial. He will be convicted and punished simply for the assault.

Sometimes the definitions of offences will admittedly include what looks like a reference to a particular vice: theft, for instance, requires 'dishonesty';[22] according to section 28 of the Crime and Disorder Act 1998, specified offences are 'racially aggravated' if they are motivated by racial hatred. Furthermore, it might be suggested that the particular vice or weakness displayed by the particular defendant should be relevant at the sentencing stage, even if it is not relevant to his conviction. However, even these definitions of offences fall well short of requiring proof of a fully fledged vice—of vicious dispositions of perception, emotion, and deliberation (Duff 2002: 169–74). And in so far as the defendant's character is relevant to sentencing at all, what matters is not the particular vice he displayed but such issues as the seriousness of the particular offence and the likely effect on him of this or that possible sentence—issues that are radically underdetermined by attention to the particular vice that his crime might have displayed.

My conclusion is, therefore, a mixed one. Virtue jurisprudents can find some comfort in the analyses of duress and provocation sketched in sections 2–3, and in the suggestion that we ought to recognize a broader defence to cover criminal actions motivated by other kinds of worthy or valuable emotion. But this falls far short of giving substantive notions of virtue or vice the kind of central role in determining or grounding criminal liability that is sometimes claimed for them. We can say that anyone who is justly convicted of a crime will have displayed some vice or weakness in the action that constituted the crime. But the offender's liability is still focused on that action, not on whatever particular vice or weakness might have lain behind it.

This conclusion should be reassuring to liberals of various kinds. The criminal law is properly interested in our wrongful actions, as they impinge on our shared world. It properly condemns and punishes us for such actions. But whilst in our private moral lives, the lives we share with family, friends, and members of other associations to which we belong, our virtues and vices are proper objects of moral interest and concern, they are not generally the business of the criminal law.

---

[22] Theft Act 1968, s. 1. See Gardner 1998: 575–6: the definition of theft, he claims, builds 'a standard of character' into the criteria of criminal liability.

5

Habituation as *Mimesis*

Hallvard J. Fossheim

I shall be asking what motivation there might be to become virtuous; or, to put it as Myles Burnyeat and John Cooper have put it, what motivation there might be to become responsive to the noble. I believe that the most important single clue to understanding this motivation is provided not in the *Ethics* but in the *Poetics*. My point of departure is Aristotle's first condition on action that is good or noble: namely, that it be done for its own sake. I shall end by showing how my interpretation fits in with what Aristotle says about the educational formation of the child, in the *Nicomachean Ethics* and in the *Politics*.

1 BURNYEAT'S SOLUTION: LEARNING BY ADVICE

In his already classic paper 'Aristotle on Learning to be Good', Myles Burnyeat has provided one of the very few sustained accounts of how, according to Aristotle, someone can develop to the point where 'the noble' is established as a proper principle of action, capable of transcending and even opposing the original rule of mere pleasure and pain. According to Burnyeat 1980: 74–8, habituation consists, in the first place, of being told what is really noble and just. This happens both when we are verbally told by parents and others what is fine and just ('knowing that'), and when we are experiencing the things in question by actual practice (which gives us knowledge by acquaintance). In the latter mode, the person learning to be good (I shall call him 'the learner') is able to see for himself the truth of what is said, to experience the fineness or virtue in good action in a way that is not accessible to one who must merely take the word of others for it.

These two modes of insight into the noble and good are what together constitute habituation. Burnyeat 1980: 78 combines them like this:

[P]erhaps we can give intelligible sense to the thesis that practice leads to knowledge, as follows. I may be told, and may believe, that such and such actions are just and noble, but I have not really learned for myself (taken to heart, made second nature to me) that they have this intrinsic value until I have learned to value (love) them for it, with the consequence that I take pleasure in doing them. To understand and appreciate the value that makes them enjoyable in themselves I must learn for myself to enjoy them, and that does take time and practice—in short, habituation.

The key to the proper enjoyment of the noble is that the learner should come to love the noble not as a means to something else, but in itself. Habituation, in the form of the learner's advice-directed activity, is needed in order for him to reach the point where his noble actions are enjoyed in themselves. The answer Aristotle offers to the question 'how does habituation lead to enjoyment?' is that through practising what is noble in accordance with advice, we come to enjoy it.[1]

2 LEARNING BY ASSOCIATION?

The problem with Burnyeat's solution is that it in one way seems to beg the question. What makes us experience attempts at virtuous action as enjoyable? How exactly does doing something lead to loving it? The idea that detached advice prepares us before we make our attempts to act virtuously only moves the question one step back. What is it that makes us want to take the advice to heart in the first place, before we start to practise virtue? The liking, loving, or enjoying of the good and the noble that is supposed to be explained by Burnyeat's sketch of a process of advice and practice seems, in fact, to be presupposed by it. While agreeing that practice takes time, we still need to find out what makes us desire to invest that time, to accept the advice we are given, to attempt to act in a certain way. Without such a source of engagement, it is difficult, perhaps impossible, to imagine how the learning process could even get started.

This is a question about motivation. And it is important to stress that it is not a simple one. For motivation is required for the process of habituation as well as for doing what is good and noble in the way that the fully developed character does it. And to the extent that the enjoyment proper to good actions is not a motivating source until the learner, through practice, has reached some relative degree of perfection, we need to find out what else there is to motivate the learner until that point is reached. Only then shall we have the beginnings of an explanation of how, according to Aristotle, we become good.

Burnyeat formulates a response to this challenge in one succinct sentence. The case of the guided practice and habituation that I have described is like the case of music as a cause of nobility in the listener. In both, 'the underlying idea is that the child's sense of pleasure, which to begin with and for a long while is his only motive, should be hooked up with just and noble things so that his unreasoned evaluative responses may develop in connection with the right objects' (Burnyeat 1980: 80). The suggestion seems highly promising, in that it aims at providing a way of infusing through habituation the right pursuits with a pleasure already

---

[1] Sherman 1989: 157–99 (cf. in particular 171–4) accepts Burnyeat's general picture of advice as the key to habituation, except for her stress on emotional discernment of the particulars (171) and on preserving 'the child's emotional vulnerability' (173). Cf. Sherman 1999.

available to the learner. In this way, Burnyeat offers the skeleton of an account of motivation by basing it on what to Aristotle constitutes a fundamental driving-force throughout our lives: pleasure. (Cf. *NE* 1172a23–26, Irwin's translation: 'enjoying and hating the right things seems to be most important for virtue of character. For pleasure and pain extend through the whole of our lives, and are of great importance for virtue and the happy life, since people decide to do what is pleasant, and avoid what is painful.')

However, Burnyeat does not explain how this 'hooking up' works. According to the tripartition of cognitive and motive forces in Aristotle's psychology, there are, in Burnyeat's words (1980: 86), 'three things to get right': 'Pursuit of pleasure is an inborn part of our animal nature; concern for the noble depends on a good upbringing; while the good, here specified as the advantageous, is the object of mature reflection.' Thus the learner, at an early stage, is characterized by a sense of pleasure that drives him or her towards the sensual sort of enjoyment that is shared with beasts. But what does it mean to say that this is 'hooked up' with what is good or noble?

On the simplest interpretation, habituation will take place when we learn to associate pleasure and pain with the right sort of things. Pain will move us away from the bad things, and pleasure will move us towards the good things, in a fairly simple logic of reward and punishment. An object or activity which the child initially desires becomes undesirable through its association with pain of some sort. Correspondingly, an object or activity which is truly good, and which ought to be seen as such by the child, is repeatedly associated with something the child finds pleasurable.[2] In this way, the young person's pleasures can be hooked up with the right sort of objects and so direct her towards the noble and the good.

This model might lead us to imagine that the learner's conscious motivations move seamlessly, as he progresses, from mere pleasure and pain, to the idea of the noble. However, Aristotle consistently treats these as radically distinct forms of motivation, even when they are confused in some particular agent. (Witness, for instance, his willingness in *NE* III.vi–ix to distinguish varieties of courage as better or worse to the extent that (*hosôi*, 1116a31) they are caused by aversion from what is painful, or by shame. Elsewhere, of course, there *is* no identifying the truly pleasant, unless one already has at least some knowledge on the good: see e.g. 1176a16 ff.) No amount of association, seen as a possible part of habituation, can by itself make a cognitive structure based on external pleasure and pain alone see anything but a pleasure as an aim. Certainly, both before the noble is present and once it is present, pleasures and pains can be moulded and rearranged around it. But it is hard to see how motivations based only on pleasures and pains can magically transmute into anything essentially different from themselves. Hence, mere association cannot bridge the gap between pleasure and the noble, and a

---

[2] See Tuozzo 1994 for a detailed account of how such basic associations might be set up.

'hooking up' of the good and the noble by associative training cannot be enough to give the learner access to the noble as a motivation in its own right.[3]

This irreducible gap is equally evident if we concentrate on the specifically advice-related part of an associative picture of upbringing. No amount of advice will bring into being a motivating notion of the noble. In fact, Aristotle paints a rather sombre view of the powerlessness of such tactics. In the words of *NE* 1179b23–31 (1179b4–20 is also instructive):

> Arguments and teaching surely do not influence everyone, but the soul of the student needs to have been prepared by habits for enjoying and hating nobly, like ground that is to nourish seed. For someone whose life follows his emotions would not even listen to an argument turning him away, or comprehend it; and in that state how could he be persuaded to change? And in general emotions seem to yield to force, not to argument. Hence we must already in some way have a character suitable for virtue, fond of what is noble and objecting to what is shameful.

Advice by itself moves nothing. Advice and argumentation have to grasp hold of something already present in the learner, in order for them to be able to do any further work. People who have so far, as Aristotle puts it, 'had no taste' (*ageustoi ontes*, 1179b15) of the noble cannot be helped by others' arguments; they will not listen in the first place. So at least one crucial part of habituation cannot be identified with advice or argument. And thus we come back to our original question. Given that the noble and the merely pleasant are irreducibly different sorts of motivations, and that only the pleasant is there in those who have not yet acquired virtue—what motivation can the learner have to be habituated into virtue?

Our puzzle is that we cannot, so far, see why the learner should *want* to engage in the activity which may make him or her better. The key to this puzzle is Aristotle's insistence that 'we become good by doing good actions' (*NE* 1105b10)—a remark which suggests that there must be something about practising itself which we have so far overlooked. I will go on to argue that this is indeed the case.

Before I come to that, let us quickly remind ourselves of Aristotle's criteria for good action, and of one aspect of his crucial distinction between *poiêsis* and *praxis*. The goodness of a table can be judged independently of any consideration of the carpenter. 'But', says Aristotle, 'for actions expressing virtue to be done temperately or justly [and hence well] it does not suffice that they are themselves in the right state. Rather, the agent must also be in the right state when he does them' (*NE* 1105a28–31). What does 'be in the right state' mean here? In the case of an art like carpentry, the most important requirement for its possession is knowing or being aware of the relevant facts having to do with the production. When it comes to actions expressing virtue, however, two other requirements are considered by Aristotle to be much more important: the agent must (i) choose his

---

[3] Curzer 2002 and Frankena 1965 seem to overlook this deep-seated truth about Aristotelian ethics.

actions for their own sake; and (ii) do so out of a firm and unchanging disposition (1105a31–b5).

These reminders help us to see the shape of the problem that we are addressing. One thing that we need to explain is how the young learner can come to 'choose his actions for their own sake'—not, no doubt, in the fully fledged sense in which the practically wise individual does so, but still in *some* sense. We also need to say something about how the young learner can at least begin to establish his character 'as a firm and unchanging state'. The rest of this chapter will be concerned with these questions.

3 *MIMESIS* AND MORAL DEVELOPMENT

My thesis will be that Aristotle's notion of *mimesis* helps to make sense of the requirement that good actions be done for their own sake. Of course, the notion of *mimesis* is most familiar from the *Poetics*; so I will begin by reminding the reader of Aristotle's account of *mimesis* in the *Poetics*. In chapter 4 (1448b4–10), Aristotle says this:

It can be seen that poetry was broadly engendered by a pair of causes, both natural. For it is an instinct of human beings, from childhood, to engage in *mimesis* (indeed, this distinguishes them from other animals: man is the most mimetic of all, and it is through *mimesis* that he develops his earliest understanding); and equally natural that everyone enjoys mimetic objects.   (Halliwell's Loeb translation)

Aristotle is explaining the existence and development of art; in doing so, he provides a sketch of certain traits of human nature. The sketch makes it clear that the established genres of representational art are only developed specializations of a much more pervasive human tendency. Our mimetic nature, initially referred to as 'a pair of causes', explains much more than just the representative arts. It also characterizes the early stages of human cognitive development, in the strong sense of constituting the cause of that development.

Aristotle is emphatic about the naturalness of our mimetic desire. The *Poetics* chapter 4 account of the ultimate origin of poetry from which I have just quoted stresses, both at its opening and at its ending, that mimetic pleasure is natural to the human species. Whilst most of the other animals must rest content with instincts of pursuit and avoidance, humans distinguish themselves early on by relating to their surroundings mimetically.

This notion of *mimesis* is important for Aristotle's concept of understanding. As Aristotle says, the very beginning of our learning process is through *mimesis*. Thus, Aristotle's description of our mimetic desire acts more as a specification of the *Metaphysics*' famous human 'desire to know' than as its complement.[4] It seems

---

[4] Many distinguished scholars have, implicitly or explicitly, made this point: House 1956; Golden 1962; Redfield 1975; Smithson 1983; Janko 1984: 139–42; Nussbaum 1986: 378 ff.; Halliwell 1986: 195–201; Frede 1992.

reasonable to relate Aristotle's idea that *mimesis* is a source of understanding to his oft-quoted statement (*Poetics* ix, 1451b5–11) that poetry, in contrast to history, 'aims for the universal'.[5] For Aristotle, specifically poetic *mimesis* is distinguished from history by its concern, not merely with what did happen, but with the sort of things that might happen, viewed through the lenses of probability or necessity (1451a37 ff.).

What is true of the poet's mimetic *poiêsis* will be true also of *mimesis* as an even more pervasive and basic mode of the human capacity for intellectual development. Immediately after my last quotation, Aristotle continues (1448b10–24):

we enjoy contemplating the most precise images of things whose actual sight is painful to us, such as the forms of the vilest animals and of corpses. The explanation of this too is that understanding gives great pleasure not only to philosophers but likewise to others too, though the latter have a smaller share in it. This is why people enjoy looking at images, because through contemplating them it comes about that they understand and infer what each element means, for instance that 'this person is so-and-so'. For, if one happens not to have seen the subject before, the image will not give pleasure qua *mimesis* but because of its execution or colour, or for some other such reason.

Performing a *mimesis*—representing—involves abstraction, as does the appreciation of others' representations.[6] Painting a picture of a flower means extracting something sufficiently general and characteristic about the original object, the flower, and reproducing it in paint.[7] Aristotle describes the specifically mimetic pleasure as the pleasure inherent in realizing that 'this person is so-and-so'. Recognizing that 'this is that' requires already having been in contact with 'that', because it requires (among other things) seeing what the two have in common as something which stems from 'that' and is represented or repeated in 'this'. A (rough-and-ready) notion of a universal is found in, and by, the experience of recognition.

Aristotle goes on (1448b24–27) to describe how differences in the characters of the various poets led to the development of two genres. 'Poetry branched into two, according to its creators' characters'—the more serious (*semnoteroi*) among them were inclined to represent grave and noble actions, and thus gave birth to tragedy; while the lower sort (*eutelesteroi*) went on to invent comedy.[8] This is interesting, because it lets us see the close fit between character and *mimesis*. The beginning of poetry, which is here seen as nothing but formalized or rather professionalized *mimesis*, lies in an expression of character. The early

---

[5] On whether Aristotle's contrast is fair, see de Ste Croix 1992.

[6] Although *mimesis* in Aristotle cannot unproblematically be translated as 'representation' (cf. Halliwell 2002), I find that the term conveys some of the central idea here.

[7] On this, see Heath 1991, in particular the first section, which brings out the distinction between two related senses of *kath' holou*.

[8] I am grateful to John Cooper for (among much else) stressing the importance of this passage to me.

poets performed as they did because of who they themselves were. They took the natural inclination to *mimesis* one step further, in somehow staging themselves, or rather something about themselves, in front of an audience.

The passage also helps us to explain the delight we take in the works of representational artists. The enjoyment of one's own representations and the enjoyment of others' representions are described by Aristotle as basically different enjoyments, having their sources in two natural tendencies of which neither is entirely reducible to the other. This, I take it, is the meaning of 1448b4–5's reference to *two* natural causes of poetry. There are two causes, since the pleasure in writing a tragedy is not identical to the pleasure in watching a performance of it.[9]

In creating art, the artist draws upon his or her experience with something and conveys, through suitable media, various aspects or truths about it. The early poets drew upon their experience of themselves, thus making the first tragedies and comedies a kind of expression of self-knowledge.

Here Aristotle's account gives a clue about how *mimesis* can be a factor in habituation. The joy that is natural to us and is here set forward as the joy of learning is not that of seeing the representations of others so much as that of oneself doing the representing. The process by which we take our very first steps in understanding is primarily a form of learning that takes place through representational activity.

To relate *mimesis* as a factor in the habituation of character to the more or less professionalized poetic *mimesis* which is the main topic of the *Poetics*, we need to understand poetic *mimesis* in reverse. The poet creates an action from the resources of who he already is; habituation involves establishing a character by first performing its characteristic actions. Habituation does not mean activating a formed character and thereby realizing something out there in the world; it means realizing something in the world and thereby forming a character. Here I mean 'realizing' in both senses of the word: both grasping something intellectually, and also making it real. For *mimesis* in habituation is about forming a character. And this requires both that the subject of the character-formation be exposed to some model or example, and also that he use this model—as material for a *mimesis* wherein he stages or re-enacts one or several of its manners or actions.

The general idea, then, is this. Children and young people develop their character by actively engaging in *mimesis* of others who function as models for them. The child does as others do, and learns to become a certain sort of person by emulating the actions and manners of others. To stick to the simplest of examples: just as painting a flower means extracting something general and characteristic about the object, so mimetically assuming, say, the gait of one's object of admiration,

---

[9] Not all interpreters would agree with me on the last hypothesis, that the enjoyments of doing and of perceiving, respectively, are what make up the reference of 1148b4–5. Malcolm Heath, in a note to his own translation of the passage, thinks the point is about the *Poetics'* next topic, music. However, my reading does not depend on 1148b4–5 alone.

requires that one has isolated, from the object's other features, what constitutes that way of walking, and that one has done so sufficiently 'analytically' to be able to repeat its variety of aspects. In re-enacting, one is oneself the repetition ('this') of a model ('that'). Let us, tentatively, refer to this developmental principle of human nature as 'practical *mimesis*'.

Let me deal at once with an obvious objection. Why, if *mimesis* is so important to the process of becoming good, is it not explicitly referred to in the *Ethics*? Part of the answer might be that Aristotle does not say much about the role of *mimesis*, because he just takes this role for granted. (Compare Plato's stress on *mimesis* as a principle of habituation in the *Republic*: here, as elsewhere, Aristotle takes Plato's work as a backdrop that is simply understood.) My claim is that Aristotle often presupposes models of thought that depend on the idea of *mimesis*, and that when we look closely at much of what Aristotle has to say about the ethical development of human beings, and at the framework of that development, we see a variety of *mimesis*-based structures and processes.

There is, however, another and more important reason why much of the evidence on this question is bound to be indirect. This is that Aristotle's *Ethics* was written for people who are already reasonably mature in virtue. Children and young or immature people, he tells us firmly, have no place in his courses, because they have not yet reached the point where they might benefit from them (1095a3–13). By contrast, the habituation I am describing here is what provides a young person with a viewpoint in relation to human actions and goods, a point of view or (set of) ideal(s) on which to base the sort of ethical reflection and development that the *Nicomachean Ethics* deals with. Thus, to study Aristotle's ethics at all, you need to be already beyond the stage of the basic process of *mimesis*-based habituation that is my concern here.

4 MOTIVATION

Although the notion of *mimesis* certainly does not explain everything about Aristotle's concept of habituation, it does add to our understanding of it in important ways. For one thing, because *mimesis* is natural, it is well suited to throw light on how a good upbringing can move our motivations on from the pleasure-seeking which, in Burnyeat's words, 'is an inborn part of our animal nature' to the noble and the good. For the pleasure taken in performing *mimesis* is both naturally engendered and culturally formed.

Even more importantly, whereas associative games of pleasure and pain can give no more than external support to the development of human goodness, the pleasure inherent in performing a *mimesis* of something ensures that the agent's focus is on the act itself rather than on something only accidentally co-present with it: the focus on the performance provides an intrinsic pleasure, not merely an associated pleasure. Whereas advice can help only in so far as the learner is already motivated to follow it, the basic human pleasure taken in *mimesis* provides the learner with a basic motivation. For the learner, a failure to emulate an action is a failure to perform a successful *mimesis*, and the pleasure of succeeding in such an emulation is the pleasure of successfully carrying out a *mimesis*. Crucially, the mimetic pleasure that the agent takes in activating her own ability to 'become like' ensures that she cannot see her activity as a means to something else, but only as an end in itself.

To see this, we need to consider briefly how Aristotle relates pleasure and virtue. According to Aristotle, pleasure makes any activity an aim for the performer. It subjectively perfects it for him or her, by making the agent see the activity as an end in itself rather than as a means to something else:

Pleasure completes their activities, and hence completes life, which they desire. It is reasonable, then, that they also aim at pleasure, since it completes each person's life for him, and life is choiceworthy. (*NE* 1175a14–18)

The virtues are realized only if their realisations—in virtuous actions—are seen as ends in themselves by the learner. But this attitude to virtuous actions is the very one that *mimesis* leads to. For, by definition, what is aimed at in the *mimesis* of an activity is *that activity itself*: mimetic pleasure in any performance is proper and intrinsic to that performance, and does not depend on what if anything follows upon it. Hence mimetic desire ensures that, whatever the learner fastens on, relating mimetically to it will at the same time mean relating to it as something to be savoured for its own sake. Thus an action which might otherwise be done in order to receive a reward or to avoid punishment will, if it is instead performed mimetically, be done without ulterior motives.

This view that performing activity x *qua mimesis* is in some respects the same as performing activity x *qua* activity x is also suggested by Aristotle's notion that we become something by doing it (*NE* 1103a31–b2)—that is, by his idea that a person can in important respects be said to perform a virtuous action before the person has herself become virtuous in any fully fledged sense. That she is doing the action mimetically will mean, for instance, that her attention is on carrying it out as perfectly as possible, that an important type of failure will consist in doing something which falls short of, or otherwise misses the target in relation to, the doing of x. Performing action x mimetically entails a closer affinity to its full performance than can be guaranteed if x is done by pure chance, or if it is done with a view to an ulterior reward, or if it is carried out step-by-step according to someone else's detailed instructions (cf. *NE* 1105a21–23). For none of these other modes of performance is it required that one's focus is on x in the relatively strong sense that mimetic performance requires. This is how doing x mimetically entails somehow 'doing x for its own sake'.

I again stress that our primary question concerns the learner's motivation, as in some ways different from the motivation of the fully developed character. Thus, the mimetic sense of doing something 'for its own sake' is not quite the full sense of doing something 'for its own sake' that is required for virtuous action. But it is like the full sense in the crucial respect of ensuring that the learner takes pleasure in the performance of the action, rather than in something only (perhaps even negatively) associated with it.

5 A QUALIFICATION

Of course, it should be admitted straight away that *mimesis* has as its possible object many other things beside the noble. Some things are mimetic, and are related to mimetic pleasure, without necessarily being noble. As quoted above (*Poetics* 1448b10f): 'we enjoy contemplating the most precise images of things whose actual sight is painful to us, such as the forms of the vilest animals and of corpses'. Practical *mimesis* will be like this, too: a child might take mimetic pleasure in aping the manners or actions of someone entirely void of nobility. Pretty much anything and everything can yield some degree of mimetic pleasure, including not only deeds that are disgusting or degrading, but also more mundane things like the practice of crafts.

Although our mimetic nature has a motivational function, the noble is, of course, determined by other features than by its capacity for yielding mimetic pleasure. Nor is there reason to think that the pleasure given by the noble should be thoroughly identified with the pleasure given by *mimesis*. Rather, the pleasure one takes in something because of one's own nobility must take over from mimetic pleasure to the extent that one can be said really to realize one's character in, and thus no longer to *mimeisthai*, whatever act is in question. Again, what was lacking in our account was not so much a principle for being good as for *becoming* good. Since the two are not identical, we should even expect something like this. We have to think of the desire to perform *mimesis* of a certain sort of action as gradually giving way to a stable, character-determined desire to perform the action.[10] Thus, I shall close by adding something about Aristotle's second requirement, that the agent's performance must stem from a firm and unchanging state, in such a way as to relate it to the notion of such a transition.[11]

---

[10] Aryeh Kosman 1992: 58–61, quoting Ben Johnson, interestingly brings out the possibility of such a gradual and perhaps imperceptible transition to our 'second nature'.

[11] A detailed treatment of the continuities and discontinuities between the learner's mimetic motivation and the noble-and-good person's motivation is well beyond the scope of this chapter. A full reply will consist in an analysis of the respects in which *to kalon* and mimetic motivation overlap. I think the major continuities between the two can helpfully be described under six main headings. (Some of these factors will also be crucial for grasping the basis for Aristotle's general optimism on behalf of goodness, in the sense that he thinks that, *other things being equal* (which they rarely are), good will have more force over us than bad.) (i) Being performed for its own sake; (ii) being pleasant; (iii) being a possible object of non-rational pursuit, in the Aristotelian sense of 'rational'; (iv) being correctly described in 'aesthetic' terms, as beautiful or handsome; (v) carrying with it a certain sense of obligation; and, lastly, (vi) inherently constituting a basis for, and developing into, fuller forms of understanding. Only the first, second, and sixth factor relevant for seeing the strong

6 NEGATIVE HABITUATION

A human being is a principle of action which starts out as highly malleable and plastic, and can develop many different virtues and vices, perfections and lacks, excellences and perversions. According to the present interpretation of ethical forming through practical *mimesis*, exposure to the wrong models can easily lead a person down a false path that he does not yet even know he has taken. His environment, and what it offers him for emulation, gradually forms him into something the full meaning of which will become clear to him, if ever, then only later. And, crucially, this can happen almost effortlessly, since his formation is mediated by his own desire. Given this view of habituation, it will be of the greatest importance to the child's ethical development not only to provide him with good examples to imitate, but also to protect him from the *wrong* impressions.

And, in fact, Aristotle's model for habituation clearly recognizes and stresses this point about the negative side of habituation: 'we always like best whatever comes first. And therefore youth should be kept strangers to all that is bad, and especially to things which suggest vice or hate' (*Politics* 1336b33–35, Richard Kraut's translation). In Aristotle's ideal city-state, those responsible for education 'should be careful what tales or stories the children hear, for all such things are designed to prepare the way for the business of later life' (*Politics* 1336a30–33). This, I suggest, should be seen as indirect evidence for the developmental importance of *mimesis*. There is, according to Aristotle, little psychological and motivational distance between hearing and doing, which is why 'there is nothing which the legislator should be more careful to drive away than indecency of speech; for the light utterance of shameful words leads soon to shameful actions. The young especially should never be allowed to repeat or hear anything of the sort.' (*Politics* 1336b3–8; cf. Plato, *Republic* 401b–d, where the impact of likenesses of what is bad is presented as dangerous to the young people who are exposed to them, but unable to judge about them.) The (presumably male) children should avoid in their mimetic activity 'the vulgar, tiring, and effeminate', and should likewise have as little as possible to do with slaves (1336b28–30 and 1336a39–41).

In Aristotle's view, the young character cannot easily be 're-programmed' by being exposed to something good after being exposed to the wrong thing. Aristotle applauds Plato for wisely concentrating on what comes first as what is of the greatest importance in one's upbringing—the well-known 'right from early youth, as Plato says' (*NE* 1104b11). What counts most is not what was encountered most recently in one's moral development but what was

---

degree of continuity from mimetic activity to virtuous activity in a full sense have been introduced in the above text. I hope to be able to present this part of the story on another occasion.

encountered first. Only because what one does mimetically settles into one's character, I suggest, is it so crucial that the child not be exposed to anything evil, indecent, vile, vulgar, or otherwise ethically misleading. Performance is inherently character-forming. Mimetic activity is essentially discriminatory, and also self-reinforcing because of the pleasure it provides. Indeed it is *because* it is a source of understanding that mimetic activity provides pleasure.[12]

Aristotle's claim that we become good by doing good actions conveys, even in the sophisticated setting of his ethics course, the idea that in this sphere, performing is the *via regia* to being. And what is true of the mature individual seeking ethical improvement is, as both the *Politics* and the *Nicomachean Ethics* attest, all the more true for the eager and unshaped material of youth. Thus, protecting the young ethical learner is not primarily needed because there are things that the child might find horrible or vile to contemplate. Rather, it is the fact that the child has as yet no proper understanding of what is truly horrible or vile that makes the protection so important. The danger is not that the child should find these things horrible or vile, but that he should find them *pleasant*. Behind the desire to become this or that is the deeper and more general human desire simply to become (to be like) *whatever* is presented as an option for *mimesis*. Hence the educational importance of controlling and limiting the child's range of available exemplars. A well-thought-out education *via* habituation must not only guide the learner towards the good and the noble, but also away from the bad and the vile.

Mimesis has its dangerously misleading power over us, simply because it has power over us; *mimesis* can forcefully motivate us to go the wrong way, simply because it can forcefully motivate us.

7 CONCLUDING REMARK

As we have seen, practical *mimesis* is not to be identified with the noble. Considered as a motivational way into the noble, however, practical *mimesis* might provide a final hint concerning the transition. For one aspect of the Aristotelian noble seems to be how it always instantiates, for want of a better expression, a fullness of existence. Coming to realize *to kalon* seems, in this specific sense, to constitute a completion. (Contrast the lack or shortcoming that might go with duty, or the

---

[12] Concerning the tendency inherent in performance towards stable traits, the above argument opens most readily towards it in terms of cognitive development: you become what you do because your (attempted) actions shape how you see yourself and the surrounding world. And, indeed, much of what Aristotle has to say seems strongly to support such a reading. Compare, e.g., the link from linguistic articulation to action at 1336a30–33, b3–8 (quoted above). (Note that this level of cognition belongs on the side of *arête êthikê* rather than on that of intellectual virtue.) This is certainly not an exclusive option, however. In particular, one which would belong naturally in any proper investigation into Aristotelian character-settling is the more material or bodily aspect of human agency factors, exemplified by *De Anima*'s 'boiling about the heart'.

relative homogeneity that goes with mere association.) It is a matter of actually being what one does, of fully living up to what one perceives as one's ideal self. And as such, it would seem to fit well into a position as the perfection of performance that is gradually realized in practical *mimesis*. From only more or less succeeding in appearing like something without yet being it, one ends up bringing it entirely to reality. The noble is not only this fullness or bringing to reality, but it is that too.[13]

[13] Much of the present investigation has been devoted to addressing some of the issues that were left hanging in my 'Mimesis in Aristotle's Ethics', in Øivind Andersen and Jon Haarberg (eds), *Making Sense of Aristotle: Essays in Poetics.* London: Duckworth, 2001, 73–86. A draft of this chapter was read at a meeting of the Oslo Happiness Project at the University of Oslo in April 2004, and then at the Values and Virtues conference at the University of Dundee. I am grateful to both audiences for their fruitful comments. I am also indebted to the Oslo Happiness Project for financially supporting my research for this chapter. I am especially grateful to Eyjólfur Emilsson and Stephen Halliwell, as well as to the editor, for their detailed responses to earlier versions of this chapter.

6

Moral Incompetence

Adam Morton

'I never knew a man who had better motives for all the trouble he caused.'
Graham Greene, *The Quiet American*

1 INTRODUCTION

In this chapter I describe a family of ways in which well-intentioned people, well equipped with the standard moral virtues, can do wrong. It is no news that good people can make decisions that turn out badly, and we all recognize that a morally admirable person could lack some practical skill required for realizing some of her intentions. She could have a bad memory or be bad at scheduling actions. The phenomenon that I am discussing is different from both bad luck and impracticality. It concerns the *moral* failings of decent people. The claim is that there are ways in which good will and virtue are consistent with a tendency to make the wrong choices in some kinds of moral problems. Such tendencies are what I refer to as moral incompetence. I expect that most people will agree not just that decent people can make a mess of things, but that there can be systematic patterns in the moral disasters of even morally admirable individuals. This is a very weak version of the claim I am making. The main claim is that *there are widespread characteristics of agents which are consistent with their being kind, thoughtful, responsible, brave, and so on, and which lead specifically to their bungling moral situations.* (And what is it to bungle a moral situation? I'll get to that.) I shall argue that there is at least a case for a stronger claim too, call it the extreme claim: *there are characteristics that lead agents to bungle moral situations and which are more likely to be manifested in morally ambitious—high-principled, admirable, un-complacent, morally uncompromising—people.*

There are two general difficulties in arguing for these claims. The first lies in distinguishing the effects of specifically moral incompetences from those of more general practical failings: social limitations, difficulties in planning and executing complex projects, and so on. The second lies in distinguishing competence from virtue, that is, in answering the question 'If someone is prone to making a mess of a class of moral situations, does this not just show that there is a moral virtue, perhaps one that we do not have a familiar name for, which the person lacks?' The solutions to both of these difficulties are clearest in the case of morally admirable agents, and therefore in the domain to which the extreme claim applies. So my strategy will not be to defend the less startling main claim first, and then move on cautiously to the extreme claim. Instead, I shall begin a defence of the main claim, with examples of everyday moral failure, and proceed to a point where considerations about the extreme claim, with examples of failure of great moral ambition, support points relevant to both.

2 EVERYDAY EXAMPLES

I begin with three examples. They are intended to show that an agent can fail to do the right thing by virtue of failing to think through the moral situation well, even though she applies the right moral principles and possesses at least some of the right virtues. (I say 'some of the right virtues' since, as remarked above, competence might itself be taken as a virtue, an issue to return to later.) Moreover, the failure in these examples is not one of general thinking power, but of the capacity to handle specifically moral aspects of problem-solving. I mean the examples throughout the chapter to give a picture of what it is like to wrestle with moral problems, a picture that suggests that asking 'what would a kind—just, generous, brave—person do?' leaves out something fundamental about what it takes to find a morally acceptable outcome.

Painful Truths

A professor, Ruth, has chaired an oral exam for a graduate student, Sam. The committee is prepared to pass Sam, but with some hesitation. In fact, there is a consensus that Sam, though intelligent and hard-working, is not well suited for advanced work in the subject. It would be in his interest if he would seriously consider dropping out. Sam meets Ruth in her office and she tells him he has passed. And then she says: 'There's something else you should know; most of us think you don't really have what it takes to do research.' Sam is visibly distressed, and so Ruth assures him that his intelligence and diligence are recognized and that the department will write strong letters for him if he decides to go to law school instead. She then realizes that she has a class to teach, and offers to discuss the matter further with Sam if he makes an appointment during the following week.

Sam is devastated. He had no idea that the faculty was not impressed with him, and all his plans centre on academic life. He leaves Ruth's office bewildered and upset, and soon spins into a dangerous depression. Suicide seems attractive, until another professor pushes him into the hands of the university health service, who help him through the first serious set-back of his life.

The best-intentioned plans can go wrong, and most of us would hesitate to condemn Ruth for saying what had to be said, one way or another. Suppose, though, that these things keep happening to Ruth: in interactions with students and colleagues the emotional message with which she intends to surround the content of what she says never gets transmitted. She does not know this, because she is too confident in the correctness of her intentions to take much note of the results. If she had known how little her attempts at being tactful succeed, she might have considered some alternatives. She could have first spoken to colleagues who knew Sam better, to get a sense of his vulnerabilities. She could have begun a long conversation about his future plans, waiting to get a sense of how bad her bad news was. But she does not consider any of these.

The example is not interesting unless we assume that it was right to tell Sam the faculty consensus, in a way that made it sink in, and unless we also assume that there was a duty, in telling him, to put it as kindly as possible. There is a tension between these two aims. Someone in Ruth's position has to get the truth across while doing minimal harm, and her way of doing this might have been a good one, if, in fact, she had just the right control over her manner. She would have to be able to pick up signs of distress and choose her words in response to them so that she would use the most direct formulation that didn't do major harm. Let us assume that Ruth knew how delicate it was to balance truth and kindness, and thought she could do it, showing a confidence that manifests itself particularly when she is in a position of responsibility. *It is particularly when she has an obligation to balance some person's interests against an institutional duty that she ventures beyond her social capacities.*

This incident does not reveal Ruth to be a bad person, in the sense of being unkind, unjust, cowardly, or lacking in any of the other standard virtues. It does reveal a fault, though, and it is a morally relevant fault. Ruth has a tendency to do the wrong thing, in a specific respect. When she is in a position of responsibility, she lets her awareness of that responsibility blunt her capacity for social delicacy. As a result, she blunders around doing harm. She may be more of a menace than someone who we would criticize for a slight lack of kindness or fairness. If we were wishing people to be different—*for the reasons that we wish people were kinder, fairer, and more courageous*—we would wish that Ruth took better stock of her actual social skills before embarking on what she takes to be right.

Incompatible Promises

Ruth's is a case in which it is clear what generally ought to be done, though it is not easy to do it. There are examples which turn on the fact that it is not clear what ought to be done. Consider George. His friend Michael asks him for a job recommendation, and he agrees. In fact, he says that he will write saying that Michael is the best person for the job. The job is one that Michael really needs to get, and in the period between applying and lining up his referees Michael is going on a hiking holiday, to get into the right frame of mind for a possible interview. While Michael is away George is approached by a friend of another, younger, colleague, Wilma, who has also decided to apply for the job. Would he be willing to write for her? In fact, the request comes just as George is reviewing some work that Wilma has done, which is of the very highest quality. In his enthusiasm, George says 'Yes, of course, I'd be delighted to write for her, in fact I would write that there couldn't be a better person for the job.'

George is no fool, and it doesn't take him long to realize what he has done. And in fact the situation is even more tangled, as George and Michael were once lovers, and George believes strongly in keeping a separation between the personal and the professional. He should not have agreed to write for Michael at all, he now thinks, and he should not have promised either candidate that he would give them top ranking. But, having promised to give Michael top ranking, he should not have also promised to rank Wilma top. He has a long hard think. Perhaps when one has made incompatible promises the first made takes precedence. Perhaps the fact that getting the job is crucial to Michael and less so to Wilma is relevant. Perhaps the fact that he should not have agreed to write for Michael means that he is less obliged to write in the strongest terms for him. Perhaps the fact that he didn't make the second promise to Wilma but to her friend makes that promise less binding, even if he is sure that his words will be conveyed to Wilma. Perhaps if he writes more strongly for Wilma, then since he should not have agreed to write for Michael it would be OK to lie to him, saying that he did all that he could. Perhaps he ought to write to Michael apologizing and saying that he cannot write for him. Perhaps he ought to write to Wilma apologizing and saying that he cannot guarantee to give her top ranking. Eventually he decides what to do.

Some people will take George to have got himself into a dilemma from which all exits have high and incompatible prices. This might suggest that he can take any of a number of resolutions of the problem, as long as he acknowledges the force of the others.[1] Others will choose some particular solution as the right one. (An option that seems to me promising is to give the stronger recommendation to whoever he thinks is better for the job, and simultaneously write to both Michael and Wilma saying that he must retract his promise to give him or her top ranking, since such promises should not be made. This may harm his relations with both of them, but this may just be the price for doing the right thing in a mess of one's own making.) Crucial to any option is George's capacity to carry it out, leaving behind as little outrage and actual harm as possible.

---

[1] The literature on moral dilemmas rarely faces directly up to the question 'when both of two available courses are wrong, and neither is clearly more than the other, are both equally permissible?' But an implicit consensus is that both are indeed permissible, as long as the appropriate retrospective emotions are experienced. See 'Moral Luck', in Williams 1981; and Stocker 1990. In Morton 1990 I explore the subsequent patterns of action that might be motivated by the retrospective emotions.

Suppose that there are better and worse ways out of the mess. Suppose that, though he does nothing awful or stupid, George takes one of the worse ones. One of many ways this can happen is that he does not consider options that he can in fact carry out satisfactorily. Either they do not occur to him, or in considering them he does not imagine very accurately how the play of his own attempts and others' reactions will develop.

George's failings are of anticipation and of imagination. Warning bells do not go off in his head when they should. This may be a sign of a generous, impulsive, optimistic nature, the down-side of real virtues. But although George's actions sometimes turn out well, they are often accompanied by a tendency to crisis. It may also be, though, that the warning bells particularly fail to tell him of likely moral problems. They do not warn him of the likelihood that he will later have reason to think that his action was unjust or ungenerous or inconsiderate. Then his failings are deficiencies of moral competence.

Pseudosupererogation

Moral philosophy is full of examples in which a person does a better thing than is required of them. Many such examples can be tweaked so that the act is *not* the best that the person could do. The person in the next example, Teresa, has applied for a promotion. She learns that someone else in her office, Sanjip, has also applied. Sanjip really wants the promotion, and Teresa knows that only one of them will get it. She is moved by sympathy for him and withdraws her application.

Teresa is kind and self-sacrificing. We have evidence that she is in conventional terms a good person. But has she made the best choice? It may be that it would be no better if Sanjip got the promotion; the cases are equal or incomparable in that there is no more value, all things considered, in either of them getting the promotion. So her choice is at most tied for best. An impartial observer would not have recommended that she make it. It may also be that it would be better if Teresa got it. She might have children to support; it might be her last chance and not Sanjip's. If so, then Teresa is making a mistake in withdrawing her application.

It is a moral mistake to discount your own interest too much; you are one of the people whose life you ought to care about. You can indeed waive your own rights to some extent; you can give yourself permission to give someone else's rights or interests some priority over yours. But only up to a point. Sometimes permission should be ignored, as when one person permits you to favour another person's trivial interest over her own vital interest. So too when it is a matter of your own interests: sometimes you should resist your generous inclinations and treat what you need with the same seriousness with which, if you are a decent person, you treat the needs of others.

But it is very hard to know when these occasions are. It requires a lot of self-knowledge, a firm resolve, and a sense of the limits beyond which someone's interests should be protected even if they are willing to see them eroded. These limits are different in the different cases of moral rights, fundamental needs, and general well-being. No wonder it is easier simply to give in to generosity. But to do so, on important matters, is just as much to bungle moral choice as it would be to act without enough thought on impulses that are fundamentally ungenerous.

3 MORAL CAPACITIES

In the cases I have described, people face situations that are too hard for them. There are many more such situations. Philosophical discussions of many moral topics—acts/omissions, trolleyology, the limits of obligation—will provide many examples that can be adapted to make the point. (Work through the examples in Kamm 1996 if you are convinced that you can grasp the essence of any moral problem without mental strain.) Many of these situations are too hard for anyone to find a perfect solution to them—I would argue that for nearly all complex situations there are better solutions than normal human beings will find—but for each type of situation there are some people who do conspicuously less well than others. Their failings can be due to many factors: lack of self-knowledge, inability to manage a complex body of information, lack of understanding of others. These factors will result in less-good choices with respect to the non-moral aspects of situations also. So perhaps the conclusion to draw is simply that moral decisions can be hard, so that a variety of cognitive failings can cause us to bungle them.

I don't think this is the whole story, and I have phrased the examples above so as to bring out ways in which it may not be. A person can be capable of performing reasonably well at thoughtful tasks in general, but be a persistent bungler of some particular aspect of moral problems. The claim is not that there is a specific moral faculty, failure of which can be dissociated from general intellectual failure. Rather, the claim is that among the large and varied bundle of competences that allow us to handle life's problems some specific combinations of them are particularly relevant to finding acceptable ways through moral problems.

Here is an analogy. Some people can ride unicycles and some cannot. Of the people who cannot, some have a weak sense of balance—but some who cannot ride unicycles can walk tightropes. Some of them are physically uncoordinated—but there are people who are physically coordinated and have a reasonable sense of balance who can only with great difficulty learn to ride the unicycle. And there are a few who have only average balance and coordination for whom after half an hour of falling off it suddenly clicks, and from then on they can jump on and go. The obvious explanation is that some combinations of balance, coordination, timing, strength, and, no doubt, other capacities make a potential unicyclist, and that a unicyclist needs to be able to make some one of these combinations work. The unicyclist needs to be able to draw on these different capacities and combine them in ways that enable her to wobble ahead. There need be no unicycle-riding faculty.

Similarly, moral situations require that we mobilize our capacities to manage complex information, imagine the situation of others, steer between general principles and special factors, adjudicate incomparable objectives, assess our own future reactions, understand our own motives, predict consequences, and more. These are, of course, our common-sense labels for skills that may, in fact, be the result of a set of quite different fundamental human capacities by whose overlaps they are constituted. Someone could be quite well equipped with these capacities, as humans go, and not have the particular combinations of them, or not be able to make them combine, that are required to deal with moral issues.

What are specifically moral issues? We should not expect a definition in non-moral terms. Moral issues are about how to deal with one another fairly, decently, and honourably, and with respect for one another as individual bearers of value. I don't think there is a less loaded way of putting it. One can describe in non-moral terms some of the themes that run through such issues: love and hate; admiration and contempt; cooperation and cheating. Early in our evolutionary history we developed specific mental capacities for handling these themes: cheater-detection modules and fair-distribution procedures. Later, human civilizations linked these capacities to a special vocabulary and a body of lore and ways of thinking to back it up, concerning rights, interests, obligations, duties, and moral character. This vocabulary, with its many complex connections, maps out a domain of problems and solutions, which has a fragile conceptual unity and also a rough unity in terms of the capacities it requires. Some of the capacities it requires link the ancient innate moral sensibilities, a grasp of the culturally acquired lore, and an understanding of the human situation at hand. Someone who has these capacities in one part of the moral domain tends to have them in other parts. There are many exceptions to this, but the correlations are good enough that we have the concept of the wise, morally capable, person, a person whose decisions we take very seriously and whose advice we seek. The reason we have this concept is that we invented the domain to single out a class of problems that arise in the project of cooperative living, competence with which varies significantly from person to person.

There are many ways that individuals can augment their moral competence. I shall describe two, which I shall call the Aristotelian way, and the Kantian way. Each reveals a space for specifically moral incompetence and, in particular, moral incompetence consistent with good intentions and possession of the standard moral virtues.

The Aristotelian way focuses on a person's exposure to other more experienced people navigating through moral situations. From early on in one's life, one is both a passive observer and a participant with others in situations involving delicate interaction and complex social thinking. One sees strategies and attitudes that succeed and others that fail. One chooses some other individuals as models for forming one's own moral character. To some extent one internalizes the personalities of these models, and one learns their ways of coping with difficult situations. One builds up in one's mind a large collection of past situations and approaches to them that were or were not successful. It is like a chess player's collection of combinations; a jazz musician's collection of harmonic possibilities; a philosopher's or a lawyer's collection of argumentative moves. Eventually, when one is in a difficult situation oneself, with no wise older person to guide one, one can draw on one's training in two ways. The first is to ask what one's role models would have done or, more profoundly, how they would have approached the problem. The second is to compare the situation with one that one has seen handled before, and to work out an analogous solution. Neither of these is automatic, even if one has successfully internalized the role models and built up the database of model solutions. For the situation at hand is nearly always novel in important respects, so one has to see resemblances which engage them either with one's internalized models or with one's accumulation of past situations.

Moral competence, seen the Aristotelian way, is based on comparing the situation in hand to situations one has seen managed in the past. In hard situations it is not obvious which comparisons will lead to outcomes that are satisfactory to those concerned or which later reflection will endorse. Then the competent moral agent has to find the kinds of connections that will be clear in retrospect, though hard to make out until they are found. In really hard situations—those that are like riding a unicycle across a tightrope in a blizzard—the virtuoso moral agent will be able to make creative analogies between new and old, analogies that mean reorganizing the structure of the existing database.

Moral incompetence is inevitable on this picture. Some people will not have fastened on suitable role models; some will not have build up a rich collection of examples; some will not have an effective way of organizing the collection; and, most importantly, some will not be able to see plausible similarities between present situations and collected ones. In fact, for every person there will be novel situations whose links to previously digested ones are obscure. The links are easiest to see when there is some conspicuous theme linking them, in particular the themes associated with the virtues made prominent in one's culture. Given a novel situation, one may well be able to see how it connects with familiar ones in terms of courage, benevolence, or justice, but not be able to put all these together with another and with other facts, about obligations, risks, and other factors. So a person may be capable of acting bravely, kindly, and fairly, even in this new situation, but not be capable of acting in a way that later, looking back, she and others will accept as the right thing to have done.

The Kantian way of describing moral competence focuses on the relation between general rules and particular acts. A person picks up from her culture a battery of labels that pick out morally relevant features of situations: lying, helping, killing, returning favours, resisting threats. In terms of these she can create much more complicated labels, such as 'keeping a promise that one made under duress', and in terms of both simple and complicated labels she can formulate general principles or maxims, such as 'always keep promises unless they were made under duress' or 'always at least consider helping people who have helped you'. Then when faced with a situation requiring moral attention the first thing is to characterize it, to give it a suitably complex label that recognizes its morally relevant features. The next thing is to formulate a general principle to govern one's behaviour in a situation so characterized. And then one must test this principle, to see if, in fact, it could represent the way a moral agent would act in situations like that. It is this last step that is the focus of Kantian moral philosophy, but it is not the most important element for present purposes. Moral competence, from this perspective, consists in having a good set of labels and principles and the capacity to construct new ones that fit the situation at hand. A general principle fits a situation when in that and future situations relevantly like it the results of acting in accordance with it will be acceptable to all concerned. (The creative aspect of the labelling, the way we make the labels, and the resemblances between situations is a theme of Christine Korsgaard's reading of Kant (Korsgaard 1996). 'Relevantly like', 'results', and 'acceptable' are obviously going to be understood differently in different Kantian accounts.)

On this view also, moral competence is a special and delicate accomplishment, and the existence of moral incompetence is unsurprising. An agent needs to have accumulated a stock of action-labels and of general principles that can be elaborated to fit the current situation, and needs to be able to find or create a label and a principle that fit the situation in an illuminating way. (And, further, needs to be able to test how morally helpful the principle is; something that Kant may have thought was easy, but which most subsequent Kantian thinkers have seen as decidedly complicated and bungle-able.) All these things can be done more and less well. Doing them less well is clearly consistent with doing many other things very well, and with benevolence, honesty, and sincerity. And so, in spite of Kant's famous assertion that nothing matters except a good will, it is clear that, from a Kantian perspective, there will be many qualities—moral qualities—in addition to a good will that we should encourage in one another.

On both the Kantian and the Aristotelian account, moral incompetence is to be expected, in the weak sense that we can expect that moral problems will often defeat even intelligent, well-intentioned people. But they also support a stronger conclusion, that we can expect there to be specific deficits of competence arising in moral thinking. They do this because they both describe moral thinking in terms of a sensitivity to a certain class of subtle patterns, the choices in particular circumstances characteristic of the virtues and the maxims appropriate to those circumstances, which are hard to describe in non-moral terms but which run through a wide range of decision-making situations. The important point is that moral sensitivity is a distinct sensitivity, with a fair amount of independence from the other sensitivities required in a complex life. Since it is distinct, the conceptual capacities that are recruited and combined to serve it will be selected for their capacity to serve that particular sensitivity. (Think of the combinations of capacities that can serve the sensitivity to three-dimensional moving disequilibrium required for unicycling.) So the exact combination available to one person will very often not be found in another, and two people who have the same capacities for, say, risk-management, salesmanship, and oratory, may have very different capacities for sensing when courage is called for, or when an act is best described as deception rather than persuasion.[2]

The three examples earlier in the chapter can easily be fitted into this framework. Ruth's difficulties in sensing when other people are likely to be hurt *in ways that she has an obligation to anticipate* may not be linked to any above-average incapacity to know how people will react to unexpected situations. George's difficulties in anticipating situations *in which he will incur obligations*, and in imagining the details of situations *where different people's interests are delicately balanced*, may not be linked to any above-average incapacity to anticipate or imagine. And Teresa's tendency not to allow herself *what she deserves* may not be linked to any above-average incapacity to compare her wants to those of others. In all these cases, and countless others, a person can perform at below-average competence in morally relevant aspects of her life while performing with normal competence in very similar, less morally relevant aspects.

The conclusion to draw is that it is not hard to see how specifically moral incompetence can come about. In most real cases, however, it will be almost impossible to tell how specifically moral a person's problem-solving difficulties are. Perhaps paradoxically, the cases that reveal a gap between moral and general competence most clearly involve high-principled or morally ambitious people. I turn to these cases next.

4 MORAL INCOMPETENCE IN TWO MEN OF HIGH PRINCIPLE: CATO AND WILSON

In my examples so far the field of moral incompetence has been personal life, and the theme has been the compatibility of incompetence and good will. This compatibility is an important point, since we misjudge many situations by ignoring it. But moral incompetence also emerges on a larger, more public, canvas, where the stakes are higher and the moral demands on people are higher.

---

[2] Though this argument is based on Kantian and Aristotelian premises, neither Kant's nor Aristotle's account of thought would support it right to the end. Kant or Aristotle could get to the weaker conclusion at the beginning of the paragraph. To get to the stronger conclusion at the end you need a contemporary conception of thought as the selective recruitment of capacities from a large biologically given pool.

My examples of people with the confidence and ambition to accept these higher stakes are Cato the younger and Woodrow Wilson.

Cato: Choosing the Wrong Moment

Marcus Porcius Cato was a leader of the Roman Senate in the last years of the Republic. He exemplified the Roman public virtues. According to the standard contemporary work on that period:

Cato extolled the virtues that won empire for Rome in ancient days, denounced the undeserving rich, and strove to recall the aristocracy to the duties of their station. This was not convention, pretence or delusion. Upright and austere, a ferocious defender of his own class, a hard drinker and an astute politician, the authentic Cato, so far from being a visionary, claimed to be a realist of traditional Roman temper and tenacity, not inferior to the great ancestor whom he emulated almost to a parody, Cato the Censor. But it was not character and integrity only that gave Cato the primacy before consulars: he controlled a nexus of political alliances among the *nobiles*.   (Syme 1960: 26)

A man of principle, then, incorruptible, brave, and honest, with an agenda of preserving the traditional values and political structure of Rome. (And a student of Hellenistic philosophy.) Yet by the time of his suicide his cause had utterly failed. The Republic was in ruins and a new cynical and autocratic state, the Rome of the Caesars, could be seen approaching. Moreover, this transition had occurred in large part *because* of Cato's principled uncompromising defence of the values of the old order. How can this be?

It wasn't just bad luck. Cato's defence of traditional senatorial rule extended to a blindness about its shortcomings. He tended to ignore how political conditions had changed since the old days, in particular how armies had to be appeased. In opposing individual threats to the Republic, he failed to think of how his opposition could make these threats combine. His principled objections to types of people whose power threatened the Republic—generals, non-Romans—led him to value the humiliation of individuals of these types, for its own sake. So he persuaded the Senate not to reward the successful general Pompey (a provincial, too) with rewards for his troops and ratification of his treaties; he sabotaged attempts to get support from the wealthy middle class for the aristocratic Senate; and he refused Julius Caesar acknowledgement (a triumph) for his good work in Spain. The result was that the wealthy, the generals, and the troops combined to force the Senate to grant what he had refused. From that moment on, it was obvious where the real power lay, and that the Senate was a device that could be used by whoever had enough real power.

Cato's failing was this: he chose disastrous moments to stand on principle. In particular, he ignored the effects of the combinations of stands he was committed to. To see his actions as misjudged we do not have to speculate about what would have happened had he acted differently. We need only see him as facing difficult situations, requiring both firm principle and the ability to accommodate social realities, both of which he possessed, but which he combined in such a way as to produce the collapse of his deepest aims. The Cato honoured by later ages as 'the last of the Romans' was so in part because of his own moral incompetence.

Wilson: The Arrogance of Principle

Woodrow Wilson was a man of outstanding intelligence, with unusual gifts for administration and eloquence. Though his experience of public life was extremely limited before he became president of the United States in 1913, he was elected largely because he was seen for what he was: honest, capable, progressive. He aimed to provide America with democratic institutions equal to the complexity of twentieth-century life. Early in his first presidency he oversaw the introduction of a systematic tariff reduction, largely independent of special interests, the first progressive income tax, the formation of the federal reserve, and he successfully defended his nomination of Brandeis to the Supreme Court against an openly anti-semitic opposition. These all fitted his vision of an open, efficient, and meritocratic society. To other social issues, whose connection with this vision he did not see, he was less responsive. He did not support the extension of the suffrage to women, and during his presidency Washington became racially segregated by law.

The great failure of Wilson's career is the American failure to join the League of Nations. The League was largely Wilson's idea and he had persuaded generally reluctant European allies at the end of the First World War to make it an integral part of the peace settlement. The price he paid with the allies was his acquiescence in the imposition of crippling reparations on Germany. These were to set the stage for the Second World War, and the Holocaust, which might have been prevented by a sufficiently powerful League, with America at its heart. But America did not join. Wilson could persuade neither the people nor Congress. The reasons lie in a failure of imagination and a failure to compromise. Wilson saw all opposition to the treaty as misguided or political. He could not understand the point of view of progressives who saw the treaty as enmeshing the United States with an incurably un-egalitarian Europe. Nor could he imagine the attitude of ordinary Americans who wanted to be left out of the troubles of the rest of the world. Still, there would have been support in the Senate for a treaty that embodied certain compromises. But he rejected any watering down of the League, and appealed directly for popular support. His campaign was extremely unsuccessful: he had lost touch with the mentality behind both progressive and conservative opposition to the League. To have persuaded the American people in 1919 to an uncompromising adherence to the League would have required overwhelming rhetorical and personal powers, and whether or not Wilson's powers were ever equal to the task, they certainly were not at this stage in his life.

There seem to me to be three core failings here. The first is a failure to see when it is better to compromise than to fail. An accommodation with the Senate could have been achieved, but Wilson's conviction that the project was too important to dilute prevented him from seriously considering it. The second is a blindness to the motives of others. Wilson's sense of the rightness of his cause made it impossible to see that others could have principled objections to it, so that, instead of arguing or persuading at this stage of his life he tended to elegant vituperation. The third is a mis-estimation of his own powers to make others see the rightness of his cause. Tired and ill, trying to convince people in a country with which he had lost touch, he could not hope to succeed, even if his course would have been what an ideally equipped moral agent would have undertaken.

All three failings have a common root. They all testify to the blinding effect of moral conviction. Knowing that one's cause is right can make one see all compromises, less than total realizations of it, as worthless. It can make one underestimate the depth and seriousness of the opposition. And it can make one think that once the point is put clearly any sensible person will be converted. A more cynical person would not have these problems; a more cynical person in the service of Wilson's principles might have achieved more. Not that cynical adherence to principle does not bring its own problems: the point is the extreme demands that real-life politics place on principled agents, and the moral requirement that they find a delicate path through the maze.

There are other ways of reading the histories of these two men. I may be wrong about their motives, their characters, and the causes of their failures. That doesn't really matter. What matters is the phenomena that my renditions of the histories highlight, and the fact that these phenomena are universals of human life. (Or, to put it differently, if you object to my diagnosis of Cato or Wilson, you are likely either to suggest different incompetences which had the same effects, or to contrast my stories with others in which the failures I describe are more plausibly found.) Everywhere in public life people have to decide when to stand on principle and when to compromise; how to grasp, morally and psychologically, the motives of the opposition; and when to take a chance on the effectiveness of one's powers to persuade. These are extremely demanding tasks. Only a very rare person gets it right when the stakes are high, and the consequences of getting it wrong can be catastrophic. One source of catastrophe is the fact that extremely capable, practically and socially competent, people, undertaking the tasks that their abilities make available to them, can easily get into situations where the moral complexities are too great for them. It is because they are intelligent, organized, diligent, and trustworthy that we can see more clearly that there are other basic capacities that they have to a less impressive degree.

My way of telling the two stories brings out reasons why moral incompetence can be most evident in the most admirable people. First of all, as I have just remarked, admirable and capable people are the ones we are likely to choose to lead us when faced with questions of large-scale moral import. Besides this, there is the factor of moral ambition and confidence. To manage relatively simple low-stakes moral questions highly admirable people, like the rest of us, rely on the virtues, categorizations, and instincts that they have acquired throughout their life. These have their limits: they are likely to be treacherous when people suddenly find themselves out of their depth. In both the Cato story and the Wilson story we can see a man equipped with firm virtues but much less well equipped with the capacity to see their areas of unreliability. Cato and Wilson do not see when their sense of what is honourable or fair may be wrong, or when they should suspect that a pair of virtues—honour and prudence in Cato's case; fairness and respect in Wilson's case—may be in conflict in a way that requires a fundamental re-thinking. In fact, neither man would have achieved the eminence that they did had they had less confidence in their capacities. There is a kind of paradox here: we inevitably choose as leaders the kinds of morally confident people who are unlikely to know the boundaries of their competence.

5 COMPETENCES, VIRTUES, META-VIRTUES

Incompetence is the absence of competence. The capacities I am discussing are directed at difficult situations, some so difficult that no person can handle them perfectly. So we cannot contrast the morally incompetent person with the morally capable, fully virtuous, person who can emerge with a good solution to all moral problems. There are no such people. I do not think that we can conceive of creatures anything like human beings that do not often encounter moral problems which exceed their capacities.[3] So there are no fully competent people. Moral competence and incompetence come in degrees, and by 'moral incompetence' we must sometimes mean unusually incompetent, sometimes incompetent relative to the situation at hand, and sometimes incompetent in some interesting way. This is true of the individual competences that contribute to moral competence, too. The capacity to know when and how to stand on principle is never fully or perfectly exercised by anyone. Neither is the capacity to anticipate other people's judgements of the character of one's motives. But the same is true of many traditional virtues, such as courage. There are situations which would terrify any real human being from doing the right thing.

---

[3] Until recently, few philosophers have used examples involving resolutions of multiple inconsistent promises or reactions to unreasonable, but deeply felt, demands of others, or the like. One reason for this is that philosophers have wanted to show that their theories deliver what their readers will agree are the right answers. So the test cases are ones to which the readers and the philosophers know what the answers are. This makes it harder to see the existence of moral incompetence. It also makes it harder to see how easily decent people can become participants in atrocity. I have discussed this latter theme in Morton 2004a.

Are moral competences virtues, then? Are moral incompetences vices? I am not sure that it matters how we draw the demarcation lines, as long as we are clear that the capacities I am discussing, although vital to moral life, are in significant ways different from the usual examples of moral virtues. To end this chapter I shall list some of the differences, and for each one I shall give reasons both for considering moral competence to be distinct from virtue, and for considering moral competences to be virtues, though of a special kind. They are moral meta-virtues. (For more on meta-virtues see the final section of Morton 2004b.)

Incompetence is not Vice

Ruth, in this chapter's first example, is not a bad person. She is trying, and making a mess of it. That alone does not prevent her social clumsiness from being a lack of moral virtue, since many people who fail to show courage or kindness when it is called for are not, all things considered, bad people. But there is a difference. When someone is cowardly or unkind we condemn them; we adopt a particular attitude whose full character is notoriously hard to describe, but which is definitely different from the kind of criticism we make when we point out that someone is misinformed or has not appreciated some distinction or has made a mistake in reasoning. We can condemn our friends: condemnation is consistent with affection, though it erodes it. Moral criticism has at least an edge of hostility to it; one of its aims is to change the direction its target is heading. If we understand Ruth, though, we want to take her aside and suggest she learn more about her social limitations, but we don't want to condemn her, to urge that she should have fundamentally different aims in life. Her judgement about what is a good eventual outcome is perfectly sound. The same is true of Cato. He is a man of principle and stubborn devotion to his values, and we admire that. We think his grasp of social and practical reality is flawed, in a way that makes his efforts largely counter-productive. If we are his contemporaries, we wish for a moral capacity that is surely beyond our powers: to get him to see how he is choosing the wrong times and places to resist his enemies. (In this connection, see section 8, 'On Moral Blindness', of Brewer 2002.)

Ruth's and Cato's failings are not matters of motivation; moral virtues are concerned with wanting the right thing at the right moment; therefore the capacities they lack are not virtues. Courage is not wanting to flee when flight would be a bad idea; generosity is wanting to help others when help is called for; prudence—in the familiar sense in which it is *not* a synonym for *phronesis*—is not wanting more danger than is called for. Moral competence is quite different from this. To put it in Christine Swanton's terms, it does not have a definite target. Or, in Rosalind Hursthouse's terms, acting competently does not consist in acting out of a sense of duty linked to that particular aspect of action: one does not think anything like 'this is what competence demands'. (See Swanton 2003: ch. 11 section (iii); Hursthouse 1999: ch. 6.)

On the other hand, there are precedents. Take prudence (in the same sense as the last paragraph's), where the dangers to be avoided are dangers to individual others and to one's own moral standing. It cannot consist just in wanting to avoid such dangers. It must also require one to think through what situations are dangerous, and how dangerous they are. This is hard; one can get it wrong, and as a result act imprudently, not by any flaw in one's motives but because of an incapacity to handle the complexity of risks, including moral risks. Surely that is a kind of moral incompetence, very similar to the others I have been discussing. Consider complex cases in which prudence involves adjudicating between higher and lower likelihoods of one's own benefit, one's own self-respect, respect to others, and benefit to others. Prudence then requires a capacity to know when one's rough estimates of danger and of the comparative weights to attach to all these competing factors are right. It requires the meta-virtue of knowing when one's sense of danger and one's sense of the value of things is accurate, and when instead of acting in accord with simple first order virtues one ought instead to reflect further. This is a virtue-like capacity to know the limits of one's standard armoury of virtues.

Competences do not Exhibit Means

An Aristotelian virtue of character typically entails a mean. That is, the virtuous person cannot identify some quality of outcome or motive and simply go for it. That results in imprudence rather than courage; cowardice rather than prudence; soft-heartedness rather than generosity. Instead, famously, the virtuous person must exercise a very delicate capacity to know how much and when. This capacity cannot consist in knowing a graspable set of truths; if it could be the virtue would be redundant given simply intelligence and good intentions. Contrast this with the capacities that fail in moral incompetence. You cannot have too much grasp of others' likely reactions, or of others' construal of your own motives, or of techniques for balancing between principle and expediency. You never need an inner voice whispering 'this is the wrong moment to see that the other guy has principles too.' Instead, since moral competence is engaged in an unequal struggle with the complexity of moral life we simply need as much of it as we can get. No means.

Again, if we look more closely, we can still assimilate competences to more standard-issue virtues of character. Suppose we accept that moral competence is usually more a matter of knowing how than knowing when. It is not as if virtues on the traditional lists do not also require a lot of knowing how. Generosity, for example, often requires that one know how to benefit people without making them feel demeaned. Traditional virtues of character also involve means, of course, but finding the mean often involves just the kind of wrestling with complexity and unpredictability that is the focus of this chapter. To know if this is the right moment to stand one's ground courageously against a bully requires thinking through the likelihood of losing the confrontation, and the consequences this might have. And, more subtly, it requires considering the possible adverse consequences of winning (the bully might turn his anger on someone more vulnerable; his loss of face might allow some yet more malign force an opportunity). If all things considered this is the wrong moment to stand up to the bully, doing so is not an exhibition of virtuous courage, even if it is a brave thing to do. So part of the thinking involved in moral competence is also needed to negotiate the mean of a traditional virtue.

Add to this fact another consideration. There *are* means with respect to, for example, knowing when to stand on principle. Sometimes though you could think more about whether this is the right moment, and as a result know better whether it is, more thinking is not what is called for. You just have to use the little understanding you have and jump in, or hold back. This is the mean of a higher-order virtue, much like the higher-order mean of knowing when you have reflected enough on whether this is the moment for courage. There is a virtue of reflecting just the right amount. And, as with the complex cases of prudence I discussed above, it can be reasonably described as a meta-virtue governing the limits and applications of the moral capacities that are used in more routine cases.

Moral Competence is not Learned by Imitation

An Aristotelian virtue is acquired by absorbing the manner of others who are in various ways admirable. One way this can work is by providing a great number of examples of right action, from which the learner can generalize, usually in a pattern-recognizing rather than a principle-formulating way. Another way is by a kind of empathetic identification with the admired model, which fine-tunes many subtle psychological factors.[4] But moral incompetence can be exhibited by highly admirable people, when they face situations that are too subtle or too complex for them. So a young Roman who had hung around Cato would acquire courage, respect for principled action, resoluteness, and sociability. But this would not guarantee that he would not fail as Cato did, when faced with the same challenges. In fact, there are no exemplars of moral competence to imitate. There are exemplars of various kinds of incompetence, and individuals who handle many situations competently and then fail when things get too hard.

On the other hand, something similar is true for all virtues. You can learn something about courage from the company of a wise and brave person, and, all going well, you will absorb something of what she has. But in situations that test your and her courage you may still do less well than she, or it may turn out that she fails the test and you do not. The contrast between, for example, knowing how to steer between competing obligations and knowing when to stand up to an aggressor is not that either can be learned perfectly, because neither can

---

[4] On imitation cf. Fossheim's chapter in this volume.

ever be acquired perfectly, but that the former much more than the latter can be demonstrated in simple paradigm situations, from which something can be learned that is of some use in more messy and challenging ones. Most of the competences whose absence makes for moral incompetence are not like that. So if they are virtues they are rather special ones. But, still, they are acquired and the presence of role models may often be important when they are.

A conclusion? I don't think it is very important whether we classify the capacities whose absence or insufficiency results in moral incompetence as virtues. My own preference would be to restrict 'virtue' to those moral traits which involve a definite pattern of motivation and action governed by an Aristotelian mean, the character traits discussed in books 2 to 5 of the *Nicomachean Ethics*. I would then prefer to classify the qualities of intellect and self-control whose failures this chapter focuses on as just that, intellectual qualities for handling the morally relevant aspects of social complexity, inadequacy of information, conflict of obligation, and the like. Within these qualities I would make a basic distinction between failures in handling the kinds of complex thinking demanded by hard moral problems, and failures in understanding and negotiating the limits of the simple virtues that get one through run-of-the-mill situations. The latter are what I am calling meta-virtues. Their failure is particularly associated with the moral incompetence of high-principled morally ambitious people. But the morally over-extended situations of such people simply make more visible the delicacy of tasks that we all undertake, sometimes successfully and sometimes disastrously, as part of shared human life.[5]

[5] I have had extremely helpful comments on drafts of this chapter from Timothy Chappell, Susan Dwyer, Glen Koehn, and Holly Smith. The audience at the Dundee Values and Virtues conference in May 2004 gave me an amiably hard time, which resulted in a number of changes.

7

The Variety of Life and the Unity of Practical Wisdom

Timothy Chappell

1 THREE PROBLEMS ABOUT PRACTICAL WISDOM

It can seem that there is no such thing as the virtue of practical wisdom.[1] For virtues are particular dispositions, with particular fields of operation. So, for example, courage is a particular disposition—the disposition that makes you stand firm in *ta tharralea*, tight corners and frightening crises—and it has a particular field of operation: tight corners and frightening crises. Again temperance is a particular disposition—the disposition whereby you resist when the lures of pleasure or the goads of pain tempt you beyond propriety—and it has a particular field of operation: dealing with the lures of pleasure and the goads of pain.

By contrast practical wisdom, *phronêsis*, is defined by Aristotle (*NE* 1140b5–7) as 'a truthful disposition' (*hexin alêthê*), one which is accompanied by reason (*meta logou*) and practical (*praktikên*), and which is 'concerned with what is good or bad for humans' (*peri ta anthrôpôi agatha kai kaka*).[2] It sounds, then, like practical wisdom is simply a disposition *to get things right in action*. But it is hard to see why we[3] should want to say that there is any *one* disposition to do that. And there are three reasons not to say it.

First, the 'things' that need to be 'got right in action' seem too various for it to be possible that a single disposition could apply to all of them. Here practical wisdom contrasts unfavourably with other virtues, such as temperance

---

[1] Readers who detect a Thomist phrasing here should compare *Summa Theologiae* 2a2ae.47.4–5.

[2] Unless I say otherwise, all the translations used in this chapter are my own.

[3] It is unfortunately rare for philosophical authors to identify their 'we's; but here 'we' = 'we neo-Aristotelians'—those of us in ethics who would like to appropriate for contemporary purposes as much as possible of Aristotle's approach. How much *is* possible is, of course, a standing question, and not just for this essay.

and courage. What unifies temperance as a disposition is its tight relation to what is recognizably a single aspect of human affairs—pleasure and pain; what unifies courage as a disposition is its tight relation to an equally unitary aspect—fear and defiance. What aspect of human affairs would likewise serve as a focus to unify practical wisdom as a single disposition? I suppose it would have to be *the good and the bad*. But the whole point of having a list of different virtues, such as Aristotle himself offers, is that 'the good and the bad' is precisely *not* a single aspect of human affairs, but a way of talking about *every* aspect.[4] The supposition that there is a single virtue of practical wisdom, a single disposition 'to get things right', seems to ignore this fact. Call this the *unity problem*.

(You might think that justice poses the unity problem too: 'there are, in the old jargon, many parts of justice—there are many strands plaited together, and each strand carries many knotty problems' (Geach 1977: 110). For all that, the complexity of justice does not prevent Justinian and Aquinas from defining it as a clearly unitary disposition: *iustitia est constans et perpetua voluntas ius suum unicuique tribuens*, 'justice is a constant and abiding will that renders every person his desert' (*Summa Theologiae* 2a2ae.58.1; cp. Justinian, *Digest* 1.1.10). No similarly unitary account of practical wisdom is available. Strikingly, the *Summa Theologiae* has no *quaestio* headed *Quid sit prudentia*.)

Second, even if there could be a single disposition with so many utterly different applications, that single disposition would then threaten to 'crowd out' the other virtues: it would apply wherever they apply and, in fact, do all their work, leaving them with nothing to do. This prospect might have appealed to the Socrates of the *Protagoras*; but it surely does not appeal to Aristotle (see *NE* 1144b17–30), and, I think, should not appeal to us either. However, the danger of collapse into a single-virtue view is surely present in the most obvious manœuvres that spring to mind as ways of reintroducing practical wisdom alongside any of the other virtues, for example by saying (roughly) that the other virtues provide prima-facie motivations which practical wisdom refines into all-things-considered motivations. Whether this sort of manœuvre (for the prototype of which see e.g. *NE* 1144a8–9, on one reading), or something like it, can, in fact, be avoided by any good response to the present problem is a question that I fear will still be in the air at the end of this chapter. Be that as it may, the manœuvre clearly has a dangerous tendency towards the conclusion that the other virtues are not really virtues at all—they are just raw material on which the single virtue of practical wisdom operates.

If, on the other hand, we try to resist practical wisdom's tendency to 'crowd out' the other virtues, there is the danger that practical wisdom itself will get 'crowded out'. If we take it as our starting-point, as I have already suggested, that the different virtues are genuinely different because each of them has a distinctive field, and is based on a distinctive disposition, then a full list of the different

---

[4] Cp. Adam Morton's discussion of 'Moral Incompetence' (Ch. 6, this volume).

virtues will presumably cover all of the different fields that together make up human life, and will specify all the various dispositions that humans need to cope well in these various fields. But once we have specified *all* the fields that together make up human life, and assigned a particular virtue to each of these fields, there seems to be no field, no distinctive role, left over for practical wisdom. And thus practical wisdom itself gets 'crowded out'. Call this the *overlap problem*.

A third reason not to say that practical wisdom is a single disposition to 'get things right in action' is that this claim sounds suspiciously like a lapse into magic, or triviality, or both. As Aristotle himself comes close to pointing out, it would be a poor explanation of medical skill to say that you are a good doctor if and only if you have the disposition to do what the skill of medicine prescribes (*NE* 1138b32). The claim that there is, central to ethics, a disposition to get things right in action seems equally opaque and uninformative. Call this the *triviality problem.*

Here we see the reason why anyone should care about my question whether there is such a thing as the virtue of practical wisdom. As Plato might have put it, the reason is this: Because practical wisdom will be teachable only if there is such a thing as the virtue of practical wisdom. The question sets up a choice between these alternatives:

(1) There is (in a non-trivial sense) a virtue, a unitary disposition, of practical wisdom;

(2) There is such a thing as practical wisdom, but it is not (in any non-trivial sense) a unitary disposition, and hence not a virtue. Rather, 'practical wisdom' is a name for a shapeless disunity of different dispositions and their interactions.

We can reasonably hope for an illuminating account of what practical wisdom is, and how we may directly and non-accidentally understand it, perhaps even acquire it, only if (1) is true and (2) is false. For unless (1) is true, practical wisdom will not have a *shape*, a definite outline. There will be nothing substantive or informative to be said about what practical wisdom is like, or how to get hold of it, that we are not told by being told about the other virtues, and how to get hold of *them*. At best, the acquisition of practical wisdom will supervene on the acquisition of the other virtues; and it will be the other virtues, not practical wisdom, that are teachable *per se*—practical wisdom will only be teachable *per accidens*, as a side-effect of the teaching of the other virtues.

Having an illuminating and non-trivial account of practical wisdom is not only a necessary condition of its teachability. It is also a necessary condition of what I shall call its *discussability*: of the possibility of rationally structured and disciplined debate about how to cash out practical wisdom in our practice, and of whether this or that particular action or policy instantiates practical wisdom. As Williamson 2004: 17 puts a similar point:

A philosopher treats some common-sense judgement as if it carried no authority whatsoever but implicitly relies on other judgements that are found pre-philosophically obvious: exactly which such judgements are supposed to carry authority? When law and order break down, the result is not freedom or anarchy but the capricious tyranny of petty feuding warlords. Similarly, the unclarity of constraints in philosophy leads to authoritarianism. Whether an argument is widely accepted depends not on publicly accessible criteria that we can all apply for ourselves but on the say-so of charismatic authority figures. Pupils cannot become autonomous from their teachers because they cannot securely learn the standards by which their teachers judge. A modicum of wilful unpredictability in the application of standards is a good policy for a professor who does not want his students to gain too much independence.

For us to cooperate in formulating rational decisions about the detail of how we should live together, it needs to be possible for us to have an open and equal debate about it. This debate needs to have substantive content and structure; it needs to be, in principle, possible for any participant to win it, if he presents good enough arguments; and it needs to be a debate that cannot simply be halted, whenever it suits, by brusque announcements of one side or the other's superior moral perception. That practical wisdom should be discussable in this sense seems to be essential for any open society: it is no accident that Aristotle identifies practical wisdom with the *politikê tekhnê* (*NE* 1141a21). Perhaps such considerations about discussability give us even more reason to care about the question whether there is such a thing as the virtue of practical wisdom than the last paragraph's considerations about teachability.

Unity, overlap, triviality: here are three connected problems about the alleged virtue of practical wisdom. In teachability and discussability, we have two practical reasons why these problems might be worth a little attention. There are scholarly reasons, too: these problems have something to teach us about the nature of practical wisdom, and about its place in Aristotle's, or any plausible, ethics. So let us look at them more closely.

2 THE UNITY OF DISPOSITIONS

First I shall set aside the technical question of how, in general, we are to give individuation or identity-conditions for any disposition. I am not going to make much fuss about this question here. For sure, dispositions are not very hard-edged entities. *Pace* Quine, that is not to say they are not entities at all. Equally for sure, we could atomize any apparently single disposition, no matter how unitary-seeming, into indefinitely many subsidiary dispositions.

If you think (like Ryle 1949: 43; Prior 1985: 29) that truths about dispositions reduce to truths about counter-factuals, then you can slice your dispositions as thick or thin as you like, depending on how general are the terms you use e.g. in subject-place in these counterfactuals. There can be unitary dispositions *of humans*, and unitary dispositions *of Joe the human*, or even *of the human timeslice Joe-from-t1-to-t2*. For present purposes this is not an advantage of the counterfactual analysis, since it seems to imply that it is always arbitrary how we individuate dispositions. But it surely matters *sometimes*—for example, in the case of practical wisdom.

Participants in the contemporary debate are more likely to say that dispositions are be individuated either (1) by their stimulus and manifestation conditions (a proposal close to the counterfactual proposal) or (2) by their causal bases in the object's structure or constitution. (For the debate see for example, Mumford 2003; or Crane 1997.) I doubt these proposals are really competitors: we shall probably need to draw on both for a full understanding of any sort of disposition, including virtues.

However, as I say, I need not settle these issues here. No matter which way the technical debates go, our intuitive grip on the unity or otherwise of dispositions is easily clear enough for my purposes here. Intuitively, courage and temperance are single dispositions; intuitively, a disposition 'to get things right' is not. It is this kind of intuitive judgement of unity that interests me here—whatever its basis may be.

For more evidence of our intuitive sense of how to individuate dispositions, think about this. At the practice field, Jonny Wilkinson kicks four drop-goals out of four; fortuitously enough, so do I. But only one of them I kick without the intervention of some fluke. As to the other three, for the first I hit the target only because I slip in the mud as I'm lining up the ball; for the second, I hit the target only because a gun goes off just behind me as I kick; for the third, I hit the target only because I'm drunk. No normal person will hesitate to say, for example, that Jonny operates *the same disposition every time*; that I, by contrast, operate *different dispositions* (four, perhaps?) during my four kicks; that for only one of my kicks do I operate *the same disposition as Jonny* operates for all of his; and so on. Whatever it may be that entitles us to this intuitive confidence about the individuation, enumeration, and identification of Jonny's and my kicking dispositions, we have the very same entitlement in our discriminations of the dispositions that are the virtues. That entitlement is enough for present purposes.[5]

3 THE DISTINCTION BETWEEN MORAL AND INTELLECTUAL VIRTUES

At first sight there seems to be a simple solution to our three problems. It turns on a crucial Aristotelian distinction that has been shamelessly ignored in my

---

[5] I once heard Anthony Price suggest a 'fluid' account of emotions, on which there is no strict way of individuating emotions any more than there is a strict way of individuating waves on the sea. Emotions have what identity they have merely as particular fuzzy-edged parts of a larger continuum (call it 'emotion' in the singular). Presumably (this is my suggestion, not Price's) something parallel might be said about dispositions. If so, interesting; but not a problem for my argument.

discussion so far: namely, the distinction between the virtues of character and the intellectual virtues.[6]

'You find it surprising' (a critic might say) 'that practical wisdom fails to behave like a typical virtue of character. But this isn't surprising, for practical wisdom isn't a virtue of character at all. It is a virtue of intellect, and distinguished from the other virtues of intellect by being concerned with matters of action. No wonder, then, that practical wisdom fails to have any specific field of the sort that (say) temperance or courage have, while none the less relating to every virtue of character in the same way. This explains why your "overlap problem" is not really a problem: because the non-trivial unity of practical wisdom is the unity of an intellectual virtue, not of a virtue of character.'

Or, as Aquinas puts it, in a typically lucid summary of Aristotle's doctrine (*Summa Theologiae* 2a2ae.47.5c):

Since the place of practical wisdom (*prudentia*) is in the reason, it is distinguished from the other intellectual virtues by the material diversity of their objects. Speculative wisdom, science, and intellect (*sapientia, scientia, et intellectus*) are concerned with (*sunt circa*) what is necessary, craft (*ars*) and practical wisdom with what is contingent. Craft is concerned with things that can be produced (*factibilia*), things which are constituted by a process that takes place in an external medium, like a house, a knife, and so on; whereas practical wisdom is concerned with things that can be done (*agibilia*), things which are constituted in the very agent himself (*quae scilicet in ipso operante consistunt*). On the other hand, practical wisdom is distinguished from the virtues of character by the different formal definitions of the capacities from which, respectively, they arise. For practical wisdom arises from our cognitive capacity, whereas the virtues of character arise from our appetitive capacity.

If we want to see how specific the scope of practical wisdom is, we can see this by contrasting it with the other intellectual virtues, which it will make it clear that the field of *ta prakta*—*agibilia*, possible actions—is not after all an entirely unlimited field: thinking about how to act and live together is a different sort of intellectual exercise from thinking about God, or the first principles of science, or how to make a statue. If, on the other hand, we want to see how general is the range of practical wisdom, we can see this by contrasting the different ways in which practical wisdom and the virtues of character contribute to particular actions. As Aquinas puts it, their contributions are respectively cognitive and appetitive.

4 PRACTICAL TRUTH

This distinction helps us a bit with section 1's three problems; but not enough. Until we know more about *how* practical wisdom cooperates with the virtues of

---

[6] As section 3 will show, I ignored this distinction only temporarily and tactically. Other philosophers, it seems, ignore it permanently and strategically. See Bakhurst 2001: 161 (quoted in § 7).

character to bring about particular virtuous actions, we still shall not be able to explain in any very satisfactory detail how the overlap problem is avoided—how it is that both practical wisdom and, say, courage play separate roles in bringing about a particular courageous act. Nor shall we be able to dismiss the problems of unity and triviality until we understand what makes practical wisdom a non-trivially *single* disposition, distinct from the dispositions that are the other virtues (moral or intellectual); and how that disposition operates, or might be acquired.

What we need is a substantive account of practical wisdom: something that takes us further than we are got by, for instance, Aristotle's remark (*NE* 1141b11) that 'practical wisdom's most characteristic realisation is good deliberation'. On its own, this still does not explain why good deliberation should be the product of any clearly and non-trivially *single* disposition: so it is useless against the triviality and unity problems. On its own, moreover, it immediately reopens the overlap problem: if practical wisdom is a disposition to deliberate well, then why can't that disposition alone do all the work that typically needs to be done to produce virtuous actions? What we need to know is what, in detail, good deliberation consists in.

Aristotle's answer is that it consists in grasping 'practical truth', *hê alêtheia praktikê* (1139a27; cp. Anscombe 1965). Practical wisdom, as we saw in section 3, is the practical species of the genus intellectual virtue; and the generic function of any intellectual virtue is to *attain the truth* (*NE* 1139a15). So the function of any particular species of intellectual virtue is to attain some particular species of truth. Thus *epistêmê* is demonstrative knowledge of necessary truth (*NE* 1139b18–36); *tekhnê* is 'a disposition of production (*hexis poiêtikê*) accompanied by true *logos*' (*NE* 1140a21). (Interestingly, then, Aristotle thinks that the good artist or craftsman has a kind of knowledge: perhaps (cp. *NE* 1106b10–13) he would even agree with Keats that, at least for the artist, beauty is truth.) Accordingly, practical wisdom will be the disposition of the mind that grasps *practical* truth.

Of course, if there is such a thing as practical truth, then Aristotle's view must be that the attainment of truth is the function not only of the intellectual virtues, but of the moral virtues, too; for the practical is the field of the moral virtues. And this does seem to be Aristotle's view; thus he says at *NE* 1139b12 that attaining truth is the function of both *nous*, the cognitive faculty in general, and of *orexis*, the appetitive faculty in general (cp. *NE* 1144a2).

So far, then, our account says that practical wisdom means, or is characterized by, good deliberation, which consists in grasping practical truth. To solve my three original problems—unity, overlap, triviality—we now need some more about what it is to grasp practical truth; how this grasping can be the work of what can informatively and non-trivially called a single disposition; and how that single disposition cooperates with other virtues without either making them redundant, or being made redundant by them. What more might be added?

5 PRACTICAL TRUTH AND THE DOCTRINE OF THE MEAN

One thing we might well add is the doctrine of the mean. That this is what we should add is, you might think, the clear implication of Aristotle's definition of moral virtue (*NE* 1106b36–1107a1):

Thus virtue is a disposition of choice, lying in the mean that is relative to us—the mean that is determined[7] by reason, and as the man of practical wisdom would determine it.

In Aristotle's view, one important difference between the intellectual virtues and the moral virtues is this (1138b26–9): the intellectual virtues are not, and the moral virtues are, subject to the doctrine of the mean in any non-trivial sense. (Perhaps *tekhnê* is an exception to this, *NE* 1106b10–13.) As we have seen, the intellectual virtues typically aim not at the mean but at truth, and each intellectual virtue at its own sort of truth.[8] There again, any truth whatever can be supposed to have a symmetrical search-space around it[9]—so we might even say that attaining truth is the equivalent, for intellectual virtues, of hitting the mean. Conversely, we can also suggest that hitting the mean is itself a form of attaining truth: it is that form of attaining truth which is germane to human action—in other words, *practical* truth.

If so, then the picture emerging is this. Practical wisdom is the virtue that reasons to find the mean in which each of the virtues of character lies. So practical wisdom can be an intellectual virtue—a form of grasping truth—because reasoning to find this mean is the grasping of *practical* truth of which section 4 spoke. Practical wisdom so understood will be something reasonably distinctive and unitary. This helps to solve the unity problem. Again, since finding the mean is a (relatively) unified aspect of human affairs, the disposition that looks for this mean can be something the specification of which is a good deal better than trivial; and this helps to solve the triviality problem.

It is not yet so obvious that the overlap problem is solved. The picture is that, for each of the other virtues—courage, for example—practical wisdom uses reason to find the mean in which that virtue lies. But then what sense could there possibly be in talking of the virtue of courage *apart from* practical wisdom?

---

[7] Reading *hôrismenêi* with Bywater, who follows Alexander, Aspasius, and William of Moerbeke. The manuscripts have *hôrismenê*, which would mean that what was determined by reason was *virtue*, not the mean that virtue lies in. Bywater is surely right to reject this banal alternative.

[8] I come at the contrast between intellectual and moral virtue from another angle in Chappell 2005.

[9] Even if, for most truths, it is more natural to think of this space as two- or three-dimensional than as one-dimensional like the arrays that are most characteristic of the classic doctrine of the mean—Aristotle's triads of excess, mean, and deficiency. Cp. Broadie and Rowe 2002: 20 for the suggestion that, even on the classic doctrine, there may be 'a whole gamut of dimensions in which a response might go wrong'.

If we take seriously Aristotle's view that courage lies in a mean, then the problem is not just (as we might have expected) that it is hard to see how someone could be *perfectly* courageous without having practical wisdom, too. The problem is how anyone could have any courage at all without practical wisdom. There will be *no* courage unless the mean between rashness and cowardice is struck; and that mean, we now hear, will only be struck by practical wisdom. It looks as if Aristotle thinks that practical wisdom is necessary for courage in no weaker a sense than Socrates thinks this (*Protagoras* 350c1–4). It also looks sometimes as if Aristotle thinks that practical wisdom is sufficient for courage and the other moral virtues: for example, *NE* 1145a1: 'When practical wisdom alone is present in someone, at once all the other virtues will be present in him.'

The return of the overlap problem can, I think, be resisted, just so long as we can keep two things separate. One is the possibility that practical wisdom might make, to every action in accordance with each virtue, its own contribution; the other is the possibility that practical wisdom might make, to every action in accordance with each virtue, *the same contribution as that virtue*. It is only the latter possibility that brings in the overlap problem. So long as practical wisdom and, for example, courage make *different* contributions to every courageous action, they will still remain distinct virtues.

I take it that Aristotle's distinction (*NE* 1144b1–32) between 'natural virtue' (*physikê aretê*) and 'virtue in the proper sense' (*kyriôs aretê*) is intended at least partly as a way of making this point. He means that the natural virtue of courage will be a disposition that, as a matter of genetic and physical endowment, makes me good at dealing with tight corners and frightening crises; but I shall not have the full and proper virtue of courage until this natural endowment has been shaped by reason into a disposition for dealing well with tight corners and frightening crises by determining the mean in them *in the kind of way that reason and the practically wise person would determine it*. Hence, courage retains its specific application to a particular field, the field of fear and defiance; and practical wisdom retains *its* specific application to a particular field, the field of using reason to identify the mean, for courage and for the other virtues. Even though practical wisdom will be manifested whenever and wherever courage is manifested, it will not be true to say that courage just *is* (one application of) practical wisdom. The two dispositions remain separate, and continue to do separate work in each case where both apply, so that their relation avoids the problem of overlap. Moreover, what we can say about practical wisdom and courage can no doubt be paralleled by what we can say about practical wisdom and each of the other virtues; so it looks like this solution to the problem of overlap generalizes.

Our proposal that practical wisdom is the disposition to use reasoning to find the mean in which the virtues of character lie thus seems usefully able to resolve section 1's three puzzles. Moreover, by resolving the unity problem, the proposal also enables us to be (relatively) *specific* about the nature of practical wisdom. On this proposal practical wisdom is not, as it is on some modern views (such as particularism, of which more in section 7), a vague shapeless catch-all, an indeterminate rag-bag for all the odds and ends we cannot accommodate anywhere else in our ethical theory. Nor is this doctrine of practical wisdom mere obscurantism, like too many contemporary statements of particularism:[10] it is not just a lofty refusal to tell us anything much about right and wrong, beyond saying that they are whatever superior men (or, occasionally, women) tell us they are. (The classic instance of this lofty refusal is McDowell 1998: 73: 'Occasion by occasion, one knows what to do, if one does, not by applying universal principles but by being a certain kind of person: one who sees situations in a certain distinctive way.') Again, the view cannot reasonably be charged, like some other accounts of practical wisdom, with any objectionable sort of intuitionism. While there is room in the view for a perceptual element to be at work, helping us to 'see' where the mean lies, the proposal is also sensitive to a crucial restriction on moral perception, one which is too little noticed by enthusiasts for a purely perceptual understanding of practical wisdom, that Aristotle imposes at 1139a20: 'perception is not the source of any action'.[11] And it does not make the implausible claim that practical wisdom is nothing but a sort of extra-sensory (or extra sensory?) perception.[12] Practical wisdom remains a form of *reasoning* about practical matters, of which 'perceiving the particulars' is only one part. And it displays enough rational structure and substantive, stateable content to be both teachable and, in section 1's sense, discussable.

6 THE FALSITY OF THE DOCTRINE OF THE MEAN

That, then, is how we might spell out the proposal to rest our account of practical truth, and hence of practical wisdom, on the doctrine of the mean. The

---

[10] For a more thorough engagement with the leading contemporary version of particularism, Jonathan Dancy's, see Chappell 2005a.

[11] In context, of course, 'perception' here refers to a capacity that is being contrasted with *nous* and *orexis*; so it may be open to the fan of moral perception to dismiss this passage as irrelevant to *moral* perception. All the same, it would be better if we could avoid so dismissing it.

[12] Aristotle's remarks on moral perception are confusing. *NE* 1142a26–30 says that it is the role of practical wisdom to perceive 'the last term'. *NE* 1143a25–b6, however, in a longer and clearer discussion, ascribes this role to *nous*. And we have already been told (*NE* 1142b26) that practical wisdom *antikeitai tôi nôi*. This could mean that practical wisdom is antithetical, or that it is analogous, to *nous*. Either way, it clearly implies that they are distinct. These three passages seem to conflict.

I suggest the following resolution. *NE* 1142a26–30 means that the intellectual virtue of practical wisdom parallels the intellectual virtue of *nous* (*nous* strictly so called, mathematical *nous*); for part of practical wisdom is the perception of moral facts which have a kind of basicity that parallels the basicity of certain mathematical facts which are perceived by *nous*. Then *NE* 1143a25–b6 begins to use *nous* in a broader way, as a name for this quasi-perceptual ability in moral matters, which is part of practical wisdom, but not the same thing as practical wisdom. This shift in terminology should not matter, provided we are not tempted to identify practical wisdom as a whole with either *nous* or moral perception.

proposal is worth spelling out, because there is *some* evidence that this is what Aristotle himself wants to do. After all, as we saw in section 5, Aristotle builds his definition of moral virtue around the doctrine of the mean, making in the process a conceptual link with the notion of practical wisdom; he also devotes a lot of space, in books 2 and 4 of the *Nicomachean Ethics*, to developing and illustrating the doctrine of the mean. A much stronger case than you would gather from many modern commentators on Aristotle can be developed for the view that the doctrine of the mean is really the heart of Aristotle's ethics.

There is, however, a very simple difficulty with this view. This is that the doctrine of the mean is false. As Lloyd 1968: 221 points out, the doctrine can hardly be meant to give us the universal and absolute rule 'Always do the thing (or favour the disposition) which is intermediate'—even where we know what being intermediate comes to. The doctrine does not provide us—and obviously cannot provide us—with any worthwhile decision procedure.

Only slightly less obviously, it provides us with no worthwhile criterion of rightness either: as Sarah Broadie aptly asks: 'What does a person do too much or too little of when he agrees to sell secrets to a foreign power?' (Broadie 1991: 100). It *might* be true that, if we are looking for a neat and schematic way to begin a theoretical exploration of the virtues, then the thought that virtues *usually* have flanking vices might be a convenient starting-point. But even that thought about how to arrange our exposition will not get us as far as a full-blown doctrine of the mean of the sort developed in section 5. As has often been pointed out, the idea that all virtues have flanking vices cannot be sustained even in the case of social virtues like justice. (Despite *NE* 1133b33, justice is obviously not a mean between suffering and doing injustice, but something that altogether excludes both; nor is justice a distributive mid-point in any non-trivial sense, since one person might *deserve* far more than another.) But even where that idea can be sustained, it is obviously far too easy to legitimate any disposition whatever simply by contriving a pair of flanking 'vices' on either side of it, and announcing that the disposition in question must be a mean just because it is so flanked.

The doctrine of the mean was often taken by later classical thinkers as a way of cashing out philosophically the commonplace Greek maxim of moderation, *mêden agan*. (In the Roman tradition see, for instance, Horace, *Odes* 2.10.5 on *aurea mediocritas*, and Apollo's well-known advice to Icarus at Ovid, *Metamorphoses* 2.134–7: 'In the middle is the safest path'.) But this connection is obviously a loose one: advocacy of a *median* disposition is in no way the same thing as advocacy of a *moderate* disposition. Perhaps Aristotle is sometimes guilty of this elision of the intermediate and the moderate: see, for example, *Nicomachean Ethics* 1119a12 *ho de sòphròn mesòs peri taut' ekhei*; and *Politicus* 284e and *Laws* 716c–d for the later Plato's anticipations (if that, chronologically, is in fact what they were) of Aristotle's view. Such a move is not only a gratuitous logical blunder, it is also inconsistent with the *im*moderate pursuit of the theoretic ideal that is recommended towards the end of the *Nicomachean Ethics*. *Eph' hoson endekhetai* *athanatizein* (1177b36) is no languid gentlemanly aristocrat's rule of life: it tells us 'to become like the Immortals', not 'so far as fits with the injunction "Nothing too much"', but '*as far as possible*'. Going beyond Aristotle's own moral universe, we can see, too, how ill the doctrine of the mean, understood in this loose way as a doctrine of moderation, fits notorious absentees from Aristotle's list of virtues such as the virtue of benevolence, or love in the New-Testament sense. There might in some cases be reason to talk of *misguided* benevolence or love, but it is not obvious that there would ever be reason to talk of *excessive* benevolence or love.[13]

Whether the doctrine of the mean enjoins intermediateness or moderation, it still seems obviously false. This fact leads many faithful Aristotelians to the view that Aristotle did not really give the doctrine a central place in his thought. Certainly there is *some* evidence for this view. (There is *some* evidence for all sorts of views in Aristotle.) But if my argument so far has demonstrated anything, it is that the doctrine of the mean does have a central place in the structure of Aristotle's account of practical wisdom. My initial questions, recall, were how to understand how practical wisdom could be a unified disposition; how it might have a sufficiently non-trivial unity to be something that we can learn, describe, explain, and debate; and how it interacts and co-operates with the other virtues, moral and intellectual. All of these questions are answered for Aristotle by showing how practical wisdom is the intellectual virtue, the disposition of the mind, that reasons to find the mean, relative to each of the moral virtues, that constitutes practical truth.

Too bad, then, that the doctrine of the mean turns out to be false. Its falsity entails that there is *no* mean constituting practical truth for each virtue; and so, that there is no work for a mean-locating rational disposition to do. Without the doctrine of the mean, the present explanation of the non-trivial unity of practical wisdom, and of how it cooperates with the other virtues, simply falls apart.

7 IMPASSE, AND THE PARTICULARIST WAY OUT

What are we to do about this *impasse*? We could reject the reading of Aristotle that has led to it, but I have already said that I shall not be doing that here. I might add that anyone else's reason for rejecting this reading of Aristotle had better not just be that it implies that Aristotle's view is committed to a large-scale falsehood. That may be a disappointing result, but it is hardly an impossible one.

A second response is simply to accept the *impasse*, and admit that there is no non-trivially unitary form of reasoning that practical wisdom can operate; hence,

---

[13] Cp. Coope, Ch. 1, this volume. Unlike Coope, I take charity/love/benevolence to be a virtue. Though his suspicion that this virtue is a shapeless make-do, designed to fill any conceptual gap that appears, is too like my own suspicion about practical wisdom for me not to endorse it, I think that suspicion can be answered for love, as it can for practical wisdom.

practical wisdom is indeed not a unitary disposition, and the problems that I began section 1 with are insoluble. Or we could stick at the point reached by the end of section 4, and insist that, although the doctrine of the mean is false, still practical wisdom does have *some* sort of unity: namely the unity of a disposition *to find practical truth*—however much unity that may be, and perhaps it is not very much.

To take either of these alternatives is to offer a more or less 'particularist' response to the impasse. I have already suggested (sections 1 and 5) some reasons for finding the particularist response inadequate. The further we go in the particularist drection, the less we can have to say about what specifically the disposition of practical wisdom consists in. We shall have to be at least moderately generalist to be able to give an account of the disposition of practical wisdom that is sufficiently specific to make it plausible that practical wisdom is a genuinely and non-trivially unitary disposition, and hence both identifiably distinct from the moral virtues with which it interacts, and also—the real prize—teachable and discussable.

Aristotle himself, in passages like *NE* 1104a3–10, is famously one of the main inspirations for contemporary particularists. Aristotle's own particularism, or rather alleged particularism, is represented by his famous remark that ethics is concerned with *tòn hòs epi to polu* (*NE* 1094b21), with matters where generalizations hold only for the most part. Clearly this remark tells us to pay *some* attention to the uncodifiable in life. But it does not say what you might expect Aristotle to say, if you had read some of his recent particularist interpreters: that no ethical generalization is any use at all. 'The most part' of life is, after all, quite a lot of it. Perhaps we shall be confronted with two hundred cases that *do* fall straightforwardly under a rule telling us not to lie, before we ever meet even one case where it takes careful judgement to decide whether or not we ought, or are permitted, to lie. Or perhaps Aristotle's generalization that ethical generalizations admit of exceptions itself admits of exceptions—and there are some ethical generalizations that we *can* take as universally and absolutely binding. (At *NE* 1107a12 Aristotle himself takes just this view of the generalizations: 'Do not commit adultery, theft, murder'.)[14] In any case, the idea that ethics involves the exercise of uncodifiable judgement is not proprietary to the particularists: even to decide that some case falls straightforwardly under some rule is itself an exercise of uncodifiable judgement. So exercising judgement in ethics is one thing; doing ethics more or less entirely without rules or principles, as some particularists propose (e.g. Dancy 2004), is quite another.

Particularist readings of Aristotle run into a number of other problems too. Here, for instance, is David Bakhurst on McDowell (Bakhurst 2001: 161):

Drawing on Aristotle, McDowell argues that the ability to discern moral reasons involves the exercise of a form of practical wisdom (*phronesis*). McDowell's position is contexualist

---

[14] See Coope, Ch. 1: pp. 38–9, for the same suggestion.

in that it sees practical wisdom as a capacity acquired in enculturation. . . Its acquisition represents our coming to occupy the moral point of view, from within which alone moral demands can be rendered fully perspicuous. . . practical wisdom is viewed as akin to a perceptual capacity (to discern the good). . .

About this certainly McDowellian, and allegedly Aristotelian, view Bakhurst has a variety of interesting comments to make. One thing he does *not* say is that Aristotle so read has no obvious use for the distinction that I stressed in section 3, between moral and intellectual virtues. (Nor does Bakhurst remark, as I would, that Aristotle so read is wide open to the three objections I began with.) This seems to me to be an important obstacle to the particularist reading of Aristotle.

Here is another problem, which connects with the overall particularist tendency that I am criticizing to turn practical wisdom into a catch-all virtue. This tendency is widespread, and not confined to particularists. The popular equation between practical wisdom and something nebulous called 'judgement' is, for instance, accepted unhesitatingly by Thomas Nagel:

The fact that one cannot say why a particular decision is the correct one, given a particular balance of conflicting reasons, does not mean that the claim to correctness is meaningless. . . What makes this possible is *judgement*, essentially the faculty Aristotle described as practical wisdom, which reveals itself over time in individual decisions rather than in the enunciation of general principles.   (Nagel 1979: 135)

Maybe there is such a thing as judgement in Nagel's sense—an uncodifiable knack for choosing right between conflicting reasons; maybe we even need judgement in this sense. The problem is that Aristotle certainly never describes *phronesis* as such a knack. The catch-all or rag-bag view of *phronesis* is here at its full development—and has lose contact altogether with anything that Aristotle actually says.

Another common (mis-)reading of Aristotle which is popular with particularists has him saying that practical wisdom determines the aim of life as well as *ta pros ton skopon*. For this reading, see McDowell 1998: 30: 'Aristotle can equate practical wisdom both with the perceptual capacity (*NE* 1142a23–30) and with a true conception of the end (*NE* 1142b33).' McDowell's proof text here is 1142b33. But what 1142b33 actually says is that *euboulia*, deliberative excellence, is defined as 'a rightness with respect to what is advantageous towards the end, of which practical wisdom is a true grasp' (*orthotês kata to sympheron pros to telos, hou hê phronesis alêthês hypolêpsis estin*). The crucially ambiguous word here is the underlined *hou*, 'of which'. Does Aristotle mean that practical wisdom is a true grasp *of the end*, or *of what is advantageous towards the end*? The text can be read either way: Broadie and Rowe, perhaps deliberately, leave it ambiguous. But since Aristotle does not say that practical wisdom is a grasp of the end anywhere else, and explicitly denies that claim at *NE* 1144a9, it seems much better to take *hou* as abbreviating *tou sympherontos*, not *tou telous*.

Particularism fails us, both as exegesis of Aristotle and as a way out of our *impasse*. So let us look for something else to fill the gap that has been left by the demise of the doctrine of the mean. Maybe we can say something else to explain what practical wisdom is; and maybe this alternative account of practical wisdom will not face the crushing objections that the doctrine of the mean faces. This is what I shall try to do in sections 8–9. In the process, I too shall go well beyond Aristotle. But at least I shall be frank about this; and at least I shall begin from something Aristotle does actually say, that 'practical wisdom's most characteristic realisation is good deliberation (*to eu bouleuesthai*)' (*NE* 1141b11), and say nothing (so far as I can see) that is inconsistent with what Aristotle says.

My suggestion is that, to understand the specific work of practical wisdom, what we need to do is take a closer look at what deliberation involves. To scrutinize this, I turn from Aristotle to Hume.

8 WHY NOT ALL MOTIVATIONS ARE DESIRES

As every schoolboy knows, Hume says that every intrinsic motivation is a desire. This claim is enormously popular among philosophers nowadays; which is odd, because, at the commonsensical level, the evidence is very much against the claim. Almost everyone, almost everywhere, is constantly doing intentionally things that they say they *don't* want to do: visit the dentist, change their babies' nappies, rescue people in wheelchairs from burning buildings, and so on. So there are quite a lot of cases that suggest that a motivation to φ does not always result from a desire to φ.

There are even cases that suggest that what results from a desire to φ can sometimes be a motivation *not* to φ, and/or a desire to get rid of the desire to φ. Think, for instance, about finding yourself desiring to lynch Jews, or to molest small children. Finding that you have *this* desire, you are, quite rightly, appalled at yourself. Since you are (for the most part) a reasonable and decent person, you are in no way motivated to act on this desire. On the contrary, your desire to lynch Jews or molest children motivates you *not* to lynch Jews or molest children; and motivates you more strongly than you would otherwise be motivated in that direction. It also motivates you to do whatever you can to lose that desire. 'The existence of a desire for x does not as such generate a reason to promote x, but at most is able to generate a reason either to promote x or to rid oneself of the desire for x' (Murphy 2001: 74). In such cases, the presence of the desire not only does not motivate; it actually, so to speak, *anti-motivates*.

Of course, the Humean has an obvious way of dealing with such counter-examples. She can say that my choices show that I prefer having my teeth drilled to getting holes in them; that I prefer a clean baby to a smelly one; that I prefer that the disabled should be rescued rather than burned; that I prefer not to be a child-molester and to fight my child-molesting tendencies—and so on.

This response may look like an easy fix; but, in fact, it creates serious further problems. The Humean who offers this response needs to interpret 'prefer', as it occurs in these explanations, as meaning 'desire more than'. (In the case of fighting my child-molesting tendencies, the Humean will credit me with a second-order desire that opposes a first-order desire.) Now, of course, saying that I prefer a clean baby, drilled teeth, a rescued wheelchair-user, and not to be a child-molester might mean that I *desire it more* that my teeth should be drilled, the baby should be clean, etc. However, that is not the only way of interpreting these occurrences of 'prefer'. They could equally mean that I *think it better* that my teeth should be drilled, the baby should be clean, and so on. But in that case, to say that my actions are motivated by my preferences is not to say that they are motivated by my *desires*. It is to say that they are motivated by my *beliefs about what is better*. If we can say that, then we have the conclusion that beliefs can and do motivate, which is just what the Humean view was supposed to rule out.

Here it will not do merely to camouflage these difficulties behind some such catch-all term as 'pro-attitude', which can be used (see Davidson 1980: 3–4) to gesture vaguely towards a category of unanalysed preferences, desires, and the like, all of which are then conveniently placed on the passion side of the familiar Humean dichotomy, without the question ever coming up whether some of them are not more like (for example) moral beliefs, or beliefs about what we have reason to do, than desires. (Hume himself engages in a similar camouflaging exercise when he distinguishes the 'violent passions' from the 'calm' (*Treatise* 2.3.3)—or, as we might also put it, the passions that behave like passions from the passions that do not.) We need an *argument*, and a non-question-begging one, to show why we must interpret 'prefer' as the Humean wants us to: to mean 'desire more than' rather than 'think better than'.

The trouble is not only that we get no such argument. It is also that, for quite a few cases, the Humean interpretation of 'prefer' seems positively perverse. If I am anything like most normal people, there will be no natural sense of 'desire' in which I *desire* to risk my life saving the wheelchair-user from the fire, *more than* I desire to avoid this risk. If I am a normal person then, in all probability, I shall not do the rescue because I want to more than I want not to; I shall do it because I think I ought to. And if the Humean responds at this point that I only ever do what I think I ought to because I *want to* do what I think I ought to, then he is just uninterestingly repeating himself; he is not adding any new argument for his thesis that moral beliefs do not motivate without accompanying desires.

So far, the Humean has produced no non-question-begging argument for his doctrine that only desires or passions can be intrinsic motivations. He also seems to be in danger of trivializing that doctrine to accommodate the most difficult counter-examples, such as heroic actions which are, on the face of it, directly contrary to the agent's desires, and motivated instead by the agent's moral beliefs.

But perhaps, in fairness to the Humean doctrine, we should dig a bit deeper, and ask: what does it mean, anyway, to claim that desires alone are 'intrinsically motivating'?[15]

At a first stab, you might expect this phrase to mean that desires are capable of motivating actions *all on their own*. But this cannot be right, even on Hume's own account. Suppose I have a desire for toast. Humeans will agree that, to motivate toast-seeking actions, my desire needs to be accompanied by *beliefs* about toast; for example, a belief that there is some toast on the table might be a useful accompaniment to a desire for toast.

So apparently—and I stress that this is still Hume's own account that I am expounding here—desires no more motivate action all on their own than beliefs do. To parody Kant: even if beliefs without desires are empty, still desires without beliefs are blind. To have any plausibility at all, the Humean doctrine will have to be that both desires and beliefs are necessary conditions of action. But then, if the Humean view is that both desires and beliefs are necessary conditions of action, in what sense are desires intrinsic motivations, and beliefs not intrinsic motivations?

The answer, I think, lies in a picture of the relation of desire and belief (or of passion and reason) that was first suggested by, of all people, Plato:

Our ruling part is charioteer to a pair of horses; but though one of his horses is honourable and good, and of good and honourable stock, the other horse—and his forebears too—are of the opposite kind; and this necessarily makes our chariot wayward and difficult to drive.   (*Phaedrus* 246b1–6)

What Hume takes from Plato's famous image is not its distinction between rationally controllable desire (the 'honourable and good' horse) and rationally uncontrolled desire (the other horse). It is its distinction between desire of any sort (both the horses together) and the steering or guiding of those desires by something beyond them that is not desire (the charioteer). What Hume means, then, by saying that reason in itself is 'perfectly inert', and that desire alone is a motivation, is that reason does not *move* anything, any more than the charioteer moves the chariot. It takes the horses to get the chariot moving. The role of the charioteer is only to steer those horses, not to move the chariot. Likewise, it takes a desire to get an agent moving into action. The role of the agent's reason is not to get the agent moving, but to steer and guide him as to which direction to move in: "'tis evident . . . that the impulse arises not from reason, but is only directed by it . . . reason has no *original* influence' (Hume, *Treatise* 2.3.3, italics added).

This picture of motivation is an interesting one; but it still faces the serious problem noted above, about the trivialization of the notion of desire. To repeat: as a matter of experience, and restricting ourselves to the most ordinary sense of

---

[15] For the argument of the next few pages, cp. Chappell 1995.

the word 'desire', it just is not true that everything we ever do is motivated by any desire at all. Phenomenologically speaking, doing something out of a sense of duty, or because you think you have reason to, is nothing like taking another chocolate because you succumb to an urge for chocolate. And, as before, it gets us nowhere to insist that anyone who acts out of a sense of duty, or because they think they have reason to, must have a *desire* to act on duty or reason lurking somewhere in their psychology.

Suppose we take the other alternative, and accept that an agent can be motivated by her sense of duty, and/or by her beliefs about her reasons, as well as by her desires. Then what becomes of the *Phaedrus* model of the relation of reason and passion? Beliefs about my reasons or my duties surely belong, for Hume if not for Plato, on the reason side of the reason/passion dichotomy; so these beliefs should be on the charioteer side of the *Phaedrus* model. But if we admit that they are motivations, then they are on the horse side of that model as well. So they end up on *both* sides? Here the *Phaedrus* model breaks down.

9 WHY NO MOTIVATIONS ARE DESIRES

So far the picture is that not only desires are motivations: some beliefs about my reasons, or my duties, can be motivations too if desires can. If this is right, and only some motivations are desires, that takes us a long way from the Humean view that all motivations are desires. My next argument takes us even further away, by showing not merely that *only some* motivations are desires, but that *no* motivations are desires.

The argument is this. The Humean desire-belief model of motivation sets two necessary conditions for an agent to act: it says that there must be (1) a desire and (2) a belief in that agent. (Or rather, of course, a *nexus* of desires, and a *nexus* of beliefs: the complication is important, and I'll come back to it in a moment.) If we accept the Humean desire-belief model, then the next question is: are these two *necessary* conditions of action also *sufficient* conditions for action, when taken together?

Crucially, the answer to this question is No. A desire (say) for toast, and a belief (say) that there is some toast on the table, are not going to motivate me to take toast from the table unless a further condition is met: that I should *put my desire and my belief together in my practical thinking*. Unless I see the mutual relevance of this desire and this belief, they will not bring me to do anything at all. So we should add a third necessary condition, alongside the conditions requiring the presence of a belief and a desire respectively. We should also require that the belief and the desire *should be seen by the agent to be practically relevant to each other*.

So far I have been hedging round expressing this by talking about reasons, but now let me put it this way. In general, desires and beliefs will do no motivational work at all until they are perceived by the agent as *combining to give her reasons*. Thus, for example, a desire and a belief about toast can combine in the following way:

> (D) I want toast;
> (B) This here is toast;
> So
> (R) (D) and (B) together give me reason to eat this.[16]

In this simple practical syllogism—to use the usual term—'D' stands for 'desire'. 'B' stands for 'belief'. And 'R' stands for what you get by combining this desire and this belief to get something genuinely capable of motivating action in its own right: namely, of course, a *reason*.

My claim is that only items of the (R)-variety are capable of the intrinsic motivation of actions. (I thus reach, by a different route, the same conclusion as Jennifer Hornsby (2004: 2): 'My objection to the standard [desire-belief] story of agency will be that . . . *the story leaves agents out*.') It is only when we reach the (R)-line that we have something that can lead the agent to bring about something that will, so to speak, be *his own doing*: something not produced by the operation of the laws of the world upon him, but by *his operation* of the laws of the world. (Compare Kant 1785: 24: 'Everything in nature works in accordance with laws. Only a rational being has the capacity to act *in accordance with the representation* of laws, that is, according to principles, or has a *will*.')

Since it is only items of the (R)-variety that are capable of intrinsic motivation, it should now be clear why I deny not only that *all* intrinsic motivations are desires, but also that any desire at all is ever intrinsically motivating. I would equally deny, of course, that any belief at all is ever intrinsically motivating—unless it is a belief about reasons of the form exemplified by (R).

('But why should we think that the (R)-line can motivate on its own? Don't we need an extra line after the (R)-line, saying that the agent desires to do what she recognizes she has reason to do?' No we do not. To insist that we do is simply to refuse to be budged from a dogmatic Humeanism. Also, if we *did* need this fourth line, it is hard to see why we would not be equally entitled to insist on

---

[16] In discussion, nearly ten years ago now, Rüdiger Bittner and the late lamented Martin Hollis (to whose memory I dedicate this chapter) both suggested that the distinctive feature of my account of the practical syllogism—the (R)-line—risks generating a vicious regress of the Achilles-and-the-tortoise sort. I reject this suggestion. The regress is real, but harmless. It is no more vicious than the parallel regress which starts off with '(E) There's evidence that p' and (ER) 'The fact that there's evidence that p gives me epistemic reason to believe that p'. Of course, thinking the (R)-thought *might* lead you to think an (R')-thought: '(R') (R), (D) and (B) together give me reason to eat this'. But I see no reason why it *must* lead you to think that thought. The point about the (R)-line, relative to a possible regress of (R')-, (R'')-, (etc.) lines, is that it is the first line in the regress that *first adds a rationalization of the action* to the story. All the subsequent lines in the regress rationalize the action, too (again, the epistemic parallel is instructive). But I see no particular reason why an agent needs to think them, given that the first line already gives him all he needs to get on and act.

a fifth line, saying that the agent has reason to do (what she desires to do and recognizes she has reason to do), and a sixth line, saying that the agent desires to do (what she has reason to do, namely (what she desires to do and recognizes she has reason to do))—and so on into a regress.)

There is a further point about the (D)-side of such practical syllogisms: which is that, despite its name, the (D)-side does not need to be occupied by a desire. It can be, of course; but for reasons explained above, it can also be occupied by beliefs about my duty or (in a general sense) about my reasons for action, which will then combine with information drawn from the (B)-side to yield more specific beliefs about my reasons. A still more strongly anti-Humean moral follows from this last point: namely that there can be actions whose motivational aetiology does not involve desire even at the (D)-stage.

However, of course, the aetiology of actions is more complex than my simple practical syllogism might seem to suggest. I have already pointed out that there will normally be not a single belief or desire in the (B) and (D) lines of the practical syllogism but a whole nexus of such items. This fact strengthens my anti-Humean case; for it helps to show that reason has a further role to play in motivation. This is the selection of which beliefs or groups of beliefs it is appropriate to act upon; and the selection of which desires—or groups of desires, or groups of desires and beliefs about my duty and beliefs about my reasons—it is appropriate to act upon. In thus selecting and making judgements of appropriateness, our rationality has a role to play that shows us much about the nature, not only of practical reason but also, by easy extension, of practical wisdom. Remember *NE* 1141b11: what is practical wisdom, if not practical reasoning *performed well?*

The performance of a practical syllogism is rarely, if ever, as straightforward a matter as the toast example I have been working with. Even in that case, there will be many other factors to consider; at the bare minimum, there will be the consideration that 'Nothing else is relevant besides these factors'. How could we reach the judgement (R) from the premises (D) and (B) if a friend were bleeding to death in the corner of the breakfast room? In that case, (D) and (B) obviously would *not* 'give me reason to eat the toast'; for I have reason to do something else that clearly overrides this reason. Thus the anti-Humean line about motivation that I have sketched here enables us to see how what we call practical *reason* (when we are thinking of simple cases like the toast case) shades off into what we call practical *wisdom* (when we are thinking of harder cases than the toast case; or when we are thinking harder about the toast case).

10 ALL'S WELL THAT ENDS WELL

Inter alia, the conception of action upon reasons that sections 8–9 have developed shows us how we might connect the notions of motivation, explanation, and justification. In the present context, the view, of course, has another important application. This is that it shows us, in outline at least, how to give an account of practical wisdom that, while not Aristotle's own, is reasonably Aristotelian in spirit, and which also deals with the three problems that I began with. Roughly, the idea will be this: seeing practical wisdom as the ability to make appropriate and rational connections between our desire-sets and our belief-sets enables us to see practical wisdom as one specific disposition (thus solving the unity problem). So to describe practical wisdom is not to make it something trivial: this account of practical wisdom makes the finding of 'practical truth' consist in the finding of appropriate and rational combinations of desires and beliefs to yield reasons. This is a pretty definite and non-trivial activity—which solves the triviality problem. It also enables us to see how this disposition does not 'crowd out' other dispositions such as the moral virtues; although it does help those virtues to reach their ends, by showing them what kind of actions might further those ends. Conversely, those virtues do not 'crowd out' practical wisdom: they set limits on its operation—by setting the ends that it is to aim at bringing about, and also by making some options salient and others not salient, or perhaps not even thinkable (Williams 1992; Chappell 2001). But the roles of the different moral virtues will remain distinct both from each other, and from the role of practical wisdom: the moral virtues will set the ends, practical wisdom will find the right ways towards those ends (*NE* 1144a9: 'practical wisdom is concerned with means, not ends'); and the co-operation of practical wisdom and the moral virtues will be what enables the agent to arrive at practical truth in his actions. This also settles the third of my opening problems, the overlap problem.

It is, of course, true that there is much more to say about practical wisdom, so described, than I can say here. In particular, there is this: if practical wisdom is, as I have claimed, the ability to make appropriate and rational connections between our desire-sets and our belief-sets, then we need to know more about what criteria for appropriateness and rationality are applicable. The answer to this question has been left wide open by my argument here. What is needed to answer it is no more and no less than a normative ethical theory; and I obviously cannot try to supply one of those in this chapter.

Now particularism is, among other roles it serves, one sort of normative ethical theory. So it is still possible that the particularist answer to the question what appropriateness and rationality come to, when we are thinking about combining desire-sets and belief-sets, might be the right one. If that were right, then first, all the objections that I have raised here (especially in section 7) to particularism as an account of practical wisdom would resurface as objections to particularism as a normative ethical theory; and second, with or without those objections, it would not follow that we have made no progress here. If we have narrowed down the question what *phronesis* is to the question how to combine desire-sets and belief-sets so as to see what we have reason to do, that seems like very significant progress to me. It may still mean that, if practical wisdom has the unity of a single disposition, then it has that unity fairly loosely. But *some* looseness in our account of practical wisdom seems entirely inevitable, if we are to find a way of doing justice not only to the unity of practical wisdom but also to the variety of life.[17]

[17] I first tried to express the worry about Aristotelian *phronesis* that is the starting-point for this chapter in conversation with Sarah Broadie. Thanks to her, and also, for other helpful discussions and comments, to Alexander Bird, Tal Brewer, Andy Clark, John Collins, Christopher Coope, Neil Cooper, Nicholas Denyer, Francis Dunlop, Nick Everitt, Lloyd Fields, Christopher Hookway, Dan Jacobsen, Rachel Jones, Andrew Mason, Peter Milne, Adam Morton, Mark Nelson, Tim O'Hagan, Catherine Osborne, Rupert Read, Angus Ross, Dory Scaltsas, Peter Sheldon-Green, Pepa Toribio, and numerous others in audiences in Edinburgh, Stirling, Norwich, Manchester, and Dundee.

8

Moral Sense and Virtue in Hume's Ethics

Paul Russell [1]

> This constant habit of surveying ourselves, as it were, in reflection, keeps alive all the sentiments of right and wrong, and begets, in noble natures, a certain reverence for themselves as well as others, which is the surest guardian of every virtue.
>
> Hume, *Enquiry Concerning the Principles of Morals* 9.10 [2]

1 MORAL SENSE AND 'MORAL BEAUTY'

On the face of it, Hume's understanding of the relationship between virtue and moral sense seems clear enough. According to Hume, a virtue is a quality of mind or character trait that produces approval, and vice a quality of mind that produces blame (*T* 614; cp. 473,575). This relationship between virtue and vice and our moral sentiments is described and analysed by Hume as part of his wider and more general account of the mechanism of the indirect passions. Any quality or object, Hume maintains, that is closely related to a person and that produces either pleasure or pain will give rise to an indirect passion. In the case of pride and humility the quality or object must be closely related to myself, whereas in the case of love and hate the quality or object must belong or be related to some other person. When the quality or object is pleasant we shall feel either pride or love, when it is painful I feel either humility or hate. To illustrate this, Hume provides the example of a beautiful house (*T* 279, 289, 330, 516, 584, 617).

[1] I am grateful to my audience at the *Values and Virtues Conference* (Dundee, May 2004) for their helpful comments and discussion. I would especially like to thank Tim Chappell for his philosophical and editorial assistance.

[2] All page references are to the Selby-Bigge/Nidditch edns. of Hume's *A Treatise of Human Nature* [*T*], 2nd edn. (Oxford: Oxford University Press, 1978) and his *Enquiries* [*EU/EM*], 3rd edn. (Oxford: Oxford University Press, 1975). Other references to Hume's writings are to *A Letter from a Gentleman to his friend in Edinburgh*, ed. by E. C. Mossner and J. V. Price (Edinburgh: Edinburgh University Press, 1967); *Essays: Moral, Political, and Literary* [*ESY*], rev. edn. by E. F. Miller (Indianapolis: Liberty Classics, 1985); Dialogues Concerning Natural Religion [*D*], ed. by N. Kemp Smith, 2nd edn. (Edinburgh: Nelson, 1947).

When a house is viewed as giving pleasure and comfort and it belongs to myself, it produces an independent and distinct pleasurable feeling, which is pride. If the same house is sold or given to another person, it will generate love (i.e. as directed at that person). If the house is found to be in any way unfit for occupancy or poorly designed, then it will produce either humility or hate, depending on whether the house belongs to me or to some other person.[3]

Hume suggests that there are several different kinds of things that may give rise to pride and humility, love and hate. These include, most notably, virtues and vices (i.e. qualities of mind); beauty and deformity (i.e. qualities of body); along with property and riches. It is an important aspect of Hume's system of ethics, therefore, that our senses of approval and disapproval (i.e. our moral sentiments) find their place in the wider fabric of our emotional responses to the pleasant and painful features and qualities that belong to all human beings. Related to these observations, Hume maintains that, through the influence of sympathy, we come to feel in ourselves not only the immediate pleasure and pain that our own personal qualities and related objects may produce in others but we also come to share the 'secondary' influence of the approval and disapproval, love and hate, that they feel towards us on this account (*T* 316, 332, 362–5). Simply put, when a person causes pleasure or pain in others, she becomes pleasant or painful to herself, through the influence of sympathy and the indirect passions. This influence is compounded by the love and hate that we arouse in others on the basis of our various qualities and characteristics. For this reason, our personal happiness depends to a significant extent on our 'reputation' as determined by 'the sentiments of others'. While the operations and influence of sympathy is significant as it concerns *all* of those features about us that affect the sentiments of others, Hume maintains that this is *especially* true of the virtues and vices (*T* 285, 295).

In several different contexts Hume defines virtue and vice in terms of their power to produce the relevant indirect passions.

Now since every quality in ourselves or others which gives pleasure, always causes pride or love; as every one, that produces uneasiness, excites humility or hatred: It follows, that these two particulars are to be consider'd as equivalent, with regard to our mental qualities, *virtue* and the power of producing love or pride, *vice* and the power of producing humility or hatred. In every case, therefore, we must judge the one by the other; and may pronounce any quality of the mind virtuous, which causes love or pride; and any one vicious which causes hatred and humility.   (*T* 575; cp. 296, 473, 614)

Clearly, then, it is Hume's view that our moral sentiments serve not only to distinguish virtue and vice, by way of making us *feel* a satisfaction or uneasiness on the contemplation of a character (*T* 471), but that these sentiments also serve the purpose of securing some general correlation between virtue and happiness,

---

[3] Here I skirt around the details of Hume's complex account of the mechanism that produces the indirect passions. Fundamental to Hume's description is the double association of impressions and ideas. For more on this, see Russell 1995: 61–2.

vice and misery. On this view of things, human moral sense serves as a kind of 'back-up' or 'support' system for the virtues, whereby the moral sentiments generated by virtues and vices will directly affect on a person's happiness, in so far as she contemplates her own character or is made aware of the sentiments of others (*T* 365, 576–7, 591, 620; *EM* 276–7, 289).

Hume's account of virtue leans heavily on the analogy involved in the phrase 'moral beauty'. (This analogy is also prominent in Shaftesbury 1711 and Hutcheson 1725.) Any beautiful object, he points out, will give some sensible pleasure or satisfaction to those who contemplate it. In the case of inanimate objects, such as tables or houses, their beauty is chiefly derived from their utility (*T* 299, 364, 472). However, a beautiful house or table will not produce love or pride unless the object is related to a person in some relevant way whereby the person becomes the object of this sentiment. In the case of physical or bodily beauty the relevant close relationship is easily identified and will produce love or pride for the beautiful person (*T* 300). Moral beauty operates on our passions and affects our happiness in much the same manner (*T* 295, 596, 618–21; *EM* 276). One difficulty with the 'moral beauty' analogy is obvious. We do not generally regard people as morally responsible or accountable for qualities that are not chosen or do not reflect their own will in any respect. The difference between virtue and beauty, as it is generally understood, is not based simply on a distinction between mental and physical traits, but also between traits that do or do not reflect a person's will and choices in life. Nevertheless, Hume, as his analogy suggests, plainly rejects this perspective on the distinction between virtue and beauty.

The unorthodox nature of this aspect of Hume's account of virtue is perhaps most apparent in his discussion of natural abilities. Hume rejects the suggestion that there is any significant distinction to be drawn between 'natural abilities', such as intelligence and imagination, and moral virtues more narrowly conceived (justice, truthfulness, benevolence, etc.). In both cases, Hume argues, the qualities under consideration 'procure the love and esteem of mankind' (*T* 607; *EM*, 321–2). Hume also rejects the suggestion that the moral virtues are somehow more voluntary than physical beauty or the natural abilities. He admits that the distinction may be supposed to be of some significance, since we cannot use rewards and punishments or praise and blame to alter people's conduct very much in respect of their natural abilities, though we can in respect of justice, truthfulness and the other moral virtues (*T* 609; cp. Plato, *Protagoras* 323c–d). This concession does not, however, alter Hume's basic position: that our natural abilities are found pleasurable, and give rise to sentiments of love and approval, just like the moral virtues.[4]

---

[4] There are, of course, two questions about voluntariness and virtue in Hume that need to be distinguished. One is: are moral virtues concerned only with dispositions of choice—is acting 'in accordance with virtue' solely a matter of our choices or decisions? The other is: must moral virtues

Hume's presentation of virtue as 'moral beauty' raises a number of puzzles about how exactly he understands the relationship between virtue and moral sense. On Hume's analysis, both beauty and virtue affect people pleasurably, and that pleasure gives rise to some form of love and approval. It is also clear, however, that a beautiful person need not herself have any sense of beauty or deformity in order to be beautiful or become an object of love as produced by the pleasure she occasions. These observations raise the question of whether a person can be thought virtuous if they lack any *moral sense*. Is there is any essential connection or dependency, logical or psychological, between being capable of virtue and possessing moral sense? Surprisingly, Hume provides no clear statement about where he stands on this important issue.

This puzzle relates to another concerning the moral status of animals in Hume's theory. Hume points out that 'animals have little or no sense of virtue and vice' (*T* 326). It does not follow from this that animals lack pleasant or painful qualities of mind that may arouse moral sentiments in those who contemplate these traits. In fact, Hume makes clear that animals 'are endow'd with thought and reason as well as men' (*T* 176) and they are no less capable of sympathy and passions such as love and hate (*T* 363, 397 f., 448; and cp. *EM* 302). It cannot be Hume's view that animals are incapable of virtue and vice simply because they acquire their mental traits *involuntarily*, since he is, as we have noted, careful to dismiss this as the basis of any account of virtue. Moreover, while it is true that human beings are superior to animals in respect of their powers of reason, Hume points out that differences of this kind can also be found from one person to another (*T* 610). Given these observations, we may also ask whether Hume's account of virtue extends to cover the mental qualities of 'mad-men' (*T* 404) and infant children. In these cases, the individuals in question are obviously *people* and, as such, are, according to Hume's principles, natural objects of the indirect passions (*EM* 213 n.). Since they too possess mental qualities that are pleasurable or painful, isn't Hume bound to regard people in these categories as legitimate objects of moral sentiment (however incapacitated they may be in respect of reason, moral sense, and so on)?

2 MORAL SENSE AND VIRTUE: EXTRINSIC AND INTRINSIC VIEWS

I have argued elsewhere (Russell 1995: 91–3, 179–80) that Hume's views about the nature of moral virtue run into serious difficulties on these questions, and that

---

always be voluntarily acquired? Hume takes the same permissive approach to both questions; his position on the status of natural abilities makes it clear that he does not regard the moral virtues as limited in either of these ways. Someone can be properly called virtuous in ways that go beyond the nature of his dispositions of choice; and virtues need not be voluntarily acquired to be real. (Contrast Aristotle.) I discuss these points in more detail in Russell 1995: ch. 9.

this is indicative of his general failure to provide any adequate account of moral capacity. For present purposes, however, I want to focus attention on the specific relationship between virtue and moral sense as presented in Hume's system. It may be argued, consistent with Hume's wider set of commitments on this subject, that there is something more to be said about the absence of moral sense in animals, the insane, and infant children as it relates to their limited capacity for virtue. More specifically, there may be a deeper connection between moral virtue and the capacity for moral sense than a casual glance through Hume's writings seems to suggest. Hume may have overlooked or downplayed the significance of this relationship because he has—unlike Aristotle—little or nothing to say in his major writings about how the virtues are actually acquired, developed, and sustained. One obvious possibility here is that our 'moral sentiments' or 'moral sense'—as Hume uses these phrases, to denote our general capacity for moral approval and disapproval—have an important role to play in the way that we acquire the virtues and provide support for them. It is this suggestion, as it relates to Hume's ethics, that I want to consider more closely.

Hume draws a basic distinction between the natural virtues (for example, generosity, benevolence, and compassion) and the artificial virtues (for example, justice and loyalty). In the case of the artificial virtues, he is primarily concerned with a system of conventions and rules that determine property and its distribution in society. Hume describes in some detail how these conventions arise and the way in which self-interest is our original motive for establishing and complying with them. He also points out, however, that injustice will displease us even when it is 'so distant from us, as no way to affect our interest' (*T* 499). The psychological basis for this is that we naturally sympathize with the effects of unjust conduct on other people; for this reason we shall view even 'remote' cases of injustice as vice. (Thus we *moralize* the conventions of justice.) Given our interest in justice, and our moral attitudes in respect of the rules involved, children quickly learn, according to Hume, the advantages of following the conventions that have been laid down, as well as the importance of their 'reputation' for justice (*T* 486, 500–1, 522, 533–4; *EM* 192). Our moral sentiments, therefore, play an essential role in cultivating our reliability and trustworthiness in respect of the virtue of justice. Hume observes that parent and politicians alike rely on this mechanism to support artificial virtues of this kind. When an individual ceases to care about her honour and reputation as it concerns justice and honesty, we can no longer be confident that this person will follow those conventions on which our society and mutual cooperation entirely depends.

If, on Hume's account, moral sense plays a crucial role in developing and supporting the artificial virtue of justice, then the next question is: does moral sense play any similar role with respect to the natural virtues? Although Hume pays less attention to this issue, very similar considerations apply. As a child grows up she is made aware that her mental qualities, as they affect others and herself, will inevitably give rise to moral sentiments in the people she comes into contact with. When a person is generous and benevolent, not only will she be treated well by others, she will become aware that she is being treated well *because* other people approve of her virtue. Through the influence of sympathy, the approval of others will itself become an independent source of her own happiness and provide further grounds for feeling proud or approving of herself. This entire process of becoming aware of the moral sentiments of others, and then 'surveying ourselves as we appear to others', is one that serves to develop and sustain the natural virtues just as well as the artificial virtues (*T* 576–7, 589, 591, 620; *EM* 276, 314). Experience of this kind gradually makes a child aware of those dispositions and traits of character that bring approval; and this approval serves as a fundamental source of happiness for the virtuous person, thereby supporting and sustaining these dispositions. This whole process depends on the individual's not only having a capacity for the particular natural virtues but also a capacity to experience the kinds of moral sentiments that cultivate and sustain these virtues.

Whether we are concerned with the relationship between natural virtue and moral sense, or the relationship between artificial virtue and moral sense, two different interpretations of Hume's views seem possible. The first, which I shall call the *extrinsic* view, denies that there is any role for moral sense in cultivating and sustaining the virtues. On this view, the role of moral sense is limited to distinguishing between virtue and vice, and providing some mechanism that correlates virtue with happiness and vice with misery (i.e. as might also be done in a future state). There is, on this view, no suggestion that the virtuous agent must also be capable of experiencing and interpreting moral sentiments in order to *become* virtuous. It must be granted that Hume's relative reticence on the question about the relationship between virtue and moral sense, and his apparent lack of interest in providing any detailed account of how we acquire and sustain the virtues, may seem to suggest that he takes the extrinsic view.

In contrast with the extrinsic view, the *intrinsic* view maintains that virtue is acquired and sustained through the activity and influence of moral sentiments or moral sense. More specifically, according to this view it is because people have acquired the habit of 'surveying themselves as they appear to others', and aim to 'bear their own survey', that these people are able to acquire the virtues that they have. It is this pattern of moral development, on the intrinsic account, that is essential for the full and stable creation of a virtuous character.[5] My claim is that, although Hume's remarks on this subject are scattered and disconnected, a number of his remarks and observations are consistent with the intrinsic view; and a case can be made for saying that this is the view that he takes.

[5] For a discussion of moral emotions in moral development, see Damon 1988: ch. 2. On the role of reflection in Hume's moral theory see Annette Baker, *A Progress of Sentiments* (Cambridge MA: Harvard University Press, 1991), esp. ch. 8.

3 THE INTRINSIC VIEW AND THE ROLE OF MORAL REFLECTION

What is the significance of the intrinsic view of the relationship between virtue and moral sense for our understanding of Hume's wider ethical scheme? It is, as I have already suggested, a general failing of Hume's account of virtue and vice that he has so little to say about moral capacity and incapacity. More specifically, Hume's suggestion that virtues and vices should be understood simply in terms of pleasurable and painful qualities of mind seems both implausible and incomplete. However, perhaps the intrinsic view of the relationship between virtue and moral sense can help us here. If moral sense is required for the full development and stability of a virtuous character, we may ask, what is required to develop and preserve moral sense?

It is commonplace to give a rather 'thin' reading of Hume's account of the nature of moral sense, taking it to be constituted simply by pleasant or painful feelings of a peculiar kind (*T* 472). But this reading does not do proper justice to the complexity and subtlety of Hume's account. In a number of contexts, and most notably in the first section of the second *Enquiry*, Hume argues that moral evaluation of conduct and character involves the activity of both reason and sentiment.

The final sentence, it is probable, which pronounces characters and actions amiable or odious, praiseworthy or blameable; that which stamps on them the mark of honour or infamy, approbation or censure; that which renders morality an active principle and constitutes virtue our happiness and vice our misery: it is probable, I say, that this final sentence depends on some internal sense or feeling, which nature has made universal in the whole species . . . But in order to pave the way for such a sentiment, and give a proper discernment of its object, it is often necessary, we find, that much reasoning should precede, that nice distinctions be made, just conclusions drawn, distinct comparisons formed, complicated relations examined, and general facts fixed and ascertained. (*EM* 172–3)

It is evident, then, that according to Hume, the exercise of moral sense involves a considerable degree of activity by our 'intellectual faculties' (*EM* 173). Hume further explains this feature of his ethical system by returning to the analogy of 'moral beauty'.

There are, Hume claims, two different species of beauty that require different kinds of response from us. In the case of natural beauty our approbation is immediately aroused and reasoning has little influence over our response one way or the other. On the other hand, the kind of beauty that we associate with the 'finer arts' does require a considerable amount of reasoning 'in order to feel the proper sentiment; and a false relish may frequently be corrected by argument and reflection' (*EM* 173). Hume argues that 'moral beauty partakes of this latter species, and demands the assistance of our intellectual faculties, in order to give it a suitable influence on the human mind' (*EM* 173). The sort of 'intellectual' activities required include, not only learning from experience the specific tendencies of certain kinds of character and conduct, as well as the ability to distinguish accurately among them, but also the ability to evaluate character and conduct from 'some steady and general point of view' (*T* 581; *EM* 227 ff.). Our ability to enter this general point of view and evaluate a person's character and conduct from this perspective, is essential, on Hume's account, if we are to be able to formulate a 'standard of merit' that we can *all* share and refer to (*T* 583, 603). When we evaluate a person's character—including our own—from this wider perspective, we find that this more 'distant' and 'impartial' view of our object of evaluation generates calm passions, which may easily be confused with the effects of reason alone (*T* 583, 603; and cp. *T* 417–18, 470).

The significance of this account of how our moral sense depends on the activity and influence of our 'intellectual faculties' in relation to virtue is clear. In so far as the cultivation and sustenance of virtue depends on moral sense, it follows that virtue also requires the intellectual faculties involved in the exercise of moral sense. An animal, infant child, or insane person obviously lacks the ability to perform the intellectual tasks involved in producing moral sentiment. It will therefore not be capable of acquiring those virtues that depend on moral sentiment. It follows that we cannot expect the virtues that are so dependent to be present when the relevant psychological capacities are absent or underdeveloped. It is evident, then, that on Hume's account, there is more to moral sense than mere pleasant or painful feelings. No one who lacks the reasonably high degree of intellectual development required for moral reflection from 'the general point of view' is capable of moral sense, nor can they acquire and maintain the moral virtues that depend upon it.

4 MORAL REFLECTION AS A MASTER VIRTUE

The question I now want to turn to is whether moral sense can itself express or manifest a virtue of any kind. Once again, Hume's analogy of 'moral beauty' sheds some light on this issue. The cultured or refined individual, who shows appreciation for 'the finer arts', is a person who possesses a 'delicacy of taste' (*ESY* 235). This capacity to become a refined and cultivated person requires training, experience, and (again) intelligence of a certain kind. The 'true judge' in respect of these matters, Hume says, has a 'strong sense, united to delicate sentiment, improved by practice, perfected by comparison, and cleared of all prejudice' (*ESY* 241). To possess refined taste is itself, according to Hume, a manifestation of a 'valuable character' (*ESY* 241). Hume's analogy of 'moral beauty' suggests that the virtuous person must also develop an ability to measure his own merit and that of others by means of some relevant 'standard of virtue and morality' (*T* 583, 591, 603; *EM* 229). For this reason, we should no more expect a virtuous person to lack any reliable moral sense than we expect to find a refined person who lacks any 'delicacy of taste'. Moreover, as we have noted, the moral sense, no less than delicacy of taste, requires experience, comparison, and an impartial perspective. Clearly, then, virtue, like refinement, must be cultivated through relevant forms of experience and training that are filtered through the lens of a disinterested and impartial 'general point of view'. An individual who regularly and reliably 'surveys' herself in this way is best placed to 'correct' her own character and conduct where it strays from the relevant shared standard.[6]

The development of moral sense begins with an awareness of being the object of the moral sentiments in the context of family and friends, but we then learn to view ourselves in this same light—in Burns's phrase, 'to see ourselves as others see us' (*T* 292, 303, 320–2, 486, 589).[7] This disposition to 'survey ourselves' and seek our own 'peace and satisfaction' is, as Hume says, 'the surest guardian of every virtue' (*EM* 276). It may be argued, therefore, that moral reflection, where we direct our moral sense at ourselves, and review our own character and conduct from a general point of view, serves as a *master virtue*, whereby a person is able to cultivate and sustain other, more particular, virtues. A person with this disposition of moral reflection is one who we might otherwise describe as 'conscientious' or 'morally aware'—moral awareness being a character trait that is, on Hume's account, essential to acquiring a fully developed and steady moral character. On the other hand, an agent who entirely lacks this disposition is a person who will be shameless. Such a person will inevitably lack all those virtues that depend on moral reflection for their development and support.

The role of moral sentiment is crucial, on this interpretation of Hume, for cultivating and sustaining the moral virtues. However, Hume also points out certain limits and complexities that are arise here. For example, as we have noted, Hume points out that, although the natural abilities and moral virtues are 'on the same footing' in respect of their common tendency to produce the indirect passions of approval and disapproval, he also acknowledges that praise and blame have little influence in changing the former (*T* 609). It may be argued, going beyond Hume's own observations, that one of the reasons we draw a significant *distinction* between the natural abilities and moral virtues is precisely that the development and cultivation of the former prove to be generally *insensitive* to the role of praise and blame or moral reflection. That is to say, in other words, that the natural abilities, like our physical attributes and qualities, are 'deaf' to praise and blame in a way that the moral virtues are not. Both the stupid and ugly person may be acutely aware how their qualities affect others, but this awareness does

---

[6] It is worth noting, however, that the beautiful person, unlike either the refined or virtuous person, need not herself possess any relevant 'standard' of beauty in order to be beautiful. On the other hand, a refined delicacy of taste may help a person to cultivate her own (physical) beauty.

[7] Cp. Smith 1976: 83, 110, 111 n., for the metaphor of holding up a 'mirror' to ourselves so that we can 'judge of ourselves as we judge of others'.

little or nothing to improve or change their qualities and characteristics. This is not to say that the moral virtues can be chosen or altered at will—obviously the situation is not as simple as this. It is, rather, that through a *process* of moral reflection and awareness of the moral sentiments of others the agent's will can be *gradually* transformed or modified, especially when the agent is still young and her character remains malleable. The natural abilities are generally less sensitive to any influence of this kind.[8]

I have argued elsewhere (Russell 1995, 91 f. and 126 f.) that Hume's interpretation of moral virtue in terms of pleasurable (or painful) qualities of mind is too wide. More specifically, our moral sentiments should be understood in terms of *reactive value*—we value people according to how they express or manifest value for themselves and others. This is why neither the ugly nor the stupid person can be judged an appropriate object of *moral* disapproval. This observation relates to the general point that I have made above about the relevance of moral sense to moral virtue. When an agent is an object of reactive value (i.e. moral sentiments) this may serve to restructure her own value commitments in some relevant way. There is no similar possibility in relation to fundamental physical qualities or natural abilities since they are not themselves bearers of value commitments.

It may be argued that, in some contexts, Hume expresses considerable scepticism about the power of moral reflection to alter or change our moral character. For example, in the *Treatise* Hume suggests that it is 'almost impossible for the mind to change its character in any considerable article, or cure itself of a passionate or splenetic temper, when they are natural to it' (*T* 608; cp. 517; and *EM* 321; *ESY* 169, 244). At the same time, however, he is equally insistent that our 'constant habit of surveying ourselves, as it were, in reflection, keeps alive all the sentiments of right and wrong, and begets in noble natures, a certain reverence for themselves as well as others, *which is the surest guardian of every virtue*' (*EM* 276; cp., 314; *T* 620). Moreover, where we find ourselves lacking some motive required for virtuous conduct, we shall he says, hate ourselves on that account and may nevertheless perform the action 'from a certain sense of duty, in order to acquire by practice, that virtuous principle, or at least to disguise to himself, as much as possible, his want of it' (*T* 479). Moral sentiments, therefore, serve to 'correct' and restructure our conduct and character in such a way that the mind is able to 'bear its own survey' (*T* 620). This is, indeed, the most powerful influence available to promote and preserve a virtuous character.

Clearly, then, while Hume acknowledges that there are some limits to the influence of moral reflection, it has, nevertheless, considerable influence on our character and conduct. In his essay 'The Sceptic' Hume perhaps expresses his 'complex' view on this subject with more precision than he does elsewhere in his philosophical writings. In this essay he begins by pointing out that 'mankind are

---

[8] Even here, however, this limitation can be exaggerated. Clearly work, study, and application can always *develop* our talents—in so far as we have talents.

almost entirely guided by constitution and temper', but he goes on to qualify this claim in some important respects:

> If a man have a lively sense of honour and virtue, with moderate passions, his conduct will always be comfortable to the rules of morality; or if he depart from them his return will be easy and expeditious. On the other hand, where one is born of so perverse a frame of mind, of so callous and insensible a disposition, as to have no relish for virtue and humanity, no sympathy with his fellow-creatures, no desire of esteem and applause; such a one must be allowed entirely incurable... He feels no remorse to control his vicious inclinations: He has not even that sense or taste, which is required to make him a better character.   (*ESY* 169)

This kind of character clearly bears close resemblance to Hume's much-discussed 'sensible knave', who appears in the 'Conclusion' of the second *Enquiry* (*EM* 282–3). This is an individual who has 'lost a considerable motive to virtue'—which is an 'inward peace of mind, consciousness of integrity, a satisfactory review of our own conduct' (*EM* 283). The problem with the sensible knave is that he is not disposed to moral reflection, and so is capable neither of the happiness derived from virtue nor of the particular form of misery occasioned by vice. Without the master virtue of moral reflection the sensible knave lacks an especially important motive to virtue, and without this we may, as Hume observes, expect that his 'practice will be accountable to his speculation' (*EM* 283).

If our 'sense of honour and virtue' is 'the surest guardian' of our moral character, how, we may ask, can we cultivate this disposition to moral reflection and self-correction? Hume's remarks in his essay 'The Sceptic' make clear that no philosophical system or method can provide a reliable 'remedy' to the predicament of the 'sensible knave'. There is, however, an 'indirect manner' by which we can cultivate a 'sense of honour and virtue'. In the first place, Hume suggests, 'a serious attention to the sciences and liberal arts softens and humanises the temper, and cherishes those fine emotions, in which true virtue and honour consists' (*ESY* 170). According to Hume, a person 'of taste and learning... feels more fully a moral distinction in characters and manners; nor is his sense of this kind diminished, but, on the contrary, it is much encreased, by speculation' (*ESY* 170). (This description, of course, closely follows Hume's account of the 'true judge' in respect of matters of taste.) Hume goes on to note that along with the influence of 'speculative studies' in cultivating a sense of virtue and honour, we may also add the importance of habit and having a person 'propose to himself a model of a character, which he approves' (*ESY* 170). Clearly, then, there is, Hume suggests, a degree of truth in the suggestion that we can learn to be good. This process begins, on his account, with the cultivation of a sense of virtue and honour through 'speculative studies' and the sort of intellectual disciplines that facilitate, among many other things, moral reflection.

5 CONCLUSION: THREE FALLIBLE BUT RELIABLE CORRELATIONS

Let me conclude this chapter returning to the problem that we began with. I have been primarily concerned to show that although Hume has little to say of a direct nature about the relationship between moral sense and moral virtue, we can, nevertheless, fill out a more complete understanding of his position by putting together a number of scattered and disjointed observations that he makes. The most important of these observations, I have argued, lead us to Hume's 'intrinsic' understanding of the relationship between virtue and moral sense. It is Hume's view that a person's ability to cultivate and sustain the virtues depends to a considerable extent on her possessing a moral sense. More specifically, it is the disposition to moral reflection—the constant habit of surveying ourselves from the general point of view—that is 'the surest guardian of every virtue'. For this reason, as I have explained, the disposition to moral reflection, as based on our moral sense, may well be described as a 'master virtue' for Hume's system of ethics. This point suggests that there are interesting parallels between Hume's 'master virtue' of moral reflection and Aristotle's account of practical wisdom as a master virtue (i.e. one which is always involved where the virtues are present) (*NE* 1144b20).

With another reminiscence of Aristotle, our moral sense as Hume understands it may be described as functioning like the rudder on a ship, which keeps us sailing in the direction of virtue, away from the rocks of vice (cp. Aristotle's use of *oiakizontes* at *Nicomachean Ethics* 1172a21). This rudder, however, cannot guide us by means of either reason or feeling on its own. On the contrary, for moral sense to guide us in the direction of virtue we must first exercise those 'intellectual faculties' that 'pave the way' for our sentiments of approval and disapproval. Our moral sense, therefore, operates effectively to promote virtue only through the *fusion* of reason and sentiment.[9]

One final set of points needs to be made if we are to remain faithful to the full complexity of Hume's final position on moral sense and virtue. The relationships that structure Hume's system of ethics are those between virtue and happiness; moral sense and virtue; and moral education and moral sense. In the case of virtue and happiness, though it is clear that our happiness depends on more than being virtuous, and that even the most virtuous person may not enjoy 'the highest felicity' (*ESY* 178), it is still Hume's basic contention that 'the happiest disposition of mind is the virtuous' (*ESY* 168; cp. *EM* 140). The

---

[9] Cp. Chappell, Ch. 7 of this volume on practical wisdom as knowing how to combine desire and belief inputs to form reasons.

general correlation that Hume sees between virtue and happiness is not infallible, but it is strong and steady enough to support moral and social life.

Similar qualifications apply, as we have noted, to the correlation between virtue and moral sense. The presence of moral sense is not a *perfect* guarantor that a person will always act in a morally admirable manner. It is, however, a reliable sign that this person will be strongly motivated to virtue, and that whenever she departs from the rules of morality she will aim to reform her conduct. The same imperfect but sufficiently reliable connection holds between moral education and moral sense. There is no philosophical programme or system, Hume maintains, that can provide us with a perfect formula that will always succeed in producing a sense of virtue and honour. Nevertheless, by means of 'speculative studies' and philosophical reflection, we may employ our 'intellectual faculties' to 'pave the way' for those refined sentiments which will generally serve to support and sustain a tolerably virtuous character.

Any philosophical system or programme that aims to provide us with correlations more perfect than these, Hume suggests, depends on illusion and encourages vain hopes and expectations. The important point for Hume's purposes is that the relevant correlations between virtue and happiness, moral sense and virtue, and moral education and moral sense are all steady and strong enough to support moral life as we actually live and experience it. The modest task of Hume's philosophy is simply to identify and describe these general correlations, and to show us their influence and importance in the operations of the moral world.

9

Can Nietzsche be Both an Existentialist and a Virtue Ethicist?

Christine Swanton

1 INTRODUCTION

Nietzsche is reasonably seen as an important figure in the Continental Existentialist tradition. This fact, it seems, poses large problems for understanding him as a virtue ethicist. Two major ones, to be addressed in this chapter, are:

(1) Existentialism does not provide, and may even be opposed to, 'morality'. In Nietzsche's writings at least, the emphasis on subjectivity and individuality results in the accusation that his thought deserves the label 'immoralist'.

(2) Existentialism is opposed to the idea of a human nature, and thereby a general account of virtue and vice, whereas virtue ethics bases its conceptions of virtue on a view of human nature.

I shall argue that the existentialist and virtue-ethical strands of Nietzsche's thought can be reconciled by showing that Nietzsche's allusions to virtue and vice have a common theme.[1] later built on by both existentialist writers and the psychoanalytic dissection of the inferiority complex. The theme is escape from self—its uniqueness, its freedom, its creativity, its suffering, its memories, its impotence, its vulnerability. Throughout his writings Nietzsche emphasizes this feature, for example:

Haste is universal because everyone is in flight from himself . . . [we] live in fear of memory and of turning inward.[2]

---

[1] My claim is not that Nietzsche's focus on this theme leads him to provide a full account of virtue and vice. On the objections to any such claim, see my 'Nietzschean Virtue Ethics', forthcoming in Stephen M. Gardiner (ed.), *Virtue Ethics Old and New* (Ithaca: Cornell University Press).

[2] 'Schopenhauer as Educator' in *Untimely Meditations*, trans. R. J. Hollingdale (Cambridge: Cambridge University Press, 1983), 158.

One must learn to love oneself—thus I teach—with a wholesome and healthy love, so that one can bear to be with oneself and need not roam.[3]

One kind of understanding of Nietzsche's existentialist thought certainly creates insuperable problems for a virtue ethical reading of him: an understanding described thus by Julian Young:

[Nietzsche] none the less retains the Cartesian view of the self as a disconnected, self-sufficient, atomic individual: an individual . . . with 'free' 'horizons' (*The Gay Science* 343), a blank sheet characterized by nothing but the power of free choice.[4]

Free (in a sense), disconnected, and self sufficient (to an extent) human beings may be, but a blank sheet? Not on Nietzsche's view. Or so I shall argue. Central to this argument is taking seriously Nietzsche's claim that value resides in the depths and not on surfaces:

. . . among us immoralists at least the suspicion has arisen that. . .the decisive value of an action resides precisely in that which is *not intentional* in it, and that all that in it which is intentional, all of it that can be seen, known, 'conscious', still belongs to its surface and skin—which, like every skin, betrays something but *conceals* still more . . ..[5]

The depth analysis of value to which Nietzsche is alluding, including his analysis of resentment, is pivotal to a virtue-ethical reading of him. For a virtue is not a surface phenomenon—not a surface intention, let alone a mere action or choice, but a disposition of character embracing at least motivational and affective states, including those not transparent. Of course, the above quotation from Nietzsche does not of itself point to the existence of character traits, but Nietzsche quite standardly characterizes our behaviour in virtue and vice terms, where, I shall argue, the distinction between virtue and vice is understood through the analysis of depth motivation.

Before I make out a case for this claim, we need to see how it is possible for Nietzsche's existentialist tendencies to be compatible with his virtue ethics. For existentialism itself is standardly thought to be either devoid of moral content, amoral, or, in Nietzsche's incarnation especially, downright immoral. In the next section I shall argue that at least much of existentialist thought can be understood in a different light: in a way that is friendly to my reading of Nietzsche. True, existentialism does not necessarily provide a complete ethics, but that is not its point. However, its central focus and question is the same as Aristotle's: what are the fundamental flaws to which humans are subject, inhibiting their prospects of living a good life (whether or not that life is properly to be held meaningful, in some sense)? And how should those flaws be remedied or avoided?

---

[3] Nietzsche, *Thus Spake Zarathustra*, in *The Portable Nietzsche* ed. and trans. Walter Kaufmann, (Harmondsworth: Penguin Books, 1982), Prologue 5, 129.

[4] Nietzsche, *Thus Spoke Zarathustra*, in *The Portable Nietzsche*, ed. and trans. Walter Kaufmann (New York: Penguin Books, 1959), Part III, 'On the Spirit of Gravity, 2', 305.

[5] Julian Young, *The Death of God and the Meaning of Life* (London, New York: Routledge, 2003), 96.

2 EXISTENTIALISM AND VIRTUE ETHICS

For Aristotle, the fundamental problem of the human condition is our tendency to hedonism: so temperance is perhaps the fundamental virtue. Without temperance, according to Aristotle, we go wrong in our handling of all the 'external goods': money, power, honours, friends. In much existentialist thought, integrity and moral/intellectual courage are fundamental, for these correct our variously expressed tendencies to escape the self by living the inauthentic, comfortable, cowardly life of the 'they', the herd, within the conventions and ceremonies of religion or social roles. The concerns of existentialists—despair, facing one's death, the sense of absurdity or pointlessness, fear of freedom—were not the concerns of Aristotle.

None the less, existentialist thought, like Aristotelian thought, is targeted on central tendencies and failings in human beings for which the cultivation of certain attitudes is a corrective.[6] The central common thread in existentialist thought is the emphasis on the individual: the profound sense in which she is not just a mere part of a comforting and comfortable whole, the responsibility that this entails, and the anxiety and fear that is its concomitant. For Kierkegaard, the religious commitment is not just a matter of being part of a tradition, but involves 'fear and trembling' in one's passionate and personal commitment to faith. For Heidegger, the individual's greatest task and fear is facing her own death, which essentially has to be done on her own. For Sartre, the real terror is freedom, and personal responsibility for one's own choices, as opposed to passive acquiescence in role duties and expectations. For Camus, the problem is the ultimate absurdity and meaninglessness of one's life, and the individual's personal task is to face this fact, and take a suitable fearless approach to it.

Nietzsche is squarely within this tradition. The comforting and comfortable whole from which the individual must extricate herself is the mediocre herd, concerned only about their small pleasures, into which the 'last man' sinks without trace into a quagmire of passivity and will-lessness. Creativity is the energizer which allows the individual to escape from hedonism, comfort, and mediocrity. Expressed thus, is the existentialist tradition in general at odds with virtue ethics? My answer is: no. In fact I shall go further. Virtue ethics in the analytic tradition would do well to supplement itself with a discussion of many of the insights of continental thought. For its own distinctive take on human problems considerably enriches the discussion of virtues needed as 'correctives' to characteristic human weaknesses. Let me provide some illustrations.

Both Kierkegaard and Camus focus on a proper attitude towards the features of individual lives which make us, as individuals, seem absurd, worthless,

---

[6] *Beyond Good and Evil*, trans. R. J. Hollingdale (London: Penguin Books, 1973), § 32, 63.

insignificant. Kierkegaard's answer is to have a proper attitude to the subjective, through commitment and involvement in the 'warp and woof'[7] of life, and to avoid the perspective of what I have elsewhere called hyperobjective vice—the disposition to see the world, intellectually and emotionally, from the perspective of the Cosmos, the world-historical, of one detached from all personal features, including her bonds and commitments.[8] A master of portraying hyperobjective vice is Camus. One's work is seen as meaningless since it cannot be differentiated from the meaningless activity of Sisyphus. From the perspective of the Cosmos all is equally meaningless or insignificant. One's friends are seen as not really friends because they are just, fundamentally, undifferentiated persons:

I say 'my friends' moreover as a convention. I have no more friends; I have nothing but accomplices. To make up for this their number has increased; they are the whole human race. And within the human race, you first of all. Whoever is at hand is always the first.[9]

Camus attempts to portray a proper disposition towards the temptations described. The perspective of the Cosmos—the 'point of view of Sirius'[10] as he puts it—is the intellectually correct perspective. The vice consists in taking this perspective seriously at an emotional level, falling into despair as a consequence. Virtue consists in laying 'one's heart open to the benign indifference of the universe',[11] in fully embracing the absurd by rebelling randomly against all and sundry, in realizing that life will be 'lived all the better if it has no meaning'. For him, 'Living is keeping the absurd alive.'[12] Hope is not a virtue, for this attitude has to 'involve the certainty of a crushing fate, without the resignation that ought to accompany it'.[13]

Kierkegaard's solution is superior in my view because Camus' insistence that the hyperobjective perspective of Sirius is the correct objective perspective leads him to embrace an *emotional/practical* solution to potential despair consisting in what (in *Virtue Ethics: A Pluralistic View*) I call hypersubjectivity—an endorsement of the lifestyles of the absurd in which resignation gives licence to self-indulgence and lack of restraint. Kierkegaard, by contrast, contrasts the life of commitment, the properly objective life, to the aimless 'aesthetic' lifestyle of hypersubjectivity, and the hyperobjective stance of the world-historical.[14]

---

[7] Here I am indebted to the important insights of Philippa Foot. See her *Virtues and Vices* (Oxford: Blackwell, 1978), 1–18. I am not, of course, committed to the details of her analysis, nor to the idea that all virtues should be understood in this way or that this is all there is to the understanding of virtue.

[8] *Concluding Unscientific Postscript*, trans. D. F. Swenson and W. Lowrie (Princeton, NJ: Princeton University Press, 1941).

[9] C. Swanton, *Virtue Ethics: A Pluralistic View* (Oxford: Oxford University Press, 2003), ch. 8.

[10] Camus, from *The Fall*, in R. Solomon (ed.), *Existentialism* (New York: Random House, 1974), 189.

[11] Camus, *The Myth of Sisyphus and Other Essays*, trans. Justin O'Brien (New York: Vintage Books, 1955), 58.

[12] From *The Stranger*, ed. Solomon, 177.			[13] From *The Myth of Sisyphus*, ed. Solomon, 183.

[14] Ed. Solomon, 183.

Heidegger's discussion of being-towards-death also concerns the proper attitude to a fundamental problem of the human condition. If, in the contemplation of one's death, one immerses oneself in the 'they' (*das Man*—Heidegger's term for the collectivity of which one is a member, under an aspect where individuals are relatively undifferentiated) one also manifests a form of hyperobjective vice—'indifferent tranquillity as to the "fact" that one dies'.[15] 'The "they" does not permit us the courage of anxiety in the face of death' but rather a 'constant tranquillization' because one experiences dying as 'in no case is it I myself', and death 'belongs to nobody in particular.' Fleeing in this way needs to be replaced by the 'courage of anxiety', which is distinguished from its perverted form, 'cowardly fear'.[16] The courage of anxiety is occasioned by the realization that our being is essentially one for which we have a 'concern'. To flee from this concern is to have the wrong perspective on our nature: it is to think of ourselves wrongly as beings which simply occur. Heidegger's discussion thus highlights an important virtue—intellectual and moral courage.

Sartre's emphasis on freedom and personal responsibility for choice also highlights the virtues of moral courage and integrity. In his famous discussion of the waiter, Sartre illustrates the latter virtue. The discussion does not advocate a lack of commitment to being in a role: on the contrary, the authentic waiter of integrity is one who does not see the role as a game in which one 'plays' at being a waiter. One should not see one's job through the eyes merely of convention, or ceremony, which are demanded by, as Heidegger would put it, *das Man*. There is nothing wrong with fulfilling the function of a waiter, but there is something wrong with doing so mechanically, for then one infects one's being a waiter with 'nothingness', in the way that a pupil who 'exhausts himself in playing the attentive role'[17] 'ends up by no longer hearing anything'.[18] As Sartre puts it, I would then be a waiter 'in the mode of *being what I am not*'.[19] Sartre is not advocating a light-minded or irresponsible desertion of others or dereliction of role duties. Suddenly abandoning one's employer on the grounds of existential insight is not a mark of courage or integrity, but is narcissistic.

Integrity, then, is the expression of practical choice as opposed to a drifting into modes of behaviour and comportment which deny, or are an escape from, self. Like Aristotle's practical wisdom, integrity is the precondition or core of virtue, though not necessarily the whole of virtue.[20]

---

[15] From *Being and Time*, ed. Solomon, 111.
[16] Ibid. 116. This position changed, according to Julian Young, in the later Heidegger (See his *Heidegger's Later Philosophy* (Cambridge University Press, 2002).)
[17] From *Being and Nothingness*, ed. Solomon, 214.   [18] Ibid.   [19] Ibid.
[20] For an advocate of this view, see Robert C. Solomon, 'Corporate Roles, Personal Virtues: An Aristotelian Approach to Business Ethics', in Daniel Statman (ed.), *Virtue Ethics: A Critical Reader* (Edinburgh: Edinburgh University Press, 1997), 205–26. Solomon claims that integrity is the 'linchpin of all the virtues' (215).

I have argued that existentialism focuses on traits which are necessary to lead a good life. Central to the goodness of a life is that it is not, in one way or another, a fleeing from self. However, this very individualism may be seen as a problem for a virtue-ethical take on existentialist thought, and on Nietzsche in particular. For does not the use of virtue and vice terms to describe properties of individuals go right against the existentialist insistence that one not rigidly define oneself? What is problematic, however, is not accurate self-description but a kind of fleeing or insulating oneself from future possibilities by taking refuge in comforting self-ascriptions. There lies the road to ossification and rigidity, precluding self improvement—self-overcoming as Nietzsche puts it.[21] For one is never in full possession of a virtue, and to ascribe to oneself virtues in a way which suggests 'one has arrived' is a mark not of virtue but of complacency, arrogance, or self-righteousness.

There is another, related problem in reading existentialist/Nietzschean thought as compatible with virtue ethics. According to virtue ethics in the Aristotelian tradition, virtue is a state of harmony. This picture of virtue has been questioned in so far as there are, or at least are thought to be, problems with the distinction between virtue and self-control.[22] However, the harmony thesis is even more problematic for the existentialist tradition, given that tradition's pessimistic outlook on the world, and Nietzsche's claims that we are the sickest of all sick animals.[23] If anxiety is a structural feature of human life, and full health or virtue is impossible, we are always in a state of convalescence, as Nietzsche puts it. This view should not be seen, however, as structurally dissimilar to that of Aristotle, who not only distinguishes between the *megalopsychos* who is capable of great virtue, and ordinary beings, but who recognizes that approximating to (perfect) virtue is a lifelong project.[24] Nietzsche, however, goes beyond Aristotle in his greater sophistication in the treatment of the convalescent, and his recognition that there are virtues proper to them.[25]

I have suggested that the individualism of Nietzsche's existentialism is compatible with a virtue ethics whose focus is avoiding fleeing from self. However, is that individualism really an advocacy of egoistic vice: the gratification of self

[21] How virtue ethics in general can cope with the phenomenon of self-improvement is a topic I cannot pursue here. For a discussion of problems, see Robert N. Johnson, 'Virtue and Right', in *Ethics*, 113 (2003); 810–34.

[22] For an excellent discussion, see Karen E. Stohr, 'Moral Cacophony: When Continence is a Virtue', *The Journal of Ethics*, 7(2003), 339–63.

[23] *The Genealogy of Morals*, trans. Douglas Smith (Oxford: Oxford University Press, 1996), essay III, §§ 13–14.

[24] Unless, of course, one takes a strict reading of Aristotle's claim that at a certain stage in life one's character is determined and unalterable. See *Nicomachean Ethics*, trans. J. A. K. Thomson, rev. H. Tredennick (Harmondsworth: Penguin Books, 1976), 1114a8–27.

[25] See further my 'Nietzschean Virtue Ethics'.

without constraint? If a virtue-ethical reading of Nietzsche is to succeed, we must deal with the charge of immoralism. Only then can we provide a positive account of the foundation of virtue in Nietzsche.

3 NIETZSCHE'S SUPPOSED IMMORALISM

There are two kinds of deniers of morality.—'To deny morality'—this can mean, *first*: to deny that the moral motives which men claim have inspired their actions really have done so . . . *Then* it can mean: to deny that moral judgments are based on truths. Here it is admitted that they really are motives of action, but that in this way it is *errors* which, as the basis of all moral judgment, impel men to their moral actions. This is *my* point of view . . . It goes without saying that I do not deny—unless I am a fool—that many actions called immoral ought to be avoided and resisted, or that many called moral ought to be done and encouraged—but I think the one should be encouraged and the other avoided *for other reasons than hitherto*. We have to learn to think differently—in order at last, perhaps very late on, to attain even more: *to feel differently*.[26]

This passage makes it clear that Nietzsche does not recommend immoral actions, or even say that we are invariably wrong in what actions we call immoral. Rather, he is a revisionist about depth phenomena: what is wrong lies in our feelings, our motives, our general orientation towards the world. He is, in short, a revisionist about the nature of virtue. Before we develop this point, however, we need to clear away some misunderstandings which lead to immoralist interpretations.

There are two main ways in which Nietzsche's philosophy of 'life affirmation' may be thought to support species of immoralism. The first is that the life-affirming individual is thought to live a life free of constraint, especially moral constraint. Thus cruelty, conquest, wanton destruction, are held to be permitted, indeed prized. The second way speaks more clearly against the virtues of justice and less directly against virtues of benevolence and non-maleficence. This is the reading of Nietzsche as an elitist: the philosophy of life-affirmation concerns the life-affirmation of the few, rather than of all.

I shall dispute these views in this section. My argument rests on a claim that it is absolutely essential to distinguish the various layers of Nietzsche's philosophy. The charges of immoralism cannot be sustained unless we either muddle these layers, or simply ignore them.

The layers I mean are these.

(1) An account of the nature of the Cosmos. With the Death of God, we must face the fact that, as Iris Murdoch puts it, 'the world is chancy

---

[26] Nietzsche, *Daybreak: Thoughts on the Prejudices of Morality*, trans. R. J. Hollingdale (Cambridge: Cambridge University Press, 1982), Book II, § 103, P. 103.

and huge'.[27] There is no order designed to be safe for humans—there is pain, suffering, and destruction which has no purpose.

(2) The evaluation of types of human being and moralities. Nietzsche speaks of 'moralities' of types of human, e.g. herd, slave, noble, master. These can be ranked as higher or lower.

> *Morality is in Europe today herd-animal morality*—that is to say, as we understand the thing, only *one* kind of human morality beside which, before which, after which many other, above all *higher*, moralities are possible or ought to be possible.[28]

(3) Practical activity from the point of view of society as a whole. This layer provides an ethics of civil and political society.

(4) Practical activity from the point of view of the individual. This layer provides an account of individual virtue.

To confuse one layer of Nietzsche's philosophy with another is to invite a charge of immoralism in one or other of its guises. Confusion between (1) and (4) leads to a view that just as the world is harsh and cruel, so individuals have licence to be harsh and cruel; to confuse (2) with (4) is to suggest that Nietzsche is a relativist; and confusing (3) with (4) invites a charge that Nietzsche subscribes to a form of elitism incompatible with justice.

Consider first confusion between (1) and (4). Nietzsche's understanding of the world as lacking any benign order congenial to our interests may have led to a belief that, for him, a correct response to it must be radically individualistic, egoistic, even capricious and arbitrary. However, to move from the idea that from the perspective of the Cosmos the world of the everyday is superficial to the idea that we ourselves can treat that world with lack of moral regard, is to confuse (1) with (4). Nietzsche's discussion is aimed at removing the illusions of bad philosophy, so that we can create an attitude of proper objectivity, as opposed to the hyperobjectivity of the Cosmic point of view according to which, in Colin McGinn's words, 'nothing matters very much'.[29] There is no implication that because the universe is purposeless, the individuals within it must cultivate an attitude of extreme and purposeless subjectivity, where whatever desires one happens to have are left as they are, without refinement, cultivation, sublimation, discipline, to be satisfied at whim.

We turn now to the confusion of (2) with (4), another confusion giving rise to the charge of immoralism. Nietzsche claims, in his genealogical mode, that

---

[27] 'The Sovereignty of Good Over Other Concepts', in *The Sovereignty of the Good* (London: Routledge, 1970), 77–104, 100.

[28] *Beyond Good and Evil*, § 202, p. 125.

[29] Review of T. Nagel, 'The View from Nowhere,' *Mind*, 96 (1987), pp. 263–72.

history may require the occurrence of harsh 'moralities' if the social climate for moral progress is to take place. Where Nietzsche speaks of types of morality, he uses 'good' or 'healthy' in an attributive sense, so that he speaks of 'good' or 'healthy' aristocracy, meaning 'good *qua* aristocracy'. He does not mean that from the perspective of (3) and (4), aristocratic morality is good *simpliciter*; but he does claim that a good healthy aristocracy may be necessary for moral progress. Indeed, this is precisely what is going on in the following passage:

Preparatory men. I welcome all signs that a more manly, a warlike, age is about to begin, an age which, above all, will give honour to valour once again. For this age will prepare the way for one yet higher, and it will gather the strength which this higher age will need one day.[30]

Consider now a typical section from *On the Genealogy of Morals*, a section which at first sight supports the charge of immoralism:

As I said, the pathos of nobility and distance, the enduring, dominating, and fundamental overall feeling of a higher ruling kind in relation to a lower kind, to a 'below'—*that* is the origin of the opposition between 'good' and 'bad' . . . it follows from this origin that there is from the outset absolutely *no* necessary connection between the word 'good' and 'unegoistic' actions, as the superstition of the genealogists of morals would have it. Rather, it is only with the decline of aristocratic value-judgments that this whole opposition between 'egoistic' and 'unegoistic' comes to impose itself increasingly on the human conscience. . . .[31]

In this decline, the 'poisonous eye' of resentment (slave morality) gives the conception of goodness 'a new colour, interpretation, and aspect . . .'[32]

However, are we to assume from this genealogy that noble or aristocratic morality represents the highest morality to which we can aspire? The answer is an emphatic 'no'. What is lauded in the lives of the noble types is a range of social virtues: fidelity, tenderness, friendship, consideration. However, according to Nietzsche, the noble types eventually see these as fetters: they need to *escape* from these constraints. They '*regress*' to the predatory animal instincts deep within. Then they are no better than 'predators on the rampage', where civilized instincts, manifested in their social peaceable lives, are ruthlessly repressed. So the noble type, too, in his barbarity, manifests a form of a general neurosis—the need to escape from self in hostility towards others. In the slave type, the neurosis takes a different form: secretive manipulativeness and resentment, to be discussed in the next section.

It *is* true that Nietzsche prefers the noble type to the slave type:

One may have every right to remain fearful and suspicious of the blond beast beneath all noble races: but who would not a hundred times prefer fear accompanied by the possibility of admiration to *freedom* from fear accompanied by the disgusting sight of the failed, atrophied, and poisoned?[33]

---

[30] 'The Gay Science', in *The Portable Nietzsche*, § 283, p. 97.
[31] *Genealogy of Morals*, Essay 1, 2, p. 13.   [32] Ibid. 25.   [33] Ibid. 27

Again Nietzsche claims:

The active, attacking, encroaching man is still a hundred paces closer to justice than his reactive counterpart; to the extent that he has no need to evaluate his object in a false and prejudiced manner as the reactive man does.[34]

However, a preference for one bad thing over a worse thing can hardly be seen as an endorsement of the former.

Now it is true that Nietzsche refrains from labelling the noble type 'bad'. But the reason is instructive. We cannot expect leopards to change their spots: strength (of a certain type) cannot be expressed as weakness.[35] Note, however, that Nietzsche is not here claiming that strength (of an inferior type) cannot be transformed with time into a superior or greater strength. He does after all have the concept of the 'convalescent' who, though warned (in *Zarathustra*) not to be virtuous beyond his strength,[36] is surely capable of self improvement. Later, Nietzsche describes the process of this improvement: 'the transformation of cruelty into something more spiritual and divine', 'a process which runs through the whole history of higher culture (and in a significant sense even constitutes it)'.[37] It was impossible, he claims, to conceive of a noble household 'without a creature upon whom one could vent one's malice and cruel teasing. . . '.[38] And there used to be 'no festivity without cruelty' and 'even in relatively recent times' important festivities 'were inconceivable without executions, torture. . . '.[39] Does this look like an endorsement of cruelty? On the contrary, what we have here is a genealogy: an account of moral progress through a civilizing of our baser tendencies. Notice, however, that the process of civilizing can be distorted; so much so that, in slave morality, the cure is worse than the disease.

Untangling the difference between (1) and (3) is essential to undermining the claim that Nietzsche's political and social philosophy is elitist in the sense that it endorses the following claim: social and political institutions are to be constructed in such a way that the development of the best members of society is maximized. However, this interpretation of Nietzsche confuses (1) and (3) in a way which is starkly repudiated by Nietzsche in the following passage, where he distinguishes between the 'end' of humanity and its (practical) 'goal':

It is a task of history to be the mediator between these [great] individuals and thus again and again to inspire and lend the strength for the production of the greater human being. No, *the goal of humanity* cannot lie in its end, but only *in its highest exemplars*.[40]

---

[34] *Genealogy of Morals*, Essay 2, 11, p. 55.
[35] *Genealogy of Morals*, Essay 1, 13, p. 29.   [36] Part 4, 'On the Higher Man', 13, p. 403.
[37] *Genealogy of Morals*, Essay 2, 6, p. 47.   [38] Ibid. 47–8.   [39] Ibid. 47.
[40] *Untimely Meditations: On the Uses and Disadvantages of History for Life*, trans. R. J. Hollingdale (Cambridge: Cambridge University Press, 1983), 111 (trans. amended by James Conant).

However, it is not the task of political and civil society directly to aim at the production of these 'highest exemplars'. Its task is not to produce excellent specimens; rather it is to provide a nourishing environment for all to improve themselves:

Two kinds of equality.—The thirst for equality can express itself either as a desire to draw everyone down to oneself (through diminishing them, spying on them, obstructing their progress) or to raise oneself and everyone else up (through recognizing their virtues, helping them, rejoicing in their success).[41]

No single set of individuals in power can usurp the 'function' of history or evolution, *itself* deciding who the splendid types are or might be, or even how they are to be understood. For there lies the path of ossifying ideology, stagnation, or worse.

As James Conant argues,[42] the notion of an exemplar is not the notion of a specimen. The notion of a specimen is at home in the context of (1); that of an exemplar in the context of (4). The latter notion is essential to understanding Nietzsche's conception of personal morality for, Conant claims, according to that morality, each individual should have a certain type of relationship to an exemplar. This is necessary to improve oneself: for 'self-overcoming'.

To show that Nietzsche is not an immoralist is not to show that he should be read as an existentialist type of virtue ethicist. We turn now to the second difficulty in reading Nietzsche as a virtue ethicist—namely that existentialist philosophy, and Nietzsche in particular, rejects conceptions of human nature. Can Nietzsche be credited with providing a conception of human nature which might ground a notion of human excellence? This is the issue addressed in the next section.

4 VIRTUE ETHICS, NIETZSCHE, AND HUMAN NATURE

It is well known that virtue ethics is naturalistic in the sense that, according to virtue ethics, what counts as a virtue (an excellence of character) is at least partly determined by a correct conception of human nature. It is then often thought that virtue ethics is also eudaimonistic in the sense that what makes a trait a virtue is that it (characteristically) is partially constitutive, or constitutes the flourishing, of its possessor. The second claim about the nature of virtue ethics does not follow from the first, so even if Nietzsche were hostile to the second claim it would not follow that a virtue ethical reading of him is impossible. At any rate, Nietzsche's rejection of eudaimonism is based on a suspect understanding.

In *Beyond Good and Evil*, Nietzsche explicitly condemns eudaimonism (as he understands it) and philosophies of well-being.

[41] *Human, All Too Human*, trans. R. J. Hollingdale (Cambridge: Cambridge University Press, 1986), i 300 (trans. amended by James Conant).
[42] In 'Nietzsche's Perfectionism: A Reading of *Schopenhauer as Educator*', in Richard Schacht (ed.), *Nietzsche's Postmoralism: Essays on Nietzsche's Prelude to Philosophy's Future* (Cambridge: Cambridge University Press, 2001), 181–257.

Whether it be hedonism or pessimism or utilitarianism or eudaimonism: all these modes of thought which assess the value of things according to *pleasure* and *pain*, that is to say according to attendant and secondary phenomena, are foreground modes of thought and naiveties which anyone conscious of *creative* powers and an artist's conscience will look down on with derision, though not without pity.[43]

However, Aristotle and Nietzsche have more in common than Nietzsche's attack on eudaimonism and philosophies of well-being may suggest. It should be remembered that Aristotle himself does not believe that pleasure is an intrinsic good: what is 'good without qualification' is pleasure handled excellently. It is true that Aristotle, unlike Nietzsche, does not have much to say about suffering—he is far more concerned about the evils of unrestrained pursuit of pleasure. So temperance is a key virtue, understood as an excellent attitude towards the bodily pleasures; but there is no reason not to incorporate a virtue concerned with an excellent attitude towards suffering, and the excellent handling of suffering. Surprisingly we do not (I think) have a name for such a virtue—the nearest perhaps is stoicism, but I fear Nietzsche would not approve. For stoicism now has the somewhat mundane connotation of 'stiff upper lip'—a banal substitute for the kind of embracing of meaningful suffering of which Nietzsche speaks:

The discipline of suffering, of *great* suffering—do you not know that it is *this* discipline alone which has created every elevation of mankind hitherto? That tension of the soul in misfortune which cultivates its strength . . . its inventiveness and bravery in undergoing, enduring . . . has it not been bestowed through suffering, through the discipline of great suffering?[44]

The fact that Nietzsche rejects welfarist conceptions of human nature does not imply that he has *no* conception of human nature. For Nietzsche, as for Aristotle, a basic biological conception of humanity is the starting-point of his conception of health or excellence, but that starting-point is constituted by a thin rather than a thick conception of human nature. The linchpin of Aristotle's conception—delivered by the *ergon* argument—is the idea of distinctively human rationality. This thin conception of the human *ergon* is thickened throughout the *Nicomachean Ethics* by substantive normative conceptions of various emotions, conceptions of fine or noble human ends, and by his accounts of *phronesis* (practical wisdom), *prohairesis* (deliberative desire), and *nous*. In Nietzsche, the catch-cry is 'will to power'. The thin conception offered in *Beyond Good and Evil*—'A living thing desires above all to vent its strength—life as such is will to power'—[45] is likewise fleshed out throughout his writings by substantive accounts, and examples, of distorted or sick manifestations of 'will to power'.[46]

---

[43] *Beyond Good and Evil*, § 225, 154–5.
[44] Ibid. 155.   [45] Ibid. 13, 44.
[46] In highlighting the importance of this notion for Nietzsche's psychology/ethics, I am not dissenting from Bernd Magnus's view that the notion has but little general ontological/metaphysical

As in Aristotle, the transformation of the thin account of human nature into the thick is irreducibly normative. In Aristotle, rational activity as characteristic human activity is transformed into substantive conceptions of the fine and the noble. In Nietzsche, 'will to power' as a venting of strength and energy, expansion, and growth, is transformed into substantive conceptions of life-affirming or healthy expressions via contrasts with a variety of 'neuroses'—sick or life-denying forms. In both Nietzsche and Aristotle these normative transformations are the basis of accounts of virtue and vice in Nietzsche.

5 ACCEPTANCE OR SELF-LOVE

We need now to flesh out some of the transformations of the thin conception of will to power so we can obtain a more substantive idea of virtue and vice.

At the core of undistorted will to power or, put positively, life-affirming or healthy will to power,[47] are two key features, acceptance or self-love, and creativity. Acceptance or self-love is the basis of health. Genuine health as acceptance is not just mere *adjustment* to reality. As the humanist psychologist Abraham Maslow recognized,[48] it also requires self-actualization or self-realization. This for Nietzsche is constituted by joyfulness, a zest for life, courage for experimentation. Without acceptance, we fall into the vices of despair, resentment, hopelessness, cynicism: vices which are energy-sapping, because energy is dissipated into anger and anxiety. Creativity is also a component of of life affirmation (though it need not always be 'healthy'). Without creativity, we fall into vices of laziness, complacency, self-satisfaction, passivity, non-assertiveness—again all manifestations of lack of energy, and a shrinking rather than a growing process. If we lack creativity and acceptance or self-love, we become inauthentic—part of the herd, or resentful—part of slave morality.

I have space here only to discuss acceptance or self-love. It is self-love which enables us to distinguish acceptance as a core of virtue from bad acceptance, complacency, or self-satisfaction, hated by Nietzsche. Paradoxically, self-love involves a dissatisfied, even contemptuous, attitude towards the self as it is now. For Nietzsche, self-love is part of a dynamic psychology where the individual thinks himself worthy of further discovery and improvement while being dissatisfied with his present state. It is this which allows for affirmation as opposed to complacency (a sense that one has arrived) to be a part of self-love. Not only must self-love

significance: 'Discussions of will to power in larger ontological contexts, in contexts other than the psychological or organic, occur primarily in only *two* entries Nietzsche chose to publish . . .', 'The Use and Abuse of *The Will to Power*', in Robert C. Solomon and Kathleen M. Higgins (eds.), *Reading Nietzsche* (New York, Oxford: Oxford University Press, 1998), 218–35, 226–7.

[47] These are not necessarily the same: for some possible points of difference, see my 'Nietzschean Virtue Ethics', forthcoming.

[48] See, e.g., his *Toward a Psychology of Being*, 2nd edn. (New York: Van Nostrand Reinhold Co., 1968).

be distinguished from self-satisfaction, but love of other, incorporating self-love, must be distinguished from 'love' ('bad love') of other that is not so based:

> Do I recommend love of the neighbour to you? . . . You cannot endure yourselves and do not love yourselves enough: now you want to seduce your neighbour to love, and then gild yourselves with his error.[49]

Three aspects of self-love are discussed by Nietzsche:

(a) loving one's past;
(b) absence of resentment against other people;
(c) overflowing, joyfulness, and embracing of life and the world.

In all these areas, virtue can be understood in terms of self-affirmation or self-love, and vice in terms of self-hate and escape from self. For example, within category (a), strong forgetfulness is to be distinguished from that kind of forgetfulness which is an opiate designed to repress the past. Within category (b) strong forgetfulness (of slights and harms) is to be distinguished from vengefulness, and envy from the creative spirit. Cleverness, a self-effacing, manipulative, secretive, form of 'wisdom', is to be distinguished from the wisdom of the strong, described thus: 'Even the most courageous among us only rarely has the courage for what he really knows.'[50]

Within category (c), the gift-giving virtues are to be distinguished from pity, where the self 'wilts away'[51] (through escape into otherness). The 'loneliness' of solitude (escape from the sick)[52] is to be distinguished from the loneliness of resignation and withdrawal (escape of the sick). Limited friendship is contrasted with an inability to be alone, manifested in excessive sociability: 'We are afraid that when we are alone and quiet something will be whispered into our ear, and so we hate quietness and deafen ourselves with sociability.'[53]

Hastiness—a form of escape from self—is not to be confused with the overflowing urgent passion of creativity. Discipline is to be distinguished from self-flagellating asceticism (escape from the flesh), and from laziness and pleasure-seeking (escape from one's potential 'for genius', for creativity).

Within category (c), too, Nietzsche distinguishes a virtue of joyfulness displayed towards the world in all its particularity, messiness, and commonplace features, from the resignatory vices, including the philosopher's vice of escape into a world of purity, simplification, abstraction, and systematicity: 'I mistrust all systematizers and I avoid them. The will to a system is a lack of integrity.'[54]

In a depth-psychological analysis of Nietzsche's multi-faceted theme of escape from various aspects of self, we can detect three major types of escape.

---

[49] *Zarathustra*, Part 1, On Love of the Neighbour, 173.
[50] *Twilight of the Idols*, in *The Portable Nietzsche*, 'Maxims and Arrows', 2, p. 466.
[51] *Twilight of the Idols*, 'Skirmishes of an Untimely Man', 35, p.535.
[52] *Zarathustra*, Part 3, 'Upon the Mount of Olives', 267.
[53] *Schopenhauer as Educator*, 158.   [54] *Twilight of the Idols*, Maxims and Arrows, 26.

1. Self-effacement or self-abasement where one's sense of oneself as inferior is dominant. Resentment is the externalized form of this type of escape;

2. Overblown, grandiose adherence to what Alfred Adler calls the ego ideal:[55] the sense of oneself as powerful or strong;

3. Resignation or retreat (including, for example, retreat into a philosophical world of purity or abstraction).[56]

In all cases, there is repression due to an inability satisfactorily to resolve the gap between the self that one despises and the image of one's self as great, conquering, or powerful in some way. This gap, if not satisfactorily resolved, causes the psychic conflict labelled by Adler the inferiority complex, which is manifested in the types of neuroses—unsatisfactory solutions to the inferiority complex—identified above. In the first (the self-effacing solution), the 'ego ideal' is repressed; in the second (which Horney calls the expansionist solution of mastery), the sense of one's self as inferior or impotent is repressed; and in the third (the resignatory solution), one 'withdraws from the psychic battle'.

The first of these types of 'neuroses' is expressed in resentment, discussed below. The second, as we saw above, is exhibited by the noble type who cannot be constrained by, disciplined by, standards of sociability and peacefulness: he sees his society as a cage which bores him, and from which he needs to escape violently in acts of barbarism. However, in some incarnations, Nietzsche seems to give positive value to some forms of the expansionist solution.[57]

I have shown in general terms how Nietzsche's existentialist theme of the strength not to escape from self (self-love) can be understood in virtue-theoretic terms, as opposed to the 'blank slate' interpretation of some existentialist thought. Let us now fill out this picture by discussing the three aspects of Nietzsche's discussion of self-loving attitudes identified above.

The first aspect of self-love, loving one's past, is famously outlined in Nietz-sche's doctrine of the eternal recurrence:

How, if some day or night a demon were to sneak after you into your loneliest loneliness and say to you, 'This life as you now live it and have lived it, you will have to live once more and innumerable times more; and there will be nothing new in it, but every pain and every joy and every thought . . . must return to you—all in the same succession and sequence—even this spider and this moonlight between the trees . . . the eternal hourglass of existence is turned over and over, and you with it a grain of dust . . . 'The question in each and everything, 'Do you want this once more and innumerable times more?' would weigh upon your actions as the greatest stress. Or how well disposed would you have to become to your self and to life to *crave nothing more fervently* than this ultimate eternal confirmation and seal?[58]

---

[55] *Understanding Human Nature*, trans. W. B. Wolfe (London: Allen & Unwin, 1932).

[56] All these types of 'escape from self' are discussed at length in Karen Horney's *Neurosis and Human Growth: The Struggle Toward Self Realization* (New York: Norton, 1970).

[57] For more on this issue, see my 'Nietzschean Virtue Ethics'.

[58] *The Gay Science*, from *The Portable Nietzsche*, § 341, pp. 101–2.

What is being claimed here? First, the experiment makes sense only in the context of that with which it is compared. The contrast is with evaluating one's life from the perspective of the Cosmos: from that perspective, everything in your life, great and small, is but a speck of dust. Nietzsche is saying that this is the perspective to be avoided. If one dwells on it one sees one's life as insignificant—one does not have a life-affirming perspective. Secondly, notice that the wish for endless repetition of one's life is qualified. Perhaps it is fitting that only the strongest or most virtuous wish for this. If we lesser mortals were to do this we would be bereft of resources to criticize our lives as wasted or vicious, or full of suffering that is *not* meaningful (because, for example, unconnected with creativity). 'What does not destroy me, makes me stronger,'[59] even if true, does not entail that *all* suffering is good, and is to be *affirmed* as opposed to accepted without endless bitterness, or withdrawal from the world. Life-affirmation and self-love, indeed, demand avoidance of the perspective of the Cosmos, but that does not imply a demand to affirm each moment in the strongest possible way. The epistemic virtue of (proper) perspective is not attained.[60]

Certainly Nietzsche is arguing against escape from self via escape from memories—a part of oneself. But there is an issue of what counts as avoiding a weak or less than virtuous escape from self in relation to one's past. For us lesser mortals—the convalescent—accepting all aspects of our past in the sense of forgiving ourselves for wrongs done[61] is not the same as affirming it in Nietzsche's strong sense. There is a related problem in understanding Nietzsche's virtue of forgetfulness. Forgetfulness as a virtue is a tendency not to dwell on one's past with obsessive guilt or bitterness. However, strong forgetfulness as a virtue must be distinguished from two related vices. The first is weak forgetfulness which is a form of escape from self. Here one's past is repressed in order to escape the pains of memory. The second is an attitude of non-caring or insouciance about harms that one has caused, or harms to loved ones, even where the harms are serious. This latter vice is forgetfulness to excess, and is related to the expansionist errors of the second neurotic solution to the inferiority complex (the psychic conflict resulting from the gap between the sense of self as impotent, and the ego ideal) identified above under (2).

The second aspect of self-love discussed by Nietzsche is the absence of resentment—a feature of the self-effacing neurotic solution to the inferiority complex. Resentment is essentially a special form of externalized self-hate. It is one of the several forms of fleeing from self—in this case an escape from one's

---

[59] Nietzsche, *Twilight of the Idols*, from *The Portable Nietzsche*, 'Maxims and Arrows', 8, p. 467.

[60] For an interesting discussion of this virtue, see Valerie Tiberius, 'Perspective: A Prudential Virtue', *American Philosophical Quarterly*, 39 (2002), 305–24.

[61] What counts as forgiveness is a large topic which I cannot develop here. Suffice to say that (virtuous) forgiveness should be distinguished from a range of things, including excusing the wrong done to one (by, e.g., understanding it), and downgrading its seriousness.

sense of impotence. The self-hate of resentment, as Nietzsche discusses it, has two main features.

1. It is externalized, for it is manifested in forms of bringing others down, which may be subtle (as in pity), or more overt: undermining other's achievements, or their ability to take pride in them (the so-called 'tall poppy' syndrome).

2. It is self-effacing (as opposed to expansionist, to use Karen Horney's terms), since the forms of bringing down are not through cruelty, overt aggression, or conquering, but through constructing a morality designed to serve the interests of the weak. As Karen Horney expresses it, resentment is a form of 'streamlined' solution to the inferiority complex, where the sense of self as inferior is salient and the 'ego-ideal' of strength and superiority is repressed. A major symptom of this repression is the 'slave' types' 'revaluation of values'. What Nietzsche calls the heroic values are turned on their head: equality (of the first kind described in the quotation above, p. 177), meekness (self-abasing) humility, pity, are all prized.[62]

The political/ethical manifestations of resentment are expressed in a range of vices which are discussed in Nietzsche's writings. Perhaps the best-known discussion is that of pity, which has misled people into thinking that Nietzsche rejects altruism in favour of egoism. But Nietzsche distinguishes virtuous from non-virtuous altruism on the basis of their depth-motivational springs. Pity, as discussed in *Daybreak*, is a vice, for it is an externalized form of self-hate—an escape from a sense of vulnerability. This sense, though repressed in one's escape through others, is still a disguised, subtle form of revenge[63]—a repressed anger at one's own susceptibility to the fate that has befallen the one pitied. By contrast, 'overflowing' generosity is a virtue, since it springs from self-love, and a sense of having enough to give away to others. The directing of the self to others is not an escape from self; rather it is a self-love which overflows to others with whom one has a bond.

6 CONCLUSION

Nietzsche is squarely within an existentialist tradition which emphasizes individualism. However, the individualism so emphasized is not egoism. It is premissed

---

[62] There is an issue about whether this 'revaluation' is creative or merely a set of beliefs that grow on one. See Rüdiger Bittner, 'Ressentiment', in Richard Schacht (ed.), *Nietzsche, Genealogy, Morality: Essays on Nietzsche's Genealogy of Morals* (Berkeley: University of California Press, 1994), 127–38. Bittner argues that Nietzsche is wrong to think of it as creative. I claim it is creative for Nietzsche, but only in the following sense—it is a 'poisonous eye' which gives values 'a new colour, interpretation and aspect'. Given Nietzsche's depth-psychological view of phenomena, he would be generally sceptical of fully intentional rational creativity—it is rather more or less an expression of sick or healthy natures.

[63] *Daybreak*, trans. R. J. Hollingdale (Cambridge: Cambridge University Press), § 133, 84.

on self-love—a healthy bonding with oneself where one does not flee from oneself. The motif of escape from self as the basis of vice is a constant refrain in Nietzsche, and this is an existentialist theme. Furthermore, he discusses many different types of escape. Here are some:

> escape from suffering in hedonism;
> escape from the messiness and detail of the world through the abstract philosophy of pure reason;
> escape from effort in laziness and complacency;
> escape from one's uniqueness in herd attitudes and behaviour;
> escape from a sense of vulnerability in pity;
> escape from a sense of impotence in resentment and envy;
> escape from boredom or sense of impotence in cruelty;
> escape from one's body in asceticism and self flagellation;
> escape from others in loneliness (escape of the sick) as opposed to solitude (escape from the sick).

We would do well as virtue ethicists to look at traditions which emphasize obstacles to the good life different from those discussed in traditional sources for virtue ethics.

10

Manners, Morals, and Practical Wisdom

Karen Stohr

'There certainly was some great mismanagement in the education of those two young men. One has got all the goodness, and the other all the appearance of it.'

Jane Austen, *Pride and Prejudice*[1]

So says Elizabeth Bennet upon her realization that the charming Mr Wickham is a cad underneath, and that Mr Darcy, for all his haughtiness and unpleasant social manners, has a fundamentally good moral character. It is not surprising that she should be so deceived; what *is* surprising, at least to modern readers, is that Elizabeth apparently expects manners and morals to track one another. In the world of Jane Austen's fiction, it is not simply a happy accident that good manners and good morals are ordinarily found together; rather, a person's manners are the outward expression of her moral character.

In this chapter, I want to explore that claim, which is implicit in Austen's novels and, I shall suggest, resonates especially well with Aristotelian virtue ethics. I shall argue that the capacity to behave appropriately in social settings is properly understood as a virtue. Genuinely good manners contribute to, and are expressive of, morally important ends, the ends to which someone with full Aristotelian virtue is committed. They thus form an essential component of virtuous conduct.

The standard contemporary view of manners is that they are a façade, a matter of mere surface appearances. According to this view, manners can tell us little, if anything, about a person's underlying character, which is what really matters. At best, good manners are a pleasing garnish; at worst, they can deceive us into believing that a person's character is better than it is, as in the case of George Wickham, whose agreeable manners conceal malevolent aims. I shall argue here that while good manners are indeed pleasing, they have a moral significance that goes considerably beyond that. Good manners are central to moral life because

[1] The quotation is from the Oxford Illustrated Jane Austen series, ed. R. W. Chapman, 3rd edn. (Oxford: Oxford University Press), 225. All references to Austen's novels in this chapter are from this series.

they serve as the vehicle through which moral commitments are expressed and moral ends are accomplished. Thus, good manners in this sense are tied directly to an agent's grasp of moral concepts.

In this chapter, I shall defend two claims about the relationship between manners and morals. The first claim is that there is an important sense of 'good manners' in which having them is possible only in conjunction with the right moral commitments. Good manners play an important moral function, and this function can be discharged effectively only by someone whose manners express those commitments. This moralized conception of manners is what Austen, in fact, defends in her novels, and I shall follow her in defending it here. The claim implies that a vicious person like Wickham cannot have truly good manners in this sense, however charming he may be. This may seem counter-intuitive in the face of Wickham's considerable social skills. An advantage of my account of the relationship between manners and morals is that it will enable me to explain how it is that Wickham can possess such skills while nevertheless lacking good manners in the moralized sense.

The second claim is that the capacity to behave in a well-mannered way is a proper part of virtue and that in so far as a person lacks this capacity, she falls short of full virtue. It is possible to have the right moral commitments without also having the skill of acting in ways that manifest those commitments in social life. Such is the plight of Mrs Jennings from Austen's *Sense and Sensibility*. The inner workings of Mrs Jennings's kind heart are often obscured by her brash behavior and impertinent remarks. Moral principles need a vehicle for expression in social life, and good manners are a crucial part of that vehicle. The cultivation of good manners is thus an essential element of becoming virtuous.

These two claims, I shall argue, find a comfortable home in Aristotle's account of virtue, particularly the intellectual virtue of practical wisdom. I shall show how good manners, in the moralized sense, can be understood as an element of Aristotelian practical wisdom. The knowledge of what constitutes well-mannered behavior in a given situation and the skill associated with acting accordingly are part of the virtue.

The moral knowledge associated with the virtue of practical wisdom is not unitary. Rather, the exercise of practical wisdom in any given situation requires a host of concepts, skills, and dispositions. It is possible to possess some of the concepts, skills, and dispositions associated with practical wisdom without possessing others and, hence, without possessing the virtue in full. This is the case with both Mr Wickham and Mrs Jennings. Wickham is vicious indeed, but this does not preclude him from having something in common with the virtuous, and my account will explain what that is. Likewise, my account will explain what has gone wrong from a moral standpoint with someone like Mrs Jennings, whose heart is good but whose manners offend.

In the first section of the chapter, I shall give an account of what I mean by good manners and argue for their moral significance. I shall defend the two claims I described above: first, that good manners in the sense that interests me are possible only in conjunction with the right moral commitments; and second, that the capacity for good manners is an element of virtue. In the second section, I shall give an account of Aristotelian practical wisdom that can accommodate these two claims. This account of practical wisdom has considerable explanatory power when it comes to flaws in both manners and morals of the sort that Austen describes so masterfully in her characters.

1 THE IMPORTANCE OF BEING AMIABLE: WHY MANNERS MATTER

Trivial? Compared to what? World hunger? Yes, the little customs of society are less important than that. So is just about anything else. It is only once people are able to manage physical survival that manners become crucial. Then tradition is what gives a society meaning and the rules by which it lives are what make it work. We call that civilization.[2]   [Miss Manners]

It is customary to think of the rules of etiquette as more or less window-dressing on social behavior. The practice of manners is often thought to be something in which one may permissibly be interested, but not a subject for serious moral inquiry. After all, etiquette concerns itself with matters like table settings and wedding invitations, and it is hard to see the proper placement of an oyster fork as a moral issue. Moreover, the rules governing etiquette are highly conventional. The only justification that can be offered as to why an oyster fork should be placed in the soup spoon rather than with the other forks is that this is how it's 'supposed' to be done. Understandably, people are skeptical of assigning moral import to a system that cannot defend its rules more robustly than that.

Even worse, rules of etiquette can be, and indeed sometimes are, used in the service of immoral aims, such as when they are used to humiliate or embarrass people. There are some circumstances in which knowledge of proper etiquette is understood to be an indication of social class and, hence, of social worth. Those who are not in the know are occasionally treated dismissively or even contemptuously by those with 'proper' manners, who seem smug or unappealingly self-righteous as a consequence. When etiquette is used as a tool of snobbery or humiliation, it is worse than trivial; it becomes downright inimical to moral aims.

All this shows, however, is that etiquette is capable of being misused and, hence, not good without qualification in Kant's sense. It does not follow that etiquette should be dismissed as generally pernicious. Moreover, one might take the view, as American etiquette writer Judith Martin (a.k.a. Miss Manners) does,

---

[2] Judith Martin, *Miss Manners Rescues Civilization from Sexual Harassment, Frivolous Lawsuits, Dissing, and Other Lapses in Civility* (New York: Crown Publishers, 1996), 11.

that genuinely good manners preclude the use of etiquette in the service of immoral ends. On this view, using the rules of etiquette to express scorn, disdain, or disapproval towards innocent parties itself constitutes a violation of etiquette.[3] Whether one's behaviour counts as polite thus depends in part on what one is trying to accomplish. So the person who sets out to embarrass a dinner guest by deliberately serving a meal requiring unusual forks and spoons that she knows her guest cannot identify is, in fact, behaving rudely.[4] On Martin's view, the rules of etiquette are not simply morally neutral social customs; they are linked to an agent's moral aims and commitments.

What about the concern that etiquette is trivial? The importance one assigns to the rules of etiquette will be influenced by what one takes the boundaries of etiquette to be. If the realm of etiquette extends no further than table settings and invitations, then of course it is not particularly important. But, in practice, etiquette columnists are often asked questions with clear moral import, such as how to respond when someone tells a racist joke, or how to express sympathy to a bereaved friend. Good answers to such questions show careful attention to moral nuance.[5] Whether one should feel, say, moral disapproval in a given circumstance might be a question for moral theory, but moral theories generally have little to say about the best methods for conveying moral disapproval. Knowing *that* one should respond indignantly to a racist joke is not the same as knowing *how* to respond to a racist joke—with what words, with what facial expressions, with what actions. This is where the rules of etiquette step in, because what they provide us with is precisely a way of communicating these essential moral attitudes to others.[6]

Martin draws a useful distinction between the rules of etiquette, which are subject to conventions of time and place, and the principles of manners that ground those conventions, which are not.[7] She gives as an example of a principle of manners the principle that guests must show respect for their hosts. There are, of course, different rules of etiquette that govern how this is done in different

---

[3] It matters that the person is innocent. Martin thinks that known scoundrels may be met with polite scorn. I shall have more to say about this below.

[4] Of course, a dinner guest can feel humiliated by his ineptitude with forks even when there is no intention on anyone's part to make him feel inept. But if, as Martin's conception of manners implies, it is rude even to notice whether someone else is using the wrong fork, a person who accidentally uses his dinner fork to eat his salad in company should no more feel humiliated than if he did so while dining alone. Sarah Buss has more to say on this in her discussion of codes of bad manners and the misuses of codes of good manners. See her 'Appearing Respectful: The Moral Significance of Manners', *Ethics*, 109 (1999), 795–826.

[5] Etiquette writers vary considerably in their ability to notice and capture this sort of moral nuance. Among American writers, Martin is clearly one of the best. At least some of what she does in her books and columns is, I would say, properly considered applied moral philosophy.

[6] The case for this has been made by Buss, as well as by Cheshire Calhoun, 'The Virtue of Civility', *Philosophy and Public Affairs*, 29 (2000) 251–75. See also Nancy Sherman, 'Manners and Morals', in *Stoic Warriors* (Oxford: Oxford University Press, 2005). Sherman focuses especially on the relationship between emotional demeanour and moral attitudes.

[7] 'Miss Manners Rescues Civilization,' 29–30.

cultures. In some cultures, one takes off one's shoes before entering a house to show respect for one's host; in other cultures, the same action might be seen as presumptuous or even insolent. The rules vary, and perhaps even conflict, but the underlying principle of manners is the same in both cases. We might put it this way: the rules of etiquette are the particular forms of expression that principles of manners take in social life. The rules have meaning in so far as they are instantiations of the principles of manners, and the meaning will vary along with the social norms and customs of a given culture.

It is through the principles of manners that rules of etiquette get their moral implications, because the principles of manners, as Martin understands them, clearly carry moral import. The claim that we should show respect to other people is, of course, a moral claim, as are the claims that we should offer sympathy, show kindness, be loyal, give aid to those in need, and express indignation where appropriate. What the rules of etiquette do is to provide us with conventionally meaningful vehicles for showing respect or kindness, offering sympathy or aid, making loyalty or moral indignation evident. They give us concrete tools with which we can communicate our underlying moral attitudes effectively.

In American culture, addressing a stranger by her title and last name rather than by her first name, shaking her hand upon introduction, and meeting her eyes when speaking to her are all ways of expressing respect for her. In using these forms, I convey a moral attitude about someone in a way that will be understood by her and by others who witness the exchange. Likewise, by deliberately refraining from using the standard forms of greeting, I can express moral disapproval or indignation. Suppose the person to whom I am being introduced is a known leader of white supremacist group, or a former corporate executive who deliberately and unapologetically plundered employee pensions to fund his personal extravagances. If I respond to his introduction with a curt nod, rather than an extended hand and a smile, I make clear to him and others that I think his behaviour bad enough to warrant a certain level of social exclusion.[8]

This is not to say that rules of etiquette are always used to express morally significant attitudes. Some rules of etiquette serve the goals of expedience more than the goals of morality. For instance, social custom in the United States dictates that when walking on a crowded pavement, one should stay to the right, rather than the left. The point, of course, is to permit efficient foot travel, but that is not an important moral good. In keeping right on the pavement, I do not

---

[8] See 'Miss Manners' Guide for the Turn of the Millennium' (New York: Simon & Schuster, 1983), 70. I can imagine people disagreeing on this point, arguing that cutting someone off from social notice this way is a violation of basic human respect. It may be true that even evildoers always deserve at least minimal social acknowledgement, although I'm not sure Martin agrees with this. Regardless, we are surely not required to smile pleasantly and shake the hand of someone whose company we find morally repulsive and who we think we have moral reason not to engage in conversation. (Martin is careful to note that we must reserve such condemnation for proven wrongdoing.)

necessarily communicate a moral attitude.[9] Moreover, some rules of etiquette can be altered at whim, such as when family members decide that when they set the table in their own house, they will always place the knives on the left. The exact placement of the knives has no expressive point. It merely facilitates pleasant dining by ensuring that everyone can find needed utensils.

But when the rules of etiquette do have an expressive function, we have moral reason to make sure that our behaviour expresses what we want to express, and that others understand what we are communicating through our actions. What we intend to express through our actions and what others understand by those same actions can, of course, come apart. I may, for instance, intend to express respect by using American conventions for introductions when I am in Japan or Iran, but what I communicate through my behaviour may not be respect at all.[10] In order to express respect effectively, I must know which social conventions are appropriate to the situation and what meaning they convey.

Martin points out that when it comes to the rules of etiquette, originality is not usually a virtue.[11] When people decide to abandon standard forms and locutions for expressing moral attitudes in favour of something more creative or sincere, they sometimes come up with appalling substitutes. We thus get people attempting to offer sympathy by telling the bereaved that the death of a seriously ill spouse is a blessing, or reminding them that they can have another child to replace the one they have just lost. Parents welcoming a second or third child of the same sex are consoled rather than congratulated; couples planning to marry are warned about rising divorce rates. Such comments, Martin points out, may be more original than saying simply 'I'm so sorry' and 'Congratulations', but they are hardly an improvement and, indeed, can serve as an impediment to the expressive function of manners. The point of having standard locutions at all is to enable us to convey the meaning that one is supposed to convey on the occasion. It is through saying, 'I'm so terribly sorry' that one expresses sympathy in a way that will be understood by the one to whom it is offered. The person who says instead, 'you're better off this way' may indeed be feeling very sympathetic, but if her goal is to offer comfort, she will very likely miss her target. Not all remarks or actions offered with sympathy manage to convey sympathy to the other party.

---

[9] It would be disrespectful to block someone's way on purpose, and moving out of someone's way can indeed express respect in many circumstances. But this is not normally what happens when I move to the right as I walk.

[10] Whether I am, in fact, expressing respect depends, of course, on why I am using the American forms. A failure to use another culture's social forms can be disrespectful when it is motivated by arrogance or culpable ignorance. But it is not always so. It may, for instance, be hard for someone ingrained in the habit of handshaking to remember that many Muslims do not normally shake hands (or even, for that matter, to discern whether a given person is a Muslim who does not wish to shake hands).

[11] *Miss Manners' Basic Training: The Right Thing to Say* (New York: Crown Publishers, 1998), 1. I'm grateful to Maggie Little for reminding me of this.

For instance, etiquette requires that sympathy letters or cards be handwritten in blue or black ink. The rules may seem trivial, particularly to those who firmly believe that 'it's the thought that counts,' but consider what else is conveyed when one expresses one's sympathetic thoughts via fax or jotted down in purple ink on a sticky note. Writing a message by hand and putting it in the mail (or hand-delivering it) is more time-consuming than faxing or emailing one, but that is precisely the point. Death is, after all, the kind of event that warrants extra trouble. Efficiency—however appealing in other circumstances—should not normally be a goal when one is attempting to express sympathy. And since death is also a solemn occasion, avoiding the appearance of lightheartedness in one's choice of paper or ink is also required. If I fail to take this into account, my attempts at expressing sympathy will very likely go awry, because they will convey something other than what I intend (or at least, what I ought to intend). This does not mean that the rules must be followed to the point of rigidity; a close friend of a bereaved person, or an inspired eulogist, can often say things beyond 'I'm so terribly sorry' that offer great comfort. But the conventions are the starting-point and for many of us, much of the time, the ending-point as well. The thought may be what counts, but the vehicle for expressing it is itself part of the thought. By following the standard conventions for conveying sympathy, it is usually possible to express the sentiments that good people want to express on such occasions and to avoid saying or doing things that will cause additional pain.

Of course, some conventions are not worth following. The meaning expressed by rules of etiquette is, after all, not always a meaning that we should endorse. Consider, the long-standing rules of etiquette that regulate certain social behaviours by men towards women. According to custom, men are supposed to open doors for women, give up their seats to them, avoid using vulgar language in their presence, and so forth. All of these have traditionally been understood as ways of showing respect for women. Showing respect for women is still, of course, a principle of manners. Yet most people now recognize that many of these behaviours do not *really* show respect for women, because they are governed by unsustainable assumptions about women as especially weak or fragile, or creatures whose purity must be preserved. The reformation of the principle of manners 'Show respect for women' requires a parallel reformation of the rules of etiquette that are supposed to express that respect. As we improve our grasp on the underlying principles of manners through more careful moral consideration, we see that rules of etiquette often require updating and transformation. Rules of etiquette need not be, and indeed are not, static. They are (and should be) responsive to refinements in the underlying principles of manners. Over time, an action that expressed one attitude in the past can come to express something else entirely.[12]

---

[12] Of course, not everyone gets the message right away, but it is possible to be culpable for one's ignorance of changing etiquette rules. Calhoun makes the important point that treating someone with respect is not always compatible with displaying or communicating respect (264). It's possible

Thus far, I have argued that the rules of etiquette are based in principles of manners, which reflect underlying moral commitments. In acting in accordance with the rules, we express those commitments. And yet, it is possible for someone, such as George Wickham, to behave according to prevailing etiquette rules without being committed to the underlying principles of manners. This might seem to imply that good manners need not always play the expressive role I have assigned to them.

Consider a salesman who takes off his shoes when visiting his Japanese host not to show respect, but because he wants the host to give him a lucrative contract. He certainly has the appearance of good manners, and perhaps there is a sense in which it is natural to say that he has good manners, especially if all it means to have good manners is to follow the rules of etiquette. But the salesman cannot have good manners in the sense that I have described, because he is not using manners in a way that allows them to carry out their central expressive function.

The salesman's observance of the rules of etiquette is detached from any sort of commitment to the principles of manners or acknowledgement of their moral force. Borrowing from Kant, we might look at it this way: his reasons for behaving according to the rules of etiquette are tied to his business goals, not to any real appreciation for the moral aims of treating others with respect. The connection between his goals and his good behaviour is an accidental one.[13] If one day it turns out that he can increase his sales volume by offending a particular host (perhaps because it would amuse another guest who is an even better customer), then we would imagine that he will be all too happy to flout the rules of etiquette. His commitment to the rules ends where those rules cease to correspond with his non-moral aims. As such, his respectful behaviour is a kind of pretense; it does not reflect or express his true attitudes.

Although the salesman is engaging in behaviour that is ordinarily respectful, notice how odd it is to say that he is expressing or showing respect through it, given his motivational structure. What he aims at is the *appearance* of respectful behaviour; this is all he needs in order to accomplish his aims. There is a sense in which one can 'be respectful' simply by behaving in a certain way, and certainly, the salesman is not being *dis*respectful by removing his shoes. Yet his behaviour falls short of actually expressing respect. It has to, since there is no underlying respectful attitude to *be* expressed.[14]

---

that opening the door for a woman might communicate respect while still falling short of treating her with respect.

[13] My argument here parallels Barbara Herman's argument about why, in Kant's thought, duty is required as a motive in order for an action to have moral worth. The problem is not that that acting from sympathy is likely to produce inconsistent results, although it might; rather, the problem is that sympathetic motives generate right actions accidentally, not necessarily. The link between the two is not of the right sort. See 'On the Value of Acting from the Motive of Duty', in *The Practice of Moral Judgment* (Cambridge: Harvard University Press, 1993), 5.

[14] Calhoun draws a useful distinction between treating people with respect and displaying or communicating respect, the latter of which she associates with civility. On her view, however, the

So while there is some sense in which we can say that the salesman is behaving respectfully, in so far as his external behaviour mimics the behaviour of someone genuinely respectful, there is another sense in which he is not. He is not *showing* respect; he is not *expressing* respect through his actions. He wishes not to offend, but this is not the same thing. True, if the salesman is a good enough actor, he may fool others into thinking that he is showing respect, but what he is, in fact, doing differs in a morally significant way from the behaviour of someone who is really expressing respect for his host.

The reasons the salesman has for following the rules have nothing to do with manners themselves; his reasons are entirely external to the essential point of manners. As such, what he is doing when he takes off his shoes is not the same thing as what someone who is genuinely trying to show respect is doing. The truly respectful person expresses respect through taking off his shoes; the salesman does not, and indeed, cannot, given his actual lack of respect. What he is doing, therefore, is not practicing good manners themselves, but feigning good manners in my sense.

In Austen's world, those who merely feign good manners usually slip up at some point, revealing their true aims in the process. Once Wickham's real character becomes known to Elizabeth, she comes to realize that she has not seen his behaviour properly before. In retrospect, she notices indiscretions and lapses in his manners that her own vanity and prejudices had caused her to overlook.[15] From that point on, she no longer finds his manners charming. Her perception of his social behaviour has been permanently altered by her new understanding of the moral concerns, or lack thereof, that underlie that behaviour.

In real life, we cannot always count on being able to distinguish those who are really expressing moral commitments through their good manners from those for whom the manners are nothing more than a façade for immoral aims. It is reasonable to expect some inconsistency from those who fall into the latter group. After all, it isn't likely that good manners will always be conducive to their immoral aims; they are undoubtedly more likely to behave badly at some point, to someone, than those whose manners express their true moral commitments. The problem, however, is not simply that people who lack the commitment to the underlying principles are more likely to be inconsistent in their well-mannered behaviour. Rather, the problem is that when they *are* behaving well, that behaviour is not expressing what it ought to express. Good manners ought to express respect, sympathy, loyalty, and so forth. What Elizabeth comes to understand

salesman would likely count as treating his host with respect. I would disagree, but the disagreement may be nothing more than a semantic one.

[15] The newly enlightened Elizabeth reflects on Wickham's behaviour thus: 'She was *now* struck with the impropriety of such communications to a stranger, and wondered it had escaped her before. She saw the indelicacy of putting himself forward as he had done, and the inconsistence of his professions with his conduct. . . . How differently did every thing now appear in which he was concerned!' (207).

about Wickham is that his seemingly well-mannered actions never did express these things, and she was mistaken in thinking that they did. When she finally sees Wickham in the proper light, his apparently respectful actions come to look sycophantic. The sense in which he continues to have good manners in her eyes is a very thin sense indeed, since she no longer sees his good manners as expressive of anything morally admirable in his character.

Recall that my first claim was that there is an important sense of good manners according to which having good manners requires the right kinds of moral commitments. This is, I have argued, because good manners in this sense play an expressive function in social life. Following the rules of etiquette is one way in which we carry out the task of conveying respect, sympathy, and so forth. In the case of someone who follows the rules while lacking the commitments, such as the salesman or George Wickham, an essential element of good manners is absent. Although the external behaviour is there, the behaviour cannot express the underlying moral aims of manners. The forms of social life are for Wickham, only that—something to be manipulated according to his own desires without any regard for their essential moral function.

This is not to say that rules of etiquette never have value when they are not expressive of the underlying moral aims. True, the community of Hertfordshire would have benefited had Wickham's manners been worse, in so far as his good manners fooled people into thinking he had the moral character to match. I shall return to this point at the end of the chapter. But even less-than-fully sincere polite behaviour can have a moral point when it serves as an acknowledgement of something with moral significance. If I know that someone is capable of offering only polite remarks and not genuine sympathy in response to my loss, I might still want her to offer those polite remarks. This is because in going through with the social forms, she acknowledges the loss as something that calls for a response, even if she cannot marshal the full expressive force of sympathy in that response.[16] We do not, after all, always feel as sympathetic or respectful as our moral commitments direct us to feel.

One advantage of the conventions of etiquette is that they give us a way of inter-acting with the world in the way we judge that we *ought* to interact with it, rather than in the way we *feel* like interacting with it.[17] Sincerity and candour, while certainly virtues, are sometimes overrated. Etiquette does sometimes demand that we say what we do not mean or do things that imply that we feel what we do

---

[16] Then, again, I might not if I think that her polite remarks conceal a kind of malicious pleasure at my loss. But recall that on Martin's view of etiquette, using standard forms of etiquette to wound or humiliate is itself rude. So being polite in order to cause pain would not, in fact, count as being polite.

[17] In *Sense and Sensibility*, Marianne Dashwood dismisses her sister Elinor's concerns about her imprudent behaviour by insisting that her feelings are a reliable guide to moral propriety: 'if there had been any real impropriety in what I did, I should have been sensible of it at the time, for we always know when we are acting wrong . . .' (68). The novel shows Marianne to be quite wrong about this.

not feel, but this is not because etiquette values insincerity. Rather, it is because etiquette recognizes that, morally speaking, we are not always up to par, and its aim is to prevent us from letting our behaviour slide down to the level of our moods. In behaving in accordance with the rules of etiquette, it is possible to acknowledge the moral import of the principles that underlie them, even when we are incapable of expressing our commitment to those principles as fully as we should. Treating a co-worker with the forms of respect when one is thoroughly exasperated with him because he has created hours of extra work is the right thing to do because, morally speaking, he still warrants respectful treatment. My treating him respectfully when I don't feel particularly respectful towards him may seem insincere, but this is a case where insincerity has a moral point.[18] My polite behaviour expresses what I believe I should feel, if not what I do feel, and this is itself a way of expressing respect. Appearances can sometimes matter from a moral standpoint.[19]

My second claim, recall, was that failures of manners are rightly seen as failures of virtue. I said above that the rules of etiquette are the vehicle through which important moral commitments, such as respect and sympathy, are expressed in daily life. It is not that rules of etiquette are the only possible vehicles for this expression, but they serve as a crucial way of making our commitments and attitudes understood by others. As we have seen, sympathy can go badly awry when it is not expressed properly, having the effect of making the bereaved person feel worse than before. The presence of good intentions usually makes such lapses forgivable, but the mere fact that we see the lapses as requiring forgiveness tells us something about their importance. Virtuous people aim to behave in a way that reflects their moral commitments. Since social conventions serve as a primary vehicle through which those commitments are expressed, a virtuous person—if she is to act in a fully virtuous way—needs to be skilled at employing those conventions appropriately.

Austen's portrayal of Mrs Jennings in *Sense and Sensibility* illustrates what can happen when the goodness of a person's manners fails to match the goodness of her heart. Mrs Jennings is warm, generous, loyal, and certainly morally superior to most of the characters in the novel. Yet she is also meddling, tiresome, and prone seriously to embarrassing people, particularly young people whom she

---

[18] There is a world of difference between insincerity of this sort and insincerity of the kind that Wickham practises. In treating my co-worker with the forms of respect, I am treating him in accordance with what are in fact my underlying moral commitments. It's just that I am having trouble living up to them. By contrast, the forms of respect with which Wickham treats people bear no relationship to his underlying moral attitudes towards them.

[19] For more on the relationship between the appearance of morality and morality itself, see Julia Driver, 'Caesar's Wife: On the Moral Significance of Appearing Good', *The Journal of Philosophy*, 89 (1992), 331–43. Moreover, the Aristotelian account of habituation into moral virtue implies that performing right actions when we don't feel like it can be the first step towards moral improvement or even redemption. Nancy Sherman draws on contemporary psychology to show that deliberately putting on certain facial expressions can have effects on one's emotions (49–50).

fancies to be in love with each other. She regularly violates established rules of etiquette by asking impertinent questions, revealing information that she should not, and teasing people well beyond the point where they stop finding it amusing.[20] Despite her deep moral sympathies, she leaves quite a lot of minor suffering in her wake. Her considerable base of moral knowledge does not extend to the ability to see how her behaviour is affecting those around her. What she lacks—at least in part—is the proper understanding, of and appreciation for, the rules of etiquette that govern the social world of the novel and how they relate to the correct moral concepts that she already has.

It has become a standard tenet in virtue ethics that the kind of knowledge characteristic of the virtuous person is not a kind of book knowledge.[21] This is true, and indeed, I shall argue below that truly good manners require a kind of adeptness at adjusting rules to particular circumstances that is impossible without a correct grasp of moral concepts. But we shouldn't underestimate the importance of familiarity with social conventions as described in good etiquette manuals. For knowledge of etiquette is, indeed, at least partly a kind of book knowledge.[22] This is made evident by the fact that considerate people visiting foreign countries often read up on the social conventions of the relevant cultures so as to avoid causing offence by violating them. The fact that one can read up on such things at all is evidence that book learning plays an important role in acquiring the knowledge necessary to employ the skill. Before one can use the rules of etiquette to express moral attitudes, one must, after all, know what they are. The starting-point for learning the rules is through an account of the customs and conventions of a given society—just the kind of thing that one reads about in etiquette books and columns.

Of course, the knowledge that is characteristic of someone with good manners is not entirely a form of book knowledge. This is, in part, because no book can ever capture every conceivable situation in which an etiquette judgement is required, but it is also because the application of even well-established etiquette rules often requires considerable sensitivity to immediate context. Navigating the social world well—both in real life and in Austen's novels—does not consist in a kind of blind obedience to intractable social rules. Austen's heroes and heroines are cognizant of social rules and customs and take them very seriously, but they are also deeply sensitive to how those rules function in social interactions and the moral significance they carry in different contexts.

Consider, for instance, Elizabeth Bennet's decision to walk from her home at Longbourn to the fine house at Netherfield (occupied by Mr Bingley, his sisters, and Mr Darcy) in order to see her sister Jane, who has taken ill during her

---

[20] To be fair, she adheres strictly to other rules of etiquette, including rules against eavesdropping.

[21] For a discussion of this issue, see Rosalind Hursthouse, *On Virtue Ethics* (Oxford: Oxford University Press, 1999), esp. chs. 1 and 6.

[22] I do not mean to imply, of course, that reading etiquette books is the only way to acquire this knowledge.

visit there.[23] Elizabeth knows perfectly well that it is considered unseemly for a gentlewoman to undertake a solo three-mile country walk and, moreover, that by the time she arrives, her clothes will be dirtier than is appropriate for visiting, especially when those to be visited are relative strangers of high social status like those at Netherfield. Yet she goes anyway. It is not that she is deliberately flouting the rules of etiquette—she does ask her father for the carriage first, and settles upon walking only when it becomes clear that there is no other way to see Jane. But she believes that the unseemliness of her walk and subsequent physical appearance matters a good deal less than the well-being of her sister, whom she rightly judges will be helped by such a visit. In this case, Elizabeth's recognition of what has moral significance shapes her view of whether and how she ought to follow the principles of decorum that apply to her situation.

In the novel we are supposed to admire Elizabeth's choice. This is not just because we are supposed to admire Elizabeth; she makes some rather bad choices elsewhere in the novel that we need not admire. But in this scene it is the reactions of other characters that show us what we are supposed to think. The genuinely amiable Mr Bingley either doesn't notice, or (more likely) pretends not to have noticed Elizabeth's dishevelled appearance upon her arrival, and will say only that her walk indicates 'an affection for her sister that is very pleasing'.[24] He thus acknowledges the moral significance of Elizabeth's aim and the relative unimportance of the rules of etiquette in this context. Darcy, whose manners at this point in the novel still leave something to be desired, notices her appearance, admits that it violates principles of decorum, but refuses to accede to the idea that violating decorum here is evidence of a character flaw in Elizabeth. Only Mr Bingley's shallow and snobbish sisters are prepared to criticize Elizabeth's behaviour, and this is because they, unlike Bingley and Darcy, have no appreciation for the moral soundness of her judgement. They do not have the right grasp on the principles of manners underlying the rules of etiquette they take so seriously.

The Bingley sisters misunderstand the aims of the principles of manners that drive and dictate both what the rules of etiquette should be and when those rules should be altered or suspended. Their concept of respect is heavily tied to social standing and wealth, and, because of this, they do not see the relatively poor Bennet sisters as particularly worthy of respect in the first place. In their eyes, Elizabeth's disregard for the social conventions of appearance is proof of that unworthiness. The Bingley sisters thus show themselves to be ignorant of a central point to good manners, and their ignorance is what prevents them from seeing why Elizabeth's choice was a reasonable one in the circumstances.

---

[23] I am indebted to Jane Nardin's work for pointing out the significance of this scene in the overall interpretation of Austen on manners, as well as for general reflections on Austen's novels. See *Those Elegant Decorums: The Concept of Propriety in Jane Austen's Novels* (Albany: SUNY Press, 1973).

[24] *Pride and Prejudice*, 36.

In order to employ social conventions in a way that properly reflects the underlying principles of manners, one must know what matters and what does not. And in order to live in a way that expresses one's commitment to what matters, one must be able to employ social conventions in a way that make those commitments evident. In the next section, I shall argue that the Aristotelian virtue of practical wisdom captures both these elements of the relationship between manners and moral commitments.

2 PRACTICAL WISDOM, MANNERS, AND MORAL IMAGINATION

Practical wisdom (*phronesis*) is the linchpin that holds Aristotle's theory of virtue together. On his view, every virtuous action is an exercise of practical wisdom. In explaining what it is to act virtuously, we are committed to explaining what it is to act in a practically wise way. The difficulty is that practical wisdom is a notoriously difficult virtue to pin down. What Aristotle himself says about it is brief and often frustratingly opaque. Perhaps the most dominant model of practical wisdom in contemporary virtue ethics literature is a kind of 'bare perception' model, according to which acting virtuously is a matter of seeing things aright and being motivated to act accordingly.[25] There is something compelling about this model, since it draws attention to the fact that what makes an action virtuous is not the kind of thing that could ever be fully codified or specified apart from a virtuous agent's perception of the situation.

Yet, for all its appeal, the bare perception model has its limitations. For one thing, it has the unfortunate effect of making virtuous perception seem like a single, unitary skill.[26] But acting well in a given situation is usually a very complicated enterprise and, as Aristotle reminds us, there are many ways to get it wrong. Virtue ethics frequently works with a surprisingly impoverished catalogue of types of moral failure—very often only vice, incontinence, and continence. But not all moral failures can be understood or fully understood in those terms, as Austen's characters show.

Mrs Jennings, for instance, acts badly enough that we cannot call her actions perfectly virtuous, but she is neither vicious nor incontinent. Quite the contrary, she is a woman with sound moral principles and considerable self-control, who unwittingly hurts people's feelings and invades their privacy on a regular basis. And while Wickham is certainly vicious and lacks proper moral concepts,

---

[25] The primary source of the bare perception model is John McDowell's very influential account of virtue. ('Are Moral Requirements Hypothetical Imperatives?', *Proceedings of the Aristotelian Society*, suppl. vol. 52 (1978), 13–29 and 'Virtue and Reason', *Monist*, 62 (1979), 331–50.)

[26] It is unlikely that McDowell intends us to think of virtuous perception this way, but he says so little about what goes into virtuous perception that it is hard to think of it as anything but 'just seeing' what is to be done.

he nevertheless shares certain kinds of skills and dispositions with those who really are virtuous. Their respective failures are rightly understood as failures of practical wisdom, although of quite different sorts. An adequate theory of that virtue should be able to explain both how Mrs Jennings gets things wrong and what Wickham manages to get right.

The closest that Aristotle himself comes to a definition of practical wisdom is probably in Book VI, Chapter 5 of the *Nicomachean Ethics*, where he says that it is a 'state grasping the truth, involving reason, concerned with action about things that are good or bad for a human being'.[27] There is more to the story of practical wisdom in Aristotle than this definition indicates, but it is a good place to start. He has already told us back in Book I that practical wisdom is an intellectual virtue, meaning that it is an excellence of the rational part of the soul. Practical wisdom is thus a form of excellent reasoning. But about what? His answer is clear enough: about actions that pertain to the good life for human beings, or human flourishing. Aristotle, of course, is committed to the view that there *is* such a thing as the good life for a human being and that, moreover, the components of this life are more or less the same for any human being. To grasp the truth about which things are good or bad for human beings is thus to understand something about human life that is both objectively true and universal.

The person with practical wisdom knows which ends are worth pursuing in human life, a knowledge which is fundamentally dependent on the moral virtues. It is impossible to have such knowledge without the moral virtues and, moreover, the exercise of the moral virtues requires this kind of knowledge. This is the essence of the reciprocity thesis, which Aristotle makes explicit when he says: 'What we have said, then, makes it clear that we cannot be fully good without [practical wisdom] or [practically wise] without virtue of character.'[28]

It is important to see that Aristotle's view of the relationship among the virtues is quite different from the Socratic view, which is more properly called a unity thesis. Socrates thought that all virtues were forms of a single virtue, wisdom. By definition, it is impossible to have one virtue without having the others. Aristotle's thesis, however, is a weaker one, since he does not claim that the virtues are identical to one another, but rather that they cannot occur independently. Importantly, the position is not that moral virtues like courage and generosity are somehow dependent on each other. Rather, the dependency relationship is between each of the virtues and practical wisdom.[29]

---

[27] *Nicomachean Ethics*, trans. Terence Irwin, 2nd edn. (Indianapolis: Hackett, 1999), 1140b5–10. All references hereafter are to this translation.

[28] *NE* 1144b31.

[29] This matters, because some people object to the reciprocity thesis on the grounds that the dispositions needed to exercise courage are quite different from the dispositions needed to exercise generosity. But this is why Aristotle categorized courage and generosity as separate moral virtues, rather than reverting to the Socratic unity thesis. Aristotelian virtues are not simply different sides of the same coin. Each of the moral virtues has its own set of dispositions and affective responses that are characteristic of that virtue. While it is true that, on Aristotle's view, it is impossible to

The reciprocity thesis is really two theses: (a) the moral virtues cannot be exercised without practical wisdom; and (b) it is impossible to acquire practical wisdom in the absence of the moral virtues. What is the reason for thinking that either of these is true? The first thesis, that the moral virtues require practical wisdom for their exercise, is probably the more straightforward of the two. They require practical wisdom because, on Aristotle's view, the exercise of any given moral virtue is an exercise of rationality. Although Aristotle says that the moral virtues are acquired through habituation, they are not exactly habits, at least not habits like twisting one's hair or biting one's nails.

Aristotle believes that virtuous action is an expression of rational choice—the outcome of good deliberation.[30] No matter how well a person has been habituated into, say, generous feelings and responses, she will always have to make judgements about exactly what kind of response is required in the situation that calls for generosity. Even if she is inclined to give to charity, she still has to decide how much to give, which causes are most worthy of her support, and which charities use the money best. And such judgements cannot be made well in the absence of at least some grasp on the relative importance of various things to human life, which is the province of practical wisdom. The moral virtues make it possible for an agent to respond in the right way in these circumstances, but it is practical wisdom that identifies what the right way is.

This is why children who perform virtuous actions under the direction of their parents are not acting in a fully virtuous way. In such cases, the source of the judgement that *this* action should be done *here and now* is external to the agent. The capacity to make such a judgement is not part of her character, at least not yet. Habituation into the moral virtues in childhood is centrally a matter of getting children to take pleasure and pain in the right things, to acquire and maintain control over emotional responses so that those responses can be directed properly when required. The child is taught to find generous actions pleasant (and stingy ones unpleasant) and, further, to be able to produce and constrain natural emotional responses as the situation requires. She must learn to hand over the present to the birthday child happily and, moreover, to constrain her envy—or at least its expression—when a desirable toy is unwrapped. These habits of emotional expressions and restraints, we hope, will carry over into adulthood when she is faced with having to act well in more pressing circumstances. Children develop the powers of judgement that are characteristic of practical wisdom only gradually and over time. And it is only once those powers of judgement have been acquired for oneself that one is capable of acting in a fully virtuous way.

---

be courageous without also being generous, it is not because the skills and dispositions needed for courage are identical to the ones needed for generosity. Rather, it is because neither is possible without a third virtue—practical wisdom. The overlap among the virtues is only partial; what unites them is their dependence on practical wisdom for their exercise.

[30] I leave open the question whether it is impossible to act virtuously in the absence of prior deliberation. I doubt it myself, but shall not contest Aristotle's thesis here.

The reasons for the second thesis, that the moral virtues are required for practical wisdom, are somewhat more opaque. Broadly speaking, the reason is that the habituation into the feelings and emotions characteristic of the moral virtue is essential for a correct grasp of human flourishing. Aristotle puts it this way: 'for virtue makes the goal correct, and [practical wisdom] makes the things promoting the goal correct.'[31] The moral virtues make the goal correct because properly directed feelings are necessary in order to understand that the goal really is the goal. A full appreciation of the value of central human ends is impossible in the absence of attachment to those ends, and it is only through the moral virtues that we come to develop the right attachments.

Consider generosity again. It is characteristic of the stingy person that he sees material goods, or money, as having considerable value. Too much value, in fact, since he is unwilling to part with them when other considerations indicate that he should. He is overly attached to things that do not warrant that kind of attachment, at least not in those circumstances. It could be that he values the wrong things entirely, or it could be that he values the right things too much and in the wrong circumstances. Either way, his failure to have the right kinds of attachment to ends causes a kind of mismatch between his feelings and desires and the objects of those feelings and desires, in so far as his feelings about the objects do not reflect their genuine value. Lack of moral virtue thus prevents a person from properly appreciating what truly matters to a good human life, and this capacity for appreciation is part of practical wisdom.

Thus, the reciprocity thesis insists that practical wisdom is required for the exercise of the moral virtues because every virtuous act is an act of rational choice. It is a reflection of a correct judgement about the value of various human ends, as they are implicated in the particular situation. And the moral virtues are required for practical wisdom because a correct grasp of those valuable human ends is impossible unless one's attachments are in proper order.

But practical wisdom is not simply wisdom about which human ends are valuable. It is also the capacity to discern which actions and responses are conducive to those ends. Aristotle takes pains to distinguish virtue from a state he calls cleverness—the ability to engage in means–end reasoning. It will, however, turn out that the skill associated with cleverness is actually a component of practical wisdom and hence, of virtue (*NE* 1144a25–30):

There is a capacity, called cleverness, which is such as to be able to do the actions that tend to promote whatever goal is assumed and to attain them. If, then, the goal is fine, cleverness is praiseworthy, and if the goal is base, cleverness is unscrupulousness. That is why both [practically wise] and unscrupulous people are called clever. [Practical wisdom] is not cleverness, though it requires this capacity.

It is possible to be clever without being practically wise, since one might well be good at determining the best means to an end without having any knowledge of

[31] *NE* 1144a9.

the real value of that end. But, crucially, it is impossible to be practically wise in the fullest sense without also being clever.

The popularity of the 'bare perception' model can sometimes make us forget how much there is to say about the skills involved in knowing what is needed to act well in a given situation. Consider, for instance, the following remark made by Richard Sorabji:

> Whatever other roles practical wisdom may or may not play, I suggest that one role is this. It enables a man, in the light of his conception of the good life in general, to perceive what generosity requires of him, or more generally what virtue and *to kalon* require of him, in the particular case, and it instructs him to act accordingly.[32]

This is true so far as it goes, but how do we learn what is required in order 'act accordingly'? Having correctly perceived that something is required of me is, as I have said, no guarantee of success in acting on that requirement appropriately. The knowledge that, morally speaking, I ought to do something to defuse an embarrassing situation or comfort someone in pain does not immediately or automatically produce knowledge of *how* to defuse embarrassment or offer comfort. The exercise of practical wisdom requires both 'knowing that' and 'knowing how,' and cleverness is concerned primarily with the latter. Knowing how is a skill, and manners are an essential part of that skill.

There are people who, while genuinely committed to the ends of offering comfort and saving others from embarrassment, are not very good at identifying the situations in which others require comfort or rescue from embarrassment. Others, equally committed to the ends, are able to identify such situations, but yet find themselves at a loss for what to say or do in order to bring about comfort or rescue. Although both engage in a kind of cognitive failure, the cognitive failures are not exactly the same. A wide range of skills and capacities is required in order to succeed at fully virtuous action, and it is possible to possess some of these skills and capacities while lacking others.

One of the central elements of the 'knowing how' aspect of practical wisdom is the ability to make certain kinds of inferences about other people and their circumstances. Suppose I have it as my aim to protect my sensitive friend from social embarrassment. Succeeding in such an endeavour requires a number of cognitive skills. I must become aware of which kinds of situations produce embarrassment for him, be able to recognize a given situation as one of that sort, and be able to tell whether my friend is, in fact, becoming embarrassed by what passes. In each case, I need a kind of adeptness at interpreting the expressions, language, tone of voice, and postures of other people, both my friend and those with whom he is interacting. I also need to know how to defuse or deflect his embarrassment—for instance, how to redirect the conversation, or insert

---

[32] 'Aristotle on the Role of Intellect in Virtue', in *Essays on Aristotle's Ethics,* ed. Amélie Rorty (Berkeley: University of California Press, 1980), 206.

an appropriate bit of humour, or remove him from the scene without seeming obvious. Some people may indeed be more talented at this sort of thing by nature, but we cannot underestimate the degree of skill involved. Such things take experience and, indeed, even practice.

In *Pride and Prejudice* Elizabeth chastises Darcy for his actions at a ball in Hertfordshire, during which he violated rules of gentlemanly behaviour by failing to do his share of dancing with women who would otherwise have to sit out.[33] He defends himself by saying that he knew none of the women and that he is 'ill qualified to recommend himself to strangers'. Elizabeth finds this to be an inadequate reply for 'a man of sense and education, and who has lived in the world', since such a man should be expected to have greater social skill than Darcy displayed at the ball. Darcy answers by saying: 'I certainly have not the talent which some people possess . . . of conversing easily with those I have never seen before. I cannot catch their tone of conversation, or appear interested in their concerns, as I often see done.' Elizabeth is not appeased, suggesting instead that Darcy's social inadequacies, such as they are, result from his failure to practise perfecting them. Darcy's cousin, Colonel Fitzwilliam, adds that Darcy is unwilling to take the trouble to learn to do better.

Elizabeth's critique is based in her expectation that the wealthy and powerful Darcy had a gentleman's upbringing, and certainly the education of a gentleman at the time would have included training in the social graces. The idea of a gentleman's education is, of course, largely an anachronism, but the suggestion that Darcy's social failures are attributable to his unwillingness to practice them is interesting.

In the novel Darcy is much more charming when he feels in his element, such as when he is home at Pemberley, but the abilities he shows at Pemberley often fail him when he has to move much outside his intimate social circle. Where Darcy falls short is in his capacity to engage in imaginative identification with other people. He pays attention to his surroundings, but not always in a way that enables him to appreciate the situation from the perspective of someone else. Darcy manages to offend Elizabeth in the course of proposing marriage to her because he proposes to her in a way that she rightly views as insulting. Darcy doesn't initially see it as insulting because he thinks he is simply speaking the truth, which he is. But what Darcy fails to see is that speaking the truth so bluntly in these circumstances is both unnecessary and hurtful. Darcy is stunned by Elizabeth's refusal of his proposal. Although she says she would have refused him even if he had proposed 'in a more gentleman-like manner' his manners anger her in ways that he cannot appreciate because he is, at that point in the novel, incapable of hearing his remarks from her point of view.[34]

---

[33] *Pride and Prejudice*, 175. There is an interesting contrast here with *Emma*'s Mr Knightley, who perfectly embodies Austen's ideal of a gentleman. Although he hates to dance, he nevertheless asks Harriet Smith to dance for the sole purpose of sparing her serious social humiliation.

[34] *Pride and Prejudice*, 192.

Mrs Jennings is subject to a similar difficulty.[35] Virtually incapable of feeling embarrassed herself, she is a poor judge of when others are embarrassed, and has trouble imagining how her vulgar attempts at humour could wound or offend. She cannot appreciate the point of view of someone like Marianne Dashwood because she cannot imagine what it is like to see the world through Marianne's romantic eyes. Where her powers of imaginative identification are more effective, such as when she imagines Mrs Dashwood's grief over her gravely ill daughter, her manners improve greatly.

Both Darcy and Mrs Jennings have a good grasp of moral concepts. They are attached to the right ends, and they know what is and what is not worth preserving in human life.[36] But their ability to preserve what they rightly see as important is hindered by their inability to take on the perspective of other people and understand what matters to *them*. Mrs Jennings is clearly very fond of the Dashwood sisters, yet her intrusive behaviour is sometimes at odds with their flourishing, such as when she tells everyone that Marianne and Willoughby are engaged when she has neither confirmation of her claim nor permission to make it.[37] Had Mrs Jennings been more discreet, Marianne would have suffered less public embarrassment when Willoughby becomes engaged to someone else. Mrs Jennings, however, never realizes this. And Darcy, while correctly judging the value of having Elizabeth as his wife, nearly loses her through his own arrogance and lack of sympathy with her perspective. He overestimates her desire to be married to someone wealthy and powerful, and underestimates her loyalty to her sister.

Neither Darcy nor Mrs Jennings is able to live in ways that fully reflect their correct grasp on what is genuinely important. Mrs Jennings is unable to see herself and her actions from the perspective of others, but if she were, she could not endorse her own behaviour, incompatible as it is with her own moral commitments. She is a kind woman who unwittingly does things that cause pain and even harm, and she lacks the moral imagination to realize what she is doing. For her, the world exists only as it she sees it. Her interpretative powers are sharply limited by her deficiency of imagination. Darcy is luckier than Mrs Jennings in the sense that he has both greater imaginative powers than she does and the corrective influence of Elizabeth. But it is not until he takes on Elizabeth's point of view that he can appreciate the mismatch between his own moral commitments and his actual behaviour.[38]

[35] For a more extensive discussion of Mrs Jennings and her imaginative failures, see my 'Practical Wisdom and Moral Imagination' in *Sense and Sensibility*,' forthcoming in *Philosophy and Literature*.

[36] It is, of course, one of Darcy's major redeeming features that he is in love with Elizabeth, rather than Caroline Bingley. And Mrs Jennings is willing to make unpopular public stands to uphold what is right.

[37] *Sense and Sensibility*, 182.

[38] During Darcy's second proposal to Elizabeth, he engages in considerable self-recrimination, saying to Elizabeth, 'What did you say of me, that I did not deserve?' This might seem exaggerated, particularly in the face of Elizabeth's own biases against Darcy earlier in the novel, but I don't think Austen intends it to be so. Darcy really has undergone a moral transformation, and although Elizabeth does not deserve the full credit, it likely would not have happened without her.

The capacity for moral imagination may be a natural skill, but it can certainly be developed and honed. Aristotle reminds us that practical wisdom is acquired primarily through experience of the world, and this is in part because experience of the world is essential to expanding one's imaginative capacities. The more actions I perform, the better able I am to see the effect those actions have in the world and on other people, assuming that I am appropriately reflective. One of the central tasks in raising children is teaching them how to broaden their own moral horizons. Several of Austen's novels contain a subtext about the proper place of novels in moral education.[39] Austen is rightly critical of those who dismiss novels as either mere frivolity or, worse, dangerous to the developing mind.[40] After all, learning to identify with fictional characters and coming to see their worlds from their point of view is a way of exercising and extending the moral imagination.[41]

It is because he has considerable powers of moral imagination that Wickham succeeds so well in his charade.[42] He has just the kind of sensitivity to nuance and social context that Mrs Jennings so badly needs. In this respect, he resembles someone with full practical wisdom, since the kind of cleverness that Wickham exhibits is part of the virtue. Austen and Aristotle share many assumptions about the role of moral education in the development of virtue, and in Austen's novels a character's upbringing is often identified as a crucial explanation of her present behavior. Given Wickham's upbringing, his social aptitude is not surprising, particularly when we reflect on his natural intellectual and imaginative talents. He is very good at judging how things seem to others; indeed, this is how he succeeds in fooling the sharp-eyed Elizabeth. He sees that she finds him attractive and uses this to his advantage in constructing an account of himself that she will find plausible and appealing.[43] Of course, Wickham lacks the part of practical wisdom that orients him towards what is genuinely worthwhile in

---

[39] This is most apparent in *Northanger Abbey*, but the theme runs throughout her work.

[40] It cannot be accidental that Mr Collins, who ranks among the least imaginative creatures in England, refuses to read novels (*Pride and Prejudice*, 68).

[41] See especially Martha Nussbaum, 'Finely Aware and Richly Responsible: Literature and the Moral Imagination', in *Love's Knowledge* (Oxford: Oxford University Press, 1990). For more on the importance of imaginative identification, see Nancy Sherman, 'Empathy and the Imagination', in *Midwest Studies in Philosophy*, Vol. XXII, ed. P. French and H. Wettstein (Notre Dame: University of Notre Dame Press, 1998); and Nussbaum, *Upheavals of Thought* (Cambridge: Cambridge University Press, 2001).

[42] I am grateful to an anonymous reviewer for Oxford University Press for helping me to see the importance of this.

[43] Wickham, like Darcy, had a gentleman's education; indeed, they had more or less the same education, thanks to the generosity of Darcy's father. If Elizabeth expects that good social graces are the natural outcome of such an education, then it is not surprising that Wickham has them. One difficulty with *Pride and Prejudice* is that we have a hard time accounting for how Jane and Elizabeth Bennet turned out as well as they did. Mrs Bennet cannot possibly have taught them the rules of propriety so effectively, and it is hard to see the *laissez-faire* Mr Bennet taking on that role himself. Darcy takes for granted that Elizabeth spent time away from Longbourn (179), but that is not confirmed.

life—the 'knowing that' component of practical wisdom. Indeed, this is why he is vicious. His attachments are not what they ought to be; he is greedy, intemperate, and disloyal. In so far as he lacks crucial moral virtues, he necessarily lacks practical wisdom. But it is possible to lack the attachments necessary for moral wisdom while still possessing some of the skills that would enable a better disposed person to express those attachments in social life. Just as one can be clever at discerning the best means to an end without knowing what the end is worth, so one can exercise some of the skills of a virtue without having the virtue itself. Wickham's powers of discernment are considerable. Were he to employ his skills in the service of better ends, he would be quite effective at virtuous action, more so than many better-disposed characters in the novels. We might wonder whether we should consider this to be a redeeming feature in him; I am inclined to think that it is, despite the fact that he would not be so treacherous but for these skills. But I shall not argue this point.[44]

Moral imagination is necessary to appreciate the link between moral commitments and their expression in social life. A commitment to sympathy takes me only so far: without the ability to appreciate how another person's situation appears to her, I shall be unable to exercise sympathy properly. The reciprocity thesis implies that one needs the moral virtues in order to have practical wisdom. This is, as I have said, because through habituation into moral virtue, one becomes attached to the right ends and aims at what is genuinely good. But it is not enough to aim at what is good; one must also be proficient with the bow in order to be virtuous. Mrs Jennings knows where to aim, but she is seriously deficient with the bow. Wickham has the proficiency with the bow, but lacks the knowledge of where to aim. Both get something right with respect to practical wisdom, but both get something wrong as well. Certainly what Mrs Jennings has right is the more important of the two, but full virtue requires both.

If, as I have argued, the rules of etiquette serve as a primary vehicle for expressing moral commitments in social life, virtue will require skill with respect to those rules. It follows from my view that anyone who aims at being virtuous

---

[44] It is, after all, one thing to say that the world would be a better place had someone not been so courageous, intelligent, etc. It is another thing to say that he is a worse human being for that. Probably, Neville Chamberlain's decision to appease Hitler resulted from features of his character that are, in fact, virtues, although clearly the consequences of that decision were devastating. The mere fact that a trait causes bad consequences does not mean that it is not a virtue. This is the same concern that motivates Philippa Foot to speculate about whether courage can be a virtue in a bad man. See 'Virtues and Vices', in *Virtues and Vices and Other Essays in Moral Philosophy* (Oxford: Clarendon Press, 2002), 18. (Her answer is that while courage is a virtue, and while it is a virtue in this man, it does not operate as a virtue in him when he acts badly.) See also Martin, 'Miss Manners Rescues Civilization,' 131–2.

in Aristotle's sense ought to be reading good etiquette books. Practical wisdom is incomplete when it cannot be exercised effectively, and effective exercise requires knowledge of how to employ the rules of etiquette to express and reflect the aims of virtue. Likewise, the practice of etiquette is empty unless it is accompanied by an appreciation for the expressive role that manners play in our lives.[45]

[45] I am especially indebted to Maggie Little for help in thinking through the argument of this paper, as well as to Tim Chappell and an anonymous referee for OUP. I would also like to thank Jim Nelson, Rebecca Kukla, Gaby Sakamoto, and the members of an audience at the University of Dundee for useful conversations about related work. Finally, I drew general inspiration from an article by David Gallop ('Jane Austen and the Aristotelian Ethic', *Philosophy and Literature* 23 (1999): 96–109).

11

The Hardboiled Detective as Moralist: Ethics in Crime Fiction

Sandrine Berges

Although much has been written to show that literature can influence the moral character, the consensus seems to be that novels which are hard to read are good for you, and those which are not are bad. If that is the case, rather than a mere prejudice on the writers' parts, then the view that literature is morally valuable is paradoxical. What is the point of something being useful for moral education if it is only accessible to a minority of adult readers? If novels are to form a part of moral education, then they had better be accessible to most readers at an age where their characters are not yet fully formed. So it would be nice if novels which do not fall into the category of 'high literature', but not into the junk-fiction category either, were good for one's character. The argument of this chapter is that a certain kind of genre fiction can be morally valuable: the modern hardboiled detective novel. I shall begin, however, by arguing for the broader claim that literature in general, and fiction such as novels in particular, can be morally valuable.

1 WHAT WE DON'T WANT TO KNOW THAT NOVELS TELL US

There has been a debate between those who think that the reading of novels from a moral perspective ('ethical criticism') is a good thing, and those who do not: Nussbaum 1990, 1998; Booth 1988, 1998 defend ethical criticism, Posner 1997, 1998 is against it. However, the debate about ethical criticism is concerned with the evaluation of works of literature *as works of art*. It does not really address the question that interests me: whether novels may be good for something else *as well as* being good works of art. For what it is worth, my own view is that aesthetic appreciation is very rarely divorced from other concerns—moral, cultural, emotional, and so on—and that this is especially so in the case of novels. But my argument here does not need this claim. It will be enough if novels can have a moral value *alongside* their aesthetic value—whether or not the two sorts of value are connected. Thus I might agree with Posner that novels should ultimately be judged on aesthetic rather than moral grounds, while also agreeing with Nussbaum and Booth that some novels have an ethical value as moral educators or corruptors.

My purpose in this section is to show that Nussbaum and Booth are right that novels may serve as a part of our moral education, as a preliminary to arguing, in sections 2–3, that some crime fiction serves this purpose very well. For the sake of brevity, I shall focus my discussion on Nussbaum's work, and especially on her book *Poetic Justice* (Nussbaum 1995).

That book opens with the claim that a novel may be morally valuable 'because it summons powerful emotions, it disconcerts and puzzles. It inspires distrust of conventional pieties and exacts a frequently painful confrontation with one's own thoughts and intentions' (Nussbaum 1995: 5). Novels are not morally valuable because they preach, or because they present examples of morally admirable people and actions, but because they force us to work through moral dilemmas in a way that is both emotionally engaged and original. They force us away both from complacent dogmatism, and from the rehearsed middle-of-the-road attitudes which we are always tempted to adopt for sheer peace of mind. In short, reading novels can help us to develop morally good attitudes, responses, and emotions, which we can then transfer to real life.

(Here there arises the familiar objection that highly immoral people can appreciate good literature; therefore there is no transfer from reading to living. I reply that if some people are indeed like that, then it is more likely a sign that something is wrong with them than that literature cannot help moral development.)

Novels are good for us, or at least some novels are, because in reading them we identify with the characters; through this identification, we experience emotions and perceive the world in ways that would not otherwise have happened. Our identification promotes an emotional engagement which leads to a finer perception of the world. This emotional engagement and fine perception are both central to an Aristotelian ethics (Nussbaum 1995: 6):

Works that promote identification and emotional reaction cut through [our] self-protective stratagems, requiring us to see and to respond to many things that may be difficult to confront—and they make this process palatable by giving us pleasure in the very act of confrontation.

Nussbaum does not claim, of course, that all novels promote identification, or that identification is the only way in which literature can be morally valuable. Her focus is on the nineteenth-century realist novel, which, she claims, can help moral development in this way.

Being morally good, for Nussbaum, means being educated in one's perceptions and emotions (the same thing, for her: more about that below) so that one can deliberate and act beyond general rules, with an eye for what is called for by each particular situation. But can reading novels be an appropriate way of becoming good in this sense? Nussbaum's notion of moral goodness is clearly meant to be an Aristotelian one; but it faces the Aristotelian objection that the (only) appropriate way of learning to be good is habituation *through action*. In order to become virtuous, one has to act repeatedly as a virtuous person would, until one has learned to find such actions pleasurable in themselves. What non-virtuous people lack is the proper emotional involvement that only virtuous action can bring. So, for example, they feel fear of punishment instead of shame, and associate no pleasure with acting virtuously except their relief from such fear (see Burnyeat 1980). We might (says the objection) allow that *this* sort of emotional engagement could be stimulated by reading. But not the level of engagement that leads us to virtue (*NE* 1179b4):

> What argument would remould such people? It is hard, if not impossible, to remove by argument the traits that have long since been incorporated in the character.

To this objection Nussbaum can reply, first, that the morally crucial part of reading is *identification*, which is a third category alongside action and thought, and which Aristotle does not consider in his writings on ethics.[1] Reading is, of course, not the same as doing (one is not shipwrecked through reading *Robinson Crusoe*). But it is not the same as thinking either: it is one thing to be told 'if you make up your mind rashly and on the grounds of appearances, you will later regret it', and quite another to read, with engagement, about Elizabeth Bennet's discomfiture as she realizes that she has radically misjudged Darcy and Wickham. What the reader of *Pride and Prejudice* experiences is not a cogitation but an imitation of Elizabeth's own experience: a mixture of shame and anger at one's own ill-based judgements.

Now a reader of *Pride and Prejudice* can be someone who has never felt the shame that comes from misjudging somebody's character by looking only at his superficial traits. Reading the novel teaches this person, and reminds the rest of us, of something valuable: what it feels like to have such an emotion in such circumstances. It also teaches or reminds us that such an emotion *can*, perhaps *should*, be felt in those circumstances. This is valuable too.

To illustrate this, consider the sort of teenagers who mock and shun their poorer (or, for that matter, richer) classmates. They often do not realize that it is even possible, never mind appropriate, to feel ashamed of their behaviour. They know that their attitude is frowned upon by some. But they are only familiar with the *arguments* against this attitude: 'you should treat everyone equally', 'you should not be prejudiced by evidence of wealth or poverty', 'being rich or poor

---

[1] Perhaps he considers it in the *Poetics*, in his discussion of *mimesis*. Cp. Fossheim, Ch. 5, and also Zamir 2002 on the *Rhetoric*: a complete Aristotelian view of ethics and literature must look well beyond the *Ethics*.

does not make you a better or worse person', and so on. Austen's novel—and it is one that teenagers often read—does not rehearse those arguments. Instead it puts us in a fictional situation where we identify imaginatively with a heroine who makes crucial misjudgements of just this sort, and then is caught out by them. The teenager who reads *Pride and Prejudice* puts herself in a position where she not only knows that she can get people wrong by relying on appearances, and that she will be ashamed of herself if she does. More importantly, it also teaches her what this will feel like.

Nussbaum can add a second response to the objection that only action can habituate us into virtue. This is that virtue is not merely a matter of fine action; it also intrinsically involves fine moral perception. So in *Love's Knowledge* Nussbaum cites a scene from Henry James's *The Golden Bowl* as an example of such fine moral awareness (Nussbaum 1990: 152):

Moral knowledge, James suggests, is not simply intellectual grasp of propositions; it is not even simply intellectual grasp of particular facts; it is perception. It is seeing a complex, concrete reality in a highly lucid and richly responsive way; it is taking in what is there, with imagination and feeling.

So learning to see things right is a separate matter from learning to do right. Therefore, even if we can't learn much about *doing* right by reading novels (as is perhaps the case), that is no reason to think that we can't learn a lot about *seeing* things right from novels.

A good novel does not tell us that there is a correct way to think about moral issues. Instead, it teaches us to respond to the world in something like the manner that Nussbaum describes in the passage just quoted (Nussbaum 1990: 152). It presents us with pictures of the world which take in fine detail in unconventional and surprising ways, thereby stimulating the imagination and the emotions. Through Elizabeth's eyes, we first see the world as a place where pleasant, attractive people deserve our attention and sympathy more than others who are less so. Then, through her mistakes and her trials, we come to perceive the world in rather finer detail. This teaches us not just *that* the moral universe is a complex one, but also *how* we might focus our gaze to take in the relevant aspects of it. This, too, is morally valuable.

To sum up. Doing rather than thinking may be central to the process of becoming virtuous; but identification with fictional characters is neither doing nor thinking, and it, too, may have something to add to the process. The kind of identification that happens when we read a novel can help our moral development in two ways. First, it educates the emotions in a way that argument cannot, through an emotional experience that can sometimes be as vivid as anything we feel in acting. Second, the identifications that we shall experience through our reading will educate our perceptions, which are themselves a necessary part of virtue.

So much, then, in defence of the general claim, on which I concur with Nussbaum, that reading novels can contribute to moral education. Let me now turn to a particular application of that general claim which Nussbaum does *not* make: that hardboiled detective novels can be especially good educators.

2 EVIL AND THE ORDINARY: A DAY IN THE LIFE OF THE HARDBOILED DETECTIVE

Here are a few examples of hardboiled-detective novels that I believe to be morally valuable: Ian Rankin's Rebus novels; Marcia Muller's Sharon McCone series (a female hardboiled who started in the seventies and is still going); Sara Paretsky's V.I. stories; and Jean-Claude Izzo's Fabio Montale trilogy (Montale is an ex-cop in Marseille). This list of authors and novels is not meant to be definitive: there are many other authors whose novels would probably serve just as well for the points I want to make. I have chosen them simply because I know them and like them.

These books share a common heritage: they are all strongly influenced by the realism of Raymond Chandler and Dashiel Hammett. (I shall not discuss either here, since their works are often regarded as classics rather than mere examples of the crime genre. My thesis, remember, is that there can be moral value in mere *genre* novels.) In these books, the plot is defined less by the mystery of the crime than by the evil or violence that unfolds during the investigation, in the process of solving the mystery. There is never just one criminal, but a myriad of wrongdoers and people indifferent to the evil surrounding them, all somehow caught up in the web of evil. In the same way, there is never just one victim (the body at the beginning, or even the several corpses we come across in the course of the novel) but an indescribably large number of sufferers: people whose lives are affected, sometimes crippled, by an injustice which should have been righted. In Paretsky's *Hard Times*, for example, V. I. Warshawski investigates the commercial use of slave labour in a private prison. However, it is very clear that the victims she identifies are not merely those women who work in the T-Shirt factory hidden in the prison building, but all of those prisoners who were picked on by the police for dubious reasons, and kept imprisoned in disgraceful conditions with no adequate legal representation.

According to Nussbaum in *Poetic Justice*, part of what makes novels morally valuable is that they succeed in engaging our emotions in an appropriate manner; which they do by focusing on the ordinary in such a way that it forces us to reassess what we know and what we are familiar with. We feel what we do in response, because what is being discussed is close to our heart, and because it is so presented that we cannot ignore it. In a novel, familiarity *stops* breeding contempt (Nussbaum 1995: 9). Nussbaum illustrates this claim by reference to Dickens's *Hard Times*, where the reader is made to visit, in her imagination, the various scenes of the everyday life of the rich and poor; their workplaces, and homes. The effect is that the moral issues we debate when we read *Hard Times* are brought home to us: understood as real issues that we are probably already debating.

In the light of this, it is surprising that in her other works on ethics and the novel, Nussbaum's leading examples almost always come from Henry James's novels. For, with a few exceptions, James's plots are *not* about (what most of us would call) ordinary life. Most of them concern the union of a very naive American with a sophisticated, impoverished, and/or dishonest European aristocrat. The heroes and heroines then spend extraordinary long stretches of their leisured lives debating with their equally implausible friends how to salvage their almost fantastically doomed relationships (or, alternatively, how to sink them further). If we are truly concerned with praising novels which depict the ordinary, perhaps we would do better to take a look at crime literature instead.

The kind of crime fiction I am concerned with typically focuses on the portrayal of evil and of what happens when we fight it. So, clearly, there is plenty of morally important material in the plots of these novels. But, it will be asked, how does the genre deal with these pressing moral issues? Does it promote identification and emotional response? Can we *learn* from those portrayals of evil?

The answers are all positive, for the crime novel focuses on the ordinary even more than do novels like Dickens's *Hard Times*. This focus forces us to confront and reflect on the evil that we see every day (and ignore; otherwise, it would not be so omnipresent). By presenting it in the context of a criminal investigation, the crime novel makes ordinary evil extraordinary, and forces us to see it and react to it in new, unprejudiced ways.

Our emotional involvement in crime novels typically comes from our identification with the hero's or heroine's indignation with crime, and passion for justice. We see the corpses of murder victims through the eyes of the person who must now interview the victim's family, or who fears that he could have prevented the murder altogether, if only he had been faster and more efficient. By following the investigation, we meet people whom we may know only as statistics and whom we never get to talk to; people whose lives are crippled by evil that would not exist if anyone cared about them: the ghetto dwellers (Rankin, Izzo), the homeless (Paretsky, Rankin), the prisoners (Paretsky, Izzo), the immigrants legal and illegal (Muller, Izzo), and the oppressed racial minorities (Muller).

We are used to seeing evil only from our own perspective: organized crime means we might get mugged and our children might be sold drugs; corruption means that politicians whom we trusted will now have to be replaced. But the crime novel brings us, and makes us care about, the perspective of those who are more directly affected by evil: the children whose career alternatives are crime and unemployment; the mothers who have to accept slave wages from criminal employers in order to feed their children; the witnesses whose own lives turns out to be so steeped in crime that they are unable to care about the victim whose death is being investigated—and so on.

All we, the readers, normally experience of crime is no more than the tip of the iceberg—an iceberg which is, in any case, a threat to us only if we are 'at sea', and certainly not if we see it only on television. The crime novel teaches us that, in fact, we *are* 'at sea': all this horror and chaos is part of *our* everyday life, of the life of the people we pass in the street, those we work with and who live not very far from us. If we do not think that this evil is part of our lives, it is because we choose not to see it.

The crime novel emphasizes the ordinariness of evil by rarely stepping out of ordinary scenes. In the course of solving a crime, the hero or heroine lives a fairly ordinary life, has confrontations with his or her boss, does paperwork, engages or tries to stay out of office politics, goes on dates, has arguments with his or her partner, splits up, makes up or meets someone new, hangs around in bars, drives around town, or stays home. The extraordinary does occur: the detective meets great criminals, gets into danger, gets involved in car-chases or cross-country chases, gets beaten up, or tortured, has her house or office ransacked, bombed or burned . . . we would hardly keep turning the pages if it didn't! But in no way do these exceptional events dispel the reader's feeling that what is being depicted is part of our world, and that it is a part that we would do well not to ignore.

Because it forces us to confront the evil around us from the perspective of someone who knows and cares, the crime novel, I believe, qualifies as morally valuable on the criteria set out by Nussbaum. The fact that these novels are more accessible than Henry James's (and a better read than Dickens's *Hard Times*!) can be no objection to their value. Even if James's psychological and moral analysis is finer than that to be found in the typical hardboiled-detective book, all that means is that those who are already on a superior moral plane (whoever they are) may benefit from reading James. Those of us who struggle to come to terms with everyday moral dilemmas may, in fact, benefit more from crime literature.

Nussbaum may object that these novels do not deal with moral issues in a subtle enough manner, and so that they do not really educate moral perception.[2] On the contrary, the novels I focus on show that the implications of evil are endless, that an evil act must be dealt with on many levels over long periods of time before it will go away (if it ever will). More about this in the next section.

3 CASUISTRY, CARE, CHARACTER, AND CRIME

Let me spell out my claim that crime fiction can be morally valuable, by being more specific about what kind of moral thinking it encourages. I shall argue that it directs us towards an Aristotelian way of thinking about evil and justice, in that

---

[2] See Nussbaum 1995: 10; Booth 1988: 201–5. On why we read popular fiction, and why many of the things that can be said about genre fiction don't apply to crime novels, see Carroll 1994; and Knight 1994. See also Knight and McKnight 1997: 124 on how crime fiction encourages finer perception.

the main virtues the hero/heroine of the crime novel displays, and which we are encouraged to identify with, are just those most clearly identified by Aristotelian ethics.

I pick out three characteristics of the moral thinking implicit in crime fiction for special attention.

(i) First: there is a willingness to go beyond the *rules*, which are seen as inadequate guidance for action in difficult cases. Instead, the detective is typically shown as psychologically and emotionally observant, and *intuitive* to an extent that suggests that she has 'some sort of complex responsiveness to the salient features of one's concrete situation' (Nussbaum 1990: 55); something, in other words, very like what many Aristotelians call *phronesis*, or practical wisdom.

(ii) Second: what keeps the detective going through a gruelling investigation, through danger, and in the face of the criticism of just about everyone he comes across? The answer is that he *cares*, deeply. He cares for the victim and the victim's survivors; he cares for past or future victims of similar crimes; he cares for all the misery he uncovers during the investigation; and he is angry with the criminal and all those who aid him—the detective is angry that justice is not done.

(iii) Third: there is an emphasis on *character development*. The serial nature of most hardboiled-detective fiction enables the author to develop the hero or heroine. The detective is seen to change, and mature from one book to another as she experiences evil and learns to deal with it. She becomes not just scarred but also quicker of understanding, keener in her responses, actions and emotions, and more able to see the larger picture of evil that the case she is working on is part of.

Here are examples, which I shall give in fairly full detail, of each of these characteristics in turn.

(i) Rules and intuition

In Ian Rankin's *The Falls*, Siobhan Clarke reflects on why she is about to break the rules and keep an assignment with a suspect without informing her superiors in the police force (Rankin 2001: 442). She cannot quite say what moved her, if not a slight disgust with what she calls 'company players', those who stick conscientiously by every rule even when the case appears to demand that they break them. At the same time, she is worried that she might become too much like John Rebus, who breaks rules as the norm, and often keeps information to himself when he should be sharing it with colleagues. Siobhan does not want to become a 'lone wolf detective' any more than she wants to be a 'company player'. She just wants to do her job well: solve the case and ensure that justice is done.

Her assignment with a suspect is the culmination of her role in a murder investigation. The suspect is the 'quizmaster' who has been sending her 'clues' by email, which are supposed to lead her ultimately to the motive for the murder. With the help of a colleague, Siobhan has cracked the clues one by one. At first, luck and her capacity for observing details helped. Then she came to understand and anticipate the quizmaster's thought patterns, and she put that understanding together with her knowledge of the case. This and her ability to pick out, from her background of information and perception, which details are relevant when has enabled her to come to a point where she could actually find the quizmaster. As she knows so much about him, it makes no sense for anyone else to be allowed to track him down. She is the best person for the job.

By contrast, when Derek Linford, a 'company player', attempts to break the rules in another Rebus novel, *Set in Darkness*, he does it on an impulse. He has been made unhappy in love, and to feel professionally inadequate by John Rebus. To defy him, he starts tailing a suspect without authorization. When the suspect leaves the pub, Linford jumps out of his car, forgetting his mobile phone. Within minutes he is in a dark alley and the suspect jumps him, leaving him incapacitated for weeks, and unable, of course, to continue the investigation. Clearly, breaking the rules was not the best idea Derek Linford ever had.

So what is the difference between Siobhan and Derek, police officers of the same age, same training, same abilities? But they do not have the same abilities. Derek may be as intelligent and physically strong as Siobhan, but he lacks what can only be called practical wisdom, and she has it. She is able to judge the situation she finds herself in finely enough to know what is the most appropriate course of action. She is, moreover, practised in such fine judgements, as we see from her ability to solve some of the quizmaster's clues. She can pick out the 'salient features' of the situation she is in, and she can match it with an appropriate course of action. The fact that she does not quite know why she thinks her course of action is best speaks for the complexity of her response: she is moved by a huge background of information containing the 'salient features' of all the relevant situations she has been part of. This is practical wisdom in the sense Nussbaum understands it.

Derek Linford, on the other hand, does not make any fine judgements about the situation he is in. In fact, he fails to notice very obvious things such as 'it is a bad idea to follow a killer up a dark alley when no one knows where you are and you have no means of contacting them'. He hasn't even thought that it might be inappropriate to park a flash car outside a Leith pub frequented mostly by thugs. In fact, he hasn't thought at all, and it is not obvious that he would have been able to think in this manner, for such perception demands a certain degree of intuitive response and emotive involvement which he lacks. He fails to take into account what other people might feel or think. He simply assumes, for instance, that Rebus has got it in for him, thus misreading his character dramatically; and he fails to recognize that the man he is following is highly dangerous. Derek Linford does not have practical wisdom—and this is why most of the time, he chooses to stick to the rules. For him, career success can only lie in that direction.

So how are the Rankin novels ethically valuable? The novels say that the best detectives, those we are encouraged to admire and identify with, solve cases by being less abstract and more practical; by stepping back from the rules and focusing on each case as deserving a new answer; by becoming involved in an intuitive and emotional way as well as intellectually and physically; by being practised observers, not just of scene of crime details, but of human emotions and ambitions; and by learning to tap into a background of past experience which is relevant to the case at hand. In short, good detectives are *Aristotelian*: they emphasize practical wisdom rather than obedience to rules. These novels familiarize us with the idea that it is often more productive to address moral problems on a case-by-case basis, taking in the particular features of a situation, rather than by applying rules in a blind, impartial, and impersonal way.

(ii) Care

In Jean-Claude Izzo's trilogy, Fabio Montale is first a demoted cop, and then an ex-cop. His investigations take place in Marseille's, a town crippled by racism and corruption, a breeding ground for the Mafia, for the National Front, and, more recently, for Islamic Fundamentalism. What drives Montale in his fight against injustice is his anger at these evils, and his intense desire to eradicate them. In the second novel, *Chourmo*, his beloved cousin comes to him to ask for help in finding her son, who has run away to be with his girlfriend. She adds that she does not want him seeing the girl, as she is an Algerian, and 'You know what these people are like'. When he hears this he threatens to throw her out of his house. Later on in the story, he witnesses a murder and is taken to a police station to be interrogated by a corrupt police officer. When he leaves the station, he tears off a National Front election poster and throws it in the bin, knowing full well that no one who works in that station will thank him for it.

Montale is a man who feels pain every time an innocent person, or at least someone who is not totally corrupt, dies. The nephew he is looking for has been murdered. His reaction to seeing the body is 'like a red lightning inside my eyes. His blood. His death splashes me. How will I be able to shut my eyes now, without seeing his body?' (Izzo 2002a: 220) But what keeps him going through all this anger and pain is the *chourmo* spirit of the title, that is, the spirit of the old galley slaves who knew that their only chance of survival was to stick together and to help each other, a certain kind of concern and sympathy and active involvement in other people's troubles which comes from the recognition that 'we are all in it together': 'When someone was in the shit, you could only be from the same family. It was as simple as that' (Izzo 2002a: 170).

Montale's emotional involvement is informed and appropriate. He is angry at racism because he recognizes it as oppression and understands it has no rational justification. He also knows what kind of anger to display when. His anger at his cousin is a personal kind: he lets her see his feelings, hopes she will be influenced by his display, and then forgives her. In the police station his anger is both public and symbolic. He acts to make his action noticed, both by the racist police officers and by the black and North African 'suspects' who are dragged there for questioning every day: to show them that *somebody* rejects the racial and political injustice that they are involved in, and cares enough to act. Montale's emotions are wise as well as powerful. They are directed towards justice. They lead him to act morally. Again, it becomes clear that this conception of morality is Aristotelian: a virtuous person according to Aristotle feels the right kind of emotions, at the right moment, and is thus driven by them to the right course of action.

(iii) Character development

At the end of one of Marcia Muller's novels, her heroine, Sharon McCone, shoots a man. Her friend and colleague steps out of his office building; the killer who has been lying in wait for him steps out and takes aim. McCone shoots the killer from a distance, and he dies. Of course, everybody is grateful that she saved her colleague's life. Still, somehow, no one feels they are able to be close to her any more. She has shot and killed a man. They did not know she had it in her to take a life. She did not either. McCone has to deal not only with all her friends giving her the cold shoulder but with the kind of person she has become; or is it the kind of person she has turned out to be?

In each of the ensuing novels, McCone makes some progress towards regaining her friends' trust and coming to terms with the changes in her character: both the changes that led to the shooting, and the changes that it led to. In a very Californian manner, she comes to terms with it all after a long introspective night spent sitting on top of a hill with her boyfriend. What is significant here is the emphasis placed by Muller on character changes. Her heroine's character grows every time she resolves a moral challenge, which means that in the later novels she is a very different person from who she was in the early ones. It is very tempting—and I don't see any reason to resist the temptation—to see Aristotle's concept of habituation and character-maturation in this feature of crime novels. In order to become virtuous, one has to educate one's character by practising being good: that is, by practising making the right decisions through displaying the right emotions and using practical wisdom. The hardboiled detective's career is all about practising solving moral problems, so it is no surprise that we see them growing into better or worse people as the series progresses.

This is just a brief selection of evidence to show how three authors' crime fiction exemplifies three characteristics of Aristotelian virtue ethics. There is plenty more evidence that I could have given: besides Chandler and Hammett, whom I denied myself, there is also Paretsky (section 2); again, I might have referred to Sue Grafton, Reginald Hill, the French author Fred Vargas, Kathy Reichs, or Patricia Cornwell—not to mention the many hardboiled-detective authors whom I have not read. It seems to me undeniable that Fabio Montale and Sharon McCone display practical reason when they solve crimes, that Rebus, Siobhan Clarke, and McCone are emotionally engaged individuals, and that

Rebus, Clarke, and Montale's characters are depicted as changing as a result of what they go through. I hope it is equally clear from my discussion that these are Aristotelian character-traits, and that what we learn about them from these novels is morally valuable.

4 PARANOIA AND DARKNESS: TWO OBJECTIONS

Let me close by addressing two objections. The first objection, which I call the *paranoia objection*, is drawn from Jane Austen's commentary on the gothic novel in *Northanger Abbey*. The heroine of that book, Catherine Morland, is encouraged by a shallow acquaintance to read every gothic novel she can lay her hands on and discuss them at length. She becomes so obsessed with them that when she visits an ancient abbey with friends, she imagines that atrocities of the kind she has read about in Radcliffe's *Udolfo* are going on. Her suspicions are exposed, she is shamed and becomes again her sensible self, realizing she may have read rather too many gothic novels. Towards the end of the novel she discovers that the master of the abbey is, in fact, crueller than anything she had imagined in her fantasies—but in a mundane rather than a fantastical way. We are made to feel that gothic fantasies mislead, not by making us think the world is a worse place than it, in fact, is but by directing our thoughts away from the real evil in the world.

A critic of my thesis about the moral value of genre fiction might well apply Austen's criticism to crime novels. The avid reader of crime novels may become the subject of a paranoia similar to Catherine Morland's. She may begin to see corruption everywhere, suspect innocent looking neighbours of being criminals (as, for instance, James Stewart and Diane Keaton do in *Rear Window* and *Manhattan Murder Mystery*—although, of course, they turn out to be right). Such paranoia may detract the crime-fiction reader from the real evil that is going on in the world, and may stop her from becoming engaged in the fight against injustice. Why bother joining any political party, if you think that all politicians are involved in crime? Why help right social wrongs, if you are convinced that the activities of the multinationals doom our social order anyway? If crime and corruption are omnipresent, then nothing we do will change anything, so engagement is useless and presumptuous.

If this is the kind of attitude that crime novels encourage, then indeed they are not morally valuable. However, seeing evil everywhere is only paranoia if there is a fantastic element to one's vision; if it involves conspiracy theories and the suspicion of one's neighbours as a matter of principle. But if it involves realizing that many people's lives are touched by evil in such a way that can only be remedied by major social reform, by a very general understanding that such evil exists, and an equally universal desire to put a stop to it, then it is not paranoia. It is not paranoid to deplore the omnipresence of racism in the streets and in the police force, nor is it paranoid to suspect that some politicians are in cahoots with the mafia—if these are real phenomena. These sentiments, on the contrary, can help us to think of ways of remedying these evils. In so far as they are responsive to truths, the more people have them the better. The novels Jane Austen parodies distract the reader from the real evil around her, towards fantasy. But *good* crime novels, although they do arguably have some fantastic elements (maybe not all corporations are as corrupt and criminal as Sara Paretsky would have us believe—yet no doubt some are), also attempt to give a realistic picture of the everyday misery and injustice against which we often close our eyes. To come back to *Northanger Abbey*, a crime-novel reader would have suspected that General Tilney was up to something unpleasant, and that if he found out that Catherine was not rich, then he would not let her marry his son.

The second objection is more worrying. It is that hardboiled detective fiction gives us a picture of the world that is so dark and pessimistic that one may be discouraged from wanting to pursue justice. Detectives in crime fiction are often portrayed as loners, and, as they solve more cases, they seem to get lonelier and lonelier. They are often unsuccessful in their relationships; they are estranged from their families; their circle of friends diminishes with each new investigation; and they become less and less good at making new friends. In some series it is simply that the job is too demanding and that potential friends and lovers cannot accept that it takes precedence over them. Or, maybe, what is at issue is that the detective is willing to risk his life whilst those who love him wait anxiously for the end of the investigation. In some other novels, the problem is that the detective has seen too much evil: 'I stink of death', says Fabio Montale, and he is reluctant to impose this smell on people who are not so tainted by evil, people who do not deal with it as closely as he. All in all, the message seems to be: 'Don't try this at home! If you want a quiet life, if you want a decent life, leave injustice well alone.' And if that is the message, then crime novels discourage rather than encourage moral involvement.

It is hard to deny that anyone who has reasonable expectations of what their life should be like will not want to emulate the heroes and heroines of detective fiction. The ordinary person will not think it is a good idea to become a private investigator who does the police's work for them, or a police officer who works against the rules (unless of course this is one's ambition anyway). But this is not quite the same as saying that readers will be discouraged from fighting injustice. The kind of injustice that is being depicted in crime novels is mostly of the kind that exists because everybody ignores it; it is not the kind that can only be solved by a Zorro, a Batman, or a Lone Ranger. The detective in crime novels is often portrayed as ultimately powerless in the face of all pervading evil because the evil is of a kind that can only be solved by a change in society's attitudes. Racism is the root of the evil Montale fights, but the fight against racism is not a one-man job. More generally, in all of the novels I have discussed, what seems to cause the most trouble is people's unwillingness to help each other; the fact that they turn away when they witness a crime being committed; that they are reluctant to come forward as witnesses; that they refuse to see that some of their compatriots are so badly off that they have no option but a life of crime. It is this kind of omnipresent evil which makes life difficult for the hardboiled detective, rather than the few extraordinary evil and powerful characters they encounter. The latter simply make things worse in a world that is already in a very poor shape. Fighting them is the detective's job, and we would be very imprudent to try it at home. But fighting the kind of social evil that crime novels depict so realistically—that does seem to be our job, and there is no reason why it should make our lives a misery.

To conclude: I have not tried to show that crime novels are better novels than the writings of (say) Henry James, or that they give us more morally speaking. Nussbaum may well be right that the reader of Henry James will gain more moral understanding than the reader of Ian Rankin. But how many James readers are there? In order to read and appreciate James, a certain degree of cultural, intellectual, and moral refinement is necessary; and, in a way, if we already are so refined, then we are not in sore need of moral education. But what about those of us who have not the time, nor the inclination, to learn to read James? Surely the recognition that crime writing is morally valuable too will come, for us, as a relief.

12

'Like the Bloom on Youths': How Pleasure Completes our Lives

Johan Brännmark[1]

Life with little or no pleasure would be a bleak affair. One might even wonder whether such a dreary life would be worthwhile at all. Some, the philosophical hedonists, go so far as to say that pleasure is the sole thing that can make a life go well. Perhaps that is going too far; but if you are going to be a monist about the human good, then hedonism's account of this one good is a very natural one. Even if it is not where all of us end up, it is where most of us start. This suggests that hedonism is a position that should be taken more seriously than it usually is among philosophers today.

How far do a person's own experiences, and her judgements about how well things are going for her, matter for her well-being? Theorists of well-being can be distinguished by their answers to this question, along a spectrum from the objectivist extreme ('Hardly at all') to the subjectivist extreme ('They are the only thing that matters'). The hedonist account of well-being lies towards the subjectivist end of this spectrum. Simple pluralist accounts (objective-list theories, as they are often called) tend to be located towards the objectivist end. And, while a powerful case against hedonism can certainly be made, there are also familiar worries about objectivist theories.[2]

Does the truth lie in the mean between the objectivist and subjectivist extremes? That is my question in this chapter. I want to explore the possibility of an Aristotelian pluralist account of the human good in which pleasure is *good*, yet is not just another item on the list of goods. Rather, pleasure is what *completes*

[1] Earlier versions of this chapter were presented at the practical philosophy seminar in Lund and at the Values and Virtues conference at the University of Dundee, May 2004. I am grateful to the participants there in general and to the editor of this volume in particular for many helpful comments. My work on this chapter has been made possible by a generous research grant from the Bank of Sweden's Tercentenary Foundation.

[2] See e.g. Sumner 1996: ch. 2, for the objection that if we get too far from what the subject herself thinks about her welfare, it is difficult to see how what we end up with is a theory of *her* own good.

the other goods: as Aristotle himself puts it, pleasure is 'like the bloom on youths' (*NE* 1174b33–34).³

Before we look at pleasure more closely, a few words are needed about how best to articulate Aristotelian pluralism as a way of doing the theory of the human good.

1 MIXED GOODS AND THE COMPLETE LIFE

Aristotle's theory of the human good is complex. He is caught in a tension between a Platonist exaltation of quasi-divine contemplation, and a more down-to-earth appreciation of the complexities of the specifically human condition. Aristotle has been read both as a monist (the *dominant-end* interpretation) and as a pluralist (the *inclusive* interpretation). I shall not address this debate in detail; I shall simply try to elaborate a modernized form of Aristotelian pluralism.

For pluralism, numerous things have prudential value. A plausible list of goods will look something like Aristotle's list in the *Rhetoric* (1360b19–24): 'Good birth, plenty of friends, good friends, wealth, good children, plenty of children, a happy old age, also such bodily excellences as health, beauty, strength, large stature, athletic powers, together with fame, honour, good luck, and excellence.'⁴

There are reasons to be dubious about this list. It is usual to accuse such lists of cultural relativity; though with this list the charge does not really stick, except perhaps for 'athletic powers' and 'large stature'. (There may be a self-deprecating joke here; it is well attested that Aristotle was short.) Another worry about the list is that it is drawn from the *Rhetoric* rather than the *Nicomachean Ethics*. Should it be taken seriously as an Aristotelian view of the constituents of the good life? After all (it might be said), the *Rhetoric* is about the art of persuasion; so what Aristotle tells us there is how things *are commonly seen*, not how they *are*. But this worry can be set aside, for two reasons. First, Aristotle makes it clear, in the context, that he himself takes the list seriously; and second, we know from elsewhere that Aristotle takes the considered ethical opinions of 'the many and the wise' as almost incontrovertible (*NE* 1145b7).

Two more interesting reasons for doubt are these. First, most (at least) of the goods mentioned on this list should be considered as instrumental rather than as final goods; and second, the goods in this list do not lie at the right level of abstraction. Let me develop the first of these two doubts. I shall reject it, but something interesting will emerge from my discussion of it. This will clarify what is meant by the second doubt, which seems to me closer to the mark.

To begin with instrumentality, then. In everyday life we pursue all sorts of things without much thought about our real motives for doing so—whether

---

³ I use T. H. Irwin's translation of the *NE* (Irwin 1999). 'The bloom on *youth*' is more usual in English, 'the bloom on *youths*' is closer to the Greek: *hoion tois akmaiois hê hôra*.
⁴ I use W. Rhys Roberts's translation of the *Rhetoric*, in Barnes 1985.

it is for their own sake or for the sake of something else. The 'cool hours of reflection', when we think about this question without prompting, are rare, and our thinking is usually unsystematic. We may, of course, be challenged by others to make sense of our behaviour, and on such occasions we can usually say something—though not always, as Hume famously pointed out (Hume (1998): Appendix I, § 18): 'Ask a man *why he uses exercise*; he will answer, *because he desires to keep his health*. If you then enquire, *why he desires health*, he will readily reply, *because sickness is painful*. If you push your enquiries farther, and desire a reason, *why he hates pain*, it is impossible he can ever give any. This is an ultimate end, and is never referred to any other object.'

Hume's remarks here are fairly informal in intent, and are open to a number of possible interpretations. All the same, his idea that the avoidance of pain is an 'ultimate end', to which our pursuit of other ends can finally be reduced, does rather suggest a simple form of hedonism. I suspect that even opponents of hedonism can feel the force of this kind of argument.

Does Hume's line of thought echo one of Aristotle's? So it might seem: in *NE* 1097a26 ff. Aristotle distinguishes between three types of goods: instrumental goods (valuable only for the sake of something else); mixed goods (valuable both for their own sake and for the sake of something else); and purely final goods (valuable solely for their own sake). The purely final goods have pride of place in this taxonomy of value (*NE* 1097a31–35):

> We say that an end pursued in its own right is more complete than an end pursued because of something else, and that an end that is never choiceworthy because of something else is more complete than ends that are choiceworthy both in their own right and because of this end. Hence an end that is always choiceworthy in its own right, never because of something else, is complete without qualification (*haplôs teleion*).

Here we might liken Aristotle's notion of an end that is *haplôs teleion* to Hume's notion of an 'ultimate end'. On the other hand, this passage of Aristotle can also be understood as making a purely formal point: happiness *as a whole* is the highest good, is complete. Which things constitute happiness (or are means to happiness) is another matter.

If Aristotle is—as I suggest—only making this formal point, then note what follows. It is clear that Aristotle must deny that a single mixed good can be the *sole* constituent of the highest good. It is less obvious that mixed goods cannot be *among* the parts of the highest good, conceived as I am suggesting. Indeed if we take the *Rhetoric*'s list of goods seriously, we shall expect the Aristotelian pluralist to say that quite a few of the components of the human good are mixed goods. Hume, apparently, will go still further, and say that most of them are instrumental; but I doubt we should follow him in this. We should resist the Humean temptation swiftly to put aside many goods simply because they are so obviously means to something else; they can still be mixed goods. There is an important middle ground between saying that a thing's value is not solely intrinsic, and saying that its value is altogether derivative. Hume's style of thinking loses us this middle ground.

If we are drawn to the idea that pleasure has ultimate value, we could accept that pleasure is the sole thing for which no further reason can be given why it is a good, yet still deny that it is the sole constituent of well-being. There can be a whole host of mixed goods, which may all serve *mainly* as instruments for achieving other things, but which need not be *mere* means: rather, they can also contribute in their own right to making our lives go better. In fact, something like this might be true of *every* particular good. There need not be any single constituent of happiness that is *just* a purely final good. After all, even pleasure has value as a means. (So have frustration and pain, which can be highly effective incentives. So far from pain's always being non-instrumentally bad, as Hume's remarks may suggest, it can even be instrumentally good.) Feeling good facilitates all sorts of other activities, both in the sense that it makes us do them better, and in the sense that it clears away the obstacles to our doing them at all.

The relations between different values are not as vertically hierarchical as the famous Hume quotation makes them out to be. The goods constituting human happiness may well be better pictured as a network of holistically interconnected values, rather than as a hierarchy of instrumentality in which some things are purely means for other things, which are purely means for other things again. . . and so on till we reach something that is purely a final value. There would be nothing peculiar about the man in Hume's example if he continued the conversation by saying that he hates pain because it makes it so difficult to concentrate on doing other things, such as his exercise. Nor, therefore, need there be just one right way of connecting up the different values, to which everyone must subscribe on pain of irrationality.

If this is right, then the relations between prudential goods are likely to be both complex, and variable between individuals. Instead of trying to spell out our account of the human good by charting these means-end and part-whole relations in full, maybe we should ask a different question about any putative good, a question which Aristotle also asks: namely, whether a good human life would be complete without it. (If the answer is 'No', then our putative good is a genuine good.)

If we forget about trying to chart the precise instrumentality relations among goods, and ask this second question instead, this will not only make our theory a lot more workable. It will also enable us to handle the second worry mentioned above as well, namely that of finding the right level of generality or abstraction for our list goods. We should distinguish clearly between the notion of a *good* and the notion of an *instance* of a good. For example, succeeding in climbing Mount Everest is something that can make a life go better. However, it is not something without which any good life would be incomplete. So we can assume that getting up Everest is not a good in itself, but an instance of a more general good (perhaps 'accomplishment', if we accept Griffin 1986's taxonomy). In other cases we might find that something is, indeed, lost in moving to a higher level of generality or abstraction. And in this way we can proceed.

2 THE CENTRALITY OF PLEASURE

Many people seem to hold conflicting views about well-being. On the one hand, what they actually pursue in life seems to be a variety of goods more or less along the lines of Aristotle's list. On the other, when (if) they think more systematically about what counts as happiness, about why they pursue what they do, they are likely to be drawn towards hedonism, at least as a first attempt at a comprehensive conception of happiness. This tension need not be seen as a sign of confusion. Quite possibly there is something right on both sides—in which case, the two sides can presumably be brought into harmony with each other.

A simple way of resolving the tension is just to make the familiar point that pleasure is best pursued *indirectly*. So maybe most people are, indeed, hedonists—it is just that they are sophisticated enough in their hedonism to be indirect hedonists? There seems to be more to it than that. Even in a sophisticated and indirect form, classical hedonism's instrumental approach makes it notoriously bad at accommodating the feeling that most people have that some pleasurable activities are better than others, because only some involve not only pleasure but also worthwhile achievement. How can this feeling be acknowledged within a broadly hedonist approach to the theory of the good? In this section I shall approach my own answer to this question by considering someone else's: Fred Feldman's.

Feldman 2004 offers a versatile theory of the good that allows the smooth incorporation of objectivist elements into a basically hedonist account. Feldman begins by developing an understanding of the notion of pleasure itself that is quite different from classical hedonism's. Instead of concentrating on the pleasures that are feelings, Feldman focuses on what he calls the 'attitudinal pleasures'. An attitudinal pleasure is a form of *enjoyment*: it is something we take *in* things, so it always has a propositional content. (There is no *enjoying* that is not an enjoying *of something*.) Although 'attitudinal pleasure' is usually connected to sensory pleasure, it is not necessarily tied to it: think of the Stoic sage who is fully satisfied with his existence, yet does not experience sensory pleasure. While classical hedonism tends to detach pleasure from its sources, the attitudinal version manages to show that there is something very natural about our preoccupation with other things than pleasure: given attitudinal pleasure's directedness towards concrete objects of pursuit, this preoccupation is built into states of pleasure from the start.

Feldman's account suggests a number of refinements in what we should say about the prudential value of pleasures. For instance, it helps us to see how their value might be conditional on the worth of their objects. Since, on Feldman's view, most interesting and important cases of pleasure involve some propositional content, it is natural to think that pleasure in worthwhile objects involves a 'fit' between attitude and object which is itself valuable, and missing in the case of pleasure in objects that are not worth while. So which pleasures are the worthwhile ones? We could use Aristotle's list to answer this. There would then be a sense in which someone's life can be going well even when she is not taking any greater pleasure in its content: this will be true when her life includes objects that are at least pleasure-*worthy*, even though they are not giving actual pleasure.

But although Feldman is surely right to build his hedonism around a focus on the attitudinal pleasures—on enjoyment, not on feeling—we might still wonder whether his account represents a stable compromise between the objectivist and subjectivist impulses in the theory of the good. Feldman's account connects the attitudinal pleasures that it is good to have to the achievement or possession of the sort of things mentioned on Aristotle's list. Yet it is not until we have these pleasures of enjoyment that we are *really* possessors of well-being; otherwise, we merely have a life that is *apt* for enjoyment. This doesn't seem right. It seems better to say that having a life that is apt for enjoyment is *one* ingredient of well-being, and taking pleasure in—enjoying—a life that is apt for enjoyment is *another*. In which case, the objects that are pleasure-worthy will add value to our lives quite apart from the pleasure that we take in them. But this conclusion is, of course, incompatible with any position that deserves to be called hedonism. Though pleasure will still have an important place on the list of goods, it obviously will not be the *only* good.

Could the hedonist object that this hybrid position, with its emphasis on 'enjoying a life that is apt for enjoyment', involves us in a cumbersome form of double-counting? That objection would be mistaken. The distinction between what is actually enjoyed and what is apt for enjoyment is real, and usefully allows us to refine our judgements about the quality of different lives. Compare two lives: both of them contain no enjoyment, but one life involves plenty that is enjoyment-*apt*; while the second life does not even have that. The consistent hedonist must say that both of these lives are equally bad. But this does not seem reasonable; the first life is pretty obviously better than the second.

Of course, there is an air of disappointment, waste, or hollowness about the first life which is absent in the second life ('How could he have all these goods, and *still* experience no enjoyment?'). We feel, so to speak, that the first life, unlike the second, is a tragically *near miss*. But it is a near miss precisely because the person in question does not appreciate that her life is *already*, to a certain extent, going well—the second life is nowhere near. So this sense of disappointment is further evidence that there are elements of well-being that are not captured by hedonism.

A second argument for preferring the hybrid position to any form of hedonism is that it makes better sense of the ways in which we ordinarily evaluate our lives. Of course, it might be unfair to demand that a philosophical theory of the constituents of happiness that it should fit neatly with our ordinary practice: as Scanlon 1998 (ch. 3) points out, we do not think much about happiness in everyday life anyway. Still, imagine a person on her deathbed, trying to assess whether or not she has had a *good* life. Would she only count the pleasures? An indirect hedonist will say that most of us benefit from thinking, falsely, that the objects of pleasure have value apart from the pleasure they give us: this illusion is beneficial, because it enables us to gain more pleasure. The person on her deathbed has no further use for this illusion. None the less, her appraisal of her own life would surely miss something if she only counted her pleasures, and ignored both the objects of those pleasures, and other objects that *could* and *should* have given her pleasure. Of course, few people get this sort of clarity, even on their deathbeds (perhaps particularly not on their deathbeds). Still, as a model for how to evaluate your own life, the deathbed perspective surely has something to teach us. One thinks of the familiar question 'Will I die regretting that I didn't spend less time at the office?'; also of the *Phaedo*'s notion that philosophy is a preparing to die. Come to that, Aristotle's list of goods in the *Rhetoric* looks like precisely the kind of list that someone might use in a deathbed evaluation of his life.

I conclude that even a sophisticated attitudinal hedonism like Feldman's is simply too restrictive in its account of the constituents of the human good. But, having reached that conclusion, I also want to emphasize that while a pluralist position looks more reasonable, it is also true that pleasure seems to have a unique place in the plurality of prudential goods. There is no other good that is so influential in pushing people towards monism about the constituents of happiness; therefore, a satisfactory form of pluralism must capture the centrality of pleasure. This is why we should not just add pleasure as another item on the list of goods. What we need instead is an account that accords independent prudential value to a variety of goods, yet acknowledges pleasure's special place in the good life. In the next section, I shall begin to develop such an account by offering some comments on Darwall and Aristotle.

3 PLEASURE AS COMPLETION

We strive after a variety of things. Our strivings are completed when we achieve their objects. Yet something seems to be lacking if we are not *moved* by such successes. Aristotle's view of pleasure is that it is an activity (*energeia*) of the soul, but also that it is an activity which *completes* other activities. But not, Aristotle explains, 'as the state (*hexis*) does, by being present [in the activity]'; rather pleasure completes other activities 'as a sort of consequent end, like the bloom on youths' (*NE* 1174b33–35).

So our various *energeiai* can be 'completed' by achieving the ends which define them. In a different way, they can also be 'completed' by pleasure. And, as

Aristotle goes on to note, 'the proper (*oikeia*) pleasure increases the activity; for we judge each thing better and more exactly when our activity involves pleasure' (*NE* 1175a31–33). In the best case, a worthwhile 'activity' will be completed both by its successful performance, and by the consequent pleasure; furthermore, there will be positive feedback in both directions between these two forms of completion.

Compare Darwall 2002: 75: 'the best life for human beings is one of significant engagement in activities through which we come into appreciative rapport with agent-neutral values, such as aesthetic beauty, knowledge and understanding, and the worth of living beings'. In some ways Darwall's position is very similar to the Aristotelian view just outlined: notice his stress on activity, engagement, and appreciation. But there is also a Platonist tone, most obvious in Darwall's claim that what matters is to achieve 'rapport with agent-neutral values'. This seems questionable to me. That certain things are good, and that it is good that we come in appreciative rapport with them, need not mean that the important thing is to come into appreciative rapport with them as values. Indeed, while many of the things that make our lives go well, for example, deep and meaningful relationships with others, can reasonably be said to have agent-neutral value, it is not really the appreciation *of their agent-neutral value* that matters in our lives; rather, it is the appreciation *of them*. We certainly appreciate our loved ones, but to put things like Darwall is to paint a picture far too reminiscent of the kind of transcendental promiscuity that characterizes Plato's theory of love in the *Symposium*, in which love objects are really only important as 'ladders' enabling us to come in touch with the form of beauty itself, and thus quite interchangeable.

Even if it is the agent-neutral value of having friends and loved ones that makes our lives go better, what we really appreciate in our friends and loved ones is their particularities. In the cool hour of reflection, we might agree that we come into contact with some agent-neutral value(s) through them. Still, it seems far too strong to demand that these relations themselves should be infused with such an understanding, or even that we should so much as have this understanding. Even in the case of appreciating art, which is probably the area where Darwall's account might seem most plausible, it is important to keep in mind the distinction between the value of a work of art and the qualities that we appreciate in it. It is the specific details that capture us and resonate for us. Truly great works of art have agent-neutral value partly because of how many people can find things in them to appreciate; but this value itself is typically not what those people come into appreciative rapport with. In sum: the appreciation that completes our activities by adding pleasure to them is an appreciation *of particular things*—as I put it in section 1, not *goods* but *instances* of goods.

However, there is a second comment that applies here. This is that 'activity' seems not to be as important a notion as Darwall (and Aristotle) think. While many of the things that can make our lives go well by adding appreciation-value to it certainly involve a variety of *energeiai*, it seems stretched to regard them all as 'activities'. For instance, involvement in deep and meaningful relations with others does not fit the recipe for a typical Aristotelian *energeia*. Such involvement simply seems too various to count as a single discrete activity, nor is its content exhausted by any list of *energeiai* alone. Yet friendship is surely an important component of a good life. It seems reasonable to be pluralistic not just about how many things can make our lives go well, but also about which metaphysical categories (objects, properties, activities, events, state-of-affairs, and so on) these things fall into. (Not that Darwall denies this: he only claims to identify the *general form* of the key constituents in the human good; he is not saying that there are no other things which matter for how well our lives are going.) Of course, it is not true that *anything* goes in the theory of well-being. But it does seem prudent to be liberal at least on the outset, and not simply insist on some substantive metaphysics of lives that forces us into the view that lives are made up of activities.

The upshot is not that we need to give up the idea that pleasure completes. The point is rather that *what* it completes is not (or not necessarily) 'activities', but, more generally, the integration of well-being's components, whatever they are, into our lives. A person can achieve all sorts of fine and noble things, but if they give her no pleasure then there is something wrong about the way in which these things are fitted into her life. The problem is that she is alienated from these goods. Although they are in one sense part of her life, she has not embraced them: she is not getting any appreciation-value out of them. So there is a more demanding sense in which they have *not* become part of her life.

Compare the illuminating distinction made in Kagan 1994 between two questions that we can ask about anyone's individual well-being: 'How well is my life going?'; and 'How well am I doing?' The answers to these questions can diverge. *My life* might be going well, in that I am achieving the sort of things mentioned on Aristotle's list, at the same time as *I* might not be doing at all well, in that I take no joy in all of these goods. Call these two sorts of well-being 'biographical' (the perspective of my life) and 'appreciative' (the I-perspective), respectively.

This distinction between how my life has objectively been going, and what it has been like leading it, is important. However, there are, of course, interrelations between the two sides of the distinction. We can say that our overall view of how well a person's existence has been going is a function of two principal components: the *biographical* goods, which constitute parts of my life objectively seen; and the *appreciative* goods, which include the good of my taking pleasure in the biographical goods and in my life generally.

Most of what comes under this category of appreciative goods is likely to be one sort or another of pleasure; but not all of it. Quite possibly the category of appreciative goods also includes the good of my understanding, at least roughly, the nature and import of the biographical goods that I have possession of. There might even be some goods the ideal appreciation of which does not primarily take the form of pleasure. Take, for example, the appreciation of the moral goods, such as the virtues. Here the most relevant appreciative good might instead be that of understanding. It seems plausible to require that a person have an understanding of moral concerns—not a *philosophical* understanding perhaps, but at least a commonsense one—if the virtues are to be realized as prudential goods in him. Pleasure, by contrast, does *not* seem an appreciative good relevant to the moral goods; even if Aristotle himself thought that taking pleasure in one's own moral behaviour was something good, to *enjoy* one's own virtuousness simply sounds too smug. It looks better to think of something more like *not being pained by* one's possession of the virtues. (There is, of course, a question about whether the moral goods form a part of the human good at all. The view that they do is common in the Aristotelian tradition, though many other modern theorists think that the very idea of taking the moral goods as constituents of happiness tarnishes them with an egotistical taint. I shall not go into this here.)

This two-level conception of the human good is what I take Aristotelian pluralism to be all about. The picture is that human well-being is composed both of biographical goods and also of appreciative goods. Aristotle's account of the biographical goods seems broadly right to me (though, as already remarked, I need not defend the detail of his list here). The central appreciative good is pleasure as enjoyment. In section 4 of this chapter, I shall end my discussion with a closer look at the relation between the two components of the two-level conception—between biographical and appreciative goods.

4 THE CONDITIONALITY OF PRUDENTIAL GOODS

The question how biographical and appreciative goods relate to each other can be understood as the question how they form wholes. I shall consider three possibilities.

(1) Any given biographical good and the appreciative good taken in it (as above, this will normally be pleasure) are simply two goods the values of which are to be added together. On this view, the importance of having both simply comes from the fact that if we really are to suck out all the marrow of life, then we need to draw our well-being from both sources.

(2) While both biographical and appreciative goods are valuable in their own right, taken together they form a whole that is valuable in some *further* way: that is, an organic unity in Moore 1903s sense.

(3) Again, the values of the two types of goods could be conditional on each other: the value of one or both of them requires the presence of the other in order to be realized fully. We might call this the Kantian sense of organic unity.[5]

---

[5] Kant does not discuss the matter directly, but his views on the highest good suggest that final values can be conditional in the way that I sketch here. On these two kinds of organic unity,

(1) is too simplistic: it takes too little account of the crucial question *how* things are combined and balanced in our lives. Also, it clearly does not capture the distinctive role played by the appreciative goods. Where we have the biographical goods but not the appreciative, what we lack is not just one more type of well-being from the same list. Furthermore, while pleasures generally make our lives go better, they don't always. Malicious pleasures can reasonably be seen not just as morally bad, but as prudentially bad too. It would be quite reasonable for someone to conclude, in a deathbed review of her life, that it was marred—not just marred *for others*, but marred *for herself*—by an excess of malicious pleasures. Louis XIV is said to have concluded on his deathbed that he had loved war too much—and no doubt he was right.

(2), the Moorean idea, holds constant the value of both sorts of prudential goods, and adds emergent values to make sense of the ways in which combining and balancing matter. However, these emergent values are simply too detached from the matters under consideration. The life with the biographical goods but not the appreciative goods, and the life with the appreciative goods but not the biographical goods, are both fairly unattractive lives. Yet the life where we have both sorts of goods is very attractive indeed. It follows that the goodness of this third sort of life must, on the Moorean picture, arise largely from the holistic extra value created by the combination. But this does not seem quite right. In the *good* life, the *good* stuff is surely the pleasures and the realised objects of pursuit *themselves*; not some mysterious amalgam of these ingredients. And likewise with the bad stuff in a bad life: if a deathbed review of her life led someone to regret her malicious pleasures, it would be the pleasures themselves that she saw as having negative value, not some other sort of value to which those pleasures contributed. While the Moorean might be able to get the right overall results about the contribution of things like malicious pleasures, his route to these results does not fit with how we understand the goods.

Since (1) and (2) are both unsatisfactory, we turn to (3): the possibility that, in concrete circumstances, the exact value of the constituents of the human good depends on what other goods are also realized in the life in question. There are different ways of developing this possibility, depending on what the conditionals are and how they function. In Kant's own theory of the good, for instance, other goods will have their own distinctive sort of dependent value, conditional on the presence of 'good will'; but good will's value is absolutely unconditional on anything else whatsoever. Given that I have based my approach on the distinction between biographical and appreciative goods, I would prefer to suggest that the conditionality should normally run both ways. For the full value of any good of

see Hurka 1998, who calls them, respectively, the 'holistic' and the 'conditionality' interpretation of organic unity. Note that there cannot be organic unities in the Kantian sense if the Moorean understanding of final values is correct. For a general argument against the Moorean idea of the unconditionality of the value of final goods, see Olson 2004.

the one type, appreciative or biographical, to be realized fully, the corresponding good of the other type has to be realized as well.

But how does this matching of goods, biographical and appreciative, work? How much of a biographical good do we need for it to be warranted to take pleasure in it, and how much pleasure need we take in a biographical good before it can be said to be properly appreciated and therefore fully integrated into the life of the person in question? Since we do not have any metric, at least not in any interesting sense of the word, either for pleasure or for the biographical goods, this is not a question to which exact answers can be given. There are, however, still a few formal points that can be made.

Irwin 1999: 8 offers a suggestion of much value to those who start their theory of well-being, as I have done, from the Aristotelian ideal of 'a complete life'. This is that we can use the type-token distinction to fill out our understanding of this Aristotelian ideal. A given good may add value to our lives in two distinct ways. First, any additional instance of that good can make our lives better; second, when we get enough instances of that good, it will become true that we have realized a certain type-good in our lives.

So, for example, having friends is a constituent of the good life. But were I to have only a single friend, and only for a single year, then it would be reasonable to say that the type-value friendship was not realized in my life. We need a certain number of *tokens* of typical goods before we can say that we have those goods, as *types*, as parts of our lives. Of course, it is not easy to say exactly where the line between 'not enough' and 'enough' such tokens is to be drawn. This difficulty does not remove the fact that, for most of the good-types that we typically place on lists of the constituents of the human good, there is such a line. There must be, because we can generally see how it can be true that one person has, for example, the type-good of friendship in her life, and another does not, even though this second person too has *some* instances of friendship in her life. Likewise, there are always scenarios where someone might experience extra instances of a given prudential good beside those she already possesses. Clearly, then, it is only with respect to the inclusion of type-goods into our lives that we can achieve complete lives.

Given this distinction, I suggest that pleasure serves to complete our lives in two ways. First, there must be a significant amount of appreciative goods such as pleasure in my life in order for the type-good of pleasure or appreciation to be realized in my life. The bare fact of a lack of pleasure or appreciation reveals a lack in any human life. And second, the prudential value of the other type-goods—the biographical goods—is only partially realized by our mere possession of them, i.e. of sufficiently many tokens of each type, unless we also take pleasure in them, appreciate them. The mere possession of the biographical goods does make our lives go better. But for their full value to be realized in our lives, we must enjoy sufficiently many tokens of them. In this way pleasure completes the biographical goods, giving them the kind of 'sparkle' that is required for them to constitute parts of real human flourishing. (One could perhaps go even further and say that for biographical goods to have any prudential value at all, they must be appreciated. But a person that has the biographical goods seems to be in a position where she has reason to find that her life is already going well and in order to make sense of this fact it is reasonable to say that even in such a life the biographical goods still have some prudential value.)

In line with my suggestion that the conditionality should normally run both ways, the dependence runs the other way as well. If the pleasures in a life are to add up to the type-good of pleasure being fully realized in that life, the pleasures should to a sufficiently high degree be taken in worthy objects, or at least not in positively unworthy ones. (We could demand that each and every token of pleasure has to be pleasure taken in a worthy object, if it is to count. Maybe this is too stern a view. While a life entirely composed of frivolity would have something wrong with it, a bit of frivolous pleasure might be a good thing in a normal human life.)

Thus, to conclude, the composition of a good life involves a complex network of interdependencies. Maybe nothing is ever fully good in a wholly unconditioned and independent way. But, even if that is so, it seems safe to say that no other good plays such a central role as pleasure. For, while there must be things for pleasure to complete, in order for pleasure to be like the 'bloom on youths', these things are very diverse; whereas the single element pleasure (or appreciation) is quite generally involved in, and quite essential to, the realization of the full value of *every* other good. We can thus reasonably regard pleasure as a form of prudential master-value—even if it is not, *pace* hedonism, the only good there is.

13

Mixed Determinates: Pleasure, Good, and Truth

Theodore Scaltsas

The righteous, promises Aristotle, shall enjoy life (*NE* 1099a11–15):

> For most people the things that are pleasant are in conflict, because they are not such by nature, whereas to the lovers of the fine what is pleasant is what is pleasant by nature; and actions in accordance with excellence are like this, so that they are pleasant both to these people and in themselves.[1]

I shall argue that Aristotle does not deliver on his promise. We shall investigate the notion of things 'pleasant by nature' (*ta physei hêdea*) and find that it does not secure the pleasant and conflict-free life that Aristotle describes. What is of interest in this investigation is not only the lost paradise, it is also the fact that the search reveals an Aristotelian doctrine about the way that human ends, and ends of nature, realize themselves as mixed determinates. Significantly, we shall find that the doctrine of mixed determinates is a theme that recurs across Aristotle's thought, extending to the good, the true, and beyond.

1 'BEING SUCH BY NATURE': A FIRST ATTEMPT AT ITS MEANING

There are several senses of being *f* 'by nature' which can be distinguished in Aristotle's *Nicomachean Ethics*. I begin with two.

The first is what we might call 'natural through universality'. Talking about the appetites, Aristotle distinguishes those that are peculiar and acquired from those that are shared by everyone. He says that 'the appetite for nourishment is *natural* to us, since everyone has an appetite for nourishment when they lack it [i.e. the nourishment] . . . and for "bed", in Homer's phrase, when one is young and in one's physical prime' (1118b10–12). He contrasts appetites which are

---

[1] Here, as elsewhere, I quote Rowe's translation, in Broadie and Rowe 2002. For 'The righteous shall enjoy life' cp. Psalm 58: 10.

not universal because they are more specific: 'but as for the appetite for this or that sort of food, not everyone has *that*' (1118b12–13). The assumption must be that hunger and the sexual appetite are natural because they are universal in the sense of being constitutive of the organisms we are. They include essential, as well as merely necessary, appetites or dispositions. Such appetites or dispositions are included in what Aristotle calls the 'necessary pleasures' (1154a12), i.e. pleasures such as eating, but also scratching an itch. These pleasures are necessary because we do not choose to have them: they are universal and thus unavoidable. By contrast, an appetite for (say) mango is not constitutive of human being, or animal, but only peculiar to some.

In a second sense of 'natural', however, the appetite for mango is natural, too. Aristotle qualifies an appetite for a particular type of food as follows: 'it [for example, the appetite for mango] *does* have an element of the *natural* about it, since different things are pleasant for different individuals, and everyone gets more pleasure from certain things than from just anything' (1118b13–15). The reason for such natural peculiarities is variation in what is felt as pleasant, or more pleasant, between and indeed within persons. In themselves, these variable tastes tell us nothing about what is or is not natural in the first sense; they are explained either by acquired (*epithetoi*) appetites for the pleasant or by peculiar individual (*idioi*) tendencies. (Thus, for instance, the peculiar appetite for whisky can be an acquired one—though it can also, to judge by some people, be there from birth.)

That such peculiarities arise from variation in what is felt as pleasant seems to be implied by the opening sentence of *NE* III.11. This chapter introduces the topic of appetites through a dichotomy that suggests that variation is due *only* to acquisition of an appetite through habit: 'Of appetites, some seem to be shared, others peculiar and acquired' (1118b8–9). Here Aristotle associates the natural with the shared appetites, and contrasts them with the acquired ones which are not shared. By contrast, in the very next sentence he seems to want to retract and qualify his dichotomy between the natural and the peculiar/acquired, and allow that a peculiar appetite 'all the same . . . *does* have an element of the natural about it' (1118b14). What could that 'element' be, other than non-acquired, raw constitution? It is not shared by all, but nevertheless it rests on the way we are built rather than on our habits. So although variation in our tastes can in some cases be the result of habit, in others it is natural, a result of the constitution we are born with.

Aristotle talks of appetite having 'an element of the natural about it' because, in some cases, raw and acquired features can be combined, as an appetite for refined wine would combine training and raw untrained preference. In general, hobbies and sports typically result from combinations of the two, where we build up the natural which is peculiar to us through habituation and training.

So far, then, we have found Aristotle distinguishing between two senses of 'natural'.

(1): some things are 'natural' in the sense that applies to those aspects of one's universal constitution which one shares with all members of the species or genus. In this sense the 'natural' is opposed to what is peculiar to someone, or acquired;

(2): some things are 'natural' in the sense that applies to one's peculiar raw constitution, which is neither acquired nor shared with the whole species: for example, physical strength or a preference for sour flavours.

We need now to consider whether either of these two senses of the natural can be employed in order to explain the sense of being f 'by nature' that applies at 1099a13–14: 'For most people the things that are pleasant are in conflict, because they are not such by nature' (*phusei hêdea*).

Suppose being 'pleasant by nature' encompasses only activities that are universally constitutive of human beings. Aristotle does indeed say that 'being alive is something that is good and pleasant in itself' (1170a20–21), which is a state or activity that would be 'by nature' in the first sense—an instance of what is universally constitutive of human beings. But the problem with such an understanding of the expression 'by nature' would be that it excludes from being pleasant the activities of acquired traits of character, just because these are not constitutive of human beings. The offending coefficient here is acquisition, which is needed, either by teaching or by habituation, to enable virtuous activity:

Excellence being of two sorts, then, the one intellectual and the other of character, the intellectual sort mostly both comes into existence and increases as a result of teaching . . . whereas excellence of character results from habituation. (1103a15–18)

But, for Aristotle, all virtuous activity is pleasant by nature: 'generally, the things in accordance with excellence [are pleasant] to the lover of excellence . . . to the lovers of the fine, what is pleasant is what is pleasant by nature' (1099a11–12). Therefore, if being pleasant by nature encompasses only activity that is universally constitutive of human beings, it will leave out the core instances of pleasant activity—*virtuous* activity.

So it cannot be right to say that, if something is pleasant by nature, then it is universally constitutive of human beings. Nor can it be right to say that, if something is universally constitutive of human beings, then it is pleasant by nature. Consider, for instance, walking, breathing, or digesting, all of which could be painful in many circumstances. The cases of perceiving and thinking look more favourable; but even here it is doubtful that there is a sense in which their mere occurrence is sufficient for the activity to be pleasant. Let us restrict perceiving to items that are proper objects of the senses, excluding for example, looking at the sun which would be painful and damaging. Then are perceiving and thinking sufficient for experiencing pleasure? Aristotle says (*Met.* 1074b32–34):

. . . both thinking and the act of thought will belong even to one who has the worst of thoughts. Therefore, if this ought to be avoided (and it ought, for there are even some things which it is better not to see than to see) . . .[2].

Clearly Aristotle here does not find the mere act of thinking or of seeing sufficient for pleasure, if he thinks that thinking certain thoughts or seeing certain things is improper and to be avoided.

So, if 'by nature' meant 'universally constitutive of human beings', then the core instances of pleasant activity (those arising from acquired moral dispositions) would be excluded; and the activities that would be included would not by themselves secure pleasure.

By the same token, 'by nature' as used in this context cannot mean 'constitutive of the raw nature that is peculiar to the individual' either. On this understanding of 'by nature', too, the pleasures of the activities of virtue would be implausibly excluded, and all sorts of individual peculiarities would be implausibly included.

So neither of these senses of being f 'by nature' will do. We must try again.

2 INCIDENTAL PLEASURES

One important, surprising, but relatively neglected, classification that Aristotle introduces is that of the incidental pleasures. The surprise comes from the realization that the incidentally pleasant is natural in the first sense identified above, that of belonging universally to beings of that type. Eating, for example, is natural to humans because it is a universal human activity—but is only incidentally pleasant. And the importance comes, not from the instances of the incidentally pleasant themselves, but from their complement in the good moral agent. This is the things that are naturally (*phusei*) pleasant, or pleasant without qualification (*haplôs*).

To understand this notion of 'natural' which applies to the acquired, let us turn to Aristotle's explanation of the incidental pleasures. Unfortunately it is a complicated explanation.

Aristotle says that 'it is only incidentally that the processes of restoring someone to his natural disposition/state are pleasant' (1152b34–35). Furthermore, such pleasures 'are not even pleasures, but only appear so, i.e. those that are accompanied by pain and are for the sake of healing, such as sick people undergo' (1152b31–33). Why is it that—as we have seen—Aristotle classifies at least some of these pleasures as necessary, but also now as incidental, and as only apparent? To see why, we need to look into the nature of the process that brings incidental pleasures about.

---

[2] Contrast what Aristotle says at *NE* 1152b36–3a1, where reflection is the type of pleasure that is unaccompanied by pain.

We saw above that such pleasures are necessary in so far as their corresponding dispositions are part of the human constitution, for example, the urge to breathe, the hunger for food and drink, the appetite for sex, the disposition to scratch itching skin, to rest when tired, etc. But why are such necessary pleasures only incidentally pleasant? The reason is that they only *restore* a person to his natural disposition/state. Aristotle does not deny that eating is pleasant; it is just that the pleasure involved in eating belongs to it only incidentally. But if the pleasure of eating does not belong to eating in itself, to what *does* this pleasure belong in itself? And how is its restoring nature relevant to the mode of possession of the pleasure by that activity? The key to the explanation is the notion of a 'natural disposition/state'.

Aristotle's reasoning is as follows:[3] 'given that the good is part activity and part disposition/state, it is only incidentally that the processes of restoring someone to the natural disposition/state are pleasant' (1152b33–35). This piece of reasoning is contracted, to say the least. In the text that immediately follows, Aristotle describes further the incidentally pleasant, by saying that 'the activity in the case of the appetites belongs to one's residual natural disposition, since there are also pleasures unaccompanied by pain and appetite, like the activities of reflection, where there is no depletion of the natural state' (1152b35–1153a2). His claim is that in the cases where the activity restores the nature to its good and stable condition (that is, to the condition that is not in any way depleted and in need of replenishment), the pleasure of the restoration is due to the activity, not of the depleted state but of the remaining wholesome state of that nature. Although Aristotle does not flag this as the reason why the pleasure of restoration is an incidental pleasure, the point becomes clearer in a further explanation he gives in a different passage: 'What I call incidentally pleasant are the remedial sort [of pleasures]; for what makes a thing seem pleasant in this case is that one happens to be cured, thanks to the activity of the part that remains healthy' (1154b17–19).

There are two considerations here. First, the activity that is pleasurable is the activity, not of the depleted state but of the remaining healthy state that replenishes the depleted one. It is the curing activity that is pleasant, which is the activity of the healthy part. Second, what makes it pleasant is the positive value of the curing for that organism. The reason why such pleasures are incidental comes from the first consideration: the point that the restoration is pleasant due to the activity not of the depleted part but of the wholesome one. So, for example, the pleasure we get from eating is due to the restoring activity of the non-starved part of our nature. It is the activity of the non-depleted state of our nature that desires and brings about the replenishment, and so the pleasure of the replenishment is due to that activity, not to any activity generated by lack or depletion.

---

[3] Those who are less enthusiastic about the fine details of Aristotle's thought can skip to the end of this section . . . at their own peril!

Aristotle continues with a further explanation which, Ross thinks, also shows restorations to be incidentally pleasant, although I wish to dispute Ross's reading. Aristotle says:

An indication is that people do not take pleasure in the same things while their nature is being restored to completion and when it has been replenished: when it has been re-established they enjoy things that are pleasant without qualification, but while it is being restored they enjoy even things that are the contrary of these—even enjoying sharp and bitter tastes, none of which is either naturally pleasant or pleasant without qualification.   (1153a2–6)

Pace Ross, Aristotle is not here giving another reason why restorations are incidentally pleasant. Rather he is defending a different claim that he has just made (1152b36–3a1), that there are two distinct groups of pleasures: pleasures that do not come from appetite and do not have corelevant pains; and pleasures that do. In this quotation, the difference between the two groups is further indicated by the fact that the pleasures in the first group (which are the pleasurable activities of the healthy states) have different objects from the activities of the second group (which are the pleasurable activities of the depleted states).

Ross begins the translation of this passage as follows: '*That the others are incidental* is indicated by the fact that men do not enjoy the same things . . .' (in Barnes's edition, 1984). But I do not see how this passage could be an indication of the incidental status of these pleasures. The best case one could make for seeing them as incidental would appeal to the *objects* of these pleasures. The argument would be that people undergoing a process of restoration or replenishment may even enjoy things that are, without qualification, *un*pleasant; so these unpleasant things are only found pleasant because of the process of replenishment; so these things are only incidentally pleasant. And since, Aristotle tells us, pleasures are co-ordinate with their objects (1153a6–7: 'as things that are pleasant are distinguished one from another, so too are pleasures deriving from them'), it follows (so the argument would run) that the pleasure caused during replenishment by these only-incidentally-pleasant objects is itself only an incidental pleasure.

But this reasoning faces an objection. During a replenishment, one might also find something pleasurable that is itself pleasant without qualification, for example, something sweet. If the argument just given is sound, then since this sweet object is pleasant without qualification, the pleasure taken in it must be pleasant without qualification, too; and, hence, not incidentally pleasant. But Aristotle's view is that replenishment is *always* only incidentally pleasant: 'it is only incidentally that the processes restoring one to the natural state are pleasant' (1152b34–35).

So Ross's reading of this passage—according to which Aristotle is giving another reason why restorations are incidentally pleasant—cannot be sustained. Rather, what Aristotle's 'indication' shows is only that there is a *difference* between pleasures of replenishment and pleasures of the replenished nature, since their objects are different. But this difference alone does not show that pleasures of the one sort are incidentally pleasant, and pleasures of the other sort are not. By contrast, on the explanation I have offered, replenishment is an incidental pleasure *because* the pleasure of replenishment derives not from the depleted state but from the activity of the wholesome state of the organism which restores the depleted state.

Although Aristotle refers to the 'depletion of the natural state' (1153a1–2), his interest in the present line of argument is not in *any* activity of the depleted state, but in the process of restoration of the organism to its wholesome condition. Throughout the paragraph Aristotle is talking of such processes of restoration, as his three examples make clear. These are: the treatment that sick people undergo for the sake of healing (1152b32–33); processes restoring someone to the natural state (1152b34); and processes restoring someone's nature to completion (1153a2–3, a4).

By extension, we *could* include here the processes that restore someone's moral character through education and habituation; for example, when he experiences feelings of loneliness, or need for revenge. But these, in my view, are a different class of processes from the activities that someone engages in as a result of a bad state of his organism or character, as, for instance, pursuing an addiction to alcohol or exhibiting brutal behaviour.

However, Broadie's understanding of the passage takes the two classes of processes together. Commenting on 1153a2–7 (the end of which I quoted above), she says (Broadie and Rowe 2002: 401):

This passage matches the two distinctions 'without qualification'/'for someone in an abnormal condition' and 'restored state'/'process of repletion'. What the other side identify as pleasures without qualification are only pleasures for the abnormal, though . . . they are a function not of their abnormality so much as of their partial normality. It is not easy to see how this applies on the ethical as distinct from physiological level. Is taking pleasure in bullying or cheating people necessarily to be analysed as pleasure in the activity of some partly decent ethical disposition?

The answer is that taking pleasure in bullying or cheating should not be analysed as a pleasure of some residual decent ethical disposition. These pleasures are not activities of the ethical disposition at all—no more than someone's indulging his addiction is (even partly) the activity of the healthy state of his organism. The examples of bullying and cheating are not an extension of the types of activity that Aristotle has been talking about here. Although a depleted state of any kind can be thought of as an abnormal state, the processes that Aristotle repeatedly refers to in this paragraph are only processes of the restoration of the abnormal state to the normal; he does not have in mind any activity of the abnormality. Otherwise, it would not be only the extension to the ethical cases that would be paradoxical; even in the physiological cases we would be reluctant to accept Aristotle's claim that the pleasure is due to the healthy part of the organism.

Indulging the need for cocaine and the need for food are very different processes. The first aims at a depraved state of the organism; while the latter aims at the restoration of the organism to its wholesome state. The first need could not be what is desired by 'one's residual natural disposition' (1152b35–36); but the second could. Broadie's criticism of Aristotle here seems unfair, because she does not distinguish, with Aristotle, between the activities of an abnormal state *qua* abnormal, and those of the organism specifically directed towards eliminating the abnormality.

Before leaving this topic I should address a surprising comment of Aristotle's about restorative processes. He says that 'other [processes] again are not even pleasures, but only appear so, i.e. those that are accompanied by pain and are for the sake of healing, such as the ones sick people undergo' (1152b31–33). But these processes are precisely the ones he proceeds to characterize as incidentally pleasant. It is clear from the text that Aristotle is introducing a new point here which is not an explanation of what he has just stated: 'Further [*eti*], . . . it is only incidentally that the processes restoring one to the natural state are pleasant' (1152b33–35). So the claim that restorative processes are only *apparently* pleasant is different from the claim that they are only *incidentally* pleasant. Are these two claims in conflict? If not, do they reduce to the same claim, despite Aristotle's distinction between them?

No, and no. Restorative processes are apparently pleasant by comparison to the pleasant without qualification, while they are incidentally pleasant because the source of the pleasure of restoration is in the activity of the wholesome state, not the needy one. An example that may help us to understand this distinction is the colour of a white wall at sunset. When the sun's rays fall on it, the wall becomes pink, but only incidentally so, because it is the sunlight on it, rather that the wall's paint, that is pink. But it is only apparently pink in comparison to the setting sun, which (at least from a terrestrial viewpoint) is truly pink, without qualification. The wall's colour is an amalgam of pink and other (non-pink) colours, and it is only our attention to the one aspect of this colour that leads us to consider this amalgam pink, just as it is only our attention to the pleasing aspects of a restoring activity that makes us consider this amalgam of pleasure and pain a pleasurable activity.

3 OUR RELATION TO THE GOOD

Our focus on Aristotle's notion of the 'incidentally pleasant' has borne some fruit, partly because 'incidentally pleasant' is often opposed by him to 'pleasant without qualification'. A further attempt to understand the sense in which Aristotle means the pleasant *by nature*, as opposed to the pleasant for most people, will lead us to his discussion of the distinction between the good, the good for the agent, and the apparent good.

When Aristotle talks of what is 'naturally wished for' at 1113a22, he is arguing that for those philosophers who claim that the object of wish (*boulêsis*) is the apparent good, nothing is naturally wished for. The distinction he is making is the same as the one with which he begins the paragraph regarding what a wish is for (1113a15–16): 'to some, it [i.e. wish] seems to be for the good, whereas to others it seems to be for the *apparent* good'. His reasoning must be that if wish is for the apparent good, no wish will be for the actual good, even if in some cases the apparent good happens to coincide with the actual good. The opacity of the context of wishing does not allow intersubstitution of the two descriptions *real good* and *apparent good*, even if the referent is the same, so that if someone wishes for the apparent good, and this happens to be the real good, she is not thereby wishing for the real good. So when Aristotle says that 'the consequence is that there is nothing naturally wished for, [there is] only what seems an object of wish to each particular person' (1113a20–23), where what is 'naturally wished for' is contrasted to 'what seems an object of wish', we must assume that the former is the real good contrasted with the latter which is the apparent good. It is the real good that is naturally wished for.

Aristotle remarks that 'for those who say that the apparent good is wished for . . . different things appear so to different people, perhaps even contrary ones'[4] (1113a20–21). This echoes the statement with which we began our investigation (1099a11–12), that 'for most people the things that are pleasant are in conflict'. To understand Aristotle's problem about contrary apparent goods, or the pleasant things that, for the many, are in conflict, we need to see what things these are contrasted with. For Aristotle, 'the good is without qualification and in truth the object of wish, whereas what appears good to a given person is the object of wish for that person' (1113a23–25). Sarah Broadie (Broadie and Rowe 2002: 317) says that Aristotle assumes that if *x* is an object of wish, then it is an object to be wished for. If this is right, it follows that the good, *qua* true object of wish, is the object truly to be wished for. The question then poses itself: who achieves this? That is, who wishes for what should be wished for? Aristotle answers: 'for the person of excellence the object of wish is the one that is truly so' (1113a24–26); 'for the good person discriminates correctly in every set of circumstances, and in every set of circumstances what is true is apparent to him' (1113a29–32). So, since what appears good to each person is the object of wish for that person, for the person of excellence there is coincidence of the object of wish for her, which is what appears good to her, with what she should wish for, namely what is good for her, both of which are in the range of what should be wished for, namely what is good.

What, then, of the agent who is not a person of excellence? Here Aristotle's explanation is less clear. He says that 'for the bad person it is as chance will have

---

[4] I take it that what Aristotle means by 'contrary ones' is things like bitter and sweet not good and bad. See 1153a4–5 for examples.

it' (1113a26–27), which prepares us for only accidental coincidence between what appears good to that person and what is good. Indeed, this expectation is fulfilled in Aristotle's subsequent statement that 'most people are deceived [about what is a fine and pleasant thing], and the deception seems to come about because of pleasure; for it appears a good thing when it is not' (1113a33–b1). Due to deception, things that are in fact bad may appear good.

This explanation is confused by Aristotle's own illustration: 'for the bad person it is as chance will have it, just as on the physical level too the things that are truly healthful are healthful for people in good condition, whereas a different set of things is healthful for those who are diseased' (1113a25–28). The case of health and disease is not like the case of the morally bad person. What is healthful for the good person is truly healthful. What is healthful for the diseased person is truly healthful for her, but may not be healthful for a healthy person. But what is healthful for a diseased person is not 'as chance will have it'; rather, what is healthful for a diseased person is dictated by the biology of her condition. It is possible that Aristotle meant here that what is healthful for the diseased person is *unpredictable*, depending on her condition. But unpredictability should be distinguished from the genuine *chanciness* that we get in the case of a bad person's taste. What is liked by a bad person really is 'as chance would have it', but what is healthy for a diseased person is not.

So we need to distinguish the *good*, the *bad*, and the *restorative*; the *good for x*, and the *bad for x*; and the *apparent* good and the *apparent* bad. The good is what is good for, and appears good to, the person of excellence. But the good is not good for everyone. What is *good for the bad person* is not necessarily what is *good*, any more than the healthful for the diseased need be the same as the healthful for the healthy: rather, it is what would restore the bad person to a good moral condition. Again, the restorative may appear good or bad to the bad person; but what is restorative of the bad person's character is not as chance would have it. Rather, just as medicine determines what is truly healthful for the diseased, so moral wisdom determines what is truly good for the bad person's condition. Finally, what appears good to the bad person is, 'as chance would have it' fortuitous and random.

The idea that the truly healthful is what is healthful for the person in a good condition is central to Aristotle's notion of the good, and as we shall see, his notion of the pleasant, too. By contrast to the restorative, what is truly healthful is *preservative* of the condition of the agent. It is what does not upset or destroy that condition, but sustains it as it is. Extrapolating to the moral domain, what is morally healthful for the good person is what preserves and sustains her good moral condition. That will be the exercise of her developed moral dispositions in carrying out actions that are both expressive of her moral character and preservative of the disposition that is being exercised through these actions. In other words, what is morally healthful for the good moral agent is being busy being good: the exercise of moral excellence.

By contrast, actions that are not an exercise of virtue, but build up virtuous character in a person by following the advice and example of the virtuous agent, are only *incidentally* good. The notion of incidental *goodness* is introduced by Aristotle in relation to remedial pleasures which 'are remedies for a nature that is lacking... these occur in the process of restoration to completion, so that they are incidentally good' (1154a34–b2). Since no explanation is offered by Aristotle of the incidental status of their goodness, we may assume that it is the same as that of the incidental status of remedial pleasures (1152b33–35). Here, the goodness must belong to the activity of the part of the nature and, by extension, of the moral character that is good, and whose activity is restoring the goodness in the part that is lacking. Aristotle's contrast between what is truly healthful and what is healthful for the diseased person (1113a25–28) suggests that we may also posit a contrast between the truly healthful and the incidentally healthful.

4 'PLEASANT BY NATURE'

We have seen that, for Aristotle, 'the truly good' means those activities that are preservative of the good state of the moral agent; these involve the exercise of her virtue. This point is the basis for a correct understanding of the 'pleasant by nature'. The relevant activities divide into those that preserve the good state of a good moral agent, and those that build up or restore her good state. The former are good without qualification; and the latter are incidentally good. Correspondingly, the former are 'naturally pleasant or pleasant without qualification' (1153a3–6); while the latter are incidentally pleasant.

The pleasures divide in the same way: some of them are activities; while others are comings to be. Aristotle says:

... not all pleasures are comings to be, or accompanied by a coming to be, but rather they are activities, and an end, nor do they occur because a coming to be is in train but because capacities are being put to use; and not all pleasures have something else as end, but only those involved in the bringing to completion of one's nature. Hence... one should say that it [pleasure] is an activity of a natural disposition.   (1153a9–14)

The comings to be are the processes of restoration of one's nature. As such, their ends are not the comings to be themselves. Rather, they have ends which are determined by what is needed to bring one's nature back to its wholesome state. In the case of bodily needs, the ends are such things as the replenishment of nutrition or strength. But by extension, we could also think of comings to be which are training processes towards the end of restoring the moral fabric of an agent to its wholesome condition, as might be needed after suffering a catastrophe that unbalanced one's judgement or disposition towards one's fellow-citizens or even towards one's self.

What is of special interest for our investigation is the other group of pleasures, those that are not comings to be. These, Aristotle says, are activities, and are themselves their own ends. His own example is that of reflection, which we saw him describe as a pleasure that is 'unaccompanied by pain and appetite' (1152b36–3a1). In 1153a9–14, as just quoted, he says that such a pleasure is an activity of a natural disposition which occurs 'because capacities are being put to use'. These activities are precisely the preservative activities we discussed above: they are the activities of a nature in a good and wholesome state, busy being active. The purpose of such a state/disposition does not reach out to an end other than itself. Its *use* is its activation for the sake of that activity.

Aristotle comes back to these activities when distinguishing the restorative (the curative) from the non-restorative. Here he refers to the non-restorative activities as the *phusei hêdea*, the things that are pleasant by nature (1154b20–21): 'pleasant by nature I call the things that bring about activity of a nature adapted to that activity [*tēs toiasde phuseōs*]'. Ross translates this as 'things naturally pleasant are those that stimulate the action of the healthy nature'. It is indeed possible to take *toiasde* as referring back to 'the part that remains healthy' in the previous clause. But I prefer Rowe's translation because it brings out more sharply the self-containment of the non-restorative activity. Certainly, *qua* non-restorative, such an activity would be that of the healthy part of the organism. But we are being told much more than this by Aristotle. The person who is in a wholesome condition, both physically and morally, engages in activities that are their own end. Their nature is self-directed in its pursuit of the good. Healthy, virtuous natures are active for the sake of realizing their activity.

So the things that are *pleasant by nature* are the non-restorative activities of the healthy nature of a good agent. More strictly, if we heed 1153a9–14, what is pleasant by nature is the activity of a good and healthy nature when it is not contributing towards the restoration of a depleted or damaged part of its nature, since that would be an end different from the activity itself. If that were an activity's goal, then it would be possible to engage excessively in it. But Aristotle says in the same passage that 'the pleasures that are not accompanied by pains cannot be taken to excess; and these are the pleasures relating to things that are pleasant by nature [*phusei hêdea*] and not incidentally' (1154b15–17). Certainly an activity that has an end other than itself can be taken to excess, once that end is achieved. So since it is possible for the healthy part of a nature to engage in restoring a deficient part (1154b18–19) of that nature, it is not just any activity of a good nature that is 'pleasant by nature', but only its 'preservative' activities (as we called them above), as opposed to its restorative activities.

The fact that activities which are pleasant by nature are described by Aristotle as 'not accompanied by pains' seems to deliver what we have been looking for since the beginning of our investigation. There we saw that the notion that there are things that are pleasant by nature is not borne out by the experience of most people, for whom 'the things that are pleasant are in conflict, because they are not such by nature' (1099a111–13). We would expect the good agent, like the healthy body, to function smoothly and without internal conflict. But, since most people are no more good than they are healthy, the same sort of account explains why their experience is characterized by conflict and pain: because of their lack of health and their lack of a morally good disposition.

Still, even in a life that *is* healthy and good, we do not yet seem to be free of conflict. Aristotle acknowledges this when he examines what makes a pleasure bad:

> To argue that pleasures are bad because some pleasant things bring disease is the same as arguing that some healthy things are bad because they are bad for moneymaking. Both sets of things, then, are bad in this one respect, but that is not enough to make them bad, since philosophical reflection too is sometimes damaging to health.   (1153a17–20)

Given the parallel Aristotle provides here, and the position recorded at 1152b20–22, it seems probably that his point in this passage is that a thing's incidental consequences do not make *that thing* bad. His point is not the unlikely (if not 'illogical', Broadie and Rowe 2004: 402) claim that the bad consequences of *some* instances of pleasure make *all* pleasure bad. Yet this is what the text seems to say; perhaps at 1153a17 we should read *phaula*, as in a19, not *phaulas*.

I shall assume that Aristotle's position in this argument is that if *x* has bad consequences, this does not make *x* bad if the consequences are somehow indirect, with only an incidental connection between *x* and its consequences. It is presumably chance circumstances that make some healthy things bad for money-making; we could imagine circumstances changing and the bad consequences disappearing. This should be contrasted with, for instance, the bad consequences of excessive exercise for one's health. These are not chance consequences, since health depends on rest; deciding to exercise excessively is forfeiting health.

It is not of immediate interest to our investigation whether the pleasures that bring disease are just for that reason bad. But it is worth noting that if Aristotle is denying this here, he must be implying that we need a distinction between a pleasure that is bad, for example, shameful (1152b21), and a pleasure that should be only prudentially avoided, until medicine can prevent the disease it causes; if a drug can prevent the disease, then there is no badness to be associated with that pleasure, since it would not be harmful any more. Similarly, what makes philosophical reflection sometimes damaging to health will be something circumstantial about the particular condition of the individual who reflects. I take it that Aristotle's point is that even in this circumstance, this instance of philosophical reflection is not itself bad, although it is bad in this respect of an incidental harmful consequence.

What *is* of direct interest to our current investigation is that philosophical reflection, which is not only a good pleasure but the finest activity a person can engage in, can conflict with another pleasure, that of healthy living, even in the life of a good moral agent—where we expect to find no conflict. For (we have been told) in the good moral agent the pleasurable activities are those that are pleasant by nature. It is only supposed to be in those agents that are not good, 'the many', that there is conflict among pleasures, conflict which arises because their pleasures 'are not pleasant by nature [*phusei hēdea*]' (1099a11–13). How are we then to explain this new claim, that conflict is possible even among the naturally pleasant activities in the life of 'the lovers of the fine' (1099a13)?

I answer that there is a particular type of conflict that is unavoidable even in the life of the most virtuous individual. Describing this conflict reveals a pattern which we shall see applies not only to the pleasant but also to the good and to the true.

5 THE DETERMINATE

In his discussion of the state of being alive, Aristotle says (1170a19–22):

[B]eing alive is something that is good and pleasant in itself [*kath' auto*], since it is determinate (*hôrismenon*), and the determinate is of the nature of the good (*to d' hôrismenon tês t'agathou phuseôs*), and what is naturally good [*phusei agathon*] is also good for the decent person.

The passage is important because it shows us something that two of Aristotle's core moral notions, the good and the pleasant, have in common. The significance of this common feature is that it is explanatory of the presence of goodness and pleasure: something determinate is in itself good and pleasant *because* it is determinate, and being determinate is 'of the nature of the good'.

We saw in section 4 that the pleasant—the pleasant by nature—is the truly good. So if the determinate is 'of the nature of the good', of the good by nature, then the determinate qualifies whatever possesses it as pleasant as well. (Aristotle's example of the indeterminate is a bad, corrupted, or pain-wracked life: 1170a22–24.)

Aristotle sees a constitutional relation between the determinate, on the one hand, and the good and the pleasant, on the other. We have just seen that he holds the entailment in the one direction, the determinate being good and pleasant. We find the opposite direction in his discussion of the opinions of the Academics. The question at issue is whether the good and pleasure are determinate. The Academics accept that the good is determinate, but raise an objection to the claim that pleasure is determinate. Aristotle's first response is to disambiguate their argument by separating *being pleased* from *pleasure*. He first runs their argument and then responds to it, assuming that they have 'being pleased' in mind:

[T]hey say that the good is determinate, whereas pleasure is indeterminate, because it admits of more or less. Now if they reach this judgement by considering being pleased, the same will hold of justice and of the other excellences—qualities of which these thinkers openly say that the persons qualified by them are more so or less so, and act more in accordance with the excellences, or less: people can be just to a greater degree, or courageous, and they can also perform just acts or behave moderately to a greater or lesser degree.   (1173a15–22)

The conclusion that the Academics aim for is that pleasure is indeterminate. Their argument for this is that *being pleased* admits of more or less. Aristotle objects that if this argument works, then, by the same token, justice and the other excellences are also indeterminate. For the *possession* of justice and the other excellences admits of more or less: obviously people can be just, or courageous, to a greater or lesser degree. Again, people can *act* more or less in accordance with the excellences: obviously people can perform acts which are just or temperate to a greater or lesser degree. If pleasure is shown to admit of more and less, and so to be indeterminate, by the indisputable fact that people's *instantiation* or *possession* of pleasure admits of more or less, then the same is shown of justice by the indisputable fact that people's instantiation or possession of justice, too, admits of more or less. But both the Academics and Aristotle reject the idea that justice and the other excellences are indeterminate; Aristotle would consider it an absurdity. Therefore, there is no valid inference from conclusions about *being pleased* to conclusions about *pleasure*; and so the Academics' argument does not show that pleasure is indeterminate.

Next Aristotle develops his own position, using the Academics' argument as a springboard. Suppose that the Academics tried, instead, to show that pleasure is indeterminate by arguing from *pleasure*, not from *being pleased*:

> But if the judgement in question [that pleasure is indeterminate] refers to the pleasures [*sc.* to what a pleasure is, not to being pleased], they are perhaps failing to give the explanation; that is, if some pleasures are unmixed while others are mixed. And why should pleasure not be in the same case as health, which while being determinate nevertheless admits of more and less? For the same kind of balance does not exist in everyone, nor is there always some single balance in the same person, but even while it is giving way it continues to be present up to a certain point, so differing in terms of more and less. The case of pleasure too, then, may be of this sort.   (1173a22–29)

Aristotle's position is that pleasure is determinate *and* admits of more and less. That it is determinate can be clearly seen when the pleasures are unmixed; that they admit of more and less becomes clear when they are mixed. Like health, pleasures can differ in kind between different people, but even in the same person. They differ in balance-type, or qualitatively as they deteriorate away.

The key idea that allows Aristotle to say both that pleasure is determinate, *and* that it admits of more and less, is the idea that there is variation in what counts as pleasure. Compare what he says about health. In the case of health, all balances are states of health, but some balances are better than others. People can have better or worse health depending on, for example, whether they have more antibodies in their system because they have been exposed to favourable conditions for the generation of antibodies. A person with fewer antibodies would still be healthy; but not *as* healthy as the person who has more. Since the one lacks qualities of health which are present in the other, we can describe her situation as privation of health, to a degree. Similarly, there is privation of health when the balance in a person changes, and the present state of health is succeeded by another. As the first state fades away, it changes before it is lost, and in this sense it is present to a lesser degree now than before. Or, again, if someone had a disability that affected his health, or some other chronic condition that could not be changed or cured, his overall state of health would be characterized by deprivation in that respect. In all these cases, the presence of privation of health gives rise to a mixed state of health and un-health. In this sense, the state of health in different healthy people would be unmixed in some lucky few who possess the very best types of health; but in most normally healthy people it would be mixed with privation of health.

Similarly, there are different ways in which states of pleasure can be more or less pleasurable than others. Either the type is different in different people—better in some, worse in others; or the same state is present, but deteriorating; or there is some pain somehow involved with the presence of this state. One particular example of the last type is the case of the boxers. Aristotle describes their predicament in this way: 'to the boxers the end—what they do it for, i.e. the wreath and the honours—is pleasant, whereas being punched hurts them' (1117b3–4). Here the achievement of the pleasure of winning comes at a necessarily painful cost. This renders the pleasure of winning a mixed one, because, although winning is purely pleasurable in itself, it is accompanied by unavoidable pain. Aristotle concludes from this case, and that of courage more generally, that 'not all the excellences give rise to pleasant activity, except to the extent that pleasant activity touches on the end itself' (1117b15–16).

This is a very significant conclusion to reach. Here Aristotle paints the good life, the life of the virtuous agent, in quite different colours from those of the euphoric statement we encountered early in *NE*, where we began our investigation: 'for most people the things that are pleasant are in conflict, because they are not such by nature, whereas to the lovers of the fine what is pleasant is what is pleasant by nature; and actions in accordance with excellence are like this, so that they are pleasant both to these people and in themselves' (1099a11–15). In the earlier statement, conflict characterizes the lives of the *failed* agents, those that are not dedicated lovers of the fine. Of course, various degrees of failure to pursue the fine generate different degrees of conflict in one's life. The lover of the fine, however, enjoys only what is pleasant by nature: which, as we have seen, means virtuous activities which are pleasant without mutual conflict. But now, in the refined picture, virtuous life and activity comes out in darker colours. Some of the pleasures experienced by a virtuous person can be mixed, even in the best of lives. It is part of the nature of some of the excellences that they, too, should involve unavoidable pain.

But, if this is so, how is the virtuous person's life different from the life of the less perfected moral agent who is one of 'the many'?

The difference must lie in the *sorts* of conflict between pleasant things that characterise these two lives. For the many, any pleasant thing may conflict with any other pleasant thing. In each pleasant activity there is a blindness towards other pleasant activities: there is a lack of coordination that results from their not being pleasant by nature. For the virtuous person, by contrast, to whom her characteristic activities are pleasant by nature, at least the ends of these activities are not in conflict; for example, Aristotle tells us that reflection is a pleasure that is 'unaccompanied by pain' (1152b36–3a1), even if he then adds that on occasion, the conditions under which it is achieved may be harmful to health and, therefore, painful. So since 'not all the excellences give rise to pleasant activity, except to the extent that pleasant activity touches on the end itself' (1117b15–16), and since the end is by nature, in accordance with the good within a virtuous life, therefore even if the means towards these ends give rise to painful activities, the ends themselves do not, but are good and pleasant. This must be the mark of a good life, that what it aims at in the multifarious daily activities is pleasant because good. The lovers of the fine are, thereby, lovers of the pleasant, even if the way to it is not always pleasurable activity.

6 MIXED PLEASURES, GOODS, TRUTHS

The pursuit of virtue in a good life may involve activities that are harmful in one way or another: reflection may be harmful to health, just as boxing may. But Aristotle argues that the fact that pursuing these ends involves harm does not make these ends bad: these 'sets of things, then, *are* bad in this one respect, but that is not enough to make them bad' (1153a19). The means to the ends of reflection and boxing may involve activities with harmful consequences; but these bad consequences do not make boxing and reflection *themselves* bad. It does, however, make them *mixed goods*, and it does introduce some badness into the life of the virtuous agent who pursues them.

Thus the virtuous life is not a life of pure pleasure, but contains some mixed pleasures—some pleasures involving some pain. This pain is not associated with the ends of the activities of virtue, but with the necessary means towards those ends' achievement. This does not make the achievement of the ends themselves unpleasant, but it does make these activities mixed pleasures, in so far as the means towards the achievement of the pleasure involve pains. So the life of the virtuous person will be a life that contains mixed pleasures and, hence, potentially at least, conflict between the things that he finds pleasant.

Aristotle reaches this conclusion having shown that that the mark of the good and the pleasant is the determinate, but having further argued that the determinate, despite its nature as such, can accept 'the more and the less'. This doctrine of mixed determinates, as we may call it, is extended in the *Nicomachean Ethics* to a further domain, besides that of the good and that of the pleasant: the domain of the true. Aristotle says that 'correctness of judgement is truth, and at the same time everything that is the subject of a judgement is also already determinate' (1142b11–12). We may, therefore, expect that the same implications about the determinate will follow in the domain of the true as we found in the cases of the good and the pleasant.

This expectation is vindicated. We saw in the domains of the good and the pleasant that the fact that the determinate can accept the more and the less does not mean that every good thing and every pleasant thing will have their bad and painful respects. What it does mean is that some good or pleasant things are accompanied by bad consequences or painful experiences—either by chance, or sometimes, even, because of the nature of the activity itself. Correspondingly, in the case of truth we would expect, not that every judgement should have some false aspects to it, but that some judgements that even the person of full epistemic virtue will make will be false in some respects—either by chance, or sometimes, even, because of the nature of the judgement itself. And this is just what Aristotle says about moral generalizations (1107a28–32):

> we should not simply state this [about the doctrine of the mean] in general terms; we should also show how it fits the particular cases. For with discussions that relate to actions, those of a general sort [*katholou logoi*] have a wider application, but those that deal with the subject bit by bit are closer to the truth; for actions have to do with particulars, and the requirement is that we should be in accord on these.

Consider such general statements about action and the practical as Aristotle's example in this context—the claim that 'with regard to feelings of fear and boldness, courage is the intermediate state' (1107a33–b1). Such general claims do not always fit the particular cases very well; in some circumstances they might not be right at all. But such a claim will fit most cases, which is why it counts as a true statement, despite the generality that makes it only an approximate truth. It is in its nature as a general statement about action not to fit every context to which it extends. In this sense, it is a mixed truth containing some falsehood.[5]

The doctrine of mixed determinates is Aristotle's way of describing how such valuable ends as pleasure, the good, the true, are realized in the world. I believe that, for Aristotle, this doctrine extends across more domains than the ones we examined in the present investigation. In particular I find it in the domain of metaphysics, where one application is to substantial forms as determinates that nevertheless accept the more and the less in their realization across the species. The doctrine summed up by Aristotle's familiar tag 'for the most part' (*hôs epi to polu*) is another expression of the doctrine of mixed determinates. The doctrine contrasts sharply with the way that the corresponding states are realized in Platonic metaphysics, where there is nothing mixed, for instance, about the Good In Itself. For Aristotle it is a crucial truth, not only in ethics but in his philosophy at large, that—even at their best—realizations of the good, the pleasant, and the true result in impurity and mixture.

[5] Cf. Chappell Ch. 7 (p. 44); and Coope, Ch. 1 (pp. 38–39), on *NE* 1094b21.

14

Three Dogmas of Desire

Talbot Brewer

... in so far as modern ethics tends to constitute a sort of Newspeak which makes certain values non-expressible, the reasons for this are to be sought in current philosophy of mind and in the fascinating power of a certain picture of the soul. One suspects that philosophy of mind has not in fact been performing the task . . . of sorting and classifying fundamental moral issues; it has rather been imposing upon us a particular value judgement in the guise of a theory of human nature. Whether philosophy can ever do anything else is a question we shall have to consider. But in so far as modern philosophers profess to be analytic and neutral any failure to be so deserves comment. And an attempt to produce, if not a comprehensive analysis, at least a rival soul-picture which covers a greater or a different territory should make new places for philosophical reflection.

(Murdoch 1970: 2)

1 INTRODUCTION

It is a truism that our desires figure essentially in the explanation of most or all of what we do: in general, we would not act as we do if we did not have the desires we have. If this truism is correct, as truisms tend to be, then having a virtue must involve having certain characteristic desires, since otherwise having a virtue would not suffice to impart a distinctive and laudable shape to characteristic actions. Desires, then, are essential components of virtues; hence, we shall be able to understand what a virtue is only if we understand what a desire is. So it would be a serious obstacle to the formulation of an adequate virtue theory if the reigning philosophical conception of desire were badly amiss. I think that it is, and that we must retrieve a more adequate conception of desire if we are to understand the virtues of character. Until we do this, we shall lack an adequate conception of how the virtuous person can be motivated to act by the intrinsic goodness of other human beings and of certain ways of interacting with them.

The flaws in the reigning conception of desire are both fundamental and systematic. Contemporary Anglo-American ethics and action theory have been grounded in large part on three basic claims about desires. The *first* is that desires are propositional attitudes. The *second* is that desires are distinguished from other propositional attitudes by the typical or proper direction of fit between the world and the desirer's mind (or, more particularly, the proposition towards which the desirer has the attitude of desire). The *third* is that any action can be explained as the product of a belief–desire pair consisting in a belief that the action will bring the world into conformity with some proposition, and a desire that takes the same proposition as its object. I shall argue that we ought to reject all three of these dogmas of desire.

These three dogmas come naturally to us because they cohere with the thought that the point of any human action can only lie in some describable state of affairs that we desire to bring about, and intend to bring about through the action. That is, actions can be seen as intelligible only if they are portrayed as attempts to work on the world so that it comes into correspondence, or remains in correspondence, with one's desires. All action is, on this view, a mode of production guided by a determinate description of a possible world at which the action aims. This remains true even if the product at which the agent aims is nothing more than the occurrence of the action itself. Since this world-centric and pragmatic conception of human agency has a firm grip on contemporary Western culture, it is no surprise that it manifests itself in popular beliefs about desire and in the philosophical analyses of desire that take their bearings from these popular beliefs.

Here we come face to face with two basic methodological commitments around which this chapter is structured. The first of these commitments is foreshadowed in the epigraph from Iris Murdoch: it is my view that our picture of human psychology is often an alternative expression of, and not an independent basis for, our picture of what might make human actions valuable or good. Anscombe 1958 urges that we ought to get straight on certain basic concepts in philosophical psychology before we try to make progress in ethical theory. This recommendation contains a genuine insight: ethical theorists should return continually to the basic psychological and action-theoretic concepts that frame and shape their ethical views, since these might well be inadequate to the task of articulating a compelling vision of ethics. However, Anscombe's suggestion can also easily lead us astray, for it might be thought to imply that we can *postpone* ethical theory while doing philosophical psychology. Yet it is hard to see how our attempts to understand the nature of action and agency can be disentangled from our attempt to understand what makes an action choiceworthy and what it is for an agent to choose well. After all, when we try to make sense of a bit of behaviour as an action, what we are trying to do is to uncover what the agent saw in the action such that it made sense for him to choose it, and this interpretive task presupposes some picture of what might possibly confer value upon an action and of what it is to act sensibly. It is clear, at any rate, that the proponents of the three above-mentioned dogmas of desire have not managed to postpone ethical theory while investigating the nature of desire. Their accounts of desire are often presented as elements of an ethically innocent philosophical psychology that can serve as a neutral framework for philosophical debates about ethics. Yet, on closer inspection, the dogmas of desire must be regarded as integral elements of a substantive vision of ethics—a vision at once worldly, progressive, and anti-contemplative. Moreover, the vision of ethics which these dogmas help to support is a vision that cannot make optimal sense of our depth, of the intelligibility of our life quests, and of the yearnings that draw us to our ideals and to each other. To the extent that this vision has a hold not only on contemporary philosophy but on contemporary culture, this ought to be regarded not as a mere idiosyncrasy of our times but as a calamity.

This brings us to the second methodological commitment. Straightforward philosophical analysis is ideally suited to bringing out internal paradoxes and contradictions in a given domain of discourse, but it is ill-suited to the task of shedding light on the impoverishment of human life that can go hand-in-hand with an impoverished yet internally self-consistent 'soul-picture.' If philosophical analysis cleaves too closely to common beliefs and practices, it can easily generate philosophical psychologies and allied ethical theories that serve only to systematize and entrench reigning prejudices concerning the nature and point of human action. But suppose the culture at large has need of a rival 'soul-picture'—a need that manifests itself only in inarticulate disorientation and dissatisfaction with the conceptual tools ready to hand for making sense of our own lives. Where, then, might we look for a fresh start? One fruitful source is the cultural history that has shaped our understanding of the self, and that reaches its greatest degree of articulacy and self-consciousness in the classics of the philosophical tradition. Here, in the traditions of thought that have both shaped our times and been left behind by them, we might hope to find rival pictures with just the degree of 'cultural distance' from our own place and time to be of help: near enough that we shall not find it impossible to re-conceive of ourselves and our strivings in those pictures' terms; alien enough that they can distance and possibly liberate us from the pictures of the self and the good in whose light, or darkness, we have been nurtured. To invoke the history of philosophy, and to learn from it, is to transcend a narrowly analytic approach to philosophy in favour of a potentially transformative struggle with the prejudices of our times. Because they are at once historically peculiar, deeply embedded in our folk psychology, and pivotal to our conception of the nature and point of human action, the three above-mentioned dogmas of desire provide a likely point of entry for such a project of historical retrieval.

2 THE THREE DOGMAS OF DESIRE AND THEIR INTUITIVE APPEAL

The first dogma of desire, again, is that desires are propositional attitudes. On this view, the real intentional object of any desire is a proposition, and the desire itself is a particular kind of attitude towards that proposition.[1] Some desires wear their propositional structure on their sleeves. For instance, my current desire that you find this chapter illuminating relates me, the desirer, to the proposition 'You find this essay illuminating.' To claim that desires are propositional attitudes is to commit oneself to the claim that any desire can be expressed fully, without distortion or loss, as a desire that thus-and-such. Here is a representative affirmation of this first dogma, drawn from Wayne Sumner's influential book on welfare:

> That desires have objects is, of course, scarcely news; this much is ensured by the fact that every desire is *for* something or other. In the surface grammar of desire, these objects are often literally things, as when I want this book or that car. Sometimes, however, they are activities (I want to go to France) or states of affairs (I want the weather to be good for our wedding). It is a simple trick to homogenize all these ostensibly different kinds of objects into states of affairs: to want the book is to want to own it or read it, and to want to do something is to want the state of affairs which consists of your doing it. It is then a further simple trick to turn these states of affairs into propositions: to want the state of affairs which consists of my owning the book is to want the proposition 'I own this book' to be true. By this process of transformation, every desire comes to take some proposition as its intentional object.   (Sumner 1996: 124)

If we accept the first dogma of desire and agree that desires are always attitudes towards propositions, we must ask what the relevant attitude might be. The second dogma of desire is supposed to answer this question. It tells us that one has the relevant attitude towards a proposition when, other things equal, one is disposed to act on the world in ways calculated to make the proposition true.[2]

This conception of desires fits neatly together with a corollary picture of another important kind of propositional attitudes: belief. A belief is an attitude towards a proposition that typically is adjusted, and at any rate ought to be adjusted, in the face of evidence that the world does not correspond to the proposition. It is true, of course, that such adjustments are not always made. However, if one lacked any disposition whatever to alter the content of a set of propositional attitudes in the presence of clear evidence that they do not correspond with the world, then whatever these attitudes are, they cannot be beliefs. This is an application of the more general Davidsonian dictum that rationality is the constitutive ideal of the mental. The norm of rationality governing the representations we call beliefs is that they should maintain a mind-to-world direction of fit, and actual representations must at least roughly approximate this norm in order so much as to count as beliefs. Desires, by contrast, are said to be propositional attitudes with

---

[1] See e.g. Smith 1994: 107; Platts 1981: 74–7; Sumner 1996: 124; Brandom 1994: 5; Velleman 2000: 24, 182. A more tentative endorsement is found in Schueler 1995: 12.

[2] The general idea that mental states can be classified in terms of their direction of fit with the world can be traced back at least to Anscombe 1957: 56 ff. It has been affirmed in one form or another by a wide array of subsequent philosophers, including Smith 1994: 111–19; Sumner 1996: 124–5; Velleman 2000: 24, 182; Audi 1997: 129; Brink 1997: 264.

a world-to-mind direction of fit. A desire is an attitude towards a proposition that typically prompts one to adjust the world, where possible, in ways calculated to make it correspond to the proposition. It is true, of course, that such adjustments are not always made. However, if one lacked any disposition whatever to perform those actions that one believes would bring the world into correspondence with a proposition towards which one has a certain attitude, then—on this second dogma—the attitude in question cannot be desire.

This pleasingly unified and symmetrical view of desires and beliefs leads to the third dogma of desire: beliefs and desires can be paired to yield a rationalizing explanation of any action.[3] To put the point in terms of the two preceding dogmas, any action can be explained as the product of an agent's belief that the action will bring the world into correspondence with some proposition towards which the agent is related by the attitude of desire. More simply, agents act only in ways calculated to fulfil their desires. Belief–desire explanations of this sort are regarded as illuminating because they make clear what in the world agents think they are doing when they engage in intentional action. In other words, such explanations are rationalizing explanations, and that is the kind of explanation that must be produced when we want to explain that peculiar class of events known as actions. Behaviour can be made intelligible as action, on this view, only to the extent that it can be brought into view as an attempt by the agent to remake the world in the image of his desires. This explanatory paradigm, in turn, provides us with a way of identifying desires. People desire that p if and only if they are disposed to act in ways calculated to make it true that p.

The three dogmas of desire fit together into a natural package, each illuminating and lending plausibility to the others. Consider, to begin with, how the propositional account of desires supports the other two dogmas. Without a propositional account of desires, it is not clear that one could speak sensibly of a 'direction of fit' between desires and the world. For instance, if some desires had people or things as their object, it is not clear what it would mean to speak of the object's fitting or failing to fit with the world. How could a person or thing do *that*? Nor could we move directly from the attribution of a desire to the explanation of an action, since the desire for a person has a very unclear bearing on what it makes sense to do—whether, for instance, to bed or befriend or build a life with the person. To explain a particular action, it seems, one must trace it to a desire with a propositional or infinitival object (i.e. a desire to φ).[4] Even if one takes the latter alternative, the thought goes, one can use Sumner's 'simple trick' to restate any desire to φ as a desire that one φ. This seems to imply that any desire suited to explain an action can be captured fully in standard propositional form.

---

[3] Cf. Chappell, Essay 7. The most prominent exposition of this view is Davidson 1980, essays 1, 2, 4, 5, 12, 14. Smith 1994: 115–6; and Brandom 1994: 56 embrace this notion of action-explanation. Other influential expositions of this sort of view include Goldman 1970; Dretske 1988; Dennett 1987.

[4] Davidson 1980 makes this point in 'Actions, Reasons and Causes'.

The second dogma also tends to support both of the other dogmas. It does not so much bolster as complete the propositional account of desires, since it purports to tell us what *sort* of propositional attitude a desire is. And, because it accounts for desires as dispositions to act in ways calculated to bring about certain envisioned states of affairs, it seems perfectly suited to play a pivotal role in the explanation of action. When a dispositional desire of this sort is conjoined with the belief that a certain action would bring about the desired state of affairs, then the disposition can express itself directly in action. Citing a belief–desire pair, then, can provide an exhaustive rationalizing explanation of an action.

The third dogma can be regarded as a kind of confirmation of the first two dogmas, because it provides a compelling answer to the question *why* our conception of desire takes the shape specified by the first two dogmas. Our conception takes this shape, and ought to take this shape, because such a conception is optimally suited to provide illuminating explanations of what people do. We speak of desires because we want to understand, and perhaps to anticipate, the actions of others. The first two dogmas permit us to do this effectively.

It would be an exaggeration to say that these three dogmas stand or fall together. Still, given the way that they cohere with and draw support from each other, a telling objection to any of them will tend to undermine the grounds for affirming the other two. Given this, I shall sometimes take the liberty of evaluating them as a package, under the name of *the propositional account of desire* (or *propositionalism*, for short), though I realize that some readers might be tempted to accept my criticisms of some elements of the package while continuing to affirm other elements.[5] I hope to show that we should reject all three dogmas. More specifically, I hope to show: (1) that no desire really has a proposition as its intentional object; (2) that while the objects of many desires can be captured in propositional form, the objects of certain desires cannot be; (3) that some desires have ideational content with a mind-to-world rather than a world-to-mind direction of fit; and (4) that some actions are best explained as issuing forth from desires whose objects are neither propositions nor propositionally specifiable states of affairs.

3 PRELIMINARY DOUBTS ABOUT THE PROPOSITIONAL ACCOUNT OF DESIRE

The word 'desire' is slipping from ordinary speech. We often ask others what they want or would like, but it sounds just a bit servile to ask what they desire, and it sounds correspondingly presumptuous to announce to others what we

---

[5] For instance, Velleman 2000: 5–11, 24, 182 embraces the first two dogmas but holds that belief–desire combinations can provide suitable explanations only of goal-directed activity, and not of autonomous action.

desire. The word has a great deal more currency in philosophy than in ordinary speech, and this makes it difficult to hold the feet of philosophers to the fire of ordinary usage. It is worth noting, however, that when non-philosophers do make use of the word 'desire', they tend to use it in one of two ways, both of which philosophers tend either to misinterpret or to ignore entirely. In its most common use, the verb 'desire' carries a direct object, as when I say that I desire a Harley Davidson, or the sylvan fields of my youth, or (and this is probably the verb's most common use) some person. In its next most common use, 'desire' is followed by an infinitive, as when I say that I desire to be famous, to travel, or to read an author's latest book. There are intuitive reasons for doubting that all such desires can really be translated, without loss, into the supposedly standard propositional form.

Suppose that Dorothy says that she desires this Harley Davidson or that man. Must we agree that she has thus far provided a less than fully informative statement of her desire because she has not said what proposition she is disposed to make true? In the case of Dorothy's desire for this Harley Davidson, it might seem straightforward to bring a proposition onto the scene in order to specify Dorothy's aim. What Dorothy desires, it might be presumed, is that she possess this Harley. But the typical desire for a Harley Davidson is unlikely to boil down to the desire that one's name appear on the certificate of title and that one enjoy the legal incidents thereof. Dorothy might hope and expect that her desire for the Harley will continue after she comes to own it, not in the form of a running desire to continue to own it but in the form of a desire for the Harley—a desire that gives point to owning it. If this more primitive desire wore off, then presumably, as a secondary effect, she would no longer desire to own it.

Now, the propositionalist might object that his account can provide as nuanced a specification of what we desire to bring about as our command of language makes possible. Maybe Dorothy's desire takes as its object the proposition 'I own a Harley and frequently ride it on a country road with the wind in my hair and my lover clutching my hips.' But these more complex propositional formulations of the desire's object only postpone the difficulty, for it seems possible that the obtaining of any relevant state of affairs at which Dorothy can plausibly be seen as aiming would serve only as the optimal condition for the intensification of a mesmeric attraction to the machine itself, and that this attraction to the machine might be essential to any adequate explanation of Dorothy's inclination to bring about some favoured relation between herself and the machine.

When we turn from desiring things to desiring people, the propositional account begins to seem more clearly procrustean. What proposition might specify the object of Dorothy's desire for this man she loves? Well, we don't know much about Dorothy, so we can only guess. Maybe what she wants is that he clutch her hips while roaring full-throttle down Highway One. Maybe she desires that he marry her at a drive-thru chapel on the outskirts of Las Vegas. Maybe she desires that they make love after a night of blackjack. Some cases of desiring people might be exhaustively characterized by propositions of this sort. But Dorothy might find (she might *hope* to find) that her desire for this man is not satisfied, but continues to draw her to him, even when she is roaring down Highway One with him, and even when they are saying their vows in Vegas, and even when they make love after a night of blackjack. Being with him, dwelling on his words, and touching and kissing him might all figure as propitious conditions for the intensification of her desire for him rather than as satisfactions of that desire. Her desire might well spawn a wide array of actionable desires that things be thus and such, but it is far from clear that the desire itself must be analysable as a conjunction of such propositional desires.

Let us consider, finally, those ordinary uses of the verb 'desire' that take infinitival phrases as their objects. Should we agree with Sumner that the true intentional object of such a desire is a proposition, and that it is always a 'simple trick' to translate this sort of desire-talk into propositional form? It seems that an apt propositional translation can always be formulated, and this marks a difference from cases of desiring things or persons. Yet the translations could also be run in the other direction, and intuitively these latter translations seem to yield a more perspicuous representation of the true objects of desires than do the translations favoured by Sumner. In general, when we desire some determinate state of affairs (including those states of affairs in which we do something or other), the object of the desire is the state of affairs itself and not the truth of the proposition picking it out.[6] Nor can the two be equated, since we would thereby lose hold of the thought that true propositions are made true by the way the world is.[7]

This provides a decisive reason to reject *strong propositionalism*, understood as the view that the real intentional object of a desire is always a proposition rather than a state of affairs to which a proposition might relate us, and that the end towards which the desire directs us is the making true of a proposition rather than the production of some state of affairs that might be represented by a proposition. Yet the objection at hand presents no challenge to *weak propositionalism*, understood as the view that the object of any desire is *capturable* in propositional terms, in the sense that the truth of the relevant proposition is a necessary and sufficient condition for the attainment of the desire's end. While Sumner and other propositionalists have not generally distinguished between strong and weak propositionalism, it seems most charitable to attribute to them the weaker and more plausible view rather than the stronger and far less plausible

---

[6] There might be exceptions to this general rule, since it perhaps possible for someone to want it to be true that she has done something while lacking any desire actually to do the thing. Or so, at any rate, opines Darwall 2002: 93, who holds that such a person 'might just want the narrative of her life to include the performance of [some] activity'. So perhaps some desires do aim at the truth of a proposition rather than at its truth-maker, but if so this would seem to be the exception rather than the rule.

[7] I owe this argument, and the distinction between strong and weak propositionalism to which it leads, to my colleague Trenton Merricks.

view. Still, I hope to show that there are good reasons to reject even the weak form of propositionalism.

We can begin to approach the problem with weak propositionalism by noting that even if the propositionalist translation of infinitival desires can succeed in capturing a necessary and sufficient condition for attainment of the desire's end, it seems unable to capture the entire representational content of all such desires. If I want to go fishing, and my wife wants me to go fishing, then the most straightforward version of the propositional account would assign our desires the same content—that TB go fishing. But our desires might well differ markedly in their representational content. My desire might involve a tendency to dwell on the prospect of fishing, not neutrally but such that fishing is lit up for me as a good or attractive activity. My wife's desire need not involve a tendency to see anything good about the activity of fishing, but only a tendency to see something good about *my* going fishing. These desires might be directed towards the same state of affairs yet represent the appeal of that state of affairs in very different ways.

It might be thought that the problem here can be resolved by distinguishing between the proposition 'I go fishing' and the proposition 'TB goes fishing', and holding that my desire takes the first proposition as its object, while my wife's desire takes the second. But we can run into a version of the problem at hand even if we stick with first-person cases. My own desire to go fishing can itself vary in its way of representing fishing as good or choiceworthy. For instance, fishing might be lit up for me as good or choiceworthy because of the prospect of catching a tasty trout, or because it would take me up into a beautiful mountain range, or because it would involve wading in the cool rushing waters of mountain streams. These all seem to be different ways to represent going fishing as good or worth while—different ways of apprehending fishing's desirability—and it seems possible for a desire to go fishing to consist partly in one or another of these representations. Indeed, Anscombe 1957 has argued that desires must involve grasping as desirable—for example, that one could not want a saucer of mud unless on saw *something* good or worth while about getting it. Yet the propositionalist must limit the content of the desire to some purely descriptive proposition such as 'I go (or TB goes) fishing and catches a tasty trout', or 'I go (TB goes) fishing while wading in the cool rushing waters of mountain streams'. Those who accept the second dogma must deny that desires have evaluative representational content—i.e. that they involve the representation of certain possible states of affairs as good—since such content would seem to demand a mind-to-world direction of fit (even if we conclude, at the endpoint of ontological reflection, that there is nothing to which they can really be fitted).

This leads to a serious problem, for propositionalism is here in danger of losing track of the thought that desires themselves can function as the core of rationalizing explanations of those actions arising from them. This is particularly obvious if we hold that to have a propositional attitude with a world-to-mind direction of fit is merely to be disposed, other things equal, to act in ways calculated to make the relevant proposition true. If I have and act on a desire to φ, one can hardly provide a rationalizing explanation of my performance by tracing it to my disposition to behave in ways calculated to make it true that I φ. Even if we grant that this dispositional claim escapes 'dormitive powers' problems and, hence, counts as a genuine explanation, still it cannot be regarded as a *rationalizing* explanation, since it cannot plausibly be thought to lay bare a pattern of deliberation to which I have any reason to adhere. This form of explanation might help to make clear what exactly others are up to — for example, whether the parent reading the paper at breakfast is aiming to stay abreast of tumultuous world events or insulated from tumultuous household events. But such explanations rationalize actions only given the background supposition that the person sees something in the behaviour he is inclined to go for, and this is not guaranteed by the mere existence of a disposition to engage in such behaviour.

This point is best seen in the first person case. If I myself am deliberating about whether I have reason to perform a proposed action, it is neither here not there that it falls within a class of performances that I find myself disposed to perform, since these performances might strike me as entirely pointless obsessions or mere nervous tics. But the same point holds in the third person case. We cannot providing a rationalizing explanation of an episode of agency simply by tracing it to some class of performances that the agent is disposed to produce, since the agent might see no more point in these performances than in obsessions or nervous tics. This is why Anscombe claims that desiring requires that the desirer see something desirable in that which is desired.

One might try to dodge this problem by spelling out the second dogma in more decidedly normative terms. This fits with the widely held view that all kinds of mental states are to be understood functionally, and that a grasp of their constitutive function immediately yields a grasp of the ways in which their workings might go awry, or malfunction.[8] In this spirit, one might understand the claim that desires have world-to-mind direction of fit as implying that other things equal, one *should* alter the world in ways calculated to make true the propositional objects of one's desires. To fail to do so would be to malfunction. But now we must ask the question *why* desires should be thought to have this direction of fit. If a proposition's having this direction of fit is *criterial* of our having the attitude of desire towards that proposition, then the mystery at hand would disappear, but the resulting view would have the absurd consequence that all humans actually desire to bring about all things they ought to bring about. Setting aside all of the other defects of this proposal, it could hardly vindicate the capacity of desires to occupy their traditional role in the rationalizing explanation of all action, since

---

[8] Brandom and Velleman both affirm this version of the second dogma, as does Anscombe, who is sometimes credited with having originated the notion that mental states can be categorized in terms of their world-to-mind or mind-to-world directions of fit. See the references given in previous footnotes.

the capacity of desires to rationalize actions would here be purchased at the cost of their capacity to explain much of what people actually do. Nor is it clear what else the attitude of desire could *be*, such that whenever we take *that* attitude towards a proposition we suddenly come to have a new reason to bring the world into conformity with it. As we have seen, the propositionalist cannot trace the reason-giving force of desires to the way in which their objects are represented to us. It is conceptually possible to have the attitude of desire towards any state of affairs we could bring about, yet surely there are some such states of affairs whose production it would be entirely pointless, or unremittingly bad, for us to aim at. How could it be that simply by adopting a particular attitude towards such a state of affairs, we could always come to have a reason to bring it about?

At this point, one might remain a propositionalist yet give up on the idea that desires can rationalize actions—i.e. that tracing an action to a desire can exhibit the subjective point of the action. Some (for example, Velleman 2000: 5–11, 24, 182) have taken this route. The problem with this alternative is that it loses sight of the place that the notion of desire has in our everyday talk about agents and their doings. We talk about desires precisely in order to make sense of what people do or are tempted to do—to lay bare the subjective purpose or point of actual or proposed courses of action. If propositionalism cannot answer to this basic desideratum of a conception of desire, we should cast about for another conception of desire. And if propositionalism runs into problems because it banishes all evaluative representational content out of desires, the solution would seem to involve building appearances of goodness and/or practical reasons into desires. Such an approach cannot be expected to vindicate the thought that desires always provide a justificatory reason for performing the actions towards which they incline us. There is, after all, no reason to suppose that the subjective appearance of goods or reasons can guarantee their actual presence. Still, this approach does help to explain how the full elaboration of a desire's representational content can provide the core of a genuinely rationalizing explanation of the actions springing from that desire. The rationalizing explanation is given not by the state of affairs that the action promises to bring about, but by the seeming goods or values that are commended (so to speak) to the desirer's attention simply in virtue of his having the desire, and that make it seem worth while to act. To say that someone acted on a desire is to say that the person saw something as good or worth while about the action, but not yet to articulate how exactly that action showed up, for the person in question, as good. On this conception of desire, it is hard to attain a full understanding of the desires of others, and almost equally hard to become fully articulate about one's own desires. But this is no surprise: fathoming the point of human actions *is* an arduous interpretive task.

As noted above, we cannot make room in our account of desire for this extra ideational content without giving up the neat mapping of the mental according to which desires and beliefs have opposing one-way directions of fit with the world. If we experience representations of what it would be good to do, and if these set the stage for our deliberations about what to do, then we ought to see to it that these pictures track any truths there are to track in this domain. No doubt the contemporary antipathy to this picture of desire owes in part to the conviction that there are no truths to track in this vicinity, conjoined with a reluctance to suppose that we cannot sensibly take guidance from our own desires—i.e. do what we want to do—without implicitly supposing that there are.

4 DEPTH, PERFECTIBILITY, AND NARRATIVE COHERENCE

By reflecting on what it is like to have certain desires, and on why the propositional account provides a procrustean account of these desires, we have begun to see the outlines and appeal of a very different account of certain desires. On this alternative approach, which has been persuasively developed in the work of Thomas Scanlon and Dennis Stampe (Scanlon 1998: 33–55; Stampe 1987), desires are understood as subjective outlooks on the space of practical reasons or goods. Stampe 1987: 355–7, 368 claims that the *object* of a desire—that is, what it is a desire *for*—is given by a proposition picking out the state of affairs that one desires to bring about, but that this proposition does not exhaust the *representational content* of a desire, since the desirer must also represent the desired state of affairs as one that would be good. Scanlon 1998: 39 argues, in a similar vein, that in one very common sense of the term 'desire' (the 'directed attention sense'), a person has a desire that P 'if the thought of P keeps occurring to him or her in a favourable light, that is to say, if the person's attention is directed insistently toward considerations that present themselves as counting in favour of P'. Here, again, the object of desire is portrayed as a propositionally specifiable state of affairs, but the representational content of desire is more ample, and includes a picture of what counts as a reason for what. Both of these authors, then, claim that desires are subjective outlooks on goods or reasons that bear on practical reasoning and, hence, both would seem to be committed to the thought that, other things equal, desires ought to track any genuine goods or reasons with which the world presents us. That is, both are committed to the rejection of dogma number 2, even if they do not make this commitment explicit.

I have already begun to explain how this picture of desire permits us to make better sense of human concerns and actions than does the propositional approach, but there is a good deal more to be said about propositionalism's shortcomings as a tool for the intelligible interpretation of human lives. Exploring these shortcomings will be much easier if we have before us a concrete and suitably complex case rather than a quickly sketched philosophical example. Let us consider, then, the longing that serves as the unifying thread of Augustine's *Confessions*, and that he eventually comes to regard as the desire for God, in whom 'all things find their origin, their impulse, the centre of their being.'⁹ The coherence of the *Confessions* as the story of a life owes to the running presence of this single longing that takes very different and (in Augustine's considered estimation) progressively less illusory forms in the different stages of Augustine's life. At one level of description, Augustine's guiding desires are continuously changing. At different stages his life is oriented around the pursuit of sex, aesthetic pleasure, philosophical insight, public honour, purely worldly friendship, and other ends that he eventually comes to regard as misguided. Yet Augustine thinks that we would lose sight of the possibility of conversion (and, by extension, of the coherence of his and many other life stories) if we fail to see that the longing for God is present from the beginning of our lives, and that many human pursuits (including Augustine's pre-conversion pursuits) are unsatisfying displacements of a longing whose real nature is opaque to, or at least unacknowledged by, its possessor.¹⁰

Augustine, then, understands his own conversion not as the wholesale substitution of one set of desires for another, but as the attainment of a clearer and less adulterated vision of what he really longs for. This idea can seem hard to credit, since the pre-conversion 'adulterations' of that vision were themselves desires, and it might seem that they must have been desires for something other than God. If the object of a desire were given by the state of affairs that actions springing from the desire are calculated to bring about, then clearly those earlier desires could not plausibly be regarded as desires for God. However, Augustine anticipates the 'evaluative attention' account of desire in the sense that he thinks of desire as appreciative attention to some real or imagined object under the guise of the good. (The famous case of the purloined pears (*Confessions* II: 4–6) is no exception, for even if the fruit itself did not show up in the young Augustine's mind as good, the pose of rebellious independence and the approval of friends did.) If we think of desires as apprehensions of actions or ends as good, then we can make sense of the thought that the real object of Augustine's early desires was God by supposing that God answers best to the kind of goodness he imputed to the actions towards which those early desires inclined him. One might say, for instance, that his early desires involved a tendency to see the consuming aims of his pre-conversion life not just as good but as properly focal goods—i.e. as goods that outweigh or eclipse all other goods. His conversion might then be

---

⁹ Augustine, *Confessions* I: 2. Augustine is here echoing *Romans* I: 36.

¹⁰ Augustine's picture of the desire for God is a religious correlate of Plato's recollection-based answer to the paradox of inquiry: just as Plato held that we must already have some inkling of truths in order to recognize them as true, so Augustine holds that we must already have an obscure longing for God's goodness in order to respond with appreciative desire to our first glimpses of God. Augustine is not speaking only of the saved but of all humans, when he writes: 'Man is one of your creatures, Lord, and his instinct is to praise you . . . since he is part of your creation, he wishes to praise you. The thought of you stirs him so deeply that he cannot be content unless he praises you, because you made us for yourself and our hearts find no peace until they rest in you' (*Confessions* I: 1).

understood as consisting in the gradual consolidation of a conviction that these consuming longings were misdirected towards activities that did not, in fact, answer to the evaluative picture implicit in those very longings—i.e. that they did not merit the consuming attention he had directed at them—and that something else, God, did answer to that evaluative picture, hence was the real object even of his earlier, seemingly irreligious, longings. The same idea is implicit in the following saying (which is often, though apparently falsely, attributed to G. K. Chesterton): 'A man knocking on the door of a brothel is knocking for God.'[11]

The appeal of this approach to desire is that it helps us to explain a vitally important yet elusive feature of certain human desires: a feature whose synchronic aspect might be called *depth* and whose diachronic aspect might be called *perfectibility*.[12] In saying that certain desires have *depth*, I mean to bring out the fact that our grasp of their objects always exceeds our explicit articulation of their objects and, hence, presents us with an occasion for further articulation of our own concerns. This point can be applied to a wide range of perfectionist pursuits and concerns, whether secular or sacred, and not just to longings directed at some perfect divinity or Platonic form. It obtains, for instance, in the pursuit of ideals of artistic or philosophical excellence. The objects of such desires are fugitive: as the light of self-understanding pierces more deeply into the desire, the desire itself extends so as to outdistance our achieved articulation of its object. This fugitive quality owes partly to the reflexive structure of the self. The self that pursues an understanding of its own guiding concerns will find that those very concerns are altered by any success it might have in that pursuit.

To say that certain desires are perfectible is just to say that repeated efforts to articulate the goods they bring to view can provide us with an increasingly more adequate conception of these goods. By attempting to provide a faithful articulation of the goods one seems dimly to apprehend, one extends the range of the subjective appearances of value that structure one's experience. Desires are, in this particular, on all fours with apprehensions of aesthetic value. By articulating one's sense of the aesthetic value of the paintings one sees, or the novels one reads, one cultivates that self-same aesthetic gaze by extending its reach and increasing its nuance and complexity (its *articulation*).[13] Likewise, by articulating the intimations of goodness or value that are partly constitutive of one's desires, one cultivates one's capacity for experiencing such intimations of the good by extending that capacity's reach and increasing its nuance and

---

[11] According to the American Chesterton Society, the line is not to be found in Chesterton's work. The most likely source is Bruce Smith's *The World, The Flesh, and Father Smith* (1945), and Smith's actual words are: '. . . the young man who rings the bell at the brothel is unconsciously looking for God' (108). (http://www.chesterton.org/qmeister2/questions.htm)

[12] This terminology and some of the ideas developed in this section were suggested to me by Chuck Mathewes in the course of several invaluable conversations about the themes of this chapter and their relation to Augustine.

[13] For an interesting discussion of the thought that the articulation of basic concerns both puts them into words and gives them more precise form, see Taylor 1982: 111–26.

complexity. This sort of progressive attempt to articulate one's own fundamental concerns is a central element in the most coherent telling of the story of (almost) any distinctively human life.

We lose sight of this central human activity if we embrace the first two dogmas of desire as an exhaustive account of the ideational content of desire. On that approach, the ideational content of a desire would consist solely in the propositional representation of whatever states of affairs the desire disposes its possessor to make actual. If Augustine's behaviour is at one point calculated to bring it about that he sleeps with prostitutes in Carthage, and at another point that he becomes famous for his philosophical teachings, and at a third point that he attains oneness with God, then the propositional approach will picture these successive guiding concerns as entirely distinct, related only because they happen to occur in the course of the same life. They do not form a series that can explain the unity of this life; rather, the unity of the life, given entirely on other grounds, is what constitutes them as a series. A life story told solely in terms of such a succession of guiding desires would be a series of unintelligible shifts in the protagonist's manner of throwing about his causal weight in the world. What seems from the first-personal standpoint to be a gradual deepening of one's grasp of what one wants is interpreted as a series of directionless changes in what one wants. Growth is replaced with mere temporal change.

It will not do for the propositionalist to attempt to restore unity to Augustine's successive pursuits by supposing that he had an enduring desire that his life be organized around and informed by, the highest goods applicable to human life, then suggesting that his conversion consisted in a fundamental change in his beliefs about this highest good. No doubt Augustine had such a desire. But if the idea behind this suggestion is to illuminate the point and the coherence of Augustine's strivings by bringing them within the canonical belief–desire model, then the suggestion must be rejected. From the standpoint of the deliberator, the point of acting in ways calculated to make true that one live a good life, or a life organized around properly focal or authoritative goods, cannot lie in the fact that one happens to have a desire with this propositional content. We have already seen that a mere disposition to act in ways calculated to make a proposition true is not sufficient to ground a rationalizing explanation of such action. Now we see that it is not necessary either. One can offer a full rationalizing explanation of an action by showing how the action came to look good to the agent who went for it, without needing to mention that the agent happens to have a disposition to go for things that look good to him. Goodness cannot be shoehorned into the propositional account, then, as a contingent element in the propositional depiction of the states of affairs one desires to bring about, without losing its capacity to rationalize action. This should be obvious, since any property could enter into a propositional desire in *that* way, yet subjective apprehensions of the property of goodness would seem to have a *special* role in explaining what one sees in the actions one pursues.

A better approach is to understand the ideational content of a desire as an inchoate picture of some species or aspect of goodness. This approach permits us to see how an initially obscure desire can be cultivated over time so as to afford what its possessor regards as an increasingly clear apprehension of an object once seen as through a glass, darkly. It can then make sense to speak of a person's life as centred on the progressive clarification of a single, self-defining longing that has strikingly different behavioural manifestations at different times.

There is a place for propositional desires on this alternative, 'evaluative outlook' account of desires, but a subsidiary rather than a primary one. Just as a visual perception (for example, of a landscape) can give rise to a plethora of beliefs *that* things are thus and such, so too the quasi-perceptual evaluative outlooks (i.e. non-propositional desires) that provide us with our pre-deliberative sense of the good can give rise to a plethora of desires *that* things be thus and such. Yet we cannot hope to make the occurrence of these propositional desires intelligible, nor to exhaust their ideational content, by capturing them in propositional form. Furthermore, propositional desires derive any justificatory import they might have from the broader evaluative outlooks that spawn them. These broader outlooks provide the desirer with a picture of the *point* of trying to bring it about that the world answer to one or another proposition. As noted above, a propositional desire considered in itself might present the desirer with a *de facto* psychological propensity to bring it about that things are thus and such, but not with a reason to do so.[14] In sum, then, the propositional account of desires cannot succeed in making sense of the justificatory role played by desires in the course of first-personal deliberation, hence it offers an unpromising basis for devising rationalizing explanations of actions, or for interpreting one's own guiding concerns and those of one's intimates.

As mentioned above, if we abandon the propositional account of desires in favour of the 'evaluative outlook' account that I have begun to elaborate, this will count heavily against the thesis that desires and beliefs are distinguished by their opposing 'directions of fit' with the world. If a desire provides an incipient picture of some range of goods, and if this picture fails to correspond with our considered judgements concerning what is, in fact, good, then we shall generally have reason to alter our desire (if we can) so that it more nearly tracks our considered view of what really is good, and we might well be disposed to do so. This view implies that we can speak of certain desires as involving misleading outlooks on value, but it does not carry the stronger and far less plausible implication that desires can be assessed as true or false. Desires differ from beliefs in that having a desire requires no affirmation of the picture of the world that the desire involves. Hence, a desire can no more be criticized as false than can a supposition or an exercise of imagination.

---

[14] Warren Quinn makes this point very effectively in his essay 'Putting Rationality in Its Place', in Quinn 1993: 228–55, esp. 236–7.

5 A BRIEF HISTORY OF THE ECSTATIC CONCEPTION OF DESIRE

Augustine's discussion of the desire for God finds its place within a long tradition of Platonist, neo-Platonist, and Christian mystical discussions of the longing that attracts humans to the highest good, understood either as abstract form or as divine person. The propositional view cannot make good sense of this tradition, nor even of our readiness to recognize that it is a tradition of thought about what we call desire. This tradition coheres far better with the evaluative attention account of desire. Still, there is a strand of this tradition that points towards fruitful revisions to the most influential contemporary statements of the evaluative attention account. It points, in particular, towards a more illuminating picture of interpersonal desires than is yielded either by propositionalism or by currently influential versions of the evaluative attention account.

To get hold of this strand, it will help to begin with two quotes from the fourth-century Century Platonist and mystical theologian Gregory of Nyssa, who died three years before Augustine penned his *Confessions*. Here is what Gregory says about desiring God:

It is not in the nature of what is unenclosed to be grasped. But every desire (*epithumia*) for the Good which is attracted to that ascent constantly expands as one progresses in pressing on to the Good . . . This truly is the vision of God: never to be satisfied in the desire (*epithumia*) to see him. But one must always, by looking at what he can see, rekindle his desire (*epithumia*) to see more. Thus, no limit would interrupt growth in the ascent to God, since no limit to the Good can be found nor is the increasing of desire (*epithumia*) for the Good brought to an end because it is satisfied. (Gregory of Nyssa 1978, sections 238–9)

In another passage, Gregory writes:

Hope always draws the soul from the beauty which is seen to what is beyond, always kindles the desire for the hidden through what is constantly perceived. Therefore, the ardent lover of beauty although receiving what is always visible as an image of what he desires (*epithumia*), yet longs to be filled with the very stamp of the archetype. (Gregory of Nyssa 1978, section 231)[15]

---

[15] Similar passages can be found in sections 7, 225, 226, 230, 232, 233, and 242; see also Gregory of Nyssa, *Commentary on the Song of Songs*, J.31, J.32, J. 321. Gregory's conception of desire fits hand in glove with his idea that the good life consists in a continuous *epektasis*, or straining forward towards the good. This idea is explained in a particularly striking way in the following passage from this *Commentary*: 'Bodies, once they have received the initial thrust downward, are driven downward by themselves with greater speed without any additional help as long as the surface on which they move is steadily sloping and no resistance to their downward thrust is encountered. Similarly, the soul moves in the opposite direction. Once it is released from its earthly attachment, it becomes light and swift for its movement upward, soaring from below up to the heights. If nothing comes from above to hinder its upward thrust (for the nature of the Good attracts to itself those

Like the Platonic desire for the good, so too the *epithumia* here described by Gregory consists in a mesmerizing vision that, because of the seeming beauty or goodness of its apparent object, never satisfies but always heightens the selfsame *epithumia*, and thus continuously induces the desirer to bring the object of desire more clearly into view. It seems clear that 'desire' is an apt translation for the longing that Gregory has in mind, not only because his thought is immediately recognizable in English but also because he uses the term *epithumia* elsewhere in the same work to refer to forms of attraction that fall comfortably within the ambit of what we call desire.[16] Yet the desire described by Gregory does not seem to aim at the refashioning of the world so as to bring it into correspondence with any proposition. It does not seem possible to formulate a proposition whose truth is a necessary and sufficient condition for attainment of the desire's end. Indeed, the desire would seem to consist in a mesmerizing attraction to a good wholly present rather than in a disposition to bring about some as-yet-unrealized state of affairs.

Any attempt to capture the desire's end in propositional form is likely to exhibit one of two failures. If love of the Good, or of God, is mistaken for the desire that one be good, or possess the good, or be worthy of the love of God, this would be tantamount to reversing the 'direction of gaze' of the desire. What presents itself as an attraction to something *other*, longing for which might have the *indirect effect* on the desirer of making the desirer good, is misconstrued as a desire for its own indirect effect. This cannot be the desire in question, since one could have any one of these self-oriented propositional desires (i.e. that one be good, or possess the good, or be worthy of the love of God) without feeling the overwhelming and unmediated attraction to the good, or God, that Gregory is trying to characterize, and that might plausibly have the indirect effect of making one good. Indeed, this is a rather exact description of the predicament Augustine took himself to be in, just prior to his conversion in *Confessions* Book VIII. He presents himself as badly wanting it to be the case that he enter into intimate relation with God, yet as lacking the wholehearted, attention-flooding longing for God that he regards as the primary constituent of this desired condition.

---

who look to it), the soul rises ever higher and will always make its flight yet higher—by its desire of the heavenly things 'straining ahead [*sunepekteinomenê*] for what is still go come', as the Apostle says [Philippians 3: 13].'

[16] For instance, in § 271 of *The Life of Moses*, Gregory writes: 'But the people had not learned to keep in step with Moses' greatness. They were still drawn down to the slavish passions (*epithumia*) and were inclined to the Egyptian pleasures.' In § 272, he writes: 'Their unruly desires (*epithumia*) produced serpents which injected deadly poison into those they bit. The great lawgiver, however, rendered the real serpents powerless by the image of a serpent.' Again, in § 280: 'When those who were lusting (*epithumountôn*) believed in the one lifted up on the wood, the earth stopped bringing forth serpents to bite them . . . It is then, when lustful desire (*epithumia*) leaves them, that the disease of arrogance enters in its place.' Finally, in § 316: 'And when you, as a sculptor, carve in your own heart the divine oracles which you receive from God; and when you destroy the golden idol (that is, if you wipe from your life the desire (*epithumia*) of covetousness) . . . then you will draw near to the goal.'

Other likely sounding propositional translations of the desire for God fail because they only manage to capture the desire itself, in its most extreme pitch, rather than its object. The desire that I be one with God, or that I be one with the good, is best understood as a metaphorical expression of the desire that I be continuously filled with a proximate and unmediated awareness of God, or the good, as what they essentially are (for example, good). But such awareness just is the desire in question, in its most extreme pitch. Yet we cannot locate the object of the desire in the desirer's own conscious states without misunderstanding contemplative devotion as self-preoccupation. To save the embarrassment of concluding that the desire's object is neither good nor God but merely itself intensified, I think it best to say that if the desire is not illusory, it is directed at a person and not at a project. That is, its object is not a state of affairs to be brought about, but a luminous being already wholly present if not wholly appreciated. While it is true that this luminous being appears as something to be savoured and approached, the desire that displays it as such is not best interpreted as the desire that one savour or approach it. Such an interpretation would either commit the above-mentioned error of mistaking the desire for a solipsistic longing for its own intensification, or assign to the desire an object that one could desire without desiring God.

The reason we cannot compass the desire for God within the framework of propositionalism is not, as one might be tempted to suppose, that God's goodness is infinite. Infinitude in itself is no bar to propositional (as opposed, say, to pictorial) representation. The real reason is that the desire's object is not the sort of thing that can be picked out by a proposition, nor for that matter the sort of thing one could sensibly endeavour to bring about. It is a person and not a state of affairs. If Gregory's discussion of the desire for God is so much as coherent, what it shows is that the wellspring of human motivation can consist in a mesmerizing and self-augmenting vision of goodness—a vision that precedes and inspires determinate plans and projects. Further, there is an historically prominent sense of 'desire' that is broad enough to encompass such visions of goodness, even when these visions are taken in isolation from ensuing plans and projects.[17]

I shall use the phrase 'ecstatic desire' to refer to desires that consist in self-augmenting attraction to persons or objects represented under the aspect of the intrinsically good. The notion that there are such desires, and that they mediate

---

[17] At the risk of illuminating the obscure with the indecipherable, the sort of desire at issue here has clear affinities with what Emmanuel Levinas calls 'metaphysical desire' (Levinas 1969: 33–4): 'The other metaphysically desired is not "other" like the bread I eat, the land in which I dwell, the landscape I contemplate . . . I can "feed" on these realities and to a very great extent satisfy myself, as though I had simply been lacking them. The metaphysical analysis of desire tends toward *something else entirely*, toward the *absolutely other*. The customary analysis of desires cannot explain away its singular pretension . . . The metaphysical desire has another intention; it desires beyond everything that can simply complete it. It is like goodness—the Desired does not fulfil it, but deepens it . . . This remoteness is radical only if desire is not the possibility of anticipating the desirable, only if it does not think it beforehand, if it goes toward it aimlessly, that is, as toward an absolute, unanticipatable alterity, as one goes forth unto death.'

our relation to the highest good, has obvious resonances with the Platonic picture of the reasoning part of the soul's self-augmenting attraction to truth and to the form of the Good. The self-augmenting feature of this desire is brought out in a particularly vivid way by Plato's talk, in *Phaedrus* 246d–249c, of the vision of true being as the proper nourishment for the soul, capable of strengthening the plumage of the soul's wings so that it becomes increasingly able to bear itself upwards and to partake of the self-same nourishing vision. However, this conception of desire for the good might just as plausibly be said to have Aristotelian roots, as it has a distinct affinity with Aristotle's claims (in *Metaphysics* Λ.7) that the unmoved mover is the highest good and the primary object both of thought and of desire, and that this object serves as the final cause of action not in the sense that things are done for its good (it cannot be altered) but in the sense that things are done out of love for it.

The ecstatic conception of desire for the divine enters into the early Christian mystical tradition at least a century before Gregory, in the neo-Platonist writings of Plotinus. For Plotinus, the human encounter with the Good is not a passionless intellectual exercise but rather the responsiveness of reason to something that mightily attracts it and that inspires a loving desire proper to us. The good is 'the desired of every soul' (*Enneads* 1.VI.7). To see the Good is to be filled with a 'veritable love' and a 'sharp desire' for it (*Enneads* 1.VI.7). If you are gripped by such a loving desire, you will find within yourself 'a Dionysiac exultation that thrills through your being' together with 'a straining upwards of all your soul' (*Enneads* 1.VI.5). This is the sole route to becoming good, since one becomes good not by directly striving to be good but only as the by-product of loving desire oriented immediately towards the divine mind—an object that all humans grasp, at least dimly, as the proper object of their longing and contemplative attention (*Enneads* 1.II.4). Indeed, Plotinus holds that all of nature strives towards contemplation of the divine mind, though the participation of inanimate nature in the divine mind differs from the best sort of human contemplation as sleep differs from waking (*Enneads* 3. VIII. 1–5). Still, humans vary widely in their degree of wakefulness, and many strive to bring about material results in the world without realizing that the real object of their longing is not some state of affairs they might produce, but a perfection they are suited to contemplate and to participate in by means of contemplation (*Enneads* 3.VIII.4).

It is well beyond the scope of this chapter to provide even a minimally comprehensive history of this still-evolving theological conception of ecstatic desire for God. Still, to get some sense of the longevity and centrality of this notion, it will help to look briefly at a few of its more influential manifestations. The ecstatic notion of the desire for God crops up in Aquinas' discussion in *Summa Theologica* 1a2ae.I.1–5 of the 'last end' and our desire for it. Aquinas speaks of man's last end as the proper object of desire, and he characterizes this last end formally as happiness and substantively as God. All men desire happiness (*ST* 1a2ae.5, 8) but not all see that 'God alone constitutes man's happiness' and, hence, that the last end of man, hence the proper object of desire, 'is not the good of the universe, but God himself' (*ST* 1a2ae.2,8 and 3,1). The last end, in other words, is not some way that the created universe might come to be, but a perfect being who is always already wholly present though never wholly grasped by the human mind. Aquinas notes that this last end of man can be characterized either as God or as the attainment or possession of God (*ST* 1a2ae.5,8; 2,7 and 3,1). Yet, he makes clear, the first characterization is primary. Attainment or possession of God is good only because it constitutes a form of participation in a conceptually prior and independent good (*ST* 1a2ae.2,7; see also 3, 1). Hence, the goodness of God is more final than the goodness of any possible relation to God, and since the proper object of desire is the most final end, the proper object is God.

We can reach this same interpretive conclusion by focusing on Aquinas' denial that the final end could be a property or possession of the human soul. For Aquinas, happiness consists in attaining or participating in the final end, God. Yet, as Aquinas makes clear, '. . . the thing itself which is desired as end, is that which constitutes happiness, and makes men happy; but the attainment of this thing is called happiness. Consequently we must say that happiness is something belonging to the soul; but that which constitutes happiness is something outside the soul' (*ST* 1a2ae.2,7; see also 3,5). Aquinas holds that 'it is impossible for man's last end to be the soul itself or something belonging to it' (*ST* 1a2ae.2,7). Again, since the last end is the proper object of desire, the proper object of desire is God and not one's own attainment or possession of God.

Relatedly, Aquinas claims that we misunderstand the proper desire for God if we think of it as a desire to enjoy or delight in the contemplative vision of God. This would effectively reverse the 'direction of gaze' of the proper desire for God. Desire for the highest good involves a movement of the intellect towards that good. Delight is necessarily attendant upon the intellect's approach to the highest good, and that approach is, in turn, propelled by a longing for the highest good (*ST* 1a2ae.2,6 and 3,4). Those whose sole desire is for this delight itself will be unable to attain it (*ST* 1a2ae.3,4).

It might seem that Aquinas' occasional references to resting in God, or sating one's appetite for God, mark an important departure from the views of Gregory of Nyssa, who denies that it is possible to bring contemplative appreciation of God to a fully perfect form, or to satiate the desire for God. Yet this difference turns out on inspection to be superficial, since Aquinas denies that the contemplation of God's infinite perfection can itself be perfected by a finite human mind (*ST* 1a2ae.3,2; 4,3 and 5,3). Hence, the human desire for God can augment itself without end. As Aquinas puts it: '. . . the more perfectly the sovereign good is possessed, the more it is loved, and other things despised: because the more we possess it, the more we know it. Hence it is written (*Ecclus.* 24: 29): "They that eat me shall yet hunger"' (*ST* 1a2ae.2,1).

A recognizably Gregorian or ecstatic conception of desire for God can also be glimpsed in the writings of various fourteenth- and fifteenth-century Christian mystics as, for instance, in this selection from Walter Hilton's *The Ladder of Perfection*:

If, then, you feel a great longing (*desire*) in your heart for Jesus . . . and if this longing (*desire*) is so strong that its force drives out of your heart all other thoughts and desires of the world and the flesh, then you are indeed seeking your Lord Jesus. And if, when you feel this desire for (*to*) God, for (*to*) Jesus . . . you are helped and strengthened by a supernatural might so strong that it is changed into love and affection, spiritual savour and sweetness and knowledge of truth . . . then you have found something of Jesus . . . and the more fully you find Him, the more you will desire Him.   (Hilton [1957]: bk I, Ch. 46; parenthetical interpolations are from the original Old English)

Hilton writes his book for aspiring contemplatives who aim to cultivate an abiding desire for God, a love on fire with contemplation. Such contemplation cannot be perfected in this life, but only in the bliss of heaven, when 'all of the aspirations (*affection*) of the soul will be entirely Godward and spiritual' (Hilton [1957]: ii. 35). In Hilton's view, this state does not leave behind the loving desire for God, but is continually buoyed and strengthened by such loving desire—it is 'love on fire with contemplation.'[18] The sole pathway to this contemplation is to cultivate a self-augmenting desire for God—to 'seek desire by desire' (Hilton [1957]: i. 47).

   Given the Platonic and Aristotelian roots of the ecstatic conception of human desire for the highest good, and given its continued grip on Thomistic and Christian mystical theology,[19] it is no exaggeration to say that its elaboration and development has been the work of two and a half millennia. This historically influential tradition of thought is fundamentally at odds with the three dogmas of desire set out above, and one cost of our attachment to these dogmas is that they impede our efforts to understand the moral psychology and cosmology of this tradition. This same tradition coheres far more naturally with the evaluative outlook conception of desire than with the propositionalist conception. Still, we must make minor emendations to the best-known expositions of the evaluative outlook account of desires in order to accommodate the possibility of ecstatic desires. Stampe, for instance, holds that having a desire amounts to being struck by the seeming goodness of something, and, to this extent, his view seems like a natural home for ecstatic desires. However, he goes on to say that the goodness in question is always attached to the prospect of some proposition's coming to be true. Hence, he does not break with the thought that we can desire something other than the coming into actuality of a possible state of affairs.

---

[18] This is Hilton's name for the highest level of spiritual enlightenment, involving 'ecstatic union with God'. See Clifton Wolters's introduction to the above-cited edition of *The Ladder of Perfection*, xxiii.

[19] This notion of desire surfaces in the work of certain twentieth-century Christian theologians. See, for instance, von Balthasar 1986: 24–5, and 1982: 120–2.

Scanlon, for his part, thinks of desires in the 'directed attention sense' as tendencies to see certain features of one's circumstances as reasons for doing or bringing about something or another, and this rules out the possibility of a desire directed at a good or value that cannot simply be reduced to reasons to act in particular ways or bring about particular states of affairs. Indeed, Scanlon's theory of value reduces all apprehensions of goodness or value to apprehensions of reasons to have certain attitudes and to perform certain action (Scanlon 1998: ch. 2, esp. 95–100). This position seems strained when applied to aesthetic or religious experience, since such experiences seem to involve the apprehension of goods that bear on, but are not exhausted by, claims about what one ought to feel or do. Hence, it is unsurprising that Scanlon's view is subtly at odds with Platonic and Christian mystical conceptions of desire for beauty, the good, and God.

6 APPLYING THE ECSTATIC MODEL: LOVING DESIRE FOR PERSONS

I suggested above that the conception of desires as evaluative outlooks ought to be embraced because it properly captures the depth and perfectibility of desires, and provides a coherent way to make sense of a long tradition of neo-Platonic, Thomistic, and Christian mystical discussions of desire. I believe, however, that the ecstatic account of desires has other benefits that should commend it even to secular anti-Platonists. Chief among these is that it permits a more illuminating account of loving desires for other persons than does the propositional view.

No doubt a wide variety of human urges and longings could be brought, with varying degrees of verbal inventiveness or evasiveness, under the fungible description of 'loving desire'. I have no wish to stake out exclusive rights to the phrase. Still, I think that the Gregory-inspired ecstatic approach gets at a centrally valuable mode of interpersonal attraction. The approach provides a way of crediting the thought that personal love essentially involves desire without committing us to the claim that it essentially involves a project of remaking the world in the image of one's thoughts. The essence of ecstatic desire just is a mesmeric attraction to, and delight in, an element of the world already wholly given. The apparent goodness brought to light by ecstatic desire for a person is the actual goodness of someone already wholly present, if not wholly grasped, and not the hypothetical goodness of some merely possible state of affairs. The attraction is not itself a call to world-making, but rather a magnetic attraction to someone already there to be vividly appreciated. Such an attraction might induce the celebration of another's presence, but when one is moved to genuine celebration one is moved not by the thought of the *celebration*'s goodness but rather by attention to the goodness that the celebration responds to and expresses.

More generally, such an attraction might issue forth in a wide variety of plans for alteration of the world, but these subsidiary aims often have the status of expressive responses to a good already present and at least dimly apprehended, and their point cannot be understood except by reference to a more primitive attraction to this instantiation of goodness.

If we reflect on what it can mean in the best of cases to desire another person—i.e. to be drawn to them lovingly—the propositional translations of this desire all seem to omit something critical. Some fail because they distort the desire, often by portraying its object with a metaphor that cannot be taken literally without rendering the desire more possessive than ideally it ought to be (for example, 'that she be mine' or 'that I possess her'). Others fail because they describe the desiring itself rather than its object. An instance of this second class of failures is the proposition 'that I be one with her'. If this last proposition is to pick out a possibility consistent with the welcome fact of the separateness of persons, it seems to mean something like: that I attain a vivid, immediate, and fully appreciative awareness of her value (and perhaps vice versa). Yet such vivid awareness just is desire in its most intense pitch. We cannot understand loving desires as desires for their own intensification without losing hold of the most basic facts about them—i.e. that the loving desire for one person has a different object from the loving desire for another person, and that the objects of such desires are not one's own future psychological states but something wholly other than oneself.

I have been using the phrase 'ecstatic desire' to pick out the Gregory-type desires under discussion, and my reasons for favouring this terminology can perhaps now be seen. First, since such desires are attention-arresting modes of appreciation of something wholly other, they remove us from the condition of distraction, and, in particular, from that most banal and obsessive of human distractions, the self. Second, such desires extend one's concerns beyond one's standing articulation of those concerns. This is particularly obvious in the case of loving desire for other persons. It is part of our relation to other persons that if we are able to love them at all, we must love them before we grasp fully who or what they are such that they are worthy of the attention we devote to them. To love another is to be drawn to another by a generous straining to bring into focus the goodness, hence desirability, of an as yet obscure object of desire.[20] The lover stands ready to interpret the beloved's words and actions as signposts towards further discoveries about what it is good to be or to do, and this interpretive posture sustains and is sustained by attention-riveting appreciation of the other. At its best, this is a mutual and continuously reiterated process. It involves a readiness on the part of each to be guided by the example of the other

---

[20] I don't know the origin of the Buñuel film title *That Obscure Object of Desire*, but it has the ring of something ancient and borrowed, and it would be quite at home in the writings of Gregory of Nyssa.

in articulating an evolving understanding of what it is good for humans to be and do. This is an *ekstasis* of the most literal sort—a displacement of the self from the confines of the standing concerns that constitute the central element in what is sometimes called, after Korsgaard 1996, its 'practical identity', and a readiness to discern new outlines for its own guiding concerns in the person of another.

It might be objected that I have suggested an improbably ample picture of what it can mean to desire another person, since we ordinarily reserve talk of desiring persons for cases of sexual attraction. Common usage might be preferred here for its refreshingly crass picture of human longings, and my view might be dismissed as quaintly romantic. Yet one must ask whether common usage might be shaped not by clarity about the real nature of human longings but by anxious insistence to mark off a safe boundary between sexuality and other, merely Platonic, forms of interpersonal longing or attraction. Common language might be regarded here as the bearer not of our accumulated psychological wisdom but of our taboos. If we set these taboos aside, we can admit the pervasive sexual undertones to supposedly Platonic human relations, and we can acknowledge that sexual desires are often shot through with longing for a kind of access to another's being that cannot be secured but only symbolized by sex, and that heightens the interest and pleasure of the sex that is at least subliminally encountered as its symbolic enactment.[21]

---

[21] The first of these insights is standard Freudian fare. The second dates at least to Plato's *Symposium*, and who writes:

> Venus plays tricks on lovers with her game
> of images which never satisfy.
> Looking at bodies fills no vital need
> However nakedly the lovers gaze,
> However much their hands go wandering
> And still are empty—can they gather bloom
> From tender limbs? And then the time arrives
> When their embraces join, and they delight
> In the full flower of love, or almost do,
> Anticipating rapture soon to come,
> The moment of the sowing. Eagerly
> They press their bodies close, join lips and tongues,
> Their breath comes faster, faster. All in vain,
> For they can gather nothing, they cannot
> Effect real penetration, be absorbed
> Body in body, utterly. They seem
> To want to do just this. God knows they try . . .

(Lucretius, *The Way of Nature*, Book IV, 1100–12)

Lucretius' ambition here is to show that sexual desire aims at something impossible, and thereby makes us ridiculous and needlessly vulnerable, hence that we ought to reshape our sexual longings so that they direct us towards ends that can actually be realized. It is worth pointing out, though, that this wonderful description of sexual longing seems most apt for cases of loving sex and not detached or impersonal sex. Given this, there are perhaps grounds for venturing that the sort of sexual longing described by Lucretius aims at symbolic enactment of the infinite nearing of loving desire. Understood in this way, the longing might be regarded as more nearly sublime than ridiculous. To

Another problem with the objection at hand is that it makes it entirely mysterious why believers and unbelievers alike tend to accept the aptness of talk about desiring God, yet do not thereby mean to place all such desires in the same category as, say, Santa Teresa's bodily shudders of religious ecstasy. If desires for God are recognized as conceptually coherent and not necessarily sexual, and if Gregory of Nyssa's discussion of the longing for God is recognizable as an account of something it makes sense to call *desire*, then there would seem to be conceptual space for desires for other persons that are not necessarily sexual but that are partly constituted, and continuously deepened, by appreciative awareness of another's goodness.

7 APPLYING THE ECSTATIC MODEL: WHOLEHEARTED ACTIVITY AND THE VIRTUES

At the heart of the three dogmas of desire is the basic thought that desires can explain action only if they are directed at a state of affairs that does not yet obtain. This does not rule out the possibility of a desire that things now fall under some description which one knows them already to fall under. One would have such a desire if the following counterfactual were true: if one believed that the world did not correspond with said description, one would be disposed to act in ways calculated to bring it into correspondence. Nor do the three dogmas rule out desires that the world continue to answer to some description to which it already answers. However, one could have a propositional desire that things be, or remain, as they happen now to be, yet still see nothing good about how things are or about their remaining as they are. To have the desire, it suffices that one, in fact, be disposed to act in ways calculated to ensure that things remain as they are. This disposition need not imply any subjective sense that things are going well. It could take the form of a nervous compulsion. Hence, one could have a powerful desire to be doing what one is actually doing, with no further end in view, and also lack any desire to be doing anything else, yet still take no pleasure whatever in what one is doing. On the propositional account, then, desires themselves cannot explain how we cease to withhold ourselves from our own activities and become wholeheartedly engaged or delightfully absorbed in them.

The ecstatic conception of desire provides a direct and appealing explanation of how we become delightfully absorbed in those activities that we desire to engage in for their own sake. When we perpetuate an activity out of an ecstatic desire for the activity itself, this will always involve a vivid running sense of the activity's goodness—an apprehension that itself explains why we are inspired to extend our engagement with the activity. Continued engagement in the activity arises

reject such sexual longings because they aim at a physical impossibility would be like rejecting a statue of Pegasus on the ground that chunks of marble cannot possibly take wing.

from a vivid subjective sense of the goodness of the activity itself, and not from a possibly mechanical or neurotic disposition to bring it about that the activity is prolonged. Such a conception of desire provides a plausible frame for the Aristotelian notion that the truly virtuous take pleasure in their virtuous activity. Those who are virtuously constituted will have an unclouded apprehension of the intrinsic goodness of virtuous activities, and will be motivated to choose them precisely by this apprehension. This apprehension can simultaneously explain why they are motivated to prolong the activity, why they become wholeheartedly absorbed in the activity, and why the activity is a source of delight for them. (For more on this, see Brewer 2003.)

8 CONCLUDING OBSERVATIONS

As I noted above, talk of desire has become quite rare outside of philosophical circles, to the point where one of the more ordinary uses of the term 'desire' might well be, or at least be heavily influenced by, the contemporary philosophical use as guided by the dogmas under discussion. Given this, there is some danger that the philosophical accommodation of ordinary usage will lend undeserved impregnability to reigning philosophical orthodoxies. Still, we should take care not to exaggerate the degree to which the proponents of the three dogmas of desire can preen themselves on their fidelity to ordinary usage. The numerous philosophers who sign up for one or more of the above-mentioned dogmas of desire tend to use the term 'desire' in a very broad sense, encompassing all mental states whose world-to-mind direction of fit suits them to explain actions (when paired with suitable beliefs).[22] These philosophers are typically quite aware that this usage departs strikingly from ordinary usage, and they are right to insist that this alone is not an objection to their view. Philosophers ought to adopt whatever conception of desire permits them to generate the most illuminating account possible of human agency, even if this conception comes loose in certain particulars from ordinary talk of desire. The tenability of the conception of desire elaborated in this chapter depends upon whether they help us or hinder us in our efforts to formulate a coherent account of human actions and the lives they compose.

The three dogmas of desire come naturally to us because they cohere with the thought that the point of human action, if there is one, would have to lie in the states of affairs that the action is calculated to bring about (if only by constituting that state of affairs). I have tried to show that this tempting understanding of the point of action does not permit us to make good sense of our lives and their unity, of our mundane and sacred desires for other persons, or of our wholehearted activities and the pleasure we take in them. I also hope

---

[22] See, e.g., Williams, 'Internal and External Reasons', in Williams 1981: 101–13; or Smith 1994: 113–14.

to have shown that the rival 'soul-picture' I have begun to articulate can make better sense of these phenomena, while opening up 'new places for philosophical reflection' of the sort mentioned by Murdoch. In particular, I hope to have opened up fruitful places for philosophical reflection about the virtues. Any adequate conception of the virtues must explain how the virtues simultaneously confer on their possessors an unclouded apprehension of the intrinsic goods that bear on their lives and their relationships to other human beings, and motivate them to act on that apprehension of goodness. I hope to have shown that the ecstatic conception of desire provides an especially fruitful starting-point for elaborating such a conception of the virtues.

Bibliography

ABBREVIATIONS

EE   Aristotle, *Eudomian Ethics*
Met.   Aristotle, *Metaphysics*
NE   Aristotle, *Nicomachean Ethics*
Pol.   Aristotle, *Politics*
Rhet.   Aristotle, *Rhetoric*

Ackerman 1988: Felicia Ackerman, ' "A Man by Nothing is So Well Betrayed as by his Manner"? Politeness as a Virtue', in P. French, R. Uehling, and H. Wettstein (eds.), *Midwest Studies in Philosophy*, XIII. Notre Dame: University of Notre Dame Press, 1988.

Alldridge, P. 'Rules for Courts and Rules for Citizens', *Oxford Journal of Legal Studies*, 10 (1990), 487.

Annas 2004: Julia Annas, 'Being Virtuous and Doing the Right Thing', *Proceedings and Addresses of the American Philosophical Association*, 2004; htp://www.u.arizona.edu/jannas/forth/rightactionvirtue.tm.

Anscombe 1957: Elizabeth Anscombe, *Intention*. Oxford: Blackwell, 1957.

Anscombe 1957a: Elizabeth Anscombe, 'Does Oxford Moral Philosophy Corrupt Youth?', *The Listener*, 1957.

Anscombe 1958: Elizabeth Anscombe, 'Modern Moral Philosophy', *Philosophy*, 1958, 1–19, repr. in Mary Geach and Luke Gormally (eds.), *Human Life, Action, and Ethics*. Exeter: Imprint Academic, 2005, 249–51.

Anscombe 1965: 'Thought and Action in Aristotle: What is "Practical Truth"?', in Renford Bambrough (ed.), *New Essays on Plato and Aristotle*. London: Routledge, 1965, 143–58.

Anscombe 1967: Elizabeth Anscombe, 'Who is Wronged?', *The Oxford Review*, 1967, 16–17, repr. in Mary Geach and Luke Gormally (eds.), *Human Life, Action, and Ethics*. Exeter: Imprint Academic, 2005, 249–51.

Anscombe 1981: Elizabeth Anscombe, *Collected Philosophical Papers, Vol. 3*, Oxford: Blackwell, 1981.

Anscombe 2005: Elizabeth Anscombe, 'Good and Bad Human Action', in Mary Geach and Luke Gormally (eds.), *Human Life, Ethics and Action*. Exeter: Imprint Academic, 2005, 195–206.

Aquinas, *Summa Theologiae*: Blackfriars translation.

Aristotle, *Ethica Nicomachea*, ed. by I. Bywater. Oxford: Clarendon Press, repr. 1949.

Audi 1997: Robert Audi, 'Moral Judgments and Reasons for Action', in Garrett Cullity and Berys Gaut (eds.), *Ethics and Practical Reason*. Oxford: Oxford University Press, 1997.

Austen 1932: Jane Austen, *Pride and Prejudice*, ed. by R.W. Chapman, 3rd edn. Oxford: Oxford University Press, 1932.

Austen 1933: Jane Austen, *Sense and Sensibility*, ed. by R. W. Chapman, 3rd edn. Oxford: Oxford University Press, 1933.

Austen 1996: Jane Austen, *Northanger Abbey, Pride and Prejudice*, in *The Penguin Complete Novels of Jane Austen*. London: Penguin, 1996.

Bakhurst 2001: David Bakhurst, 'Ethical particularism in Context', in Brad Hooker and Margaret Little (eds.), *Moral Particularism*. Oxford: Clarendon Press, 2001.

von Balthasar 1982: Hans Urs von Balthasar, *Seeing the Form*, Vol. I of *The Glory of the Lord: A Theological Aesthetics*. Edinburgh: T&T Clark, 1982.

von Balthasar 1986: Hans Urs von Balthasar, *Prayer*. San Francisco: Ignatius Press, 1986.

Barnes 1985: Jonathan Barnes (ed.), *The Complete Works of Aristotle*. Princeton: Princeton University Press, 1985.

Barnes 1990a: Jonathan Barnes, 'Aristotle and Political Liberty', in G. Patzig (ed.), *Aristoteles Politik*. Göttingen: Vandenhoeck and Ruprecht, 1990.

Barnes 1990b: Jonathan Barnes, 'Partial Wholes', *Social Philosophy & Policy*, 8: 1 (1990), 1–23.

Baron 1997: Marcia Baron, 'Kantian Ethics', in Baron, Pettit, and Slote, 1997.

Baron, Pettit, and Slote [BPS] 1997: Marcia Baron, Philip Pettit, and Michael Slote, *Three Methods of Ethics*. Oxford: Blackwell, 1997.

Blackburn 2005: Simon Blackburn, 'Simply Wrong', TLS, September 30th 2005.

Booth 1988: Wayne Booth, *The Company We Keep: An Ethics of Fiction*. Berkeley: University of California Press, 1988.

Booth 1998: Wayne Booth, 'Why Banning Ethical Criticism is a Serious Mistake', *Philosophy and Literature*, 22: 2 (1998), 366–93.

Brandom 1994: Robert Brandom, *Making it Explicit*. Cambridge, Mass.: Harvard University Press, 1994.

Brewer 2002: Talbot Brewer, 'Maxims and Virtues', *Philosophical Review*, 111:4 (2002), 539–72.

Brewer 2003: Talbot Brewer, 'Savoring Time: Desire, Pleasure and Wholehearted Activity', in *Ethical Theory and Moral Practice*, 6 (2003), 143–60.

Brink 1997: David Brink, 'Kantian Rationalism: Inescapability, Authority and Supremacy', in Garrett Cullity and Berys Gaut (eds.), *Ethics and Practical Reason*. Oxford: Oxford University Press, 1997.

Broadie 1991: Sarah Broadie, *Ethics with Aristotle*. Oxford: Oxford University Press, 1991.

Broadie and Rowe 2002: Sarah Broadie and Christopher Rowe, *Aristotle: Nicomachean Ethics*. Oxford: Oxford University Press, 2002.

Brody 1999: Inger Sigrun Brody, 'Adventures of a Female Werther: Jane Austen's Revision of Sensibility'. *Philosophy and Literature*, 23 (1999), 110–26.

Brown 2001: Vivienne Brown, ' "Rights in Aristotle's *Politics* and *Nicomachean Ethics*?" ', *The Review of Metaphysics*, 55 (2001), 274.

Burnyeat 1980: Myles Burnyeat, 'Aristotle on Learning to Be Good', in Rorty 1980, 69–92.

Buss 1999: Sarah Buss, 'Appearing Respectful: The Moral Significance of Manners', *Ethics*, 109 (July 1999), 795–826.

Byrd 2005: B. S. Byrd, 'On Getting the Reasonable Person out of the Courtroom', *Ohio State Journal of Criminal Law*, Ohio State University, Moritz College of Law, 2 571–7.

Carroll 1994: Noel Carroll, 'The Paradox of Junk Fiction', *Philosophy and Literature*, 18 (1994).

Chappell 1995: Timothy Chappell, 'Reason, Passion and Action: The Third Condition of the Voluntary', *Philosophy*, 70 (1995), 453–9.

Chappell 1998: Timothy Chappell, *Understanding Human Goods*. Edinburgh: Edinburgh University Press, 1998.

Chappell 2001: Timothy Chappell, 'Option Ranges', *Journal of Applied Philosophy*, 18 (2001), 107–18.

Chappell 2003: Timothy Chappell, 'Practical Rationality for Pluralists about the Good', *Ethical Theory and Moral Practice*, 6 (2003), 161–77.

Chappell 2005: Timothy Chappell, ' "The Good Man is the Measure of All Things": Objectivity without World-Centredness in Aristotle's Moral Epistemology', in Christopher Gill (ed.), *Moral Objectivity in the Ancient World*. Oxford: Oxford University Press, 2005.

Chappell 2005a: Timothy Chappell, 'Critical Notice of Jonathan Dancy, *Ethics without Principles*', in *The Notre Dame Philosophical Review* at http://ndpr.nd.edu/review.cfm?id=3161

Coope 2003: Christopher Coope, 'Peter Singer in Retrospect', *Philosophical Quarterly*, (2003), 596–604.

Coope 2006: Christopher Rider Coope, 'Death Sentences', *Philosophy*, formthcoming.

Cooper 1986: John Cooper, *Reason and Human Good in Aristotle*. Indianapolis: Hackett, 1986.

Cooper 1990: John Cooper, 'Political Animals and Civic Friendship', in G. Patzig (ed.), *Aristoteles Politik*, Göttingen: Vandenhoeck & Ruprecht, 1990.

Cooper 1999: John Cooper, 'Reason, Moral Virtue, and Moral Value', in Cooper, *Reason and Emotion: Essays on Ancient Moral Psychology and Ethical Theory*. Princeton: Princeton University Press, 1999, 253–80.

Copp and Sobel 2004: David Copp and David Sobel, 'Morality and Virtue: An Assessment of Some Recent Work in Virtue Ethics', *Ethics*, 114 (2004), 514–54.

Crane 1997: Tim Crane (ed.), *Dispositions: A Debate*. London: Routledge, 1997.

Curzer 2001: Howard Curzer, 'To Become Good', http://www.bu.edu/wcp/Papers/Anci/AnciCurz.htm (accessed November 2001)

Curzer 2002: Howard Curzer, 'Aristotle's Painful Path to Virtue', *Journal of the History of Philosophy*, 40: 2 (2002), 141–62.

Damon 1988: William Damon, *The Moral Child*. New York: Free Press, 1988.

Dan-Cohen 1984: M. Dan-Cohen, 'Decision Rules and Conduct Rules', *Harvard Law Review*, 97 (1984), 625.

Dancy 2004: Jonathan Dancy, *Ethics Without Principles*. Oxford: Oxford University Press, 2004.

Darwall 2002: Stephen Darwall, *Welfare and Rational Care*. Princeton: Princeton University Press, 2002.

Davidson 1980: Donald Davidson, *Essays on Actions and Events*. Oxford: Oxford University Press, 1980.

Davies 1991: Vanessa Davies, *Abortion and Afterwards*. Bath: Ashgrove Press, 1991.

Dennett 1987: Daniel Dennett, *The Intentional Stance*. Cambridge, Mass.: MIT Press, 1987.

De Sousa 1990: Ronald De Sousa, *The Rationality of Emotions*. Cambridge, Mass.: MIT Press, 1990.

De Ste Croix 1992: De Ste Croix, G. E. M.: 'Aristotle on History and Poetry (*Poetics*, 9, 1451a36–b11)', in A.O. Rorty (ed.), *Essays on Aristotle's Poetics*. Princeton: Princeton University Press, 1992, 23–32.

Dickens 1994: Charles Dickens, *Hard Times*. London: Penguin Books, 1994.

Donnellan 1966: Keith Donnellan, 'Reference and Definite Descriptions', *Philosophical Review*, 75 (1966), 281–304.

Dretske 1988: Fred Dretske, *Explaining Behavior: Reasons in a World of Causes*. Cambridge, Mass.: MIT Press, 1988.

Driver 1992: Julia Driver, 'Caesar's Wife: On the Moral Significance of Appearing Good', *The Journal of Philosophy*, 89: 7 (July 1992), 331–43.

Duff 2002: R. A. Duff, 'Virtue, Vice and Criminal Liability', *Buffalo Criminal Law Review*, 6 (2002), 147.

Duff 2002a, 'Rule-Violations and Wrongdoings', in S Shute and A. P. Simester (eds.), *Criminal Law Theory: Doctrines of the General Part*. Oxford: Oxford University Press, 2002, 47.

Duff 2003: R. A. Duff, 'The Limits of Virtue Jurisprudence', *Metaphilosophy*, 34 (2003), 214.

Duff 2004: R. A. Duff, 'Action, the Act Requirement and Criminal Liability', in J. Hyman and H. Steward (eds.), *Action and Agency*. Cambridge: Cambridge University Press, 2004.

Dressler 1989: J. Dressler, 'Exegesis of the Law of Duress: Justifying the Excuse and Searching for its Proper Limits', *Southern California Law Review*, 62 (1989), 133.

Feinberg 1988: Joel Feinberg, *Harmless Wrongdoing*. New York: Oxford University Press, 1988.

Feldman 2000: H. I. Feldman, 'Prudence, Benevolence, and Negligence: Virtue Ethics and Tort Law', *Chicago-Kent Law Review*, 74 (2000), 1431.

Feldman 2004: Fred Feldman, *Pleasure and the Good Life*. Oxford: Clarendon Press, 2004.

Finkelstein 1995: C. Finkelstein, 'Duress: A Philosophical Account of the Defense in Law', *Arizona Law Review*, 37 (1995), 251.

Fletcher 1978: G. Fletcher, *Rethinking Criminal Law* Little, Brown, 1978, 829–35.

Foot 1967: Philippa Foot, *Theories of Ethics*. Oxford: Oxford University Press, 1967.

Foot 1978: Philippa Foot, *Virtues and Vices*. Oxford: Blackwell, 1978.

Foot 1993: Philippa Foot, 'Justice and Charity', Oxford: Oxfam, 1993.

Foot 2001: Philippa Foot, *Natural Goodness*. Oxford: Oxford University Press, 2001.

Foot 2001a: Philippa Foot, 'Elizabeth Anscombe (1919–2001)', *The Siren*, 2001.

Foot 2004: Philippa Foot, 'Rationality and Goodness', in Anthony O'Hear (ed.), *Modern Moral Philosophy*. Cambridge: Cambridge University Press, 2004.

Fortenbaugh 1975: William Fortenbaugh, *Aristotle on Emotion*. London: Duckworth, 1975.

Fortenbaugh 1977: William Fortenbaugh, 'Aristotle on Slaves and Women', in Jonathan Barnes, Malcolm Schofield, and Richard Sorabji (eds.), *Articles on Aristotle 2: Ethics and Politics*. London: Duckworth, 1977, 135–9.

Fortenbaugh 1979: William Fortenbaugh, 'Aristotle's *Rhetoric* on Emotion', in Jonathan Barnes, Malcolm Schofield, and Richard Sorabji (eds.), *Articles on Aristotle 4: Psychology and Aesthetics*. London: Duckworth, 1979, 133–53.

Fortenbaugh 1991: William Fortenbaugh, 'Aristotle's Distinction Between Moral Virtue and Practical Wisdom', in John P. Anton and Anthony Preus (eds.), *Essays in Ancient Greek Philosophy IV: Aristotle's Ethics*. New York: State University of New York Press, 1991, 97–106.

Fossheim 2001: Fossheim, Hallvard: 'Mimesis in Aristotle's Ethics', in Øivind Andersen and Jon Haarberg (eds.), *Making Sense of Aristotle: Essays in Poetics*. London: Duckworth, 2001, 73–86.

Frankena 1965: Frankena, William K.: 'Aristotle's Philosophy of Education', in W. K. Frankena, *Three Historical Philosophies of Education*. Glenview, Ill.: Scott, Foreman and Company, 1965, ch. 2.

Frede 1992: Dorothea Frede, 'Necessity, Chance, and "What Happens for the Most Part" in Aristotle's Poetics', in A. O. Rorty (ed.), *Essays on Aristotle's Poetics*. Princeton: Princeton University Press, 1992, 197–219.

Gallop 1999: David Gallop, 'Jane Austen and the Aristotelian Ethic', *Philosophy and Literature*, 23 (1999), 96–109.

Galston 2003: William A. Galston, 'The Danger of Absolutes', *The Public Interest* (Winter, 2003).

Gardner 1998: J. Gardner, 'The Gist of Excuses', *Buffalo Criminal Law Review*, 1 (1998), 575.

Gardner 2003: J. Gardner, 'The Mark of Responsibility', 23 (2003), *Oxford Journal of Legal Studies*, 157.

Gardner and Macklem 2001: J. Gardner and T. Macklem, 'Provocation and Pluralism', *Modern Law Review* 64 (2001), 815.

Gaskin 2002: Richard Gaskin, 'Do Homeric Heroes Make Real Decisions?', in Douglas L. Cairns (ed.), *Oxford Readings in Homer's Iliad*. Oxford: Oxford University Press, 2002.

Geach 1977: Peter Geach, *The Virtues*. Cambridge: Cambridge University Press, 1977.

Geach 2001: Peter Geach, *Truth and Hope*, Notre Dame: University of Notre Dame Press, 2001.

Golden 1962: Leon Golden, 'Catharsis', *Transactions and Proceedings of the American Philological Association*, 93 (1962), 51–60.

Goldman 1970: Alvin Goldman, *A Theory of Human Action*. Princeton: Princeton University Press, 1970.

Gollwitzer et al. 1956: H. Gollwitzer, K. Kuhn, and R. Schneider (eds.), *Dying We Live*, trans. R. Kuhn. London: Harvill Press, 1956.

Gregory of Nyssa, *The Life of Moses*, trans. by Abraham J. Malherbe and Everett Ferguson. New York: Paulist Press, 1978.

Griffin 1986: James Griffin, *Well-Being: Its Meaning, Measurement and Moral Importance*. Oxford: Clarendon Press, 1986.

Halliwell 1986: Stephen Halliwell, *Aristotle's Poetics*. London: Duckworth, 1986.

Halliwell 2002: Stephen Halliwell, *The Aesthetics of Mimesis: Ancient Texts and Modern Problems*. Princeton: Princeton University Press, 2002.

Halper 1999: Edward Halper, 'The Unity of the Virtues in Aristotle', *Oxford Studies in Ancient Philosophy*, Vol. XVII, Oxford: Clarendon Press, 1999, 115–43.

Hampton 1984: J. Hampton, 'The Moral Education Theory of Punishment', *Philosophy & Public Affairs*, 13 (1984), 208.

Hardie 1980: W. F. R. Hardie, *Aristotle's Ethical Theory*, 2nd edn. Oxford: Clarendon Press, 1980.

Hart 1968: H. L. A. Hart, 'Legal Responsibility and Excuses', in H. L. A. Hart, *Punishment and Responsibility*. Oxford: Oxford University Press, 1968, 28.

Heath 1991: Malcolm Heath, 'The Universality of Poetry in Aristotle's *Poetics*', *Classical Quarterly*, 41: 2 (1991), 389–402.

Hilton [1957]: Walter Hilton, *The Ladder of Perfection*, trans. by Leo Sherley-Price. New York: Penguin, 1957.

Hohfeld 1923: W. N. Hohfeld, *Fundamental Legal Conceptions as Applied in Judicial Reasoning*. New Haven: Yale University Press, 1923.

Horder 1992: J. Horder, *Provocation and Responsibility*. Oxford: Oxford University Press, 1992.

Hornsby 2004: Jennifer Hornsby, 'Agency and Actions', in J. Hyman and H. Steward (eds.), *Action and Agency*. Cambridge: Cambridge University Press, 2004.

House 1967: Humphrey House, *Aristotle's Poetics: A Course of Eight Lectures*. London: Rupert Hart-Davis, 1967, orig. 1956.

Hudson 1995: B. Hudson, 'Beyond Proportionate Punishment: Difficult Cases and the 1991 Criminal Justice Act' (1995), 22.

Huigens 1995: K. Huigens, 'Virtue and Inculpation', *Harvard Law Review*, 108 (1995), 1423.

Huigens 2002: K. Huigens, 'Homicide in Aretaic Terms', *Buffalo Criminal Law Review*, 6 (2002), 97.

Hume 1998: David Hume, *An Enquiry Concerning the Principles of Morals*, ed. Tom L. Beauchamp. Oxford: Oxford University Press, 1998.

Hurka 1998: Thomas Hurka, 'Two Kinds of Organic Unity', *The Journal of Ethics*, 2 (1998), 299–320.

Hursthouse 1987: Rosalind Hursthouse, *Beginning Lives*. Oxford: Blackwell, 1987.

Hursthouse 1991: Rosalind Hursthouse, 'Virtue Theory and Abortion', *Philosophy and Public Affairs*, 20 (1991), 223–46.

Hursthouse 1995: Rosalind Hursthouse, 'Applying Virtue Ethics', in Rosalind Hursthouse, Gavin Lawrence, and Warren Quinn (eds.), *Virtues and Reasons*. Oxford: Clarendon Press, 1995.

Hursthouse 1999: Rosalind Hursthouse, *On Virtue Ethics*. Oxford: Oxford University Press, 1999.

Hursthouse 2000: Rosalind Hursthouse, *Ethics, Humans, and Other Animals*. London: Routledge, 2000.

Hursthouse 2003: Rosalind Hursthouse, 'Virtue Ethics', *Stanford Encyclopedia of Philosophy*, http://plato.stanford.edu/entries/ethics-virtue.

Hutcheson 1725: Francis Hutcheson, *An Inquiry into the Original of our Ideas of Beauty and Virtue*, in *Two Treatises*, 1725, ed. Wolfgang Leidhold. Indianapolis: Liberty Fund, 2004.

Hutchinson: D. S. Hutchinson, 'Aristotle's Ethics', in Jonathan Barnes (ed.), *The Cambridge Companion to Aristotle*. Cambridge: Cambridge University Press, 1995, 199.

Irwin 1975: Terence Irwin, 'Aristotle on Reason, Desire, and Virtue', *The Journal of Philosophy*, 72: 17 (1975), 567–78.

Irwin 1999: Aristotle, *Nicomachean Ethics*, trans. Terence Irwin. Indianapolis: Hackett, 1999.

Irwin 1999a: Terence Irwin, 'Permanent Happiness: Aristotle and Solon', in Nancy Sherman (ed.), *Aristotle's Ethics: Critical Essays*. Lanham, Md.: Rowman & Littlefield, 1999.

Izzo 2002a: Jean-Claude Izzo, *Chourmo*. Paris: Gallimard, 2002.

Izzo 2002b: Jean-Claude Izzo, *Total Kheops*. Paris: Gallimard, 2002.

Jackson 1879: Henry Jackson, *The Fifth Book of the Nicomachean Ethics of Aristotle*. Cambridge: Cambridge University Press, 1879.

James 1999: Henry James, *The Golden Bowl*. Oxford: Oxford University Press, 1999.

Janko 1984: Richard Janko, *Aristotle on Comedy*. London: Duckworth, 1984.

Kagan 1994: Shelly Kagan, 'Me and My Life', *Proceedings of the Aristotelian Society* 94 (1994), 309–24.

Kahan and Nussbaum 1996: D. M. Kahan and M. Nussbaum, 'Two Conceptions of Emotion in Criminal Law', *Columbia Law Review*, 96 (1996), 269.

Kamm 1996: F. M. Kamm, *Morality, Mortality, Vol. II: Rights, Duties, and Status*. Oxford: Oxford University Press, 1996.

Kant 1785: Immanuel Kant, *Groundwork of the Metaphysic of Morals*, ed. Mary Gregor. Cambridge: Cambridge University Press, 1997.

Kenny 1992: Anthony Kenny: *Aristotle on the Perfect Life*. Oxford: Oxford University Press, 1992.

Kenny 2004: Anthony Kenny, *The Unknown God*. London: Continuum, 2004.

Knight 1994: Deborah Knight, 'Making Sense of Genre', *Philosophy and Film*, 2 (1994), http://www.hanover.edu/philos/film/vol_02/Kinght.htm.

Knight and McKnight 1997: Deborah Knight and George McKnight, 'The Case of the Disappearing Enigma', *Philosophy and Literature*, 21: 1, (1997).

Knox 1993: Bernard Knox, *The Oldest Dead White European Males*. New York: W. W. Norton.

Koonz 2003: Claudia Koonz, *The Nazi Conscience*. Cambridge, Mass.: Harvard University Press, 2003.

Korsgaard 1996a: Christine Korsgaard, *The Sources of Normativity*. Cambridge: Cambridge University Press, 1996.

Korsgaard 1996b: Christine Korsgaard, *Creating the Kingdom of Ends*. Cambridge: Cambridge University Press, 1996.

Kosman 1992: Aryeh Kosman: 'Acting: Drama as the *Mimêsis* of *Praxis*', in A. O. Rorty (ed.), *Essays on Aristotle's Poetics*, Princeton: Princeton University Press, 1992, 51–72.

Kripke 1980: Saul Kripke, *Naming and Necessity*. Oxford: Blackwell, 1980.

Levinas 1969: Emmanuel Levinas, *Totality and Infinity: An Essay on Exteriority*. trans. Alphonso Lingis. Pittsburgh: Duquesne University Press, 1969.

Lloyd 1968: Geoffrey Lloyd, *Aristotle*. Cambridge: Cambridge University Press, 1967.

Lucas 1980: J. R. Lucas, *On Justice*. Oxford: Clarendon Press, 1980.

McCabe 2002: Herbert McCabe, *God Still Matters*. London: Continuum, 2002.

McDowell 1980: John McDowell, 'The Role of *Eudaimonia* in Aristotle's Ethics', in Rorty 1980.

McDowell 1995: John McDowell, 'Two Sorts of Naturalism', in Rosalind Hursthouse, Gavin Lawrence, and Warren Quinn (eds.), *Reasons and Virtues: Philippa Foot and Moral Theory*. Oxford: Clarendon Press, 1995.

McDowell 1998: John McDowell, 'Are Moral Requirements Hypothetical Imperatives?', in J. McDowell, *Reason, Value, and Reality*. Cambridge, Mass.: Harvard University Press, 1998.

MacIntyre 1981: Alasdair MacIntyre, *After Virtue*. Notre Dame: University of Notre Dame Press, 1981.

MacIntyre 1984: Alasdair MacIntyre, *After Virtue*, 2nd edn. Notre Dame: University of Notre Dame Press, 1984.

MacIntyre 1988: Alasdair MacIntyre, *Whose Justice? Which Rationality?* London: Duckworth, 1988.

Miller 1995: Fred D. Miller, Jun., *Nature, Justice, and Rights in Aristotle's Politics*. Oxford: Clarendon Press, 1995.

Miller 2002: Fred D. Miller, Jun., 'Aristotelian Autonomy', in Aristide Tessitore (ed.), *Aristotle and Modern Politics: The Persistence of Political Philosophy*. Notre Dame: University of Notre Dame Press, 2002, 375–402.

Moore 1903: G. E. Moore, *Principa Ethica*. Cambridge: Cambridge University Press, 1903.

Moore 1997: M. S. Moore, *Placing Blame: A Theory of Criminal Law*. Oxford: Oxford University Press, 1997.

Morgan 1980: Susan Morgan, *In the Meantime: Character and Perception in Jane Austen's Fiction*. Chicago: The University of Chicago Press, 1980.

Morris 1981: H. Morris, 'A Paternalistic Theory of Punishment', *American Philosophical Quarterly*, 18 (1981), 263.

Morse 1998: S. Morse, 'Excusing and the New Excuse Defenses', in M. Tonry (ed.), *Crime and Justice: A Review of Research*, Vol. 23. Chicago: University of Chicago Press, 1998.

Morton 1990: Adam Morton, *Disasters and Dilemmas*. Oxford: Blackwell, 1990.

Morton (2004a): Adam Morton, *On Evil*. London: Routledge.

Morton (2004b): Adam Morton, 'Epistemic Virtues, Metavirtues, and Computational Complexity', *Nous*, 38, 3 (2004), 481–502.

Muller 1994: Marcia Muller, *Games to Keep the Dark Away*. The Women's Press, 1994.

Mumford 2003: Stephen Mumford, *Dispositions*. Oxford: Oxford University Press, 2003.

Murdoch 1970: Iris Murdoch, *The Sovereignty of Good*. London: Routledge & Kegan Paul, 1970.

Murphy 2001: Mark Murphy, *Natural Law and Practical Rationality*. Cambridge: Cambridge University Press, 2001.

Nagel 1979: Thomas Nagel, *Mortal Questions*. Cambridge: Cambridge University Press, 1979.

Nietzsche 1968: *The Twilight of the Idols and the Anti-Christ*. trans. by R. J. Hollingdale. London: Penguin, 1968.

Nietzsche 1979: *Ecce Homo*. trans. R. J. Hollingdale. London: Penguin, 1979.

Nussbaum 1986: Martha Nussbaum, *The Fragility of Goodness: Luck and Ethics in Greek Tragedy and Philosophy*. Cambridge: Cambridge University Press, 1986.

Nussbaum 1990: Martha Nussbaum, *Love's Knowledge*. New York: Oxford University Press, 1990.

Nussbaum 1994: Martha Nussbaum, *The Therapy of Desire*. Princeton: Princeton University Press, 1994.

Nussbaum 1995: Martha Nussbaum, *Poetic Justice*. Boston: Beacon Press.

Nussbaum 1998: Martha Nussbaum, 'A Defence of Ethical Criticism', *Philosophy and Literature*, 22: 2 (1998), 394–412.

Nussbaum 2001: Martha Nussbaum, *Upheavals of Thought*. Cambridge: Cambridge University Press, 2001.

Olson 2004: Jonas Olson, 'Intrinsicalism and Conditionalism about Final Value', *Ethical Theory and Moral Practice*, 7 (2004), 31–52.

Owens 1981: Joseph Owens, 'The *Kalon* in the Aristotelian Ethics', in Dominic J. O' Meara (ed.), *Studies in Aristotle*. Washington, DC: The Catholic University of America Press, 1981, 261–77.

Paretsky, Sara. *Hard Times*. New York: Delacorte Press.

Pincoffs 1985: Edmund Pincoffs, 'Two Cheers for Meno: The Definition of the Virtues', in E. E. Shelp (ed.), *Virtue and Medicine*. Dordrecht: Reidel, 1985.

Platts 1981: Mark Platts, 'Moral Reality and the End of Desire', in M. Platts *Reference, Truth and Reality*. New York: Routledge & Kegan Paul, 1981.

Plotinus, *The Enneads*. trans. by Stephen MacKenna. New York: Penguin Books, 1991.

Popper 1963: Karl Popper, *The Open Society and its Enemies*. New York: Harper & Row, 1963.

Posner 1997: Richard Posner, 'Against Ethical Criticism', *Philosophy and Literature*, 21: 1 (1997).

Posner 1998: Richard Posner, 'Against Ethical Criticism Part II'. *Philosophy and Literature*, 22: 2 (1998), 416.

Prior 1985: Elizabeth Prior, *Dispositions*. Aberdeen: Scots Philosophical Monograph Series, Aberdeen University Press, 1985.

Putnam 1975: Hilary Putnam, 'The Meaning of "Meaning"', in H. Putnam, *Mind, Language, and Reality: Philosophical Papers*, Vol. 2. Cambridge: Cambridge University Press, 1975.

Quinn 1993: Warren Quinn, *Morality and Action*. Cambridge: Cambridge University Press, 1993.

Raddatz 1979: Fritz J. Raddatz, *Karl Marx*. London: Weidenfeld & Nicolson, 1979.

Radford 1975: Colin Radford, 'How Can We be Moved by the Fate of Anna Karenina?', *Proceedings of the Aristotelian Society*, Supp. Vol. 49 (1975), 67–80.

Rankin 2000: Ian Rankin, *Set in Darkness*. London: Orion, 2000.

Rankin, 2001: Ian Rankin, *The Falls*. London: Orion Mass Market Paperback.

Redfield 1975: James Redfield, *Nature and Culture in the Iliad*. Chicago: The University of Chicago Press, 1975.

Rogers 1993: Kelly Rogers, 'Aristotle's Conception of *to kalon*', *Ancient Philosophy*, 13 (1993), 355–71.

Rorty 1980: Amélie Oksenberg Rorty, Essays on Aristotle's Ethics. Berkeley: University of California Press, 1980.

Ruderman 1995: Anne Crippen Ruderman, *The Pleasures of Virtue*. London: Rowman & Littlefield, 1995.

Russell 1995: Paul Russell, *Freedom and Moral Sentiment: Hume's Way of Naturalizing Responsibility*. Oxford: Oxford University Press, 1995.

Ryle 1949: Gilbert Ryle, *The Concept of Mind*. London: Harmondworth, 1949.

Ryle 1968: Gilbert Ryle, 'Jane Austen and the Moralists', in B. C. Southam (ed.), *Critical Essays on Jane Austen*. London: Routledge & Kegan Paul, 1968.

Scanlon 1998: T. M. Scanlon, *What We Owe to Each Other*. Cambridge, Mass.: Harvard University Press, 1998.

Schueler 1995: G. F. Schueler, *Desire: Its Role In Practical Reason and the Explanation of Action*. Cambridge, Mass.: MIT Press, 1995.

Schweitzer 1923: Albert Schweitzer, *Philosophy of Civilization*. trans. by John Naish. London: Black, 1923.

Shaftesbury 1711: Lord Shaftesbury, *Characteristics of Men, Manners, Opinions, Times* (1711).

Sherman 1989: Nancy Sherman, *The Fabric of Character: Aristotle's Theory of Virtue*. Oxford: Clarendon Press, 1989.

Sherman 1997: Nancy Sherman, *Making a Necessity of Virtue*. Cambridge: Cambridge University Press, 1997.

Sherman 1998: Nancy Sherman, 'Empathy and the Imagination', in P. French and H. Wettstein (eds.), *Midwest Studies in Philosophy*, Vol. XXII. Notre Dame: University of Notre Dame Press, 1998.

Sherman 1999: Nancy Sherman, 'The Habituation of Character', in N. Sherman (ed.), *Aristotle's Ethics: Critical Essays*. Lanham: Rowman & Littlefield, 1999, 231–60.

Sherman 2004: Nancy Sherman, 'Virtue and Emotional Demeanor', in A. Manstead, N. Frijda, and A. Fischer, (eds.), *Feelings and Emotions: Interdisciplinary Explorations*. Cambridge: Cambridge University Press, 2004.

Simester and Sullivan 2003: A. P. Simester and G. R. Sullivan, *Criminal Law: Theory and Doctrine*, 2nd edn. Oxford: Hart, 2003.

Singer 1986: R. Singer, 'On Classism and Dissonance in the Criminal Law', *Journal of Criminal Law and Criminology*, 77 (1986), 6.

Skorupski 1999: John Skorupski, *Ethical Explorations*. Oxford: Oxford Univsersity Press, 1999.

Slote 1996: Michael Slote, 'Agent Based Virtue Ethics', in Peter A. French, Theodore E. Uehling, and Howard K. Wettstein (eds.), *Moral Concepts*. Notre Dame: University of Notre Dame Press, 1996.

Slote 1997: Michael Slote, 'Virtue Ethics' in Marcia Baron, Philip Pettit, and Michael Slote (eds.), *Three Methods of Ethics*. Oxford: Blackwell, 1997.

Slote 2000: Michael Slote, 'Virtue Ethics' in Hugh LaFollette (ed.), *The Blackwell Guide to Ethical Theory*. Oxford: Blackwell, 2000.

Slote 2001: Michael Slote, *Morals from Motives*. Oxford: Oxford University Press, 2001.

Slote 2002: Michael Slote, 'Justice as a Virtue', *Stanford Encyclopedia of Philosophy*, http://plato.stanford.edu/entries/justice-virtue.

Smith 1976: Adam Smith, *The Theory of Moral Sentiments*, ed. by D. D. Raphael and A. L. Macfie. Oxford: Clarendon Press, 1976.

Smith 1994: Michael Smith, *The Moral Problem*. Oxford: Blackwell, 1994.

Smith 1996: A. D. Smith, 'Character and Intellect in Aristotle's Ethics', *Phronesis*, 41: 1 (1996), 56–74.

Smithson 1983: Isaiah Smithson, 'The Moral View of Aristotle's Poetics', *Journal of the History of Ideas*, 44 (1983), 3–18.

Smyth 1920: Herbert Weir Smyth, *Greek Grammar*, rev. Gordon M. Messing. Cambridge, Mass.: Harvard University Press, 1920.

Snell 1953: Bruno Snell, *The Discovery of the Mind: The Greek Origins of European Thought*. Cambridge, Mass.: Harvard University Press, 1953.

Solum 2003: L. Solum, 'Virtue Jurisprudence: A Virtue-Centred Theory of Judging', *Metaphilosophy*, 34 (2003), 178.

Sorabji 1980: Richard Sorabji, 'Aristotle on the Role of Intellect in Virtue', in Rorty, 1980.

Sorabji 2000: Richard Sorabji, *Emotions and Peace of Mind*. Oxford: Oxford University Press, 2000.

Stampe 1987: Dennis Stampe, 'The Authority of Desire', *The Philosophical Review*, 96: 2 (July 1987), 335–82.

Stephen 1967: J. F. Stephen, *Liberty, Equality, Fraternity*, ed. J White. Cambridge: Cambridge University Press, 1967.

Stocker 1990: Michael Stocker, *Plural and Conflicting Values*. Oxford: Oxford University Press, 1990.

Sumner 1996: Wayne Sumner, *Welfare, Happiness, and Ethics*. Oxford: Oxford University Press, 1996.

Susemihl and Hicks 1894: F. Susemihl and R. D. Hicks, *The Politics of Aristotle*. London: Macmillan, 1894.

Swanton 2003: Christine Swanton, *Virtue Ethics: A Pluralistic View*. Oxford: Oxford University Press, 2003.

Syme 1960: Ronald Syme, *The Roman Revolution*. Oxford: Oxford University Press, 1960.

Tadros 2001: V. Tadros, 'The Characters of Excuse', *Oxford Journal of Legal Studies*, 21 (2001), 495.

Taylor 1982: Charles Taylor, 'Responsibility for Self', in Gary Watson (ed.), *Free Will*. Oxford: Oxford University Press, 1982, 111–26.

Thomson 1971: J. J. Thomson, 'A Defence of Abortion', *Philosophy and Public Affairs*, 1 (1971), 47–66.

Tuozzo 1994: Thomas Tuozzo, 'Conceptualized and Unconceptualized Desire in Aristotle', *Journal of the History of Philosophy*, 32: 4 (1994), 525–49.

Velleman 2000: David Velleman, *The Possibility of Practical Reason*. Oxford: Oxford University Press, 2000.

Walton 1978: Kendall Walton, 'Fearing Fictions', *Journal of Philosophy*, 75 (1978), 5–27.

Weber 1946: Max Weber, 'Religious Rejections of the World and Their Directions', in H. H. Gerth and C. Wright Mills (eds.), *From Max Weber: Essays in Sociology*. Oxford: Oxford University Press, 1946.

Weil 1951: *Simone Weil, Waiting on God*. London: Routledge, 1951.

Weil 1962: Simone Weil, 'Human Personality', in *Simone Weil, Selected Essays, 1934–1943*, trans. by Richard Rees. London: Oxford University Press, 1962.

Westen and Mangiafico 2003: P. Westen and J. Mangiafico, 'The Criminal Defense of Duress', *Buffalo Criminal Law Review*, 6 (2003), 833.

Wiggins 1980: David Wiggins, 'Deliberation and Practical Reason', in Rorty, 1980, 221–40.

Wilkes 1980: K. Wilkes, 'The Good Man and the Good for Man in Aristotle's Ethics', in Rorty, 1980.

Williams 1980: Bernard Williams, 'Philosophy', in M. I. Finley (ed.), *The Legacy of Greece*. Oxford: Clarendon Press, 1980.

Williams 1981a: Bernard Williams, *Moral Luck*. Cambridge: Cambridge University Press, 1981.

Williams 1981b: Bernard Williams, 'Justice as a Virtue', in *Moral Luck*, Cambridge: Cambridge University Press, 1981.

Williams 1985: Bernard Williams, *Ethics and the Limits of Philosophy*. London: Penguin Books 1985.

Williams 1992: Bernard Williams, 'Moral Incapacity', *Proceedings of the Aristotelian Society*, 1992, repr. in B. Williams, *Making Series of Humanity*. Cambridge: Cambridge University Press, 1995, 46–55.

Williams 1993: Bernard Williams, *Shame and Necessity*. Berkeley: University of California Press, 1993.

Williamson 2004: Timothy Williamson, 'Must Do Better', forthcoming in M. Lynch and P. Greenough (eds.), *Proceedings of the 2004 St Andrews Conference on Realism and Truth*. Oxford: Oxford University Press.

Young (forthcoming): Charles Young, Archélogos Online Commentary on *Nicomachean Ethics* V.

Zagzebski 1996: Linda Zagzebski, *Virtues of the Mind*. Cambridge: Cambridge University Press.

Zagzebski 2003: Linda Zagzebski, 'Emotion and Moral Judgement', *Philosophy and Phenomenological Research*, 66: 1 (January 2003), 104–24.

Zagzebski 2004: Linda Zagzebski, *Divine Motivation Theory*. Cambridge: Cambridge University Press, 2004.

Zamir 2002: Tzachi Zamir, 'An Epistemological Basis for Linking Philosophy and Literature', *Metaphilosophy*, 33: 3, (2002), 321–36.

Zeller 1897: Eduard Zeller, *Aristotle and the Earlier Peripatetics*, trans. B. F. C. Costelloe and J. H. Muirhead. London: Longman's, Green, & Co., 1897.

Index